Factional Struggles

Rulers & Elites

Comparative Studies in Governance

VOLUME 10

The titles published in this series are listed at *brill.com/rule*

Factional Struggles

Divided Elites in European Cities and Courts (1400–1750)

Edited by

Mathieu Caesar

BRILL

LEIDEN | BOSTON

Cover illustration: *Grandes chroniques de France* (ca. 1460), Châteauroux, Bibliothèque Municipale, ms. 5(B. 244), fol. 171v, cliché CNRS—IRHT. Upper register: Confrontation between William of Longsword, count of Rouen, and Arnoul I count of Flanders. Lower register: murder of William of Longsword by count Arnoul. The episode took place in 942, and was part of the complex factional struggles of tenth-century France.

The Library of Congress Cataloging-in-Publication Data is available online at http://catalog.loc.gov
LC record available at http://lccn.loc.gov/2017023570

Typeface for the Latin, Greek, and Cyrillic scripts: "Brill". See and download: brill.com/brill-typeface.

ISSN 2211-4610
ISBN 978-90-04-34415-0 (hardback)
ISBN 978-90-04-34534-8 (e-book)

This book is printed on acid-free paper and produced in a sustainable manner.

Contents

List of Maps VII
Notes on Contributors VIII

Did Factions Exist? Problems and Perspectives on European Factional Struggles (1400–1750) 1
Mathieu Caesar

The Black Raven and His Gang: Politics in Augsburg in Times of Crisis (1450–1480) 18
Dominique Adrian

Changing Skin: Identities and Strategies in Late Medieval Basque *banderizo* Warfare 37
José Ramón Díaz de Durana and Arsenio Dacosta

Conciliarist Employment of Eschatology during and after the Council of Basel (1431–1460) 56
Frances Courtney Kneupper

Factions in Rome between Papal Wars and International Conflicts (1480–1530) 82
Maria Antonietta Visceglia

The Prince and the Factions: Rebellion and Political Propaganda in Sixteenth-Century Geneva 104
Mathieu Caesar

Not Only Blood: Factions on the Venetian *Terraferma* during the Early Modern Period 122
Andrea Savio

A Temperate Factionalism: Political Life in Amiens at the End of the Wars of Religion 137
Olivia Carpi

The Imperial Court during the Thirty Years War: A Battleground for Factions? 155
Rubén González Cuerva and Luis Tercero Casado

Divide and Rule? Rival Factions and Prussian State Management in Eighteenth-Century Neuchâtel 176
Nadir Weber

Factions and Parties in Early Modern Swiss Conflicts 196
Andreas Würgler

Bibliography 217
Index 247

List of Maps

1 The Hermandad of 1397 and the lineages of the Guipuzcoan *Parientes Mayores* (14th–15th c.) 42
2 The seigneurial domains around 1450 and the territorial formation of Alava (1463–1507) 43
3 The Private (banderizo) warfare (15th c.) 44

Notes on Contributors

Dominique Adrian

wrote his PhD on late medieval politics in the imperial city of Augsburg (*Augsbourg à la fin du Moyen Âge: la politique et l'espace*, Ostfildern, 2013). He is an associate researcher at the Université de Lorraine in Metz. His research is focussed on political life in the southern German imperial towns, with particular attention on texts produced by the various institutions and individual actors involved in civic life and on the political role of guilds.

Mathieu Caesar

is senior lecturer (*maître assistant*) in medieval history at the Université de Genève and a member of the Editorial Board of the of the online *Glossary on Medieval Taxation*. His research focus is on the political, social and religious history of European cities (1300–1600). He is the author of *Le pouvoir en ville. Gestion urbaine et pratiques politiques à Genève (fin XIII*^e^*–début XVI*^e^ *siècles)* (Turnhout, 2011) and *Histoire de Genève. La cité des évêques (IV*^e^*–début XVI*^e^ *s.)* (Neuchâtel, 2014), and co-editor with Marco Schnyder of *Religion et pouvoir. Ordre social et discipline morale dans les villes de l'espace suisse (XIV*^e^*–XVIII*^e^ *s.)* (Neuchâtel, 2014). He is also currently editing in collaboration with Franco Morenzoni a collective book on the House of Savoy and late medieval princely legislation: *La Loi du Prince: les Statuts de Savoie d'Amédée VIII (1430)*.

Olivia Carpi

has been a teacher and researcher at the University of Picardie-Jules Verne (Amiens, France) since 2000. Her PhD dissertation in modern history was about the Holy League in Amiens. Her interests focus on the French Wars of Religion in the north of France, the urban Holy League, municipal history and civic culture and, more recently, she has become interested in the pacification process in French Catholic towns during and after the civil conflicts of the second half of the sixteenth century. She has published several articles and two major books: *Une république imaginaire. Amiens pendant les troubles de religion* (Paris, 2005) and *Les guerres de Religion. Un conflit franco-français* (Paris, 2012).

Frances Courtney Kneupper

is Assistant Professor of History at The University of Mississippi Arch Dalrymple III Department of History. She is a historian of prophecy and religious dissent in late medieval Europe. She recently published a monograph titled

The Empire at the End of Time: Identity and Reform in Late Medieval German Prophecy (Oxford, 2016). Her other publications include articles on heresy, prophecy and Church reform. Her current projects address debates over the knowledge of the future in the later Middle Ages and late medieval representations of the Antichrist.

Arsenio Dacosta
is a Lecturer in Anthropology at the University of Salamanca and a member of the research group Power, Society and Culture at the University of Basque Country, Spain. He has been invited as a guest teacher and researcher to the University of Alcalá, National Distance Education University (UNED), Universidade Nova de Lisboa and the Research Centre for the Study of Population, Economics and Society (CEPESE) in Porto. His PhD analysed the involvement of the nobility in the social conflicts which riddled the Lordship of Biscay during the late Middle Ages. Dacosta's most recent publications discuss the lower nobility's sources of power and dynastic/genealogical memory in the Iberian Peninsula. Additionally, he is currently coordinating a project in Digital Humanities named *Hidalgos, Labradoras, Mercaderes* (www.hilame.info/web/), linked to the research group led by Professor Díaz de Durana.

José Ramón Díaz de Durana Ortiz de Urbina
is Professor of Medieval History at the University of Basque Country, Spain, and the principal investigator of the research group Power, Society and Culture. He is the author of many studies on the society, economy, and local and territorial institutions of the Basque Country. Over the last few years, he has focussed on the lesser nobility (*hidalgos*) of the northern coastal territories, in which over 75% of the population claimed noble status, the highest concentration of the privileged class in Europe. The first findings from this research can be found in *Anonymous Noblemen. The Generalisation of Hidalgo Status in the Basque Country (1250–1525)* (Turnhout, 2011).

Rubén González Cuerva
is Juan de la Cierva Postdoctoral Fellow at the Spanish National Research Council, Madrid. He specialises in Early Modern diplomacy and political communication. González Cuerva is currently working on the political networks operating between the Habsburg courts; he was recently the editor (with José Martínez Millán) of *La dinastía de los Austria: las relaciones entre la Monarquía Católica y el Imperio* (3 vols, Madrid, 2011); *Baltasar de Zúñiga: una encrucijada de la Monarquía hispana (1561–1622)* (Madrid, 2012); and the dossier

(with Valentina Caldari) "*The Secret Mechanisms of Courts: Factions in Early Modern Europe*" (*Libros de la Corte.es*, N°. Extra 2, 2015).

Andrea Savio
is a Research Fellow of Early Modern History in the Department of Historic and Geographic Sciences and the Ancient World at the University of Padua, Italy. He received his BA and MA at Ca' Foscari University of Venice and his PhD from the University of Verona. During the PhD he attended seminars at the Birkbeck College University of London as a Visiting Research Student. Savio's research project focusses on the elite in the Republic of Venice, in particular on spies and the Spanish party. He collaborates with CISA (the Andrea Palladio International Centre of Architectural Studies). He is the co-editor with L. Trevisan of *Vittorio Lombardi. Mecenate illuminato e tesoriere della conquista italiana del K2* (Verona, 2014). He is the author of *Nobiltà palladiana. La famiglia Godi fra Vicenza e l'Europa* (Rome, 2017).

Luis Tercero Casado
is a PhD doctoral candidate at the University of Vienna. His main field of research is the focus of his ongoing PhD thesis: the relations between both lines of the Habsburg dynasty between the Peace of Westphalia (1648) and the Peace of the Pyrenees (1659). Within this framework, his other fields of interest and publications are focussed on the history of the House of Austria during the seventeenth century, Early Modern diplomatic history, and courtly society at the Imperial Court of Vienna.

Maria Antonietta Visceglia
is Professor of Early Modern History at the University of Rome "La Sapienza". She is a member of the *Giunta Storica Nazionale* and a member of the Editorial Board of the *Dizionario Biografico degli italiani*. She is Director of the Journal *Dimensioni e problemi della ricerca storica* and Co-Director of the *Rivista Storica Italiana*. She was co-editor with G. Signorotto of *Court and Politics in Papal Rome 1492–1700* (Cambridge, 2002) and with J. Martínez Millán of *La Monarquía de Felipe III*, (4 vols, Madrid, 2008). She is the author of numerous works on the social history of the Kingdom of Naples in the modern age and on Rome in the sixteenth and seventeenth centuries. Her books include: *La città rituale. Roma e le sue cerimonie in età moderna* (Rome, 2002); *Riti di corte e simboli della regalità* (Rome, 2009); *Roma papale e Spagna. Diplomatici, nobili e religiosi tra due corti* (Rome, 2010); *Guerra, Diplomacia y Etiqueta en la Corte de los Papas (siglos XVI y XVII)* (Madrid 2010); *Papato e politica internazionale nella prima*

età moderna, ed. by (Rome, 2013); *Morte e elezione del papa norme, riti conflitti, L'età moderna* (Rome, 2013).

Nadir Weber

received his PhD in History from the University of Bern in 2013. His main research interests are aristocratic republics in Early Modern Europe, foreign relations and domestic policy in composite monarchies and the relationship between humans and animals in seventeenth-century courts. He is author of the book *Lokale Interessen und grosse Strategie. Das Fürstentum Neuchâtel und die politischen Beziehungen der Könige von Preussen (1707–1806)* (Cologne, 2015), and co-editor of the volume *Protegierte und Protektoren. Asymmetrische politische Beziehungen zwischen Partnerschaft und Dominanz (16. bis frühes 20. Jahrhundert)* (Cologne, 2016). His current book project is entitled *A Tamed Society? Interspecies Interactions at the Royal Court of France, 1594–1715*. After holding positions as a research assistant and lecturer at the University of Bern, he was a visiting postdoctoral fellow at the Ludwigs-Maximilians-Universität München and the École Pratique des Hautes Études Paris from 2014 to 2016. He currently holds a ZIF Marie S. Curie postdoctoral fellowship at the University of Konstanz.

Andreas Würgler

studied history and German literature at the University of Berne and the Free University of Berlin. He is now a professor of Medieval and Early Modern Swiss History at the University of Geneva. His publications include the monographs *Unruhen und Öffentlichkeit. Städtische und ländliche Protestbewegungen im 18. Jahrhundert* (1995); *Medien in der Frühen Neuzeit* (2009, 2013); *Die Tagsatzung der Eidgenossen. Politik, Kommunikation und Symbolik einer repräsentativen Institution im europäischen Kontext (1470–1798)* (2013); and the articles (in English): 'Censorship and Public Opinion: Press and Politics in the Helvetic Republic (1798–1803)', in Joris Oddens et al., eds., *The Political Culture of the Sister Republics* (2015); 'National and Transnational News Distribution 1400–1800', in *European History Online* (EGO), http://www.ieg-ego.eu/; 'Revolts in Print: Media and Communication in Early Modern Urban Conflicts', in: Rudolf Schlögl, ed., *Urban Elections and Decision-Making in Early Modern Europe, 1500–1800* (2009); 'Voices from among the 'Silent Masses'. Humble Petitions and Social Conflicts in Early Modern Central Europe', *International Review of Social History* 46 (2001), Supplement 9.

Did Factions Exist? Problems and Perspectives on European Factional Struggles (1400–1750)

Mathieu Caesar

Questioning whether factions actually existed by way of introduction to a book titled *Factional Struggles* will probably come as a surprise to the reader. However, a review of the abundant historiography on factions in European cities and courts from the twelfth to the seventeenth centuries leaves one impressed at the enormous variety and complexity of factional patterns. Often historians have developed radically opposing interpretations of the same historical circumstances, and in some cases the very existence of factions and partisanship has been disputed. The historiographical debate over the English Tudor court probably furnishes the most striking example.[1] Historians such as Greg Walker and George Bernard have seriously questioned the extent of factional disputes, and even their existence, in Henry VIII's court.[2] Simon Adams has discussed and rejected the idea that factionalism in the English court was a permanent state of affairs during the second half of the sixteenth century,[3] and recently, in a study of the later Elizabethan period, Janet Dickinson has argued that court politics in the 1590s was not at bottom a fight between two factions.[4] Similarly, other researchers have concluded that in many European towns, harsh conflicts were not always the fruit of factional rivalries, as has sometimes been hastily assumed.[5] Even when the existence of factions is not in doubt, the overwhelming variety of discordant interpretations concerning

1 Ever since the seminal work by Eric Ives, *Factions in Tudor England* (London: 1979), the debate about the place and influence of courtesan factions in Tudor England has grown significantly. For an overview and discussion of the main contributions to this debate, see Robert Shepherd, 'Court Factions in Early Modern England', *The Journal of Modern History* 64, no. 4 (December 1992), 721–45, and Natalie Mears, 'Courts, courtiers and culture in Tudor England', *Historical Journal* 46, no. 3 (2003), 703–22.

2 See in particular Greg Walker, *Persuasive Fictions: Faction, Faith and Political Culture at the Court of Henry VIII* (Aldershot, 1996), and George W. Bernard, *Power and Politics in Tudor England: Essays* (Aldershot, 2000).

3 Cf. N. Mears, 'Courts, courtiers', 708.

4 Janet Dickinson, *Court Politics and the Earl of Essex, 1589–1601* (London, 2012).

5 Christopher R. Friedrichs, *Urban Politics in Early Modern Europe* (London, 2000), 36–37; José María Monsalvo Antón, 'Violence between Factions in Medieval Salamanca: Some Problems of Interpretation', *Imago Temporis Medium Aevum*, 3 (2009), 139–70.

 | DOI 10.1163/9789004345348_002

the origins, nature and importance of factional conflicts can be puzzling. A clear definition of what makes a faction, who belonged to factions and what their aims were, often appears impossible to state. Working on the French and Imperial courts, Jeroen Duindam came to the conclusion that no single model of factions can be constructed for early modern courts.[6]

Many well-known cases demonstrate that the abundance of competing interpretations is frequently the result of historiographical twists and turns. Studies of the Italian cities provide a good first example. The long, still very much alive, historiographical discussion of the Guelphs and the Ghibellines in twelfth-century Florence, ignited in 1899 by Gaetano Salvemini's *Magnati e popolani*, has led to a bewildering variety of interpretations of the nature and composition of these two parties. Historians have shifted from describing this reality as a socioeconomic clash to analysing it as chiefly as being the result of patron-client relations.[7]

The focus of many historians studying Italian factions during the Renaissance and Early Modern periods in terms of topics such as "violence", "feuds", "honour", and "rituals", and a stress on microhistorical case studies, was dictated by the influence of anthropological and ethnographical studies.[8] More recently, some historians have drawn attention to the long-underestimated persistence and vitality of the Guelphs and Ghibellines in northern Italy during the late medieval period. Challenging the interpretation of factions as a form of irrational violence, they emphasised the structural organization of factions, showing how they were also an accepted tool for the resolution of conflicts, and a

---

6 Jeroen Duindam, *Vienna and Versailles: The Courts of Europe's Dynastic Rivals, 1550–1780* (Cambridge, 2003), 257.

7 For a synthetic view, see Sergio Raveggi, 'La lotta politica e sociale', in *Storia della civiltà toscana* (Firenze, 2000), vol. 1: Franco Cardini, ed., *Comuni e signorie*, 117–36. Also useful is Andrea Zorzi, *La trasformazione di un quadro politico. Ricerche su politica e giustizia a Firenze dal comune allo Stato territoriale* (Firenze, 2008). For recent studies, see for example, Federico Canaccini, *Ghibellini e ghibellinismo in Toscana da Montaperti a Campaldino (1260–1289)* (Roma, 2009), and Silvia Diacciati, *Popolani e magnati: società e politica nella Firenze del Duecento* (Spoleto, 2011).

8 Good examples are the important works by Edward Muir, *Mad Blood Stirring: Vendetta and Factions in Friuli During the Renaissance* (Baltimore, 1993), and by Italian early modernists close to the *microstoria* such as Osvaldo Raggio, *Faide e parentele. Lo stato genovese visto dalla Fontanabuona* (Torino, 1990), and Edoardo Grendi, *In altri termini: etnografia e storia di una società di antico regime* (Milano, 1994). On this "turn" in the research see Daniel Lord Smail, 'Factions and Vengeance in Renaissance Italy. A Review Article', *Comparative Studies in Society and History* 38, no. 4 (October, 1996), 781–89, and Marco Gentile, 'Factions and Parties: Problems and Perspectives', in Andrea Gamberini and Isabella Lazzarini, eds., *The Italian Renaissance State* (Cambridge, 2012), 307–309.

recognised method of engaging in politics, not unlike modern political parties. This reaction is connected with a re-assessment of the process which resulted in the so-called "modern state", which emphasised pluralisms and contributions from "below" to state-building and increased attention to the study of political languages and practices.[9]

Concentration on the actions and motivations of individuals, rather than groups or institutions, and the popularity of a prosopographical approach, have, beginning in the late 1970s, influenced many important studies, including the interpretation of the nature of the Guelph party in late twelfth-century Florence,[10] and Robert Descimon's influential research on the Seize and factional conflicts during the French Wars of Religion.[11] The prosopographical approach and network analysis, which have recently received further impetus from the turn to digital research, continue to be popular among historians studying factional conflicts, as shown by recent research on twelfth- and thirteenth-century Norway,[12] Byzantium in the fourteenth century,[13] cities such as Dijon, Gand and The Hague during the fifteenth and sixteenth centuries,[14]

---

9 For some of the most important publications and remarks on these trends, see Marco Gentile, ed., *Guelfi e ghibellini nell'Italia del Rinascimento* (Roma, 2005); Fabrizio Ricciardelli, *The Politics of Exclusion in Early Renaissance. Florence* (Turnhout, 2007), 60–84; Bertrand Forclaz, 'Local Conflicts and Political Authorities in the Papal State in the Second Half of the 17th century', in André Holenstein, Wim Blockmans, Jon Mathieu, eds., *Empowering Interactions. Political Cultures and the Emergence of the State in Europe, 14th-19th centuries* (Aldershot, 2009), 65–77; Michele Tamponi, *Nino Visconti di Gallura. Il dantesco Giudice Nin gentil tra Pisa e Sardegna, guelfi e ghibellini, faide cittadine e lotte isolane* (Roma, 2010); Paolo Grillo, *Milano guelfa (1302–1310)* (Roma, 2013); Serena Ferente, *Gli ultimi guelfi. Linguaggi e identità politiche in Italia nella seconda metà del Quattrocento* (Roma 2013); and Patrick Lantschner, *The Logic of Political Conflict in Medieval Cities: Italy and the Southern Low Countries, 1370–1440* (Oxford, 2015).

10 Cf. Sergio Raveggi *et al.*, eds., *Guelfi e Popolo grasso: I detentori del potere politico a Firenze nella seconda metà del Dugento* (Firenze, 1978).

11 Robert Descimon, *Qui étaient les Seize? Mythes et réalités de la Ligue parisienne (1585–1594)* (Paris, 1983).

12 Bente Opheim, 'Political networks and factions: Online Prosopography of Medieval Scandinavian Sagas', *History and Computing* 12, no. 1 (2000), 43–57.

13 See the project *Mapping Medieval Conflict* at the Österreichische Akademie der Wissenschaften and directed by Johannes Preiser-Kapeller.

14 Thierry Dutour, 'Pouvoir politique et position sociale en ville: les factions et leurs chefs à Dijon à la fin du Moyen Âge', in Jacques Paviot and Jacques Verger, eds., *Guerre, pouvoir et noblesse au Moyen Âge, Mélanges en l'honneur de Philippe Contamine* (Paris, 2000), 227–38; Jelle Haemers, *For the Common Good. State Power and Urban Revolts in the Reign of Mary of Burgundy, 1477–1482* (Turnhout, 2009); idem, 'Factionalism and State Power in the

and Alpine communities in the eighteenth century.[15] But this approach has also been criticised. In studies of the French League, for example, many historians have argued that factional struggles have been unduly reduced to social and political conflicts (a consequence of the prosopographical approach), and that the importance of religion has been underestimated. Thus, from the beginning of the 1990s, historians have begun "putting religion back into the Wars of Religion", according to the felicitous expression of Mack P. Holt,[16] which has fuelled new debates and interpretations that seem far from concluded.[17] Examples of developments in the field could be easily multiplied, but it is not the aim of this introduction to provide a full discussion of the contemporary historiography of late medieval and early modern partisanship, a topic that would require, and probably deserve, a monograph for a complete survey.[18]

Despite an overabundant number of studies and the many historiographical developments we have briefly outlined, no syntheses and only a few comparative studies have been specifically devoted to factions. The great diversity and complexity of factional struggles, historiographical boundaries and traditional periodization are probably the best explanations of why we still lack a good overview. Jacques Heers's well-known *Parties and Political Life in the Medieval West* is still the only attempt to produce a large survey of factions and parties during the medieval period, although, despite the title, it was mainly concerned with cities in northern and central Italy during the twelfth and thirteenth centuries.[19] Some interesting comparative approaches have been

---

Flemish Revolt (1477–1492)', *Journal of Social History*, 42 (2009), 1009–39; Serge ter Braake, 'Parties and Factions in the Late Middle Ages: The Case of the Hoeken and Kabeljauwen in The Hague (1483–1515)', *Journal of Medieval History* 35, (2009), 97–111.

15 Sandro Guzzi-Heeb, *Passions alpines. Sexualité et pouvoirs dans les montagnes suisses (1700–1900)* (Rennes, 2014).

16 Mack P. Holt, 'Putting Religion Back into the Wars of Religion. Review Article', *French Historical Studies* 18, no. 2 (Autumn, 1993), 524–51.

17 See the reply to Mack P. Holt in Henry Heller, 'Putting History Back into the Religious Wars: A Reply to Mack P. Holt', *French Historical Studies* 19, no. 3 (Spring, 1996), 853–61. For the historiographical debate, see Nicolas Le Roux, *Les guerres de Religion 1559–1629* (Paris, 2009) and the recent contribution of Philip Benedict, 'Were the French Wars of Religion Really Wars of Religion? Contemporary Views, Then and Now', in Wolfgang Palaver, Dietmar Regensburger, and Harriet Rudolph, eds., *The European Wars of Religion. An Interdisciplinary Reassessment of Sources, Myths, and Interpretations* (Farnham, 2016), 61–86.

18 A historiographical approach has proved to be stimulating and rewarding for a similarly entangled and complex subject: the Crusades. Cf. Norman Housley, *Contesting the Crusades* (Oxford, 2006).

19 Jacques Heers, *Parties and Political Life in the Medieval West* (Amsterdam, 1977). It must be said that the work is sometimes flawed by an excessively polemical language and reliance

proposed for the Italian Renaissance[20] and for the role of favourites in late medieval and early modern dynastic courts.[21]

This book does not pretend to fill all the existing gaps in research, nor does it claim to be an extensive survey of European factionalism during the late Middle Ages and the Early Modern period. Instead, it offers case studies which have not always been at the forefront of historiography, permitting us to broaden and deepen our understanding of European partisanship. Moreover, this book aims to be a first step towards a comparison of different forms of partisanship (within urban elites, at dynastic courts, in rural contexts, and among regional noble lineages), a comparison which has not yet been attempted over a large geographic area, at least not to my knowledge. By bringing together studies on courtly, noble and urban factions, we would also like to contribute to the discussion about the existence of a shared political society and culture, and eventual fissures in that society and culture, as well as reducing the analytical distance between court and urban studies.[22]

---

on a conception of party as an extension of family clans and their disputes. In fact, *Parties and Political Life in the Medieval West* is somehow the continuation of Heers' previous book *Le clan familial au Moyen Âge. Étude sur les structures politiques et sociales des milieux urbains* (Paris, 1974).

20 Gentile, ed., *Guelfi e Ghibellini*. See also idem, 'Factions and Parties: Problems and Perspectives', in Andrea Gamberini and Isabella Lazzarini, eds., *The Italian Renaissance State* (Cambridge, 2012), 304–22.

21 Jan Hirschbiegel and Werner Paravicini, eds., *Der Fall des Günstlings: Hofparteien in Europa vom 13. bis zum 17. Jahrhundert* (Ostfildern, 2004). See also on court factionalism, Rubén González Cuerva and Valentina Caldari, eds., *The Secret Mechanisms of Courts: Factions in Early Modern Europe*, Journal Special Issue of the *Revista Libros de la Corte, Monográfico* 2 (2015).

22 For a brief sketch of the relationships between early modern European cities and courts, see Jeroen Duindam, 'Royal Courts', in Hamish Scott, ed., *The Oxford Handbook of Early Modern European History. 1350–1750*, vol. 2: *Cultures and Power* (Oxford, 2015), 458–60. For some recent comparative approaches, see Susanne Claudine Pils, Jan Paul Niederkorn, eds., *Ein zweigeteilter Ort? Hof und Stadt in der Frühen Neuzeit* (Wien, 2005) ; Werner Paravicini, Jörg Wettlaufer, ed., *Der Hof und die Stadt. Konfrontation und Integration in Spätmittelalter und Früher Neuzeit* (Ostfildern, 2006); Jan Hirschbiegel, Werner Paravicini, Jörg Wettlaufer, eds., *Städtische Bürgertum und Hofgesellschaft. Kulturen integrativer und konkurrierender Beziehungen in Residenz und Hauptstädten vom 14. bis in 19. Jahrhundert* (Ostfieldern, 2012) and Léonard Courbon, Denis Menjot, eds., *La cour et la ville dans l'Europe du Moyen Âge et des Temps Modernes* (Turnhout, 2015). Reflections on capital cities are also rich with perspectives and suggestions, cf. especially Peter Clark, Bernard Lepetit, eds., *Capital Cities and their Hinterlands in Early Modern Europe* (Aldershot, 1996) and *Les villes capitales au Moyen Âge. XXXVI*[e] *Congrès de la* SHMES *(Istanbul, 1*[er]*-6 juin 2005)* (Paris, 2006).

Dominique Adrian examines factional conflicts in Augsburg (1450s–1480s) and the difficulties posed by sources that raise questions about the very nature of the conflict under study. The *lucha de bandos* in the provinces of the Basque country analysed by José Ramón Diaz de Durana and Arsenio Dacosta reveals how partisanship was not a simple local struggle for economic and political resources, but was closely linked to the wider political circumstances existing on a regional scale. Frances Courtney Kneupper's analysis of the use and circulation of prophecies among Conciliarists during the fifteenth century raises interesting questions about how ideas and writings were circulated among the members of a particular faction. Maria Antonietta Visceglia's contribution dives into the behaviour and language of Roman factions, carefully demonstrating how complex political struggles arose out of a mixture of personal, familial and factional decision-making. Olivia Carpi's analysis of the Catholic League in Amiens during the Wars of Religion shows the weaknesses of factionalism and how the policy of the ruling elite can be characterised by moderation towards an opposing faction. Andrea Savio's analysis of partisanship in Vicenza during the Renaissance and my own contribution on sixteenth-century Geneva demonstrate how parties can be used by sovereigns (respectively, the republic of Venice and the duke of Savoy) as political interlocutors. The imperial court and its relationship with the Spanish party are at the centre of Rubén Gonzalez Cuerva's and Luis Tercero Casado's contribution, which insists on the complicated mechanisms of decision-making at the court and describes how these mechanisms created fluid and dynamic factions instead of monolithic parties. Nadir Weber's study of the principality of Neuchâtel in the eighteenth century demonstrates how the existence of political alternatives led to factional friction within the patrician elite, and how factional struggles on a local level were intertwined with factional shifts at the distant Prussian court, as well as within the political centres of neighbouring territories. Finally, Andreas Würgler provides an overview of the importance of factional disputes in early modern conflicts within the Swiss Confederacy, revealing that although factions were mostly seen as seditious instigators of rebellion, they were nevertheless accepted "participants" in political debate.

The authors gathered in this volume have worked on a common set of questions addressing problems which are still understudied, and their papers focus in particular on the practices and dynamics of factional struggles and the language used by contemporaries to describe those struggles. Social and anthropological analysis have already been widely applied to factional conflicts, but political and ideological motivations for partisanship have often seemed relatively unimportant—despite the fact that political debate has consistently been a recognised feature at all levels of European society, from common people in Early Modern Venice to Alpine communities during the eighteenth and nineteenth centuries.[23] Can then we speak of factional ideologies? Did factions have a precise political, religious or social program? How did such notions contribute to assertions of a faction's legitimacy? Is it possible to measure the relative weight of these different factors?

The relationship between the group and the individuals composing the group deserves attention as well. Historians describe factions as heterogeneous or fluid groups. How and why did an individual join a faction? How can historians determine the factional partisanship of individuals? Were political and religious beliefs always shared within a faction? Or was it possible to establish different degrees of partisanship? Following that perspective, it would seem promising to look more carefully at internal conflicts, at the means used by a faction's leaders to establish themselves within the faction, and at the ways factions attempted to unite the group. Surprising individual memberships (from the point of view of family origin or social status) provide interesting case studies as well. Was it possible to change from one faction to another? What reasons dictated these choices, and what were the consequences for the individuals and/or their families?

Discovering the answers to such questions is surely not easy, and the answers can sometimes appear contradictory. However, the contributions in this volume provide some initial responses and offer patterns that can be used to analyse many points worth further investigation, as the pages of this introduction that follow will highlight.

Especially at lower levels of society, such as cities or villages, historians have often interpreted partisanship as a mere struggle for resources or access to power. In that view, people joined factions essentially for their self-interest and for benefits which might accrue to their family or lineage, and to these historians it is debatable whether factional realities were in any way related to political and international realities before the beginning of the seventeenth century.[24] In contrast, many studies presented here show, even if self-interested motivations were surely present, how ideology and political

---

23 Filippo de Vivo, *Patrizi, informatori, barbieri. Politica e comunicazione a Venezia nella prima età moderna* (Milano, 2012); and Guzzi-Heeb, *Passions alpines*.

24 Cf. for instance Robert von Friedeburg, 'Response to introduction: 'ideology', factions and foreign politics in early modern Europe', in David Onnekink and Gijs Rommelse, eds., *Ideology and Foreign Policy in the Early Modern Age (1650–1750)* (Farnham, 2011), 11–28. See also, for the different impacts of political ideology on the local vs. national levels, J.L. Price, *Holland and the Dutch Republic in the Seventeenth Century. The Politics of Particularism* (Oxford, 1994).

debate were in some cases important features of partisanship. Dominique Adrian's reconstruction of the harsh factional conflicts in the imperial city of Augsburg during the second half of the fifteenth century and of the role played by three main actors (Peter von Argon, Heinrich Erlbach and Ulrich Schwarz), shows that the struggles were not simply fuelled by personal antipathies and political rivalries. Political debate was deeply rooted in Augsburg's civic life, and the troubles were in part a consequence of the *Städtekrieg* (Town War) of 1449–1450, which resulted in discontent because of the war-related fiscal burden. The ruling elite, and more generally the political leaders, were divided about the best policy for the city. Olivia Carpi's reflections about the Catholic League in Amiens during the Wars of Religion in the 1580s arrive at similar conclusions. Using often-neglected municipal sources, she shows that Leaguers in Amiens were far from being simply unscrupulous people used by more powerful rulers, but rather were driven by religious and political ideals and inspired by a true civic republicanism to act for the common good.[25] From that point of view, Imperial and French urban realities do not appear so unlike those of Renaissance Italy, a world often considered unparalleled at the level of political consciousness and practices.[26]

It also appears that in many cases factions took shape as the result of debate over geopolitical choices. The Swiss scenario discussed in this volume by Andreas Würgler clearly shows that, beginning as early as the late fifteenth century, many factional conflicts arose out of differing opinions of foreign affairs. The case of Geneva at the beginning of the sixteenth century, on which my own contribution focuses, and Nadir Weber's reconstruction of factionalism in eighteenth-century Neuchâtel, clearly show that the existence of political alternatives created by dynastic and geopolitical changes led to important factional struggles. Neuchâtel's patricians split because "alternatives to Prussian patronage and rule continued to exist and had beneficiaries and supporters within the local elite". Similarly, in sixteenth-century Geneva, caught between the expansion of the Swiss cities of Bern and Fribourg and the House of Savoy's loss of power, factions formed over a disagreement as to which of these entities

25 See also the case of late medieval Bruges, where a faction grouped around Willem Moreel became politically oriented only after the catastrophic events that led to the death of the duke of Burgundy in 1477, in which the idea of the "common good" had an important influence. Cf. Jelle Haemers, *For the Common Good. State Power and Urban Revolts in the Reign of Mary of Burgundy (1477–1482)* (Turnhout, 2009).

26 Cf., for instance, Serena Ferente, 'Guelphs! Factions, Liberty and Sovereignty: Inquiries about the Quattrocento', *History of Political Thought* 28, no. 4 (2007), 571–98. See also the bibliography quoted at n. 9.

would be the best ally to protect the city, and came into serious conflict when the situation became complicated and uncertain. The same could be said for the evolution of the conflict between the Orsini and Colonna lineages in Rome, analysed by Maria Antonietta Visceglia, and for the case of Vicenza discussed by Andrea Savio. Italian political turmoil and wars in the first half of the sixteenth century strongly fuelled rivalries among lineages. What was true for cities can also be observed at dynastic courts. Rubén González Cuerva and Luis Tercero Casado observed how at the end of the Thirty Years' War, and thus the end of a climate of high uncertainty, a division between the "Spanish" and "Bavarian" parties in the imperial court ceased to be a dominant political reality. In fact, very often changes in regional or European geopolitics had important repercussions on the formation of urban and court parties, and factional struggles were often, especially at a local level, the result of debates fuelled by dynastic and political uncertainty.

These observations raise important questions. How much can European political and religious factional struggles be interpreted as efforts to face and reduce uncertainty? In an uncertain climate, the presence or absence of trust (at court, in receiving ambassadors, in negotiating with opposing factions, etc.) is crucial for interpreting the dynamics of political and religious debates and conflicts. Thus, the ways in which "trust" and "uncertainty", two concepts that have been widely employed by social-economic history,[27] can be understood by historians appears to be a new, promising and challenging field of research in religious and political history.[28]

In attempting to describe the reasons motivating factional decision-making, historians have often emphasised the role of strategic considerations, family ties, social relationships, patronage, etc. Although these elements must be taken into account, other factors were essential as well. Many of the contributors to this volume have highlighted how not every choice made by a faction was dictated by a precise strategy. Sudden political changes and unforeseen circumstances were often key factors. From this point of view, historians must never forget that historical developments, which often appear to our hindsight

27 See in particular the seminal works of Laurence Fontaine, *L'économie morale: pauvreté, crédit et confiance dans l'Europe préindustrielle* (Paris, 2008) and Daniela Luigia Caglioti, 'Trust, Business Group, and Social Capital: Building a Protestant Entrepreneurial Network in 19th Century Naples', *Journal of Modern Italian Studies*, 13/2 (2008), 219–36.

28 Cf. for interesting remarks and the path of research of Peter Kollock, 'The Emergence of Exchange Structures: An Experimental Study of Uncertainty, Commitment, and Trust', *The American Journal of Sociology*, 100/2 (1994), 313–45 and Geoffrey Hosking, *Trust: a history* (Oxford: 2014).

as clear and linear, were, for contemporaries, more opaque and unpredictable. As Andreas Würgler reminds us in his contribution to this volume, historical actors, whether individuals, groups or institutions, often had multiple options for addressing a problem, but not every option was available at any particular time.[29] Writing the history of factional struggles requires thinking about the past as a series of political alternatives and individual choices which coexisted and may have been in conflict. Thus many papers in this volume have chosen to follow and reconstruct specific events, adopting a chronological narrative that best emphasises the actual situations that people and factions faced.

Historians approaching factions, and in particular their dynamics and the language surrounding them, are often concerned with various methodological problems. In the case of municipal factions, we often bump into the silence of sources, almost a documentary *omertà*. As Daniel Lord Smail has pointed out with respect to late medieval Marseille: "the veiled references that do exist in the registers of the council deliberations make sense only if one already knows of the existence of the enmity".[30] A similar situation has been observed for Renaissance Lombardy,[31] and more generally for the documented deliberations of cities, as Andreas Würgler's overview of the Swiss Confederation reveals, which tend to report decisions but rarely discussion. Olivia Carpi wisely pointed out in her contribution to this volume that although the Amiens Catholic League can be studied in a wide range of sources, all of the sources originated from the king's circle, making it difficult to counterbalance the allegations of royal agents with witnesses from the Leaguers. And Dominique Adrian's contribution on Augsburg shows how contemporaries attempted to characterise their adversaries' actions as "factional" in order to discredit them. Similar remarks can be applied to dynastic courts. In their contribution, Rubén González Cuerva and Luis Tercero Casado discuss the difficulties of identifying a "Spanish party" from Italian sources. Italian ambassadors and other Italian observers at the Viennese court were from a political culture marked by an intense, century-long factionalism, both in the urban and courtly context, as the long-standing labels of Guelph and Ghibelline remind us. Thus Italian ambassadors were quick to see the existence of organised factions everywhere.

29 Andreas Würgler, 'Factions and Parties in Early Modern Swiss Conflicts'.

30 Smail, 'Factions and Vengeance', 116.

31 Marco Gentile, 'Discorsi sulle fazioni, discorsi delle fazioni. *Parole e demonstratione partiale* nella Lombardia del secondo Quattrocento', in Andrea Gamberini and Giuseppe Petralia, eds., *Linguaggi politici nell'Italia del Rinascimento: atti del convegno, Pisa, 9–11 novembre 2006* (Roma, 2007), 381–408.

This reminds us that the sources we use to examine partisanship and to identify and analyse a "faction" were very often written by the faction's adversaries. And very often, these texts were produced in order to retrospectively justify the acts of a triumphant party and to lend coherence to choices that, when made, were less than coherent. This is true starting from the very word "faction". The terms used by contemporaries to describe a faction, even those that appear more neutral, provide an implicit definition and a precise judgment. The terms used could rarely be characterised as "neutral descriptions". The word *factio* (lat.) (and its equivalents in later European languages) was certainly used during the Middle Ages to describe the phenomenon, but it was not the only term used, and was surely not the term most commonly used. "Party" (meaning a portion or a divided part) and the related term "partisanship" were very often used—*Pars-partialitas* (lat.), *partie* (fr.), *parte, parzialità* (it.), *parcialidad* (es.), *partîe* (de.), *partye, partyelicheyt* (ned.)—along with many other terms referring to the idea of "gang" (for example, *bando* (es.), *bàndol* (cat.), *anhang* (de.), and *bende* (ned.)) or "sect", the first meaning of which is "a group apart".

This great terminological diversity was no less important in the early modern period. In sixteenth- and eighteenth-century France, for instance, the semantic domain of factionalism was extensive. *Brigue, cabale, party, factions, ligue* and *menée* were the most common terms, often used interchangeably and very often connoting "plot", "intrigue" or "sedition".[32] As Olivia Carpi reminds us in her contribution, in France the word "faction" definitely acquired a negative connotation, as a synonym for "gang of seditious people", during the intense factional struggles of the 1580s. However, it would be wrong to assume that authors never tried to distinguish these various concepts, as the case of seventeenth-century France shows.[33] Development in the meanings of these terms is difficult to identify and describe, as much of it was the result of idiosyncratic usages and interpretations. It was only slowly and not until the end of the eighteenth century that the word "party" became the term used to describe a legal form of political association, and "faction" became increasingly used only in a negative sense, to refer to a secretly-plotting group. The article on "Faction"

32 Malina Stefanovska, *La politique du cardinal de Retz: Passion et factions* (Rennes, 2008) 111–18. Similar remarks apply to the terms used by participants in the seventeenth-century Imperial court, such as *Parthey, Faction* and *Kabal*. Cf. Ivo Cerman, '"Kabal", "Parthey", "Faction" am Hofe Kaiser Leopolds I', in Werner Paravicini and Jan Hirschbiegel, eds., *Der Fall des Günstlings. Hofparteien in Europa vom 13. bis zum 17. Jahrhundert* (Ostfildern, 2004), 235–47.

33 Jean-Marie Constant, '*Partis, cabales, factions*. Études des sensibilités politiques dans les Mémoires du temps de Louis XIII', in Malina Stefanovska and Adrien Paschoud, eds., *Littérature et politique. Factions et dissidences de la Ligue à la Fronde* (Paris, 2015), 143–58.

in the first edition of the *Encyclopédie* of Diderot and d'Alembert (1756) stated that "the principal meaning of this term is a seditious party within a state. The term party means nothing heinous in itself, as faction always does".[34] But this distinction was not universally shared across Europe at that time, as David Hume's complex use of "factions" and "parties" reminds us; for example, in his well-known *Of Parties in General* (1742), he argued against religiously grounded "parties".[35]

Urban factions especially were not only defined by generic terms or regional labels such as in the case of court factions, but by proper names or sobriquets. It is worth noticing that in many cases names were imposed by an opposing party as a way to insult their adversary. In sixteenth-century Geneva, on which I focus in my own paper, the terms "Mammelus" and "Eidguenots" began as political insults. The same can be observed in fifteenth-century Paris during the civil war, when the term "Armagnac" was used in order to offend.[36] The terms "Whig" and "Tory", whose original meanings implied "thief" and "rebel", respectively, were also initially used to mock and discredit adversaries.[37] Samuel Johnson's often-quoted assertion that "the first Whig was the Devil",[38] reveals the persistence of some propaganda tools—the connection between the devil and partisan divisions was not particularly original, as it had been frequently used to characterise the origins of more than one medieval factional struggle. Many Italian chroniclers argued that the conflict between Guelphs and Ghibellines had a devilish origin,[39] and according to some legends, the Basque Country's factional struggles between the Oñacino and Gamboíno families

---

34 *Encyclopédie ou dictionnaire raisonné des sciences, des arts et des métiers, par une société de gens de lettres, mis en ordre et publié par M. Diderot... ; & quant à la partie mathématique par M. d'Alembert* (Paris, 1756), t. 6, 360: "La principale acception de ce terme signifie un parti séditieux dans un état. Le terme de parti par lui-même n'a rien d'odieux, celui de faction l'est toujours".

35 On Hume see, Jennifer A. Herdt, *Religion and Faction in Hume's Moral Philosophy* (New York, 1997) and Marc Hanvelt, *The Politics of Eloquence: David Hume's Polite Rhetoric* (Toronto, 2012). It is also instructive that modern political science does not always consider factionalism a negative and disruptive force. See, for instance, the seminal work by Giovanni Sartori, *Parties and Party Systems. A Framework for Analysis* (Cambridge, 1976).

36 *Journal d'un bourgeois de Paris de 1405 à 1449*, Colette Beaune, ed. (Paris, 1990), 37.

37 Robert Willman, 'The Origins of Whig and Tory in English Political Language', *The Historical Journal* 17, no. 2 (June, 1974), 247–64.

38 Robert Folkenflik, 'Johnson's Politics', in Greg Clingham, ed., *The Cambridge Companion to Samuel Johnson* (Cambridge, 1997), 104.

39 Rosa Maria Dessì, 'I nomi dei guelfi e ghibellini da Carlo I d'Angio a Petrarca', in M. Gentile, ed., *Guelfi e Ghibellini*, 3–78.

had been inspired by the devil.[40] These explanations were certainly connected to mendicant preaching that characterised factions as threats to peaceful urban coexistence[41]—Bernardino da Siena had preached in his sermons that factionalism was the work of the devil and his demons.[42] This conception was still popular at the beginning of the sixteenth century: writing for the duke of Savoy, the Franciscan theologian Michele Dominici asserted that Guelph and Ghibelline were two demons, and that for this reason all people involved in partisanship were sons of demons.[43] It is less important to know the precise extent to which these views were actually believed than to stress that they were powerful weapons used to discredit an opposing party.

Keeping this in mind, many of the contributors to this volume demonstrate how political practice often diverged greatly from political theory when it came to factions. Nadir Weber's study of factionalism in the Prussian principality of Neuchâtel in the eighteenth century shows how princes used a divide-and-rule policy towards factions as a way to consolidate power. The case of Vicenza, analysed by Andrea Savio, shows how urban elites were, owing to factional struggles, able to strengthen their political networks. My study on the House of Savoy's policies towards Genevan factionalism, and Andreas Würgler's analysis of the Swiss situation also indicate how, despite arguments by theoreticians such as Bodin and members of the Franciscan Order that factions were dangerous, princes and members of urban elites could accept their existence and even use it as a modality of political competition. Attempts to stigmatise by accusations of factionalism were not primarily condemnations of partisanship, but instead were usually more an expression of disapproval of an opposing party's policies.

This bring us to another crucial question: how much were factions and their "memberships" a reality and how much a construction of their adversaries? Factional names were often bestowed in order to provide a coherent identity to groups which might have lacked one. In Holland, members of the Kabeljauw

40 See José Ramón Díaz de Durana and and Arsenio Dacosta, 'Changing skin', in this volume.

41 Cf. Francesco Bruni, *La città divisa: Le parti e il bene comune da Dante a Guicciardini* (Bologna, 2003).

42 Michael J. Bailey, 'Reformers on Sorcery and Superstition', in James D. Mixson and Bert Roest, eds., *A Companion to Observant Reform in the Late Middle Ages and Beyond* (Leiden, 2015), 248–49.

43 Michele Dominici, *Quaestio contra diabolicas partialitates guelforum et gibellinorum siue alio quocunque nomine nuncupatas. Per praeclarum sacrae theologiae magistrum & diuini uerbi praeconem celebrem fratrem Michaelem* (Torino: Giovanni Angelo e Bernardino Silva, 1522). This idea can already be found in the thirteenth century as seen in Saba Malaspina's *Historia*. Cf. R.M. Dessì, 'I nomi dei guelfi', 33.

party considered anyone against them to be "Hoeks".[44] Jeroen Duindam has shown how in the Habsburg territories the idea of a "Spanish party" was a rallying cry to unite forces against a common enemy that needed shaping and identification. It was more a label than a reality.[45] Regardless of the names applied to and used in connection with factions, it is fundamental that the boundaries of a party can be blurred and difficult to delineate, not only for historians, but for the actual people living at the time. These difficulties were described by Jean-François Paul de Gondi, the cardinal of Retz, in his *Memories* (1675–1677), where he compared the effort to understand factional dynamics to studying "a science in which [...] one could never be a doctor".[46] The real extent of factional allegiance can easily be misunderstood. Muzio Vitelleschi, the superior general of the Jesuits from 1615 to 1645, once complained that his war policy was misinterpreted: Spaniards considered him pro-French and the French saw him as pro-Spanish.[47] Similarly the view that later Elizabethan court politics constituted factional conflict between the parties of Essex and Cecil is less a reality than a construction of the facts by Essex and his followers "convinced that they were being denied power and influence by their 'enemies' at court—a set of men loosely grouped around the key figure of Robert Cecil".[48] Especially at court, various anxieties, especially the fear of failure and disgrace, could powerfully shape and lend consistency to how a group was viewed by its opponents.[49]

Propaganda, and more generally, the way in which the images of factions were shaped by their adversaries, are not the only obstacles for historians trying to understand them. The nature and dynamics of parties themselves also pose serious problems. It would surely be misleading to limit one's focus on individuals and groups to their status as actors joining more or less preformatted factions or parties. As the prematurely deceased French historian Bernard Lepetit stated: "Human beings are not in social categories like marbles in boxes, and incidentally, the boxes only have the existence that human beings (indigenous people of past times and contemporary historians in the case of the historical discipline), in a context, gave to them", and thus "social identities or social

44 Ter Braake, 'Parties and Factions', 102.

45 Duindam, *Vienna and Versailles*, 255.

46 Stefanovska, *La politique du cardinal*, 121: "une science dans laquelle [...] l'on ne pouvait jamais être docteur".

47 Robert Bireley, *The Jesuits and the Thirty Years War. Kings, Courts, and Confessors* (Cambridge, 2003), 270.

48 Dickinson, *Court Politics*, 76.

49 Cf. Alan Marshall, *The Age of Faction: Court Politics, 1660–1702* (Manchester, 1999), p. 37.

ties do not have a nature, but only usages."[50] In their study for this volume of the so-called "Spanish party", Rubén González Cuerva and Luis Tercero Casado demonstrate that the parties at court were not monoliths, but rather were constituted by "several layers of affinities and groupings" which "coexisted in addition to national identity". Maria Antonietta Visceglia has, with respect to urban Roman factions, reached a similar judgment that lineages could be divided by the opposing views of different factional branches. Courtney Kneupper's study on Conciliarists' use of prophecy shows the many fractures and diversities within that faction. Although eschatological thought was generally used to support arguments for the legitimacy of councils, such thought, in reference to the failure of the Council of Basel, was also instrumental for other purposes, such as the reform of the monastic orders. These findings are consistent with other studies showing how factions and parties were usually heterogeneous and fluid groups,[51] and that loyalties and allegiances could easily change.[52] If from factions we switch attention to individuals, it can be seen that their networks were often made up of multiple and usually overlapping circles.[53]

It is then probably useful to extend to the study of partisanship Geert Janssen's suggestion that patronage be thought of more as a "process" than a "status".[54] And, with every process, much is to be gained from a deeper analysis of the language used by contemporaries to describe it. Many contributions to this volume underline the importance contemporary witnesses assigned to the "passions" of their adversaries and to the role of leaders' personal charisma. In her analysis of Roman partisanship, Maria Antonietta Visceglia has reminded us that the sources have drawn on "a vocabulary of passions", and Olivia Carpi has noticed how factional Leaguers were described in the king's correspondence as people "driven only by 'their passions and particular affections'". Similarly, many observers insisted on the power of "seduction" wielded by factional leaders. Dominique Adrian in his paper for this volume notices that the

50 Bernard Lepetit, 'Histoire des pratiques, pratiques de l'histoire', in idem, ed., *Les formes de l'expérience. Une autre histoire sociale* (Paris, 1995), 13 : "...les hommes ne sont pas dans les catégories sociales comme des billes dans des boîtes, et que d'ailleurs les 'boîtes' n'ont d'autre existence que celles que les hommes (les indigènes du passé et les historiens d'aujourd'hui dans le cas de la discipline historique), en contexte, leur donnent. [...] les identités sociales ou les liens sociaux n'ont pas de nature, mais seulement des usages".

51 Ives, *Factions*, pp. 17–20; Gentile, 'Factions and parties', 308.

52 Duindam, *Vienna and Versailles*, 249.

53 John Watts, *The Making of Polities* (Cambridge, 2009), 153–57; Marshall, *The Age of Factions*, 36–37.

54 Janssen Geert H., *Princely power in the Dutch Republic: patronage and William Frederick of Nassau (1613–64)* (Manchester, 2008), 7.

chronicler Burkhard Zink explained Peter von Argon's personal leadership as the fruit of his friendly and seductive manners. Emotional language was more than simple rhetoric, and shows how the alleged existence of "passions" contributed to shaping the opposing party's view of a faction.

These observations surely need and deserve a more complete analysis. Relatedly, how much has character, more than religious beliefs or political views, affected decisions taken by factional leaders at court and in cities? Contemporaries were fully aware that passions and a ruler's emotions could provide a means of influence, as Bertrand Schnerb has demonstrated with respect to factions in the fifteenth-century Burgundy court, which appealed to the duke's anxieties for their own political purposes.[55] This is surely not an easy path to follow, but the important place held by emotions in historical studies encourages historians to continue working in this direction.[56] A more in-depth investigation of the role of emotions and a rediscovery of a more psychological approach to historical analysis would probably help us to better understand the political societies of medieval and early modern times.[57]

Did factions exist? They surely did—sometimes they had a tangible life over many decades, and sometimes their existence was more ephemeral, lasting only during the time of the circumstances which generated them. Sometimes they were simply the fruit of the fear, anxieties and propaganda of competing groups and individuals. It is the role of historians to disentangle these different characteristics and, if possible, to show connections (or the absence of connections) between them. The essays collected here do not pretend to provide concise definitional boundaries to the phenomenon of factional struggles.

---

55 Bertrand Schnerb, '*Familiarissimus domini ducis.* La succession des favoris à la cour de Bourgogne au début du XVe siècle', in Werner Paravicini and Jan Hirschbiegel, eds., *Der Fall des Günstlings. Hofparteien in Europa vom 13. bis zum 17. Jahrhundert* (Ostfildern, 2004), 177–89.

56 Among an increasingly rich literature, see William M. Reddy, *The Navigation of Feeling: A Framework for the History of Emotions* (New York, 2001); Damien Boquet and Piroska Nagy, *Sensible Moyen Âge. Une histoire des émotions dans l'Occident médiéval* (Paris, 2015); Barbara H. Rosenwein, *Generations of feeling: a history of emotions, 600–1700* (Cambridge: 2016); Alain Corbin, Jean-Jacques Courtine, Georges Vigarello, eds., *Histoire des émotions*, 3 vols. (Paris, 2016).

57 For some interesting analysis, see Laurent Smagghe, *Les émotions du prince. Émotions et discours politique dans l'espace bourguignon* (Paris, 2012). See also the historiographical remarks in Barbara H. Rosenwein, 'The Place of Renaissance Italy in the History of Emotions', in *Emotions, Passions, and Power in Renaissance Italy*, ed. Fabrizio Ricciardelli and Andrea Zorzi (Amsterdam: Amsterdam University Press, 2015), 15–30, which also discussed Edward Muir's use of emotions in his *Mad Blood Stirring*.

What they provide is discussion, based on concrete historical situations, of factional dynamics and of the way contemporaries saw and experienced factionalism. They demonstrate that factions contributed to the makeup of political society during the early modern period, but asking questions, as we have done here, about their existence and functioning is useful for teasing out the precise nature of factions, serving a purpose beyond just a provocative title for an introduction.

The Black Raven and His Gang: Politics in Augsburg in Times of Crisis (1450–1480)

*Dominique Adrian**

Hear now of the black raven,
How he knew the way to snap so many treasures.
When he had built his nest,
He gathered many little birds in it,
Like magpies, ravens, vultures and kites
Whose greed makes them shout all the time.
Their screams were so diverse,
Nobody could avoid their violence
With their cunning and wicked beaks,
They intended to force the good birds,
So that they could throw by their bites
Eagle, pelican, ostrich out of the house.[1]

A swarm of wicked birds against birds of better breeds: in an anonymous poem of the time, this animal metaphor exemplifies the desolate state of political life in Augsburg, one of the main southern German imperial cities, just after the execution of the mayor Ulrich Schwarz in 1478, who is the black raven of the text. We know the real names of many of the 'birds' around him, 'middle-class' craft masters who, during Schwarz's short time as the political leader of the city, reached political positions most often reserved for merchants, patricians and other wealthy citizens (although exceptions were always possible—Schwarz himself was one). As with most other cities of the region, the political system in Augsburg, since 1368, had been based on representation of the citizens through guild masters (*Zunftmeister*) and other guild representatives, who served on the town council together with privileged members of the

* I use the following abbreviation: Augsburg, Stadtarchiv = StAA.

1 Rochus von Liliencron, *Volkslieder der Deutschen vom 13. bis 16. Jahrhundert*, vol. 2 (Leipzig, 1866), 133: "Nun höret von dem schwarzen rappen,/ wie er so manichen schatz tet schnappen!/ Als er sein netz gemachet het,/ darein vil voglin versamlet tet/ von alster krauen geiern und weien,/ Die allweg nach dem geiz schreien./ Ir geschrai was gar manigfalt,/ schier niemant kund für iren gewalt;/ mit iren listen und bösen schnebel/ mainten zů nöten die gůten vögel,/ daß s' adler, pelican und strauß/ heten gebißen ab dem haus". *Strauß* (ostrich) is certainly a wordplay on the name of Jörg Strauß, one of Schwarz's main enemies.

 | DOI 10.1163/9789004345348_003

'old lineages' (*Geschlechter, Herren*, 'patricians'). In cities like Constance and Memmingen,[2] the antagonism between guild members and *Geschlechter* remained a vivid fault line with a few more or less violent episodes; in Augsburg, the common interests of the rich guild merchants and the *Geschlechter* led to a generally peaceful coexistence, helped by a relative absence of economic dynamism and the demographic decline of the *Geschlechter*.

However, civil peace was not left untroubled in late medieval Augsburg. The main episodes followed the two *Städtekriege* (Town Wars of 1387–1389 and 1449–1450), between an alliance of most southern German towns on the one hand and local lords and princes on the other. In both cases, the discontent in the city was triggered not by disagreements over issues related to the war itself, but by the fiscal load imposed by the wars' expenses: in addition to the traditional and widely-accepted *Steuer* (wealth tax), the municipality was forced to increase the rate of the *Ungeld* (sales tax on wine, wheat, etc.). With respect to the first Town War, chronicles testify to the discontent of "a part of the crafts and many poor people" following on a tax raised to finance the repair of the town walls in anticipation of the war;[3] ten years later, the authority of the town council was challenged by a strong movement of public opinion in favour of abolishing the tax, even though it was still much needed to assist with paying back the war debt.[4] Events in 1387 seem to have been limited to fierce debates in the council; the conflict was styled by the chronicler Hector Mülich around 1470 as a confrontation between "the council" and "the common", the latter of which asked and obtained just recompense in exchange for their acceptance of the new tax—in Mülich's words at least, basic civic unity remained untouched.[5]

The opponents of the tax in 1397 are described in another earlier chronicle as "secretly assembled with their banners in their sleeves";[6] they seem to have been organized even before the council discovered their intent. The major role

2 Constance: see the introduction by Konrad Beyerle in Otto Feger, *Das Rote Buch*, (Konstanz, 1949) (Konstanzer Geschichts- und Rechtsquellen 1), *1–*28; Memmingen: Dominique Adrian, 'La chronique de Memmingen', to be published in *The medieval Chronicle*, no 11 (2017). The chroniclers only show these two parties as coherent entities, without mentioning the name of their leaders.

3 Chronicles are cited under the names of their authors or under the conventional name given by the editors of the *Chroniken der deutschen Städte* series (Karl Hegel, ed., *Die Chroniken der deutschen Städte vom 14. bis ins 16. Jahhrundert*, 36 vol., (Leipzig, 1864–1968), cited as CDS). 1387: "ain tail der hantwerk und darzů vil armer lüt", *Chronik von 1368 bis 1406 (1447)* (CDS 4, 79); see there, on the *Ungeld*, the annex, 157–65.

4 Ibid., 109–110.

5 CDS 22, 29.

6 *Chronik von der Gründung der Stadt Augsburg bis 1469*, CDS 4, 316: "gesamelt mit iren panern in den örmelen haimlich". See Burkhard Zink, CDS 5, 52–53; Hector Mülich, CDS 22, 47:

here was played by five of the seventeen guilds, craft guilds as opposed to the wealthier trade guilds, with socially homogeneous memberships. This group could be identified as a "faction" —an alliance of citizens (certainly including councillors) focussed on common goals and acting in a coordinated manner— and they met with at least temporary success: the *Ungeld* was abolished over a period of a few months, before the hard realities of the town's finances became clear. What we do not see here is any hint of the identity of the opposition leaders: we know only that the leading guilds operated as a clearly delimited group, in their official capacity, far from being a small conspiratorial group, probably with the guild masters acting as spokesmen. They saw their action as a defence of the common interest, not of their own profit.

In the middle of the next century, the troubles triggered by the second Town War, troubles which lasted from 1450 to 1478, are well-documented by a wide range of documentary evidence, including many sources authored by the main actors of the successive episodes, both from the popular movement and the conservative party. During those three decades, the personal and thematic continuity of these opposing groups, as well as their capacity to pursue their goals effectively, was a dominant feature of political life in Augsburg. This article focuses on the men who supported these opposing agendas: accusations of forming an organized faction in support of specific ideas were common weapons in the political debate, since factions were seen as opposing the "common interest" every politician claimed to have in mind. Even though many leading politicians are described in the sources as isolated actors reigning through their personal charisma, these sources also allow us to analyse their interactions with other sectors of the political sphere. Three of them in succession shone as major personalities in the political debates of those few decades.

1 Three Popular Leaders: Peter von Argon, Heinrich Erlbach, Ulrich Schwarz

Peter von Argon (1414–1452)[7] is somehow an older type of popular leader, a man from the upper class leading the guilds, similar to Ulrich Kunzelmann

"bei ainander bewapnet zů den parfůssen mit iren panern" ("assembled together at the Franciscan church [in an area where many artisans lived], armed, with their banners").

7 On his political career, see Hartmut Boockmann, 'Spätmittelalterliche deutsche Stadt-Tyrannen', *Blätter für deutsche Landesgeschichte* 119 (1983), 73–91, as well as the documentary evidence in CDS 5, 395–420. Two manuscripts written by Argon with a list of his extensive possessions both in and outside the town remain virtually unexplored (StAA, Schätze 147 and 148).

in Ulm around 1325 or Rudolf Brun in Zurich from 1336.[8] His family was very likely one of the 'old lineages' who chose in 1368 to favour their economic interests over their social status and entered the merchants' guild. Peter von Argon himself was, during most of his life, the richest man in Augsburg, and he held the highest political offices of the city from an early age. The chronicler Burkhard Zink, who worked for him, draws a very critical portrait of his former master, describing him as a shameless demagogue: he "was extremely friendly to the poor people", which paved the way for him to gain a dominant position in the council, and he "was more powerful than anybody ever in this town". But it wasn't enough for him, as Zink wrote: to secure even more power, he left the city in 1444, confident that his supporters among the guild masters would make it possible to have him recalled to his previous positions of power, and so it happened in the following year—in fact, "he could be so friendly to the guild masters that they were all eager to do whatever he wanted from them."[9]

It may seem incorrect to identify such personal power as indicative of a "faction". It would be more accurate to speak of a patron and his clients—even though Zink describes something that is more akin to seduction than to tangible benefits for Argon's clients, and it is difficult indeed to discover precise political goals in his followers' actions, other than the consolidation of Argon's personal power. Why, then, include Peter von Argon and his followers/clients in this study? Because in the events surrounding his voluntary exile and consequent downfall, we have a first hint of an embryonic 'popular party' within Augsburg's civic institutions. These events took place at the dawn of a period of thirty years of political instability in the city, even before (or perhaps at the same time as) this emerging discontent was inflamed by the huge increase in the city's debt during the second Town War. So even though the guild masters may have been dependent on Peter von Argon, their coherent action in his service may have been a significant factor in structuring the popular opposition in subsequent decades.

In late 1450, though, Argon's renewed ambitions for greater personal power were thwarted and he was exiled. In the same year, the city's officials appointed

---

Peter von Argon's original name was Peter Egen. He was inspired to change his name by the ancient Greek legend.

8 Christian Keitel, 'Städtische Bevölkerung und Stadtregiment bis 1397', in Hans-Eugen Specker, ed., *Die Ulmer Bürgerschaft auf dem Weg zur Demokratie* (Ulm, 1997), 96–103 (overstating the often understated importance of the political context of the Empire); Anton Largiadèr, *Bürgermeister Rudolf Brun und die Zürcher Revolution von 1336* (Zurich, 1936) (*Neujahrsblatt der Antiquarischen Gesellschaft in Zürich* 100).

9 Zink, CDS 5, 197–99: he "was gar grausam freuntlich gegen armen leuten", "was so gewaltig als kainer nie in diser stat was"; "er kund es so freuntlich mit den zunftmaistern, daß sie im all willig waren, wes er von in begert".

a new town clerk (*Stadtschreiber*), Heinrich Erlbach,[10] whose background remains unknown to us.[11] The position was at this time mainly a technical one with few political responsibilities, but the oath he took when assuming the office[12] stated that he was required to advise the council to the best of his abilities. This clause was sufficiently vague to allow anyone with the skills to exploit the majority's opposition to the heavy tax load an opportunity to resist the council's traditional tax policy. The policy he advocated apparently found a wide range of supporters among the guild representatives, but engendered aggressive hostility from many traditional political leaders. Their opposition to Erlbach was unsuccessful until 1459, when he was dismissed from the office.

In his justificatory writings after his forced departure, Erlbach readily testified that his purpose was indeed to bring a new political orientation to the city; the council books of the years he was the town clerk provide evidence supporting this assertion and show that he enjoyed broad support in the council. One of his major achievements was the appointment of a special commission in 1456 to investigate the financial situation of the city and to propose reforms which would alleviate the tax burden: this commission, composed mainly of powerful and experienced politicians, prepared a long report with many proposals for better management of municipal finances. This report was widely disseminated, especially in guild circles, which saw it as proof of their ability to influence important decisions in the general interest of guild members as well as for the common good of whole city.

Implementation of reform measures quelled popular discontent for a time, but did not address the city's debt problem. Exactly ten years after the work of the first commission, a new commission was formed, with the same goals, but with a completely different composition.[13] This time, the commission consisted of only one patrician with 17 representatives of the guilds, one from each guild. Established politicians such as Jörg Strauß and Andreas Frickinger were confronted by a majority of delegates from the craft guilds, so that they were

10 On Erlbach, see my article 'La face cachée de la politique. Le chancelier au cœur des tensions politiques à Augsbourg au XVe siècle', *Journal des savants* (janvier-juin 2008), 107–21. A large number of sources were copied in the mid-16th century by Paul Hector Mair, a servant of the council, in his *Memoribuch*, StAA, Schätze 119, fol. 336r–472v.

11 The only information we have on his previous career comes from his Augsburg enemies (letter from 1467 to the Duke of Bavaria): Erlbach held other positions before he came to Augsburg, and when he left the city his departure "left very few regrets and complaints". (Ibid., fol. 433r).

12 StAA, Urkunden, 14 March 1450. See citation in Adrian, *Augsbourg à la fin du Moyen Âge: la politique et l'espace* (Ostfildern, 2013) 236.

13 StAA, Ratsbuch 7, 61–62.

forced to make compromises in order to reach acceptable decisions. The representative of the carpenters was Ulrich Schwarz,[14] a relatively new name in Augsburg politics: he was elected to the council for the first time by his peers in 1459, directly as a guild master, but had not yet reached a higher position in the city's government. Years later, the Benedictine monk Wilhelm Wittwer wrote a short but valuable remark on Schwarz's beginnings as a politician: Hans Vittel and Andreas Frickinger, wrote Wittwer, "helped him in many ways and promoted him in his youth, because he was Frickinger's servant and behaved laudably. This way, many people liked him, and thus, after some time, he was promoted to [guild] master, i.e. *zunftmaister*."[15]

In the following years, Schwarz rose quickly to power: he was elected as one of the three *Baumeister* (responsible for public finances) in 1467, certainly as a reward for his role in the 1466 commission; he then rose to become one of the two mayors for the first time in 1469. He was re-elected in 1471 and 1473, having respected the obligatory gap between each one-year term; from 1475 to 1478, however, he remained in office continuously for four years, "which was unheard-of in this imperial city,"[16] as Wittwer wrote. This infringement should be seen both as a mark of his continued popular support and as the result of Schwarz's efforts to secure his power over the long term. Contrary to many older and more modern views of Schwarz, his comparatively long tenure was accompanied by a real political program, explained by Schwarz to an emissary from the Freiburg council in 1476,[17] and observable in the legislative activity of the council as reflected in the council's books. Schwarz was a reformer in

14 The only thorough biography of Schwarz is the 1913 thesis by Georg Panzer, *Ulrich Schwarz, der Zunftbürgermeister von Augsburg 1422–1478*, Munich, 1913, with edited sources pp. 86–109. Some important sources edited in CDS 22, 415–43. The only modern, as well as stimulating, account of Schwarz's political career is Jörg Rogge, *Für den gemeinen Nutzen. Politisches Handeln und Politikverständnis von Rat und Bürgerschaft in Augsburg im Spätmittelalter* (*Studia Augustana* 6), Tübingen 1996, mainly 48–98.

15 Wilhelm Wittwer, 'Catalogus Abbatum monasterii SS. Udalrici et Afrae Augustensis', ed. Anton von Steichele, *Archiv für die Geschichte des Bisthums Augsburg* 3 (1860), 10–437, here 295: "Multa bona fecerunt ac promouerunt eum in juventute, quia famulus ipsius Frickinger fuit et laudabiliter se habuit, ut eciam placeret multis, ita ut successu temporis promotus fuit in magistrum id est zunftmayster". This is the only allusion to civic politics in the *Catalogus*; the source of this is very likely Frickinger himself, who sought refuge from Schwarz at St. Ulrich in 1477 and died there the following year.

16 Ibid., 295: "quod inauditum fuit in hac regali civitate".

17 Tom Scott, *Die Freiburger Enquete von 1476. Quellen zur Wirtschafts- und Verwaltungsgeschichte der Stadt Freiburg im Breisgau im fünfzehnten Jahrhundert* (Freiburg im Breisgau, 1986) (*Veröffentlichungen aus dem Archiv der Stadt Freiburg im Breisgau* 20), 21–26.

the most classic sense: his goal was a broad overhaul of the city's government through a restoration of the idealized situation of 1368, the year which gave birth to the guild system. This meant primarily re-establishing equality between the guilds, which had been destroyed by a usurpation of power by the richest (merchant) guilds allied to the patricians; Schwarz's program provided that the latter should be given no more power than any other guild. Predictably, this policy won him many enemies, and they succeeded in having him arrested and eventually executed in the spring of 1478, at which point this decades-long era of successful popular politics in Augsburg came to an end.

2 Factions in a Troubled Time

Only for the Schwarz era do we have both the names of the partisans and the adversaries of these men; these are mentioned in many documents. The list of all the actors who disappeared from the political stage during the Schwarz era is impressive—some exited the stage via execution, including both enemies during his reign and partisans after his downfall, some were exiled, and some others were merely expelled from the council. From the Erlbach years, we only have the identities of his adversaries; he named them himself in letters he wrote to defend himself after his dismissal:[18] "Heinrich Langenmantel, Andreas Frickinger, Leonhard Radauer, and some others"—Thomas Ehem, Jörg Strauß and Hans Vittel are named later in the same text.[19] All six were experienced politicians; two (Langenmantel, Radauer) were patricians, the others were not, but they all belonged to the council, and all but Ehem and Vittel had served as mayor in the pre-Erlbach period. A somewhat exceptional document shows them acting as a faction, in full conspiracy mode: a protocol of interrogation at the secret courts of Westphalia presents the intriguing testimony of a secret agent for the city, Gebhard Kepler.[20] Kepler narrates how, after a few routine missions, his patrons gave him a most unusual and difficult assignment: on the promise of a large financial compensation, the task he reluctantly accepted was nothing less than the assassination of the town clerk himself. In his statement, Kepler named a few names: he was recruited by Radauer, Strauß, Thomas Ehem, an unknown "Gessler the guild master", and Hans Vittel; the murder was ordered in Ehem's house, in the presence of Leonhard Radauer. All those names appear in Erlbach's justificatory writings, with the exception

18 Most texts copied by Paul Hector Mair in Augsburg, StAA, Schätze 119.

19 Ibid., fol. 346r.

20 Ibid., fol. 357r–359r and fol. 402r–408r (two versions of the same text, the first one only partial); see my article cited in note 10.

of the unidentified guild master Gessler. As Erlbach put it, it was impossible for him "to satisfy everyone in the council, since they were on bad terms with each other". Was Kepler's recruitment motivated from the start by hostility toward Erlbach? In any event, both Kepler's and Erlbach's testimonies give the impression of a compact faction of experienced politicians from the social elite of the city. Whether their alliance was the product of long-term opposition inside the political system or of a momentary reaction against Erlbach and his backers remains unclear.

Most importantly, the names of Erlbach's enemies are at least partially the same as Schwarz's enemies. During the Schwarz era, Frickinger fled possible prosecution for the immunity of St. Ulrich monastery (and died there); Hans Vittel was executed in 1477 with his brother Leonhard on charges of betraying the city's interests after complaining against Schwarz to the Emperor during an official mission; Jörg Strauß was one of the main architects of Schwarz's downfall and of the rebuilding a more autocratic style of government afterwards. Schwarz himself was not present on the political stage at the time of Erlbach's dismissal, and the sources do not address whether one or more politicians took on Erlbach's political goals or transmitted them to the Schwarz generation, but the common political program, the common enemies, and the events of 1466 all support a conclusion that a more or less organized party supporting popular politics continued to exist after Erlbach's tenure.

The use of the avian metaphor in the poem set forth in the introduction was prompted by the name of one of Schwarz's main opponents, Jörg Strauß: Strauß means ostrich; Frickinger's crest of arms depicted an eagle wing, and the arms of many other patrician families also depicted birds;[21] other direct allusions may be hidden to us by the scarcity of sources. In any case, their common enemy was the raven, the superlative black (*schwarz*) bird.

The sources' precise information about the political background in the short period around 1478 strongly indicate that these texts were written in the immediate aftermath of Schwarz's execution, even though most of the manuscripts available to us date from the 16th century.[22] The enemies, Schwarz's "jüngern" (disciples) as one source calls them, are known mostly—but very partially—

21 See the coats of arms hanging in the patrician meeting hall (*Herrenstube*) in Hector Mülich's copy of the Meisterlin chronicle, Staats- und Stadtbibliothek Augsburg, 2° Cod. H 1, fol. 117v–121r, reproduced in Dieter Weber, *Geschichtsschreibung in Augsburg. Hektor Mülich und die reichsstädtische Chronistik des Spätmittelalters* (Augsburg, 1984: *Archiv für die Geschichte der Stadt Augsburg* 30), no. 97–104.

22 See note 1; the exception is the poem by Hans Schneider, preserved in Munich, Bayerische Staatsbibliothek, cgm 379 (added to the end of a 1454 songbook) and its copy in Salzburg, St. Peter, cod. b IV 3 (end of the 15th century).

from records of the repressive measures taken after their patron's death and from another anti-Schwarz poem.[23] Unsurprisingly, the fiscal records show how much the wealth of Schwarz's disciples was inferior to their enemies.[24] The fiscal records also show that his disciples were far from being destitute, but it would be wrong to infer from this fact that Schwarz's reformatory policy was directed only towards those wealthier guild members—we only have information about the identities of the minority of guild representatives whose involvement with Schwarz was judged serious enough to justify punishment. We do not know the identities of all of Schwarz's supporters inside the council, and we know even less about the guild members who voted for Schwarz's supporters.[25]

Two lists of council members from the time of the Vittel brothers' death sentences appear to prove that their condemnation resulted from a broad consensus in the council. The first list of 44 names is followed by the somewhat cryptic phrase "Summa 44 Personen, darunder vier geurtailt ain zum tod 2 nit weis und ainer allain h vittel disen nit",[26] meaning approximately: "Total forty-four persons, of whom four judged [differently?]: [only?] one to death, two didn't know, one only H[ans] Vittel, but not to death [?]"; this appears to be the list of all persons who were present at the council when the death sentence against the Vittels was rendered. The second list contains 65 names after those of the two mayors: it is a fairly precise list of all the members of the Little council and the Council of Elders, a supplementary body to the Little council.[27]

23 See Liliencron, *Volkslieder der Deutschen*, 140 (Neumüller, Glatz, Hacker, Taglang, "Bartolme Schneider cramer", "der Schmidel underkeufel", Herzl "zunftmaister under den schůster", Hans Mezger).

24 See Rogge, *Für den gemeinen Nutzen*, 60 (with imprecise source indication, mostly from CDS 22, 374–375 [here the word "jüngern"] and StAA, Ratsbuch 8, fol. 100r–v). A 16th century chronicle (Staats- und Stadtbibliothek Augsburg, 2° Cod. Aug. 69, fol. 20v–22r) offers not only a list of the council members for 1478 and of those who were arrested with Schwarz, but also another list under the title "Dise nachgeschribne seind diser Zeit nit in dem Rath gewesen" ("The following were not in the council at this time"), with 22 names, among whom two "send austretten alß fraundt" ("had got away as friends", i.e. as his relatives). Those 22 names are not exclusively of well-known supporters of Schwarz, but the sense is quite clearly that most of them were not welcome at this session, in order to secure Schwarz's downfall. Erlbach described the same practice of a partial meeting of the council used by his enemies in 1459 (StAA Schätze 119, fol. 350r).

25 Council members from the guilds were elected by the general assembly of the guild; it is certain that the elites of every guild were able to exercise influence over those elections, but it is also clear that shifts in public opinion were reflected in the electoral results.

26 StAA Schätze 123, fol. 313v–315v (copy by Paul Hector Mair).

27 The Council of Elders was composed of politicians not serving on the Little council (either because they did not wish to serve or because they failed to be elected) who were occasionally summoned to sit with the Little council.

Of the 12 patricians cited in the second list, only four were present at the fateful council meeting, and there is no indication that any of these four cast a vote for clemency; the four councillors from the merchant guild were absent, as well as three of the four councillors from the *Krämer* guild, of which the Vittels were members. One other guild, the salt and wine sellers' guild, was represented by only one councillor, but that representative was not the guild's leader for the previous thirty years, Andreas Frickinger, who in 1477 was elected only to the council of Elders, certainly a bitter defeat for him; his colleague who appeared at the meeting and voted for the Vittels' death sentence was probably one of his political opponents. Of the five other councillors missing from the execution vote list, one was a wealthy merchant and a proficient adversary of any kind of popular politics, Jörg Strauß—there are no clues in the sources that would allow us determine whether he, Frickinger and the patricians were absent because Schwarz excluded them from the session or because they decided to refrain from taking part in a session with such an agenda. The four other absentees came from four different guilds and were probably genuine artisans; their absence may be explained by the low level of political involvement by the poorer guild representatives, but the identity of the three named opponents to the death sentence—a furrier, a brewer, and a loden weaver—contradicts the picture of supposedly sheepish obedience on the part of the poorer guild representatives.

The impression Schwarz intended to give is that his leadership of the urban community was based on a broadly shared conception of the common good. To show the broad support he enjoyed in the council, Schwarz twice reported results of ballots in the council, an extremely rare proceeding in Augsburg. In every election for the mayoral office beginning in 1475, he wrote, he received the same number of votes (29 out of 42 members of the council).[28] In 1475, a debate arose in the council about a peasant captured by the patrician Hans Vetter, maybe one of Vetter's serfs. Vetter probably wanted to have him condemned by the council, but Schwarz questioned the legality of this seizure and obtained the peasant's release. "28 men followed me on this verdict; Bartholome Welser, Lucas and Peter Herwart wanted to condemn him to death": those three patricians, Schwarz implied, defended the interest of their peer, while the vast majority of loyal citizens followed the common good as embodied by himself; and as always, the "faction" was the opposing party.

28 Panzer 93 (from the dossier on Schwarz by Clemens Jäger, Staatsarchiv Augsburg, Reichsstadt Augsburg MüB Literalien 105 [cited hereafter 'Jäger'], fol. 228v): "Der urtail volgent mir 28 man; aber Bartholme Welser, Lucas und Peter die Herwart, erkanten in zu dem tod".

3 Factions in Political Argumentation

3.1 *Chronicles*

Polemical writings were produced around both Erlbach and Schwarz: Erlbach was very active in justifying his actions after his dismissal in 1459, and the city answered at least partially—and rather reluctantly—his accusations;[29] Schwarz wrote a short justificatory text[30] (often called a "chronicle", rather inappropriately), and immediately became the anti-hero of five poems.[31] This body of opposing texts offers a wide range of opportunities to analyse the political arguments that circulated and how they were used, in addition to opportunities provided by narratives contained in some chronicles.[32] In most of the chronicles, however, no mention is made of "factions": Hector Mülich remarked that Erlbach made "a great discord here" and would have made even more if he could,[33] but neither with respect to Erlbach nor Schwarz does he

29 See note 17.

30 Jäger, fol. 228r–235v (16th century copy), edited by Panzer, 92–107.

31 The four anonymous poems are edited by Liliencron, *Volkslieder der Deutschen*, 126–42; Hans Schneider's work is edited by Konrad Hofmann, 'Hans Schneiders historisches Gedicht auf die Hinrichtung des Augsburger Bürgermeisters Schwarz', in *Sitzungsberichte der Königl. Bayerischen Akademie der Wissenschaften zu München*, 1870/1 (München, 1870), 500–511. See Isolde Neugart, 'Ulrich Schwarz', and Frieder Schanze, 'Schneider, Hans', in *Die deutsche Literatur des Mittelalters. Verfasserlexikon*, respectively vol. 10, 17–21 and vol. 8, 786–97 (no. 2).

32 Many other polemical texts were produced around 1548, when Emperor Charles v imposed a new political regime dominated by the *Geschlechter*. These texts were produced before this date to praise the old regime and after it to justify the new course, both mainly by Clemens Jäger. The best-known of these texts is certainly the so-called *Vorbereitung aines erbern Rats der Stat Augspurg wider die nichtig auch ongegründet und grob Anklag des Österreichers Anno 1555 Ultimo Decembris* ("Preparation of the honourable council of the City of Augsburg against the void, unfounded and gross accusation by Österreicher", December 31, 1555) in which Schwarz is a key target of the anti-guild rhetoric (StAA, Reichsstadt Augsburg MüB Literalien 97 and StAA, Schätze 55; the entire text is still unedited, but some excerpts on Ulrich Schwarz are printed in CDS 22, 416–431; see Pius Dirr, 'Clemens Jäger und seine Augsburger Ehrenbücher und Zunftchroniken. Zur Kenntnis der Historiographie des 16. Jahrhunderts', *Zeitschrift des Historischen Vereins von Schwaben* 36 (1910), 1–32, here 19–23); for Jäger's perspective on Schwarz, see Gregor Rohmann, *„Eines Ehrbaren Raths gehorsamer Amptman". Clemens Jäger und die Geschichtsschreibung des 16. Jahrhunderts* (*Studien zur Geschichte des Bayerischen Schwaben* 28) (Augsburg, 2001), 301–7 (note the intensive use of the bird metaphor in direct imitation of the poems from around 1480).

33 Mülich, CDS 22, 153–54: "groß zwieträchtigkait hie".

mention the building of coherent parties following or opposing those leaders. With respect to Schwarz, Mülich's remark that "he could reach everything he wanted" is nearly identical to Zink's words about Peter von Argon. Mülich himself, a longstanding member of the council and one of the city's richest citizens, does not appear to have belonged to any of the opposing factions: when Schwarz sent the brothers Vittel to the gallows, Mülich recorded the facts with a negative assessment of the brothers' temperaments, and when Schwarz was himself handed over to the executioner, he remarked on his excessive use of power. Mülich neither pitied the martyrs of a tyrant as the satirical poems do, nor repeated the allegations of corrupt practices contained in the poems, in Schwarz's *Urgicht* ('protocol of interrogation'), a widely diffused text which is either completely apocryphal or obtained by torture, and in the *Beruff*, the text of the proclamation announcing Schwarz's death sentence.[34]

Along with *sonderung* (separation, separate group) and *partey* (party), *Zwieträchtigkeit* (discord) was a common word for the chroniclers, showing their views on the political life of their times: their chief concern was civic unity, and civic division their cardinal fear. The creation of factions centred around a leader has little place in their political vision, perhaps because of the poor image the existence of factions would lend to the city. Schwarz's rise to power, however, was described by one unconventional chronicler as the product of factional action. Wilhelm Rem (c. 1462-c. 1529) described a group of guild masters as

> mediocre craftsmen, who had no wisdom, with bad body and bad fortune. Under them there was one called Ulrich Schwarz, from the carpenters' guild; he was a mediocre man too, but he was the most distinguished among that pack; he brought them together, and they aspired to the guild master offices in the guilds, they made one another powerful in the city and in the council, so that their voice predominated, and they were all so supportive that they made Schwarz a mayor, one became a director of the civic finances, another a tax collector, a third a customs officer; so they distributed all the city offices, to themselves and to one another, every year, because their power kept growing. And they spent time everyday

34 Both edited by Panzer, 87–90. Most of what Schwarz "confesses" are crimes he committed alone, in his private life (assassinating his wife's first husband, mixing perry with wine…) as well as ex officio (making secret keys of the city gates…), but "sein anhang"/"seine gesellen" took part in some of his misdeeds (no names are provided).

> together, they ate and drank together (…). The votes of the other councillors were worthless, and it annoyed many honourable citizens, patricians and others, that their vote was not taken into consideration, so that they came even less often to the sessions, and that was only favourable for the others.[35]

Rem was only a youth when Schwarz died, but certainly had many occasions to speak with his elders about these events. His personal views were marked by two peculiarities: his family left the patrician group in 1368, but in his chronicle he consistently championed the development of a strong elitist identity through all means of social distinction; and since 1462 his family had been excluded from the council after the misdeeds of one of its members, so that he had no direct experience of the municipal government. On themes such as the Schwarz story, what he finds in the Mülich chronicle is unsatisfactory to him. Rem's narration does not rely on earlier chronicles; it is much livelier than Mülich's chronicle because, unlike Mülich who was bound by his oath as a councillor, Rem enjoyed an outsider's freedom.

Rem's text is marked by its political bias, but describes quite clearly how a faction operated. Politics were only a part of its activity: the group was constituted even before any of them rose to power—Rem uses the word *rott*, comparing them to a criminal gang—and the group's solidarity was strengthened by common meals. Rem does not mention a political programme: what counts for him is the positions of power they conquered gradually, their strength residing in their unwavering solidarity. Rem's argumentation follows well-known patterns: his method of stressing the self-seeking interests of the other party without mentioning its political ideology is a classical way to discredit a political adversary, and the other chronicles, including Zink, used that same method of argumentation many times. The distinctive aspect of the Rem chronicle is

35 CDS 22, 371 (also ed. by Liliencron, *Volkslieder der Deutschen*, 133): "schlecht handwerchsleutt, die on weishait, leib und guet schlecht waren. Under denen was ainer, hies Ůlrich Schwartz, aus der zimerleutt zunft, der was auch ain schlecht man, doch was er der furnembst in diser rott; er hueb die andern zesamen, sy stallten auch vast nach dem zunftmaisterampt in den zünften, sy machten ainander gewalltig inn der statt und im ratt, das ir stim fürtraff, das sy so ainhellig waren, also das sy machten den Schwartzen zum burgermaister, ainen zum paumaister, den andern zů steurmaister, den dritten zum ungeltter; und also verliehen sy der statt ämpter, sy inen selbs und anainander, alle jar, wann ir gewallt meret sich. und giengen alle tag zůsamen und assen und truncken mit ainander. (…) der ander herrn rett stim galt nichtz, wann es etlich frum erber leutt von burgeren auch andern verdroß, das ir stim nichtz solt sein, das sy dest minder in ratt giengen, das was den andern nun lieb."

the coherence of its anti-guild vision: the way he used the Schwarz episode to show the inherent frailties of the guild system led directly to the authoritarian offensive of the subsequent decades, up until the abolition of the guild system by Charles V.

3.2 *Poems on Schwarz*

"Ulrich Schwarz und sein anhang" (Ulrich Schwarz and his *anhang*): the word *anhang*, probably the most precise equivalent in the contemporary texts to "faction", appears in the title given by chronicler Wilhelm Rem around 1500 to his copy of one of the five known poems about Schwarz, and the poem itself illustrates some of the implications of the word: Schwarz arranged

> that some wise, worthy and pious persons
> had to leave the council,
> and so made place to some guilds
> to have all the more followers.
> He was cunning enough,
> by his tricks and inventions,
> to get to be elected mayor
> so that they could be at ease [?].
> He prepared all that with Taglang,
> to get such a faction with him
> of all who wanted to quench their thirst
> where they wouldn't have to pay the bill.
> When he brought his faction together,
> whatever he had dreamt up with them,
> Cünlin could directly write it off,
> It would remain so in the morning.[36]

---

36 CDS 25, 357–59: Schwarz arranged "das etlich weis, erber und frummen/ da muestend aus dem ratte komen,/ und meret etlich zunft hinein,/ das seiner volg dester mer möcht sein./ Er khundt gar listigklich zuerichten/ mit seinem trachten und gedichten,/ das man in zů burgermaister machet,/ damit sy waren unversachet./ das berayt er mit dem Taglange/ im zů ainem söllichen anhange/ alle die gern waren volle,/ wo man der zech nit zallen solle./ wenn er sein anhang zůsamen bracht,/ was er sich denn mit in erdacht,/ das kündt der Cünlin anschreiben,/ des morgens solt es also beleiben." Taglang, guild master of the bakers, was one of Schwarz's main followers; Cünlin (Cunrad Fludeysen) was the assistant town clerk (he was tried after Schwarz's death and lost his office, see his protocol of interrogation in StAA, Schätze 41, fol. 5r–7v, 1479). The town clerk in office, Valentin Eber, hired in 1454 to undermine Erlbach's position, was kept in Vienna on official business, quite clearly to keep a potential adversary of Schwarz off the political stage, see Eber's letter

The entire poem insinuates that Schwarz and his faction were only after money: corruption and the use of inside information for personal profit are among the most common accusations against a political foe. In this late medieval, urban context, the absence of salaries for holders of political positions made such allegations a weapon of choice against those coming from outside the social elites: it seemed only too natural that politicians without a fortune should try to improve their condition at the expense of the civic finances. It seemed so natural indeed that modern historians have no way to distinguish the calumny from the real crimes, although it is always suspected that many such allegations are simply false—the way the supposed crimes are rehashed from text to text, from poem to "confession" and from chronicle to poem, shows a rather unique policy of setting an example. Other powerful men in Augsburg endured a sensational downfall, including Peter von Argon, Ulrich Dendrich, and Ulrich Arzt. The chronicles recorded the misdeeds of these men, and they clearly approved of the punishments, but in none of those cases was there such a vicious communication campaign designed to shape a diabolic image of a politician. What strikes us in the poems is the homogeneity of the way they deal with the Schwarz story: there is little doubt that the authors had preliminary, at least half-official texts, such as the *Beruff* or the *Urgicht*, in hand when they wrote. The avian metaphor found in two of the poems may pertain to satirical themes diffused widely outside official circles.

One of the poems describes in more detail how the *anhang* worked, who were its members and what acts justified their punishment. Fear, self-interest, and wickedness were the main levers inducing its members, each in his own way, to cooperate with Schwarz; three circles inside the *anhang* are described, one made up of those who simply attempted to avoid conflict with their leader, one of people who sought to foster their own interests, and a third following him simply out of wickedness, against the common good.[37] Unlike Rem's chronicle, however, the poems are mainly interested in the singular figure of Schwarz. That he had an *anhang* around him is obviously pointed out too, but rather as the product of his schemes to attain power and/or as a weapon at his disposal to sustain his power after being elected a mayor. Rather than depicting Schwarz's *anhang* as an indeterminate and menacing group, the poets singled out a few names, mainly that of the bakers' guild master Jos Taglang, portrayed as Schwarz's henchman: the obvious goal was both to justify the

---

from November 27, 1476, in Jäger, fol. 259r–v). The end of the text implies that municipal decisions were prepared in the evenings at a cabaret (or a guild's *Stube*?), then presented the next morning in the council.

37 Liliencron, *Volkslieder der Deutschen*, 140–42.

measures taken against these individuals and to closely delimit the criminal group from the mere fellow travellers. The instigators of this campaign saw themselves as attempting to restore civic unity, and presenting caricatured enemies to Augsburg's citizens meant at the same time offering reconciliation to Schwarz's more tepid partisans. This explains why their perspective coincided neither with the neutral narration by Mülich nor with the later uses of the Schwarz story by 16th century writers aiming to discredit the guild regime as a whole. The black legend of Schwarz, as it developed from this beginning, has shown how successful the campaign was.

3.3 *Erlbach's and Schwarz's Argumentation*

The word *anhang* was also used by Schwarz himself, not to refer to his own supporters, but in his interpretation of the Erlbach case, in reference to Erlbach's opponents, but with the same negative meaning. Erlbach, he wrote in his justificatory "chronicle", was excluded from the council by "the patricians and their faction" because "he sided with the common people".[38] The continuity between Erlbach and Schwarz is hence not only an historian's reconstruction: the Erlbach case was for Schwarz proof that the patricians allied to the richest guild members followed their own particular interests. The patricians, he implied, driven by their hatred of Erlbach, were responsible for the high costs resulting from the private war between Erlbach and the city. Schwarz did not provide any further description of the group around the *Herren*, but the outline of this group is quite clear: his targets were those citizens who benefitted from a statutorily privileged condition, i.e., the patricians and their relatives through marriage which together formed the *Herrenstube*,[39] what Schwarz allegedly called "die grossen Mayr auff der altten Stuben" (the word "Mayr" is not clear in this context: "the big pundits [?] of the old club"?)—one of the poems about Schwarz evokes his hostility to the *Herren*.[40] In Schwarz's view,

38 Jäger, fol. 232v, ed. Panzer, 100: "die von herren und ir anhang"; "der hett es mit der gemain".

39 On this quasi-public institution, see Adrian, *Augsbourg à la fin du Moyen Âge*, 284–92: the Herrenstube is the meeting hall (*Stube*) of the patricians, but throughout most of the 15th century its social importance seems to have been rather weak, in any event weaker than in many other German towns.

40 StAA, Schätze 55 ("Vorbereitung"), 116v (ed. CDS 22, 434: what 'Mayr' means in this context is unclear, but it addresses the arrogance of the members of the *Stube*; see Liliencron, *Volkslieder der Deutschen*, 132: Schwarz wanted to "der burger freihait auch vernichten,/ es solt sein ainem als dem andern alten,/ trinkstuben und tantzhaus verwalten" ("annihilate the burghers' [=patricians'] liberty,/ one had to have the same rights as the other [from the] old [families], [he wanted] to manage the *Trinkstube* and the dance house", i.e. the two strongholds of patrician identity.

his enemies did not form a conspiracy ad hoc: it was through their common origins and social network that they came together, more than through conscious, intentional organizational effort. What Schwarz describes here is less a faction than a class, although, as we saw above, some members of the social group he opposed were indeed either among his active enemies or neutral in the conflict.

Although Erlbach's writings do not identify any factions, what he described mirrored quite precisely what the anti-Schwarz polemical texts alleged: a clique of leading politicians taking control of the government to their own advantage.[41] But there are differences too: Erlbach noted that his main enemy Heinrich Langenmantel attempted to have him expelled from the council by threatening to boycott the council as long as Erlbach was present, but the two mayors did not yield to this blackmail—one of the mayors was Jörg Strauß, himself an enemy of Erlbach.[42] In this way, Erlbach drew a sharp contrast between him and his factious enemies—he was merely a disinterested servant of the common good, holding himself above the conflicting parties within the political elite. This supposed neutrality contrasts with the more charged statements of Schwarz, which is understandable since Erlbach was a city employee, not an elected politician like Schwarz. Even in this indirect way, Erlbach's writings confirm the importance of the concept of faction as one of the main political arguments employed all during this decades-long political crisis; from the brutal accusations in the poems to the subtler analysis in the chronicles and also in Schwarz's and Erlbach's writings, allegations of "faction" were an effective way to end the possibility of any theoretical discussion of civic politics. This kind of *reductio ad hominem* is one of the oldest techniques of political argumentation, but one of the most striking features of the texts discussed here is that they show clearly that the political conflicts were not merely personal antagonisms, but were firmly rooted in divergent theoretical positions concerning the best way to govern the city.

4 Conclusion

What happened to Schwarz's faction when it lost its leader? The aggressive communications campaign conducted by his adversaries certainly helped to cover up any potential dissent, and the policy of the victorious party to impose the authority of the council instead of employing a more collegial approach,

41 StAA, Schätze 119, fol. 346r.

42 Ibid., fol. 348v.

was certainly successful. Anyway, many leading figures of the Schwarz party were exiled, sentenced to death or banned from the council. But we have a small piece of evidence of an underground persistence of popular views on politics twenty years after Schwarz's death. In 1498, an enduring rumour reached the ears of the council: according to the rumour, the carpenters were about to elect Marx Neumüller as one of their representatives. This was absolutely unacceptable to the council, which prohibited the election from taking place.[43] Marx Neumüller was an old man at the time—he was elected to the Large council as early as 1466 and served many times as a guild master—but his association with the Schwarz party had earned him a lifelong exclusion from the council. His fellow guild members certainly knew that and were aware of the potential conflict Neumüller's election would cause, but the shift of opinion within the guild was strong enough to take the risk.

Circumstances at the end of the 15th century left little space for the expression of political dissent, even less to a structured movement in favour of more popular public policies. The politicians who took power after Schwarz's death did not find a miraculous way of squelching political discontent, despite their authoritarian conception of politics: conflicts arose inside the guilds—in the weavers' and shoemakers' guilds for instance.[44] What failed to materialize, however, was a confluence of popular movements forming a community of interest, having the goal of achieving comprehensive change in civic politics.

How much the latent, long-restrained popular opposition to this elitist policy contributed to the success of the Reformation, seen as an anti-institutional movement, among some social groups is beyond the scope of this paper.[45] What political life in Augsburg from 1450 to 1480 reveals is significant enough: whatever the motivations and interests of the individual actors may have been, there was a clear structural continuity in the political life of the city, with a "popular" party opposed to an "elitist" group, with a clear delineation between the groups, both in the substance of their programs and their

43 StAA, Ratsbuch 12bis, fol. 66.

44 On both, see Rogge, 107–24. Another even less structured opposition to the political elites of the city is exemplified by the chronicle of the painter Jörg Breu the Elder (edited by Friedrich Roth, CDS 29, Leipzig 1906, 18–83).

45 The short revival of the guild system in 1552 (abolished by Charles V in 1548) might possibly have been in continuity with what we saw in the preceding century, but the episode has not been evaluated to date. Clemens Jäger's *Vorbereitung*, which used the Schwarz episode as one of the cardinal arguments against the guild system, was relied on as an authority in response to a leader of the 1552 uprising, Georg Österreicher, who had certainly cited the Schwarz episode himself. On the events of 1548–1552, see Friedrich Roth, *Augsburgs Reformationsgeschichte* 4: 1547–1555 (Munich, 1911), 413–52.

personal compositions. From Erlbach to Schwarz, the popular party backed a relatively stable and structured body of concrete demands, without idealistic or millenarian tendencies, and it had real opportunities to change city policy according to its proponents' agenda. The other side were certainly not extremists either: their political horizon did not go beyond stronger control over the 1368 institutions by the political elite to a complete elimination of the political influence of the guilds. Factions were very present in the political language of actors and observers, mainly as a means of disqualifying opposing parties, but to what extent did the various leading groups function as factions? From what we have seen, it seems clear that actions were prepared and taken on both sides by a small group of men meeting outside the official decision-making bodies, whose power was thus effectively compromised—although maybe not more than by parties in modern representative systems.

Changing Skin: Identities and Strategies in Late Medieval Basque *banderizo* Warfare

José Ramón Díaz de Durana and Arsenio Dacosta[1]

1 Objectives and Scope: The *luchas de bandos* in the Basque Country

Traditionally, studies of late medieval Spanish inter-noble warfare known as the 'luchas de bandos'[2] saw it as an explanation for the endemic political unrest in the different kingdoms of the Peninsula or as an explanation for the weakness of kings or even whole dynasties. This essentially political analysis then gave way to a perspective which regarded such conflict as a symptom of structural contradictions within the feudal system. Both interpretations have now been superseded and more recently, alongside individual case-studies, the focus has been on the internal structure and dynamics of the conflict, on the interaction between the main actors and the local institutions of the different towns where it played out, on the way the conflict regulated itself, and on the relationship between the warring bands and the values and social structures of the nobility.

This study is based on the accumulated experience of a number of researchers who, in recent years, have challenged previous interpretations[3] based on

---

1 José Ramón Díaz de Durana (joseramon.diazdedurana@ehu.es) is Professor of Medieval History at University of the Basque Country (UPV/EHU). Arsenio Dacosta (adacosta@usal.es) is Lecturer of Anthropology at the University of Salamanca. This paper is part of the findings of the research project *De la Lucha de Bandos a la hidalguía universal: transformaciones sociales, políticas e ideológicas en el País Vasco (siglos XIV y XV)* (Ministry for Science and Innovation, Spain, ref. HAR 2013-44093-P), and the Basque Government Consolidated Research Group *Sociedad, poder y cultura*, ref. IT-896-16 and UFI 11/02. The text has been translated by David Peterson to whom we wish to express our thanks. The maps were composed by Ismael García.

2 Literally, 'fights between bands', and from which the adjective *banderizo*, which we shall use henceforth, is derived.

3 José Ramón Díaz de Durana, 'Historia y presente del tratamiento historiográfico sobre la Lucha de Bandos en el País Vasco: balance y perspectivas al inicio de una nueva investigación', in *La Lucha de Bandos en el País Vasco. De los Parientes Mayores a la Hidalguía universal. Guipúzcoa, de los Bandos a la Provincia* (Bilbao, 2008), 21–46. José Ángel Lema, 'Bibliografía y fuentes impresas para el estudio de la Lucha de Bandos en el País Vasco', in *La Lucha de Bandos en el País Vasco*, 557–602.

 | DOI 10.1163/9789004345348_004

the publication of a host of previously unknown medieval sources.[4] Our primary objective here is to offer a synthesis of the state of the inquiry surrounding the evolution and results of the *luchas de bandos* in the Basque Country: Álava, Guipúzcoa and Vizcaya. Far from comprising a single political unit in the Middle Ages, the history of these three territories is quite distinct; nonetheless, a series of common cultural traits, and above all the relationships and interests of certain local nobles that spanned the three territories, allow for a comparative analysis that works on several different levels.

Traditionally, the *banderizo* warfare of the Basque Country has been interpreted in terms of the conflict between the *Oñacino* and *Gamboíno* bands. We will analyse the meaning of these denominations from the perspective of political identity, showing how in each case this identity went beyond the geographical origins of the group's members or the institutional particularities of each territory, and instead was rooted in the legendary origins of the bands, as described by one of the main protagonists of the phenomenon, Lope García de Salazar (1399–1476), to whom we will return repeatedly. These identities became all the more relevant when the conflict spread beyond its original territorial confines and came to pose a political problem for the Castilian monarchs. In this context, the internal dynamics of the bands, their territorial stratification and their relationship with lineage structures and local power interests imply an extremely complex identity.

We will also attempt to shed some light on the mechanisms that led to membership in the bands, evaluating the importance of family, neighbourhood and material interests in the creation of clientship. We will attempt to show how—alongside the undoubted importance of group dynamics—individual values,

4 *Colección de Fuentes Documentales Medievales del País Vasco* (150 vols.) in http://www.eusko-ikaskuntza.org/es/publicaciones/colecciones/fuentesmedievales/. See also the edition of source material by José Ángel Lema et al., eds., *Los señores de la guerra y de la tierra: nuevos textos para el estudio de los Parientes Mayores guipuzcoanos (1265–1548)* (San Sebastián, 2000); José Ángel Lema et al., eds., *El triunfo de las elites urbanas guipuzcoanas: nuevos textos para el estudio del gobierno de las villas y de la Provincia (1412–1539)* (San Sebastián, 2002); Javier Goicolea et al., eds., *Honra de hidalgos, yugo de labradores: nuevos textos para el estudio de la sociedad rural alavesa (1332–1521)* (Bilbao, 2005); Arsenio Dacosta et al., eds., *Poder y privilegio. Nuevos textos para el estudio de la nobleza vizcaína al final de la Edad Media (1416–1527)* (Bilbao, 2010) and José Antonio Munita et al., eds., *En tiempo de ruidos y de bandos. Nuevos textos para el estudio de los linajes vizcaínos: los Barroeta de la merindad de Marquina (1355–1547)* (Bilbao, 2014). More specifically, as regards sources for the study of the *luchas de bandos* in the Basque Country, see also Arsenio Dacosta, 'La nobleza vizcaína ante un siglo de cambios', in *Poder y privilegio*, 15–105 and José Ramón Díaz de Durana, *Anonymous Noblemen: The Generalization of Hidalgo Status in the Basque Country (1250–1525)* (Turnhout, 2011), 41–44.

strategies and feelings were other important factors, although these aspects were all too often obscured by the strong sense of noble competitiveness referred to in the literature of the time (and ever since) as *valer más* (literally "being more worthy", though not just in the sense of moral worth, but also encompassing power and wealth).

Furthermore, we will consider the way the *banderizo* conflict evolved, observing the differences but also the capillary relationship between rural and urban societies in this context. Finally, we will show how the conflict came to be resolved, evaluating the importance of a mixture of internal factors—generational change, the effect on noble families of such public violence, peasant and urban resistance—and external ones, as political institutions such as urban councils, provincial brotherhoods and the Crown intervened. By way of an epilogue, we will observe the extraordinary and paradoxical way in which the *Oñacino* and *Gamboíno* bands nominally survived within the local and regional institutions of Vizcaya during the sixteenth century, seemingly with the Crown's blessing.

2 Lineages and *banderizos* in Álava, Guipúzcoa and Vizcaya: Beyond the *Oñacinos* and *Gamboínos*

Alongside the documents conserved in municipal, judicial and to a lesser extent family archives, a few historiographical works elaborated in Vizcaya during the fifteenth century afford us a fascinating insight into the *luchas de bandos*. The most outstanding example is the *Libro de las buenas andanças e fortunas* written by Lope García de Salazar, a lengthy work largely dedicated to telling the story of the *luchas de bandos* in both the Basque Country itself and in neighbouring regions such as Navarre, Labourd, eastern Cantabria and northeastern Burgos. The significance of the text is enhanced by the fact that its author had himself been one of the main protagonists of these conflicts during the mid-fifteenth century.[5]

In his account of events, García de Salazar introduces us to two concepts fundamental to and inseparable from his theme: the lineage and the band. He regarded the former as a group of individuals who recognised a common ancestor from the paternal line, although maternal ancestry was also valued. The concept of lineage extended not only to actual family members, but to artificial kin too, associated in contemporary texts with terms such as *vasallo*,

5 Consuelo Villacorta, *Libro de las buenas andanças e fortunas que fizo Lope Garçía de Salazar* (Bilbao, 2015).

amigo, *atreguado* or *acotado* (the latter two explained below). It is from these ties of family and kinship that the lineage drew its strength, and in the Basque Country this structure was the absolute protagonist during the later Middle Ages. At the head of each lineage there was the *pariente mayor*, a term which, as J.A. Marín has indicated, alludes to the superior social condition of this figurehead in comparison with all the other members of the community.[6] This privileged condition imposed on him the responsibility for protecting, administering and augmenting the lineage's patrimony, as well as maintaining the internal cohesion of the structure.

As we have said, the lineage comprised not only the immediate family and more distant blood-relations, but also those linked by marriage alliance, and others tied into it by a variety of forms of artificial kinship, geographical proximity, or feudal ties: servants, priests installed in churches over which the lineage exercised patronage,[7] men responding to a call to arms and expecting an economic reward for doing so (known as *atreguados*), and even outlaws (known as *acotados* or *encartados*) who sought refuge in the lineages' strongholds, the latter of whom were regarded as being responsible for most of the violence denounced by peasants and townsfolk.[8]

Each lineage's head, the *pariente mayor*, occupied the fortified manor house (*casa-torre*) which was the group's ancestral home and which through its name identified the lineage. As well as the manor house itself, the ancestral estate brought together all the other elements, both real and symbolic, that contributed to the lineage's prestige: the mill, the foundry, the winepress or ciderpress and the church. All of this served to reinforce awareness of the lineage's origins in a remote and common ancestor, alongside symbolic elements of enormous importance such as onomastics, the coat of arms and the family pantheon, elements which were used by the *pariente mayor* to express his feudal authority over the peasant community.

---

6 José Antonio Marín, *"Semejante Pariente Mayor". Parentesco, solar, comunidad y linaje en la institución de un Pariente Mayor en Guipuzkoa. Los señores de Oñaz y Loyola* (*siglos* XIV–XVI) (San Sebastián, 1998), 87–101.

7 Iosu Curiel, *La parroquia en el País Vasco-Cantábrico durante la baja Edad Media* (*c.* 1350–1530) (Bilbao, 2009), 319–67.

8 Jon Andoni Fernández de Larrea, 'Las fuerzas de los Parientes Mayores en Álava, Guipúzcoa y Vizcaya en la Baja Edad Media: reclutamiento y organización', *Iura Vasconiae* 4 (2007), 163–88; José Ramón Díaz de Durana and Jon Andoni Fernández de Larrea, 'Las relaciones contractuales de la nobleza y las élites urbanas en el País Vasco al final de la Edad Media', *El contrato político en la Corona de Castilla. Cultura y sociedad políticas entre los siglos* X *al* XVI (Madrid, 2008), 293–321.

The internal cohesion of the lineage and its incorporation of new members were key components in its ability to both extend its influence beyond the ancestral estate and to demonstrate the political clout of the lineage's head. In the Basque Country, alliances cemented the relationship between the different lineages that made up the *Oñacino* and *Gamboíno* bands, leading to a complex map of interrelated alliances and hostilities on local, regional and even inter-regional scales, which have been studied in Vizcaya by A. Dacosta (cf. maps 3.1, 3.2, 3.3).

In the cities of the Crown of Castile during the late Middle Ages, the different lineages were grouped together in units known as lineage-bands (*bandos-linaje*), whose sphere of action was generally local. In the Basque Country, however, these lineage-bands were often rurally based. Family and geographical proximity were vital factors for recruitment into such groups, together with a sense of identification strengthened by the existence of mutual enemies or common interests, although straightforward coercion tied some individuals to the band. Despite all these unifying factors and forces, such groups were inherently unstable, and unity relied on the success or failure of the leading *pariente mayor*'s strategies, and above all, his fulfilling the expectations placed upon him by his relatives and the communities under his control.[9]

In Castile, even more striking, though, was the tendency of the associates of some lineage-bands to further group together into what have been termed partiality-bands (*bandos-parcialidad*): unions of different noble lineages. In the Basque Country these partiality-bands might even encompass towns and rural communities. Apart from the question of scale, what further distinguished them from the lineage-bands is that they were much more highly politicised, with ambitions reaching far beyond the objectives and strategies of a particular *pariente mayor* or lineage.[10] Within the context of the Crown of Castile they would become endemic during the reigns of Juan II (1406–54) and Enrique IV (1454–74). Although on occasion they would influence each other, there were important differences of scale between great partiality-bands operating on a kingdom-wide basis and more localised versions. Lacking any

9 José Ramón Díaz de Durana, Arsenio Dacosta, 'La dimensión social del liderazgo del linaje: solidaridad, poder y violencia (País Vasco, siglo XV)', *Studia Zamorensia* 12 (2013), 87–106.

10 Marie-Claude Gerbet, *Les noblesses espagnoles au Moyen Âge. XIe–XVe siècle* (Paris, 1994), 171–72; Julio Caro Baroja, *Linajes y Bandos. A propósito de la nueva edición de las "Bienandanzas e Fortunas"* (San Sebastián, 1956), 13–61; Isabel Beceiro and Ricardo Córdoba, *Parentesco, poder y mentalidad. La nobleza castellana, siglos XII–XV* (Madrid, 1990), 310 seq.; Arsenio Dacosta, *Los linajes de Bizkaia en la baja Edad Media: poder, parentesco y conflicto* (Bilbao, 2004), 292–302.

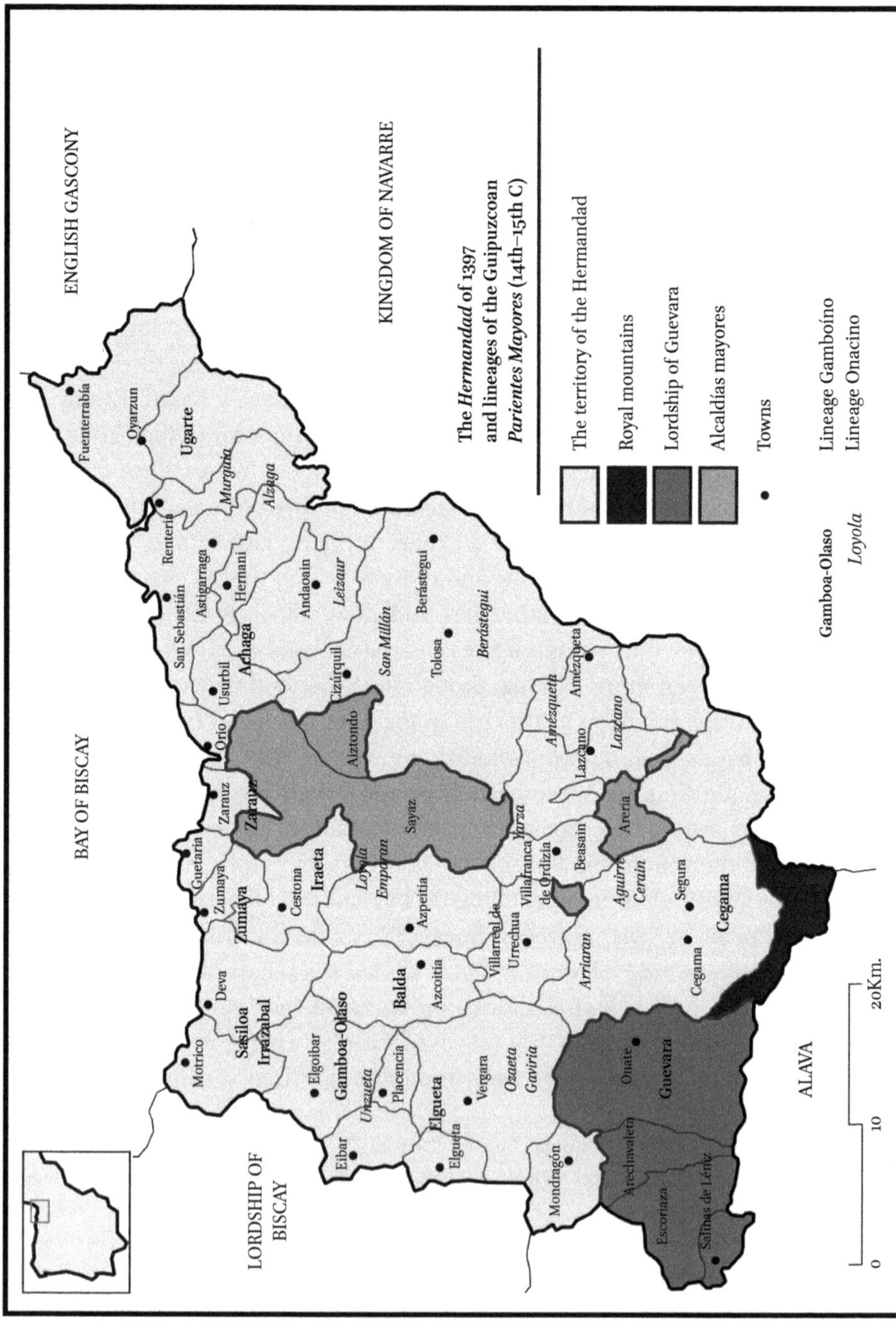
The *Hermandad* of 1397
and lineages of the Guipuzcoan
Parientes Mayores (14th–15th C)
The territory of the Hermandad
Royal mountains
Lordship of Guevara
Alcaldías mayores
Towns
Gamboa-Olaso Lineage Gamboíno
Loyola Lineage Onacino
ENGLISH GASCONY
KINGDOM OF NAVARRE
BAY OF BISCAY
LORDSHIP OF BISCAY
ALAVA
0 10 20Km.
Fuenterrabía
Oyarzun
Ugarte
Murguía
Alzaga
Rentería
Astigarraga
Hernani
San Sebastián
Andoain
Leizaur
Berástegui
Usurbil
Achaga
Cizúrquil
San Millán
Tolosa
Berástegui
Orio
Aiztondo
Amézqueta
Amézqueta
Lazcano
Lazcano
Zarauz
Zarauz
Sayaz
Yarza
Areria
Guetaria
Zumaya
Zumaya
Cestona
Iraeta
Loyola
Emparan
Azpeitia
Villafranca de Ordizia
Beasain
Aguirre
Cerain
Segura
Cegama
Villarreal de Urrechua
Arriaran
Cegama
Deva
Balda
Azcoitia
Motrico
Sasiloa
Irazabal
Elgoibar
Gamboa-Olaso
Unzueta
Placencia
Vergara
Ozaeta
Gaviria
Oñate
Guevara
Eibar
Elgueta
Elgueta
Mondragón
Arechavaleta
Escoriaza
Salinas de Léniz

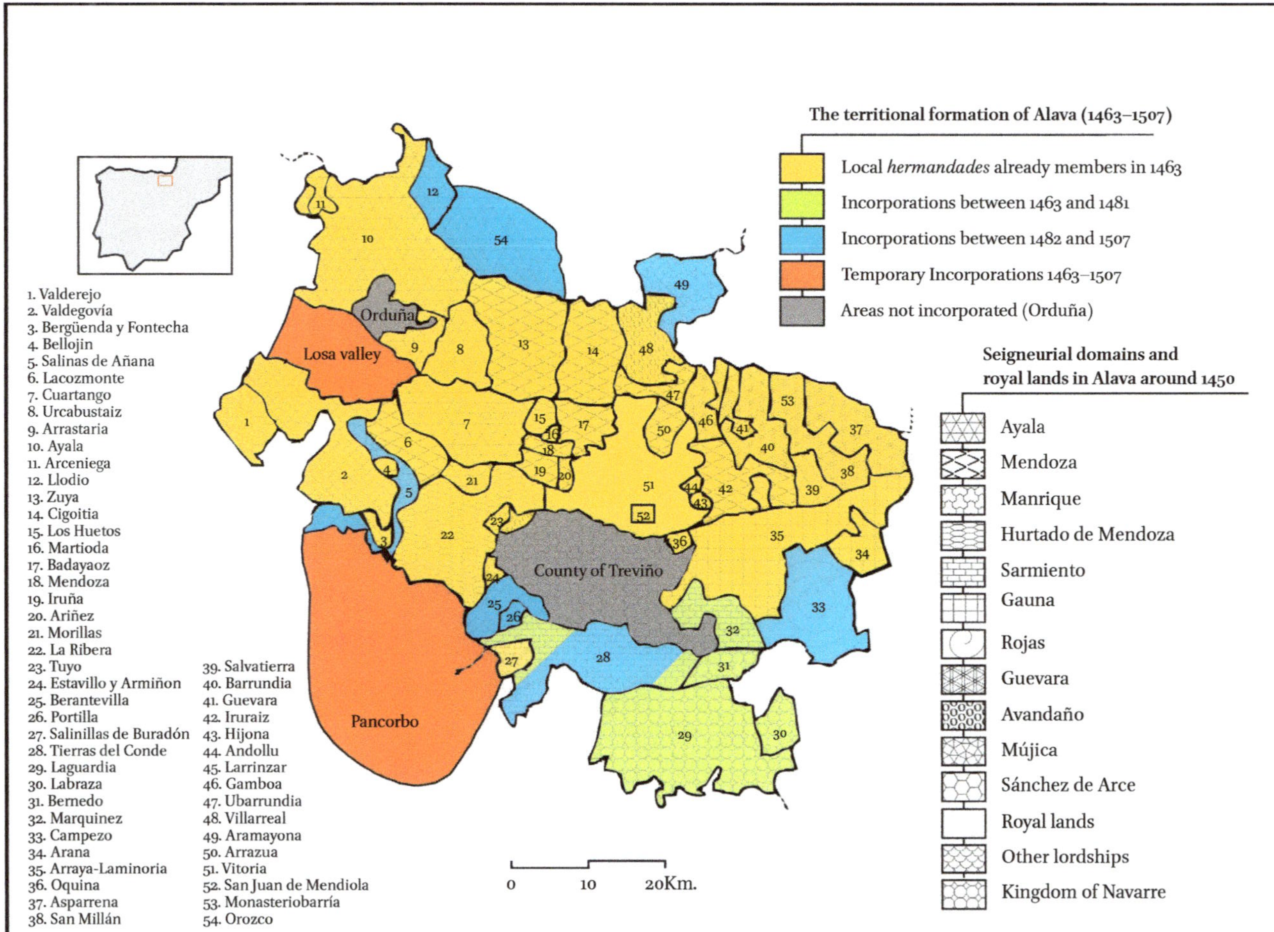

MAP 2 *The seigneurial domains around 1450 and the territorial formation of Alava (1463–1507).*

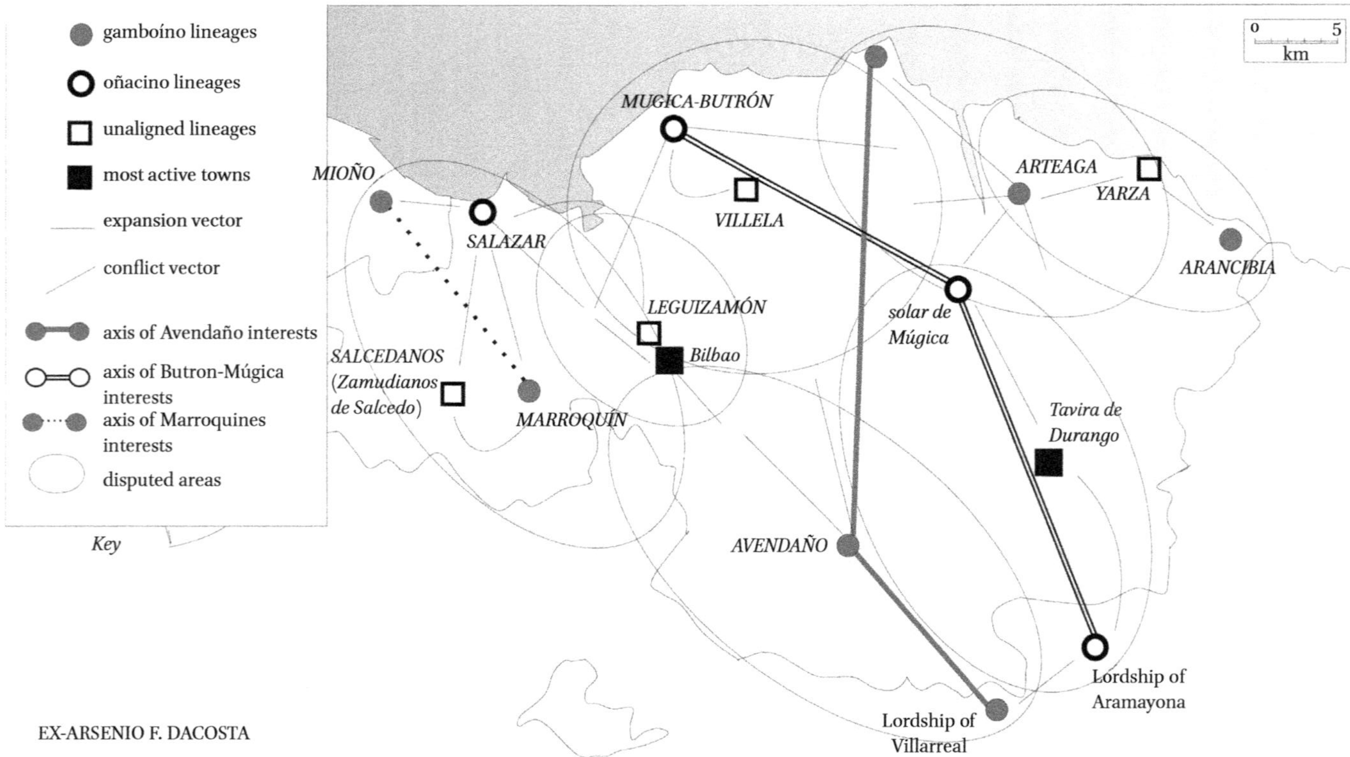

EX-ARSENIO F. DACOSTA

MAP 3 *The Private (banderizo) warfare (15th c.).*

institutional role, their mode of functioning depended enormously on their size and on the particular political context: the kingdom-wide versions were constantly reforming themselves during the period mentioned, but because of their large size tended to be less stable, while the localised Basque partiality-bands became almost permanent fixtures, for reasons we will explore.

As we have mentioned, in what is now the Basque Country these partiality-bands were known as the *Oñacinos* and the *Gamboínos*. The names were derived from those of two of the main lineages of Guipúzcoa, the Oñaz and the Gamboa, although oddly their legendary origins were, according to Lope García de Salazar, to be found in Álava. As A. Dacosta has shown, the chronicler hardly ever employed these labels when referring to the Lordship of Vizcaya, and when he did so it was only to highlight clashes between Vizcayan and Guipuzcoan lineages. The names were much more commonly used in Guipúzcoa as that is where the ancestral homes of the Gamboa and the Oñaz, sworn enemies and leaders of the respective bands, were located. In Vizcaya, on the other hand, the main conflict was between the Avendaños and the Butróns, and the Oñacino and Gamboíno labels were only used by Garcia de Salazar when fighting spread beyond the Lordship's borders. Nonetheless, paradoxically, it would be in Vizcaya where these names survived into the Early Modern period as the bands became institutionalised: the local elites nominally aligning themselves with one band or the other when assuming roles in the territory's various institutions. As for Álava, we only encounter the two labels when there are clashes between Guipuzcoan and Alavese lineages, particularly when the Guipuzcoan Lazcano lineage—aligned with the Oñacinos—was involved. At the local level the bands did not identify themselves with reference to the lineages that led them, contrary to the case in Vitoria, where the opposing bands were known as the Ayalas and the Callejas.

In urban contexts too, the elite was organised in terms of lineages. In general terms, these urban lineages were the result of the fusion of the richest merchant families with the lesser branches of rural noble lineages which, from the mid-fourteenth century had established themselves in the towns with a view to profiting from the new economic opportunities that were opening up. During the fourteenth and fifteenth centuries, as J. Mª Monsalvo has shown to be the case in Castile, as the rural nobles adapted to the urban milieu and the two groups strengthened their mutual ties, their partnership developed into a tremendously efficient operation for appropriating wealth and monopolizing power.[11] Soledad Tena, who has studied such formations in Guipúzcoa,

11 José Maria Monsalvo, 'Parentesco y sistema concejil. Observaciones sobre la funcionalidad política de los linajes urbanos en Castilla y León (siglos XIII–XV)', *Hispania* 185 (1993), 939–41.

distinguishes between two different models of evolution for this new patriciate. The first is applicable to the towns of San Sebastián and Fuenterrabía, where the creation of the elites resulted from a fusion of Gascon merchants present from the twelfth century onwards and whose origins were in nearby Bayonne, and autochthonous elite lineages with whom they subsequently merged. The second model was driven by rural lineages which established themselves in the towns of Rentería and Oyarzun. Two models then, one allochthonous, the other autochthonous, but both involving essentially the same process, led to the creation of "powerful commercial oligarchies" in each of these four towns.[12]

From the second half of the fourteenth century and throughout the fifteenth, the urban lineages, divided into bands, faced off over political control of the towns and reached a power-sharing agreement that ensured each 50% of the towns' magistracies, effectively marginalising and even negating the political representation of the common townsfolk. The struggle between these bands is best understood in the context of a struggle for control of the profits to be made from the thriving town economies and for social and political influence over the rest of the community.

Lope García de Salazar, both a leading participant in and eyewitness of the *lucha de bandos*, explains the origins of the Oñacino and Gamboíno bands in terms of a legend which, set at some time in the distant past, suggested that the devil was at the root of the conflict between the two families who had previously maintained a peaceful co-existence. Though competition and rivalry are clearly part of human nature, thus explaining why García de Salazar's legend of a feud with its origins stretching back into the mists of time would have found acceptance, we note there is no evidence that prior to the fourteenth century the noble elites had been divided into bands. Historiography has offered several non-legendary explanations for the emergence of the conflict. Layburu, writing in the late nineteenth century, observed that rooted in the origins of the hostility was the idea of social pre-eminence, generally expressed through the formula "the most worthy in the land" ("quien valía más en la tierra"), a recurrent theme in Lope García de Salazar's work. J. Caro Baroja brought this theory back into the spotlight,[13] while J.A. García de Cortázar developed it further, suggesting that questions of honour and worth would have been as quantifiable as rents and retainers.[14] A. Dacosta has further explored the notion,

12 Maria Soledad Tena, *La sociedad urbana en la Guipúzcoa costera medieval: San Sebastián, Rentería, y Fuenterrabía (1200–1500)* (San Sebastián, 1997), 375–465.

13 Caro Baroja, *Linajes y Bandos*, 13–61.

14 "…por un lado, en número contante y sonante de rentas y hombres y, por otro, en cantidad, igualmente medible para los contemporáneos, de valor, temple y honor", José Ángel

suggesting that the concept of worthiness (*valer más*) would have functioned as an ethical frame of reference and programme of action for the northern nobles.[15] The work of A. Otazu and E. Fernández de Pinedo has also suggested that *valer más* was related to late medieval social conflict. Indeed, *banderizo* warfare seems to have grown fiercer whenever the elites came under pressure, whether through a drop in income from rents in the fourteenth century, or as a result of increased inter-noble rivalry caused by the spectacular economic recovery of the fifteenth century.[16] It is within this framework that grouping together in bands of lineages with conflicting economic interests begins to make sense: some may have been allies within a band and possibly even part of the same lineage, but in conflict over the patronage of a given church, or over access to firewood and iron ore for their iron works, peasants' rents or the control of municipal magistracies.

Clashes between different lineages and bands were part of a chain of hostilities that existed for the purpose of maintaining the *parientes mayores'* hegemonic positions. The violence, while common to every valley and region, was particularly virulent in Guipúzcoa and Vizcaya. It was somewhat less so in Álava, a territory dominated by great lords with interests that extended far beyond their ancestral lands, stretching to the royal Court and other parts of the realm. By contrast, the *parientes mayores* of the two coastal territories (i.e., Guipúzcoa and Vizcaya) had relatively few interests outside their areas of origin, and neither the scale of their possessions nor of the rents they received were comparable to those of the magnates of Álava.

Although the earliest evidence of the existence of bands dates from the first half of the fourteenth century, it was not until the end of that century, and above all during the reigns of Juan II and Enrique IV of Castile in the mid-fifteenth century, that the conflict became generalised. The most serious episodes took place during the 1440s, with the burning and destruction of Mondragón in 1448, which should be regarded as the high water mark of the private warfare between lineages and bands. Thereafter the *hermandades* associations (literally 'brotherhoods') which had earlier been formed in

---

García de Cortázar, 'El fortalecimiento de la burguesía como grupo social dirigente de la sociedad vascongada a lo largo de los XIV–XV', in *La sociedad vasca rural y urbana en el marco de la crisis de los siglos XIV y XV* (Bilbao, 1973), 283–313; José Ángel García de Cortázar et al., eds. *Vizcaya en la Edad Media: evolución demográfica, económica, social y política de la Comunidad vizcaína medieval* (San Sebastián, 1985), vol. III, 350–80.

15 Dacosta, *Los linajes de Bizkaia*, 82–93.

16 Emiliano Fernández de Pinedo, '¿Lucha de bandos o conflicto social?' in *La sociedad vasca rural y urbana*, 29–42; Alfonso de Otazu, *El "igualitarismo" vasco: mito y realidad* (San Sebastián, 1973), 41–92.

Vizcaya (1394), Guipúzcoa (1397) and Álava (1417) with the aim of maintaining public order, stepped up their activities with the support of the Crown. For example, in order to combat the lineages' methods of binding and controlling their adepts based on a lineage's social and political pre-eminence and to dismantle the client networks that riddled rural society, in 1450 the Crown prohibited the participation of Guipuzcoans in indentures (*treguas*) with the *parientes mayores*. Such measures were accompanied by other occasionally effective tactics such as demolition of the *banderizo* fortified manor houses, so important to the material and symbolic power of the lineages.

In response to the *hermandades'* initiatives, in July 1456 the heads of the lineages, in a remarkable display of unity, declared war on twenty-four leading townsfolk whom they considered had been most active in the campaigns directed against them. The twenty-four were accused by the *banderizos* of demolishing their strongholds, murdering their relatives, setting them against the king, wiping their names from the countryside and depriving them of their churches. Nonetheless, the *hermandades* kept up their offensive, systematically attacking symbols of seigneurial power, and above all concentrating on the core of their power in local communities, the patronage of churches. In this context, it is no coincidence that immediately before decreeing their banishment, the king had demanded to see the legal deeds on which the rights of patronage claimed by the *parientes mayores* were based. The decree of exile of April 1457 stipulated that the leading *parientes mayores* of Guipúzcoa and Vizcaya should remain between one and four years waging war at their own expense against the Muslim enemy on the frontier with Granada. On completion of their exile, they were to swear before the king that they would henceforth obey his orders, neither usurp royal revenues and rights nor enter again into hostilities with the *hermandades*, and would even abide by the latter's ordinance books.

In the short term, the exile of 1457 implied explicit royal disauthorisation of the activities of the *parientes mayores*, and moreover temporarily de-activated their client networks and *banderizo* strategies. In the medium term, such measures were to prove particularly effective in Álava and Guipúzcoa, owing to the actions of the *hermandades*. In parallel, the royal justice system began to rule against the arbitrary obligations and abuses that the *parientes mayores* had imposed upon the peasantry and the townsfolk, while nevertheless respecting their genuine jurisdictional rights. The main political consequence of this was the distancing of the *parientes mayores* of Álava and Guipúzcoa from the new institutions of government that evolved from the *hermandades*: the General Assemblies (*Juntas Generales*). It is worth pointing out, though, that participation in these new assemblies was restricted to those who could satisfy certain requisites of wealth and land-holding, and thus these bodies were firmly in the grip of the urban elites, which through them also controlled administrative bodies at the local and provincial levels.[17]

In Vizcaya, on the other hand, measures taken against the *parientes mayores* initially proved a failure. Although the Vizcayan *hermandad* launched a powerful campaign against them between 1450 and 1452,[18] the local nobility reacted resolutely on two fronts, stepping up their own violent actions, and also initiating an institutional offensive which saw the leading *parientes mayores* temporarily overcome their differences and act in concert for the first time. This was the context of their determination in 1452 to secure confirmation of the traditional legal code, known as the *Fuero Viejo,* which effectively enshrined the nobility's privileges. The other factor to be borne in mind with regard to Vizcaya is the Castilian Civil War (1475–79), in which the majority of the Vizcayan nobles supported the parties that would later become the Catholic Monarchs (i.e. Ferdinand and Isabel), and this, together with their common front against the *hermandades,* led to a general consensus among the nobles during the 1470s. This consensus came into particularly sharp focus in 1471 when most of the Vizcayan *parientes mayores* united against an invasion by the Conde de Haro. Nonetheless, it is not these events that explain the simultaneous end of *banderizo* warfare in Álava, Vizcaya and Guipúzcoa. The explanation is rather more complex and far-reaching.

3 The End of *banderizo* Warfare: Towards a General Explanation

The *banderizo* wars in the Basque Country, characterised as they were by their duration and extreme violence, can be explained by a combination of the social composition of the noble class, a mentality insisting upon noble honour, the complex jurisdictional mosaic of these territories, and the particular conditions pertaining to Castile during the economic and political crisis of the fifteenth century that led to a growth in inter-noble competition. Consequently, the end of this warfare should be understood as a long-term process related to the evolution of each of these structural factors.

---

17 José Ángel Achón, *A voz de concejo: linaje y corporación urbana en la constitución de la Provincia de Gipuzkoa: los Báñez y Mondragón, siglos XIII–XVI* (San Sebastián, 1995), 120–95; Ernesto García Fernández, *Gobernar la ciudad en la Edad Media: Oligarquías y élites urbanas en el País Vasco* (Vitoria, 2004), 21–278.

18 Sabino Aguirre, *Las dos primeras crónicas de Vizcaya. Estudios, textos críticos y apéndices* (Bilbao, 1986), 176–181; Estanislao J. Labayru, *Historia General de Vizcaya* (Bilbao, 1897), III, 293–316.

The structure of the noble lineages and the power base of the *parientes mayores* would not undergo significant change during the transition to the Early Modern period. Nor would it seem that the *valer más* mentality changed, and there are a number of documented examples of both inter-noble conflict and hostilities between lords and local communities during the reigns of the Catholic Monarchs (1474–1516) and Charles V (Carlos I of Spain, 1516–1556). Nonetheless, new ideas and patterns of behaviour began to mould the social reality of these territories, and they were accompanied by a series of radical changes in the structure and balance of power in Álava, Vizcaya and Guipúzcoa, although with significant differences in each territory.

In Álava, a powerful anti-seigneurial alliance formed against the nobles. Comprising both townsfolk and members of rural communities, it controlled a new institutional alternative, the *Juntas Generales* of Álava, in which all the territories and towns participated irrespective of their individual jurisdiction (royal or seigneurial), and which was led implacably by the city of Vitoria. As for Guipúzcoa, practically the whole of its territory was under the jurisdiction of a group of twenty towns, the elites of which engineered an alliance based around the *hermandad* and supported by the *corregidor*, a governor appointed by the Crown. Between 1463 and 1495, the *hermandad* was transformed from an instrument for suppressing *banderizo* violence and defending the frontier with Navarre into an institution which represented the whole of the territory in the *Juntas Generales*.

As for Vizcaya, the balance of power was rather different. The institutional peculiarities of the Lordship were maintained and even strengthened with the institutional consolidation of the rural councils known as *anteiglesias*, which were effectively under the control of the *parientes mayores*. The *Juntas Generales*, assemblies in which in theory all Vizcayans were to be represented, were effectively monopolised by the nobles from the mid-fifteenth century onwards as they sought to promote themselves as the direct representatives of the Crown in the territory. They were so successful in this that the townsfolk were effectively excluded from the *Juntas*, and moreover failed to articulate an alternative representative assembly.[19] Indeed, by the end of the fifteenth century, some towns would see their jurisdictional limits eaten into by the rural *anteiglesias*, while others, with few responsibilities and little real political clout, ended up being controlled by local lords.

19 Arsenio Dacosta and José Ramón Díaz de Durana, 'Political identities in conflict: the Lordship of Vizcaya in the fourteenth and fifteenth centuries', *Journal of Medieval Iberian Studies* 7 (2015), 112–34.

The Crown was at first happy to accept this situation in return for the submission and service of the nobles. However, the stance of the Catholic Monarchs towards Vizcaya would change substantially after 1483. That year Garci López de Chinchilla was named *pesquisidor real* (Royal Inquirer) and given two main objectives: to ensure the definitive implementation of the *corregidor* system, and to reform governance in the towns, introducing what would be known as the *regimiento* model. As regards the *corregidores*, their period of office was reduced and their role was professionalised, while the crystallisation of the new territorial institutions and the end of the *luchas de bandos* helped consolidate their position. As for the governance of the towns and the new *regimiento* system, the municipal reform initiated in Vitoria in 1476 was continued, was then further developed in Bilbao (1483), and was subsequently extended to the other Basque towns (1487).[20] The process would be further consolidated by the institutionalisation of the bands in the towns of Vizcaya.[21]

The institutional and political consensus allied to the growing efficiency of crown officials permitted the introduction of royal justice as an alternative to the private justice of the *parientes mayores*. *Banderizo* activity was criminalised, and police, political and judicial mechanisms were established, led by the *corregidores* and *hermandades*, to ensure implementation of the reform. On another level, the Crown's initiatives had begun to create a radical new framework for its relationship with the nobility in these northern territories, and this in turn helped to defuse the logic behind the *luchas de bandos*. Setting aside the case of the *Juntas Generales* of Vizcaya, in which the nobility as a class were granted privileged political representation, the Crown's handling of the situation tended towards establishing personal links with each lord or head of lineage. Anticipating the logic of the modern state, the Catholic Monarchs guaranteed the rights of the nobles, but on a case by case basis. In Vizcaya, the *status quo* as regards lay patronage was respected, and the old seigneurial right was reformulated as a royal concession. In this way the *parientes mayores* in Vizcaya saw their control of the rural communities confirmed, as was its

20 José Ramón Díaz de Durana, 'La Reforma municipal de los Reyes Católicos: el Capitulado vitoriano de 1476 y su extensión por el noroeste de la Corona de Castilla', *La formación de Álava* (Vitoria, 1986), I, 213–36; Regina Polo, *El régimen municipal de la Corona de Castilla durante el reinado de los Reyes Católicos: organización, funcionamiento y ámbito de actuación* (Madrid, 1999); Javier Enríquez et al., 'Política real y control municipal en Vizcaya durante el reinado de los Reyes Católicos (1476–1516)', *Vasconia* 15 (1990), 27–42; José Ramón Díaz de Durana and Arsenio Dacosta, 'Culture politique et identité dans les villes cantabriques à la fin du Moyen Âge', *Histoire Urbaine* 40 (2014), 149–55.

21 Manuel Basas, 'La institucionalización de los bandos en la sociedad bilbaína y vizcaína al comienzo de la Edad Moderna', in *La sociedad vasca rural y urbana*, 117–60.

hereditary transmission. The nobles who benefitted from these concessions are referred to in the documentation of the period as "royal vassals", and as such they had the duty of providing the Crown with a given number of men at arms, in direct proportion to the rents they received.

Military commitments on the frontiers with Granada, Navarre and France, and in Flanders, North Africa and America made these Basques particularly valuable to the Crown. The focus of the war effort, other than the town militias and the contingents provided by the *parientes mayores* and other nobles, was mainly maritime, and the nascent State provided new opportunities for what were generically referred to as Vizcayans.[22] It was a question of social survival: in the Basque Country of the late fifteenth century, the high level of entropy, or, put differently, the informality of power structures at all levels, meant that the system was incapable of guaranteeing the survival of local elites, a problem that has similarly been found for England in this period.[23] This absence of formalised power structures allowed fluid movement from rural community to seigneurial estate to kingdom and even empire, to a degree that is surprising from our modern perspective.

In the specific case of the *parientes mayores*, their contribution to the wars of the Catholic Monarchs was centred on the conquests of Granada (1492) and the kingdom of Navarre (1512). When the king requested some 2,000 men from his Vizcayan vassals in order to complete the conquest of Navarre, command of the troops was shared evenly between two of the main *parientes mayores*, Martín Ruiz de Avendaño and Gómez de Butrón y Múgica.[24] This arrangement was at odds with their traditional *banderizo* enmity, and is an example of how influence and power was gradually being shared, or, in other words, of the institutionalisation of the bands. It was their proximity to the Crown as vassals and as a result of services rendered, which allowed them to secure these positions, in spite of the anti-seigneurial opposition's continued hostility. The case of the Múgicas and the Avendaños is particularly revealing when set in the context of the succession of lawsuits brought against them from 1485 onwards by rural communities within their seigneurial jurisdictions in Aramayona and Villarreal de Álava, respectively.[25] The support these nobles offered the

22 Alfonso de Otazu and José Ramón Díaz de Durana, *El espíritu emprendedor de los Vascos* (Madrid, 2008), 43–72. In sixteenth-century Castile the term "Vizcayan" came to denote the natives of any of the Basque provinces.

23 Peter Coss, *The origins of the English Gentry* (Cambridge, 2003), 11 and 202.

24 Micaela Portilla, *Torres y casas fuertes en Álava* (Vitoria, 1978), II, 1045.

25 José Ramón Díaz de Durana *Álava en la Baja Edad Media. Crisis, recuperación y transformaciones socioeconómicas* (*c. 1250–1525*) (Vitoria, 1986), 356–72.

Catholic Monarchs during the early years of their reign was rewarded with new grants and favours as well as a consolidation of the aristocratic *status quo*.

By way of conclusion, the direct action of the Crown was the single most decisive factor in bringing an end to *banderizo* violence in the Basque Country. The question has been well-studied by Susana Truchuelo in the case of Guipúzcoa,[26] while for Vizcaya we have summarised the process of the "domestication of the Vizcayans."[27] Nonetheless, the question goes beyond the governmental and judicial activity of the Crown in these territories. The nascent modern state of the Catholic Monarchs, with its evident monopoly on the use of violence, contributed decisively towards the creation of a new culture. In a relatively short period of time, Castilian society in general, including Basque society, accepted that warfare could no longer be a private matter, but rather that it should exist only at the service of the state. Moreover, the Crown established itself in all walks of life as the sole and irrefutable arbiter and authority, even with respect to morality, an aspect of Castilian life which was relatively undeveloped given the scant moral and jurisdictional capacity of the bishops in these territories. The Catholic Monarchs confirmed their authority physically with visits to Vitoria and Vizcaya in 1476 and 1483, respectively. This authority was of course based on the power of the new state, but also on the feudal logic of the earlier system, as we appreciate when Fernando, in November 1476, demanded that the leading *parientes mayores* of Vizcaya fulfill their traditional obligations.

This gradual shift in perception with regard to authority and, more specifically, the use of violence, would have enormous consequences for all aspects of Basque life. A new political and judicial culture was introduced along with new instruments that depended on the full acceptance of the laws of the realm and the formalisation of local legislation. Moreover, the way was opened up for new tools relating to and governing submission and pact in the political sphere, contractual formulas in economic relations, and lawsuits in the judicial arena. Faced with these new mechanisms for conflict resolution, the *luchas de bandos* had become completely discredited and obsolete. Moreover, these deep-seated changes emerged in parallel with a spectacular growth in lucrative economic activities such as maritime commerce and iron-working as well as opportunities for service at different levels of the new state, from the militia to administration.

Changes were taking place at all levels and in all spheres, and all of them were contributing towards the demise of the *banderizos*. Some of these changes

26 Susana Truchuelo, *Gipuzkoa y el poder real en la Alta Edad Moderna* (San Sebastián, 2004).

27 Arsenio Dacosta, 'La nobleza vizcaína ante un siglo de cambios', *Poder y privilegio*, 93.

are particularly worth stressing because of their relationship to the factors we have just explored. One fundamental change was the inevitable generational turnover that took place among the leading noble families. While private warfare had been accepted as entirely legitimate by the generation of *parientes mayores* who led the hostilities of 1456, the survivors who had continued in that vein until 1468 were starting to die off by the early years of the Catholic Monarchs' reign, including, for example, Juan López de Lazcano, Pedro de Avendaño *"the Elder"* and Lope García de Salazar. Violence is behaviour learned in a specific social context and its chief exponents were disappearing.

The heirs of those masters of violence inhabited a radically different world which had seen profound changes, affecting even their own lineages. On the one hand, the leading regional nobility was faced with a matrimonial market severely restricted not only by inherited enmities and *banderizo* adscriptions, but also by the logic of seeking the most advantageous alliances for their heirs. The changes made to the system of inheritance, with the steady consolidation of the *mayorazgo*,[28] which institutionalised primogeniture, would similarly have a radical effect on the members of what had until then been the relatively broad and all-encompassing lineage, leading to a surplus of younger sons in search of a living and of daughters needing to be placed in accordance with the new patrimonial logic. Moreover, the *mayorazgo* implied a significant change in the economic strategy of the lineage, which was now exclusively centred on the first-born son. All of this meant that the *pariente mayor's* capacity for redistributing income became more restricted, which in turn affected the informal system of adhesions to the lineage. Thus, though in many ways the new social system was as hierarchical as in the past, the flow of relationships and income had been restructured: the informal vertical solidarity which had allowed for the dynamics behind the *luchas de bandos* had been dissolved.

All of these factors, along with the internal dynamics of the armed conflict itself, which in its different phases had run on for some sixty years, would put an end to *banderizo* violence. Nonetheless, some of its characteristics would survive, such as the alienating mentality of *valer más*, and structural violence caused by the society's own contradictions.

The most extreme example of this generalised change was the extraordinary declaration of universal *hidalguía* (nobility) contained in the *Fuero Nuevo* of Vizcaya of 1526 and sanctioned by Charles V. Although the actual social implications of this declaration were to some extent limited, as there were still

28 The *mayorazgo* was a social practice which favoured the first-born male descendent, making him sole heir of most of the rights and possessions of the lineage and excluding other otherwise legitimate heirs.

peasants tied to estates, the fact that the condition of nobility was theoretically applied to all persons born in the territory displays a significant change in the self-perception of Vizcayans. It is worth asking whether the generation of *parientes mayores* that had declared the hostilities of 1456, or the feudal lords who had controlled Álava in the same period, would have permitted the declaration of universal *hidalguía*.[29] Their direct descendants, nonetheless, tolerated the concept—which some decades later would be extended to Guipúzcoa—and even assumed positions of leadership in the new institutions, which were transforming the political reality in these territories. A good example is Diego Martínez de Álava, from the Vitoria-based Calleja band, who would become, by appointment of Isabel I, General Deputy of Álava—i.e. the leader of the *Juntas Generales*—from 1499 to 1533. He was aware, as were many other descendants of the *banderizo* leaders, that their power and privileges were no longer founded on the bands, but instead were secured on their loyalty and service to the Crown. Thus the *banderizo* families of the past had turned into loyal servants of the Crown; shedding their old skins to adapt to new times.

---

29 José Ramón Díaz de Durana and Jon Andoni Fernández de Larrea, 'El discurso político de los protagonistas de las luchas sociales en el País Vasco al final de la Edad Media', in *Lucha política: condena y legitimación en la España Medieval* (Paris, 2004), 313–36; Díaz de Durana, *Anonymous Noblemen*, 119–30.

Conciliarist Employment of Eschatology during and after the Council of Basel (1431–1460)

Frances Courtney Kneupper

What role did Antichrist play in the factional struggles of the Council of Basel (1431–1449)? The Council of Basel represented a momentous occasion in the history of Christendom for many reasons. Perhaps most importantly, it became the battleground for the future governance of the Church. Who held the ultimate authority—the pope or a council representing the entire church? Which represented the "ship of Peter," that could not err? The conflicting answers of papalists and Baselian conciliarists drove a wedge into the fifteenth century church, a divide so deep that it brought about a new schism. In 1438, supporters of the Council of Basel went to the dramatic lengths of charging the reigning Pope Eugenius IV with heresy, deposing him, and in 1439 electing a new Pope Felix V. On the other side, Eugenius and his supporters nullified the Council of Basel, convened a new council at Ferrara and then Florence, denounced those who remained at Basel as heretics, and excommunicated them. Thus, schism appeared again in the West, only a few decades after the Papal Schism (1378–1417) had been healed. Two men claimed the title of pope, and two councils supported them, each representing opposing views on the governance of the Church. Ambassadors from both councils sought the support of European secular rulers, hence threatening again to rend the Latin Church in two.

These events were so alarming that individuals on both sides saw in them apocalyptic implications. Partisans of the various ecclesiological perspectives employed apocalyptic events as a discursive framework for interpreting the great controversies surrounding the Council of Basel. Eugenius IV and members of the papalist faction suggested that Felix V was Antichrist (and also that Felix was using the advice of sorcery). Others perceived in the schism of Basel the *discessio* or "falling away" described by Paul in 2 Thessalonians 2:3. In 1444, an astrologer by the name of Jean de Bruges wrote a treatise using astrology to calculate the dates of the End Times.[1] While he placed the Final Judgment well

1 One Jean de Bruges' *Prenosticatio*, see Jean-Patrice Boudet, 'Simon de Phares et les rapports entre astrologie et prophétie à la fin du Moyen Âge', in *Les textes prophétiques et la prophétie en Occident* (*XII–XVI siècle*) (Roma, 1999), 617–48 and Boudet, *Entre science et nigromance: astrologie, divination et magie dans l'Occident médiéval, XII*^{e}*–XV*^{e} *siècle* (Paris, 2006), 321–24. See the comments of Laura Smoller, 'Apocalyptic Calculators of the Later Middle

 | DOI 10.1163/9789004345348_005

in the future, he noted the eschatological significance of the schism between Eugenius IV and the Council of Basel, which indicated that Antichrist's arrival was imminent.

On the conciliarist side, those in support of Basel exhibited a variety of reactions. Some went out of their way to insist that the End Times were not, as their opponents intimated, at hand. Basel did not represent the *discessio*, and Antichrist was not yet walking the earth. Others turned the words of their opponents against them. Yes, the *discessio* might be at hand, but it was the papalists who had brought it about. They perceived the onslaught of apocalyptic tribulations in the form of enemies both outside and inside the Church. To their minds, the enemies without were the Ottoman Turks, but far worse were the enemies within the Church: the papalists who opposed Basel and its reform measures. Finally, some conciliarists suggested that Antichrist was in fact present in the world, and his presence explained the failures of Basel and reform more generally.

The goal of this essay is to begin to trace the role of Antichrist and the Last Days in the thinking and writing of pro-Basel conciliarists within the Holy Roman Empire. I will first establish that certain texts, such as the *Master of Rhodes' Letter* and the sermons of Vincent of Ferrer on Antichrist, were circulated among conciliarists and influenced thought about the council. I will then proceed to consider the writings of some pro-Basel conciliarists, and the presence of a shared apocalyptic framework of thinking in these writings. In the most general sense, writings about Antichrist and the End Times became part of the literature used to support the council because they suggested that the imminent future of Christendom hung in the balance and that the opponents of Basel represented the tribulations associated with Antichrist. In this scenario, it was incumbent on supporters of the council to defend themselves against Basel's opponents, in order to remain on the side of the blessed rather than the damned. This essay will further demonstrate that the conciliarist use of eschatology changed over the life of the Council of Basel and the decade following it, becoming increasingly radical. It was in the later years of the Council, and after its failure, that the most outspoken associations between the events of Basel and apocalyptic events appeared.

This essay focuses on one particular faction of conciliarists—reformed clerics of the Holy Roman Empire. I explore the ways that members of this faction

---

Ages', in *Knowing the Time, Knowing of a Time, 3rd Annual Conference of the Center of Millennial Studies Boston, Dec 6–8 1998, Conference Proceedings*, 5 note 16 (http://www.mille.org/publications/Confpro98/SMOLLER.PDF). See also Smoller, *History, Prophecy, and the Stars: The Christian Astrology of Pierre D'Ailly* (Princeton, 1994), 193–94, note 14.

employed eschatological thought to advocate for the legitimacy of the Council of Basel, and more generally for the causes of conciliarism and reform. Reformed clerics of the Holy Roman Empire were the strongest supporters of Baselian conciliarism, and they as a group held to this position longer than anyone else. Moreover, their bitterness and disillusionment (and their recourse to eschatology) had long-term implications. In particular, the reaction of reformed clerics of the Holy Roman Empire to the events of Basel influenced the Empire's increasingly anti-Roman and anti-papal trajectory, which culminated in the Protestant Reformation.

In a collection about factional struggles, it makes sense to ask in what sense this group of Baselian conciliarists constituted a faction. Put simply, they shared a set of values and an agenda—to support and defend Basel and its reform policies. However, due to the current state of research and what remains to be done, I cannot demonstrate that all of the individuals discussed here associated with each other (although some did). The writings and thoughts of the more well-known figures associated with Basel have been thoroughly scrutinized (for instance those of Denis the Carthusian, Nicholas of Cusa, John of Ragusa, and John of Segovia). Other somewhat lesser-known Basel-era conciliarists have also recently been the subject of sustained inquiry, such as Bartholomeus of Maastricht, Vincent of Aggsbach, Johannes Hagen, and Jacob of Paradise. However, the networks that existed between these figures and other less famous supporters of Basel still require further investigation. What were the mechanisms through which the pro-Basel conciliarists communicated and shared their ideas? How were letters, treatises, visions, and prophecies circulated among those interested in promoting Basel and its agenda? What role did these have in decision-making and opinion-forming (and ultimately in support or rejection of the council)? This would seem a rich area of inquiry that will involve further investigation of manuscripts and textual transmission.

Of course, supporters of a cause do not always express their support explicitly. Instead, their inclinations can be articulated much more subtly—they can be hidden within their phrasing or diction, or simply in their choice of subject matter. Such nuances might have been clear to their fellow faction members, but they are not necessarily obvious to historians working today. Thus, to follow all of the subtleties of communication among pro-Basel conciliarists will be an undertaking requiring delicacy. The intention of this essay is to consider one such area of communication, and to demonstrate that apocalyptic discourse represented a point of contact and mutual interest among pro-Basel conciliarists. As more research into conciliarist networks in the Empire appears, researchers will discover more sharing of apocalyptic ideas among individuals with conciliarist leanings.

The issues raised at Basel did not die in 1449 with the end of the council, nor did the apocalyptic discourse. In the decade after Basel, a number of Baselian conciliarists continued to advocate for the superiority of general councils and for the reform of the Church. Within the Empire, members of the pro-Basel faction also continued to use eschatology as an interpretive tool. The Last Days and the arrival of Antichrist remained significant points of reference for their interpretation of the events surrounding Basel and its failure. More than one member of this faction concluded that Basel had failed in its attempts at reform because the council occupied a moment in eschatological history when reform was no longer possible. Others concluded that God had chosen to punish the sins of Christendom by assailing it with enemies. The fall of Constantinople to the Ottoman Turks in 1453, only four years after the council's dissolution in 1449, allowed the disappointed partisans of Basel to interpret this catastrophic event as a result of the council's failure to enact reform.

Particularly within the Empire, post-Basel conciliarists used apocalyptic thought and imagery to express the following themes: disillusionment with the council fathers, blame of prelates for hindering reform, doubt that reform could succeed through human actions, and the perception that the Ottomans were sent by God to punish Christendom. These themes would outlive the conciliarist era, and would contribute to the acrimonious discourse of members of the Empire toward the Roman Church in the fifteenth and sixteenth centuries.

The Council of Basel, which met as an ecumenical council from 1431–1438 and as a rump council from 1438–1449, was called at the behest of Pope Martin V, who died before the council could begin. The decree *Frequens*, issued by the Council of Constance in an attempt to perpetuate conciliar authority, obligated Martin, and his successor Eugenius IV, to call this council. *Frequens* decreed that a general council of the Church must be called after five years, then after seven, and thereafter every ten years—thus compelling future popes to continue to call councils.

The express goal of these frequent ecumenical councils was to enable the pursuit of the process of church reform begun at Constance. Indeed, reform became the watchword of conciliar activity in the fifteenth century, during which ecumenical councils were viewed by many as the best, and possibly only, effective tool for the reform of the Church. The expectation of the participants of Basel was that the council would undertake this reform.[2] The word "reform"

2 The literature on Basel is vast. For general bibliography, see Nelson H. Minnich, *Councils of the Catholic Reformation: Pisa I (1409)-Trent (1545–63)* (Aldershot, 2008) and Minnich, *General Church Councils, 1409–1517: Oxford Bibliographies Online Research Guide* (Oxford, 2010). On the Council of Basel, see Joachim Stieber, *Pope Eugenius IV, the Council of Basel, and*

was really an umbrella under which all sorts of institutional changes stood. One may think of the phrase "reform in head and members" as a slogan, with a positive, but vague, meaning that ensured the support of many. Among the reforms attempted by the council were the curbing of the practices of simony and multiple benefices, and the abolishing of papal annates. Monastic reform was equally prominent, and members of the observant parties of religious orders eagerly utilized the council to institute spiritual renewal and reform within their orders.[3]

Another goal of the frequent ecumenical councils was less explicit, but no less concrete: to act as a potential brake on papal authority. Many conciliarists insisted that the ecumenical council's authority within the Church was superior to that of the papacy's, based on the decree *Haec Sancta*, also issued at the Council of Constance. The notion of the superiority of council to pope received strong, though hardly universal, backing throughout Christendom. Participants at the Council of Basel were especially stout in their support for *Haec Sancta* and the idea that the council was the highest authority within the Church. As William Paul Lundell noted in his study of Carthusians at the Council of Basel, many clerics who chose to participate in the council did so because they held a "vision of the legitimately-assembled general council exercising fullness of executive, legislative, and judicial power over all aspects, even the most commonplace, of religious life."[4]

Eugenius IV (1431–1447) had just been elected pope at Basel's commencement, and from the outset perceived the council as alien to his own ambitions to recover and strengthen papal prestige. Eugenius resented *Frequens* and

---

the Secular and Ecclesiastical Authorities in the Empire: The Conflict over Supreme Authority and Power in the Church (Leiden, 1978); Werner Kramer, *Konsens und Rezeption: Verfassungsprinzipien der Kirche im Basler Konziliarismus: mit Edition ausgewählter Texte* (Münster, 1980); Erich Meuthen, *Das Basler Konzil als Forschungsproblem der Europäische Geschichte* (Opladen, 1985); Johannes Helmrath, *Das Basler Konzil: 1431–1449, Forschungsstand und Probleme* (Cologne, 1987). Alexander Patschovsky and Ivan Hlaváček, eds., *Reform von Kirche und Reich zur Zeit der Konzilien von Konstanz und Basel* (Constance, 1996); Jürgen Dendorfer and Claudia Märtl, eds., *Nach dem Basler Konzil. Die Neuordnung der Kirche zwischen Konziliarismus und monarchischem Papat (ca. 1450–1475)*, (Berlin, 2008); the collected essays in Thomas M. Izbicki, and Christopher M. Bellitto, eds., *The Church, the Councils and Reform: the Legacy of the Fifteenth Century*, Gerald Christianson (Washington, D.C., 2008); Heribert Müller, ed., *Das Ende des konziliaren Zeitalters (1440–1450): Versuch einer Bilanz* (Münich, 2012).

3 Useful on reform is Kaspar Elm, ed., *Reformbemühungen und Observanzbestrebungen im spätmittelalterlichen Ordenswesen* (Berlin, 1989).

4 William Paul Lundell, *Carthusian Policy and the Council of Basel* (Dissertation thesis, University of Toronto, 1996), 81.

Haec Sancta and viewed them as threats to his papal authority. Over the period of his papacy, he would in fact use the full extent of his power and diplomatic skills to resist them. Hence, the council was destined to become the arena for the struggle between papalists and conciliarists. Nothing less was at stake than the future governance of the Church.

From the beginning, then, the council was on a collision course with the papacy. Indeed, Eugenius first attempted to dissolve the council within six months of its commencement. Using sparse attendance as a pretext, he issued a bull adjourning the council and calling for a new council to meet in Bologna. He argued that the change of venue would make the location more accessible to Greek Christians. The true reason was that if the council were in Italy, Eugenius would have a better chance of dominating its proceedings. Eugenius's attempt to dissolve the council was met with indignation, as conciliarists supposed, correctly, that the pope was attempting to undermine the principle of *Haec Sancta*. As a result, participation in the Council of Basel swelled. Indignant prelates joined the council, while secular authorities, especially within the Holy Roman Empire, maintained their backing of the gathering. Eugenius was forced to concede—at least for a time—and to accept the council as legitimate, although he refused to acknowledge its superior authority.

At its commencement, both Basel's conciliarism and its reform agenda enjoyed the backing of many individuals within the Holy Roman Empire. These included the Holy Roman Emperor Sigismund before his death in 1437, as well as the three elector-archbishops of Mainz, Trier, and Cologne, and the faculties of the universities of Vienna, Cologne, and Erfurt. Among the rank and file of the Empire, the promotion of Basel was even more apparent. A number of German clerics eagerly supported the council. This stance appears to have been strongest among religious devoted to the cause of observant reform. For instance, Joachim Stieber commented, "It would appear that the strong stand in favour of the Council of Basel by the reformed Benedictine monasteries in the Empire was based not so much on their devotion to conciliar authority as an abstract constitutional principle of church government, but rather on their experience and hope that church reform, and especially, monastic reform, could be secured most effectively with the aid of a general council."[5] The monastic orders within the Empire with the strongest devotion to the dual—and as they saw them, linked—causes of Basel and reform included observant Benedictines, Augustinian Canons, Augustinian Friars, and Carthusians.[6]

---

5 Stieber, *Pope Eugenius IV*, 96–97.

6 On the orders within the Empire and their relationship to Basel, see Stieber, *Pope Eugenius IV*. Regarding the mendicant orders, see Petra Weigel, 'Reform as Paradigma: Konzilien und

As the Council of Basel endured, the conflict with Eugenius only intensified. One point of discord was the attempt of the council to reform the papal curia and to prohibit papal reservations of benefices which had formerly been filled through election. Another point of contention was the location—leaders of the Greek Orthodox Church were willing to meet with Latin representatives to discuss the unification of Christendom, but the council fathers at Basel could not agree with Eugenius on an acceptable meeting place. In 1437 Eugenius again attempted to increase his power over the council by insisting that it move out of the Holy Roman Empire to Ferrara. This time he was more successful. In 1438 he relocated the council to Ferrara and declared null any further proceedings at Basel. Some participants followed, but many did not. In turn, Eugenius excommunicated those who remained active in Basel. The council persisted, insisting on its ecumenical standing, and in 1439 deposed Eugenius, electing Amadeus of Savoy as the new Pope Felix V. This critical moment was a litmus test for support of the conciliarist cause and the Council of Basel. Individuals and institutions now had to choose between a reigning pope and a potentially schismatic council. Those who continued to stand with the Council of Basel (and Felix V) in its second decade (1438–1449) acted to support *Haec Sancta* and *Frequens* and in open defiance of Eugenius.

After 1438, fearing the birth of a new schism, many secular and religious leaders opted for a position of neutrality in the conflict between Eugenius and Basel. The new Holy Roman Emperor, Friedrich III, was less favourably disposed towards the council than Sigismund had been. Basel could no longer rely on the unwavering support of the constituents of the Empire. Yet, a core of believers in the dual causes of reform and conciliarism continued to stand with Basel. These included many within the Empire, in particular members of observant monastic orders and the universities. The holdouts who supported the cause of Basel and Felix became even more tightly bound to each other in the face of determined opponents. The most passionate of these partisans of Basel were Carthusians, Benedictines, Augustinian Canons, Augustinian Friars, and university theologians, all bonded by their reformist and conciliarist views. At this point, they had virtually everything to lose. Beset by detractors, and wary of losing support, they bolstered their position through writing—sharing letters, commentaries, visions, and eschatological ideas.

Support for the Council of Basel and its reforms occurred in three phases. The first phase corresponds approximately to the council's first decade, 1431–1438, when many who leaned towards a conciliarist position supported

Bettelorden', *Konstanzer Arbeitskreis Vorträge und Forschungen* 67 (2007), 289–335. On the Carthusians, see Lundell, *Carthusian Policy and the Council of Basel.*

Basel during its early dispute and uneasy truce with the papacy. The second, and more radical, phase constitutes the council's schismatic decade, 1438–1449, when it operated in direct opposition to the Roman papacy. Eventually, the Council of Basel failed, and its members were forced to pledge their obedience to Nicholas v. Thus, the third phase occurred after Basel had been defeated and dispersed—in the years 1449–1460—when the most radical supporters of the council continued to assert its legitimacy and to advocate for conciliarism and reform. Certain supporters of Basel participated only in the first phase, while others held fast well after 1449.

During all three phases, pro-Baselian supporters took recourse to eschatological thought to bolster their positions or to assuage their disappointments. The use of eschatological themes changed over time, however. Eschatological texts circulated at the Council beginning with Phase One; yet, in the early years, some conciliarists expressed skepticism about any association between Basel and the End Times. Later, as the conciliar cause grew more desperate, conciliarists regularly employed apocalyptic thought to offer radical interpretations of events.

1 Phase One: The Early Years 1431–1438

I first wish to consider allusions to the End Times by advocates of Basel in its earliest years—1431–1438. The most dramatic example is the circulation of a letter proclaiming the birth of Antichrist, ostensibly written by the Master of the Hospitallers on the Island of Rhodes.[7] This "letter" announced the recent birth of Antichrist in far-away Babylon, born to a prostitute of the tribe of Dan. The birth was, the letter claimed, accompanied by portents: hail the size of ostrich eggs, fire suspended in the air, the absence of the sun in a clear and cloudless sky, and the appearance of a stone bearing the words, "He is born today who was promised in the law."[8]

The *Master of Rhodes Letter* circulated widely in late medieval Europe, and its composition predated Basel by more than fifty years. Nevertheless, the *Letter* seems to have been viewed by some as relevant to the Council of Basel, and manuscript copies of the *Master of Rhodes Letter* demonstrate that the letter

7 See Jessica Roussanov and Robert E. Lerner, "The Jerusalem Rumors: The Earliest Stage of the 'Master of Rhodes' Letter on the Birth of Antichrist", *Rivista di Storia del Cristianesimo* 2, (2005), 157–72, and Robert E. Lerner, 'The Jerusalem Rumors: An Addendum', *Rivista di Storia del Cristianesimo* 3, (2006), 541–43.

8 Roussanov and Lerner, 'The Jerusalem Rumors', Appendix 1, 167.

circulated among pro-Baselian conciliarists. One copy of the letter appears in a codex in the Basel University Library.[9] All indications suggest that this copy was made in Basel in the second quarter of the fifteenth century—most likely during the council years—and one entry was written 1440 (during the council's schismatic second decade). Because this copy of the *Letter* cannot be dated to a precise year, the evidence for this manuscript cannot be placed for certain in Phase One or Two. Perhaps it even represents the transition between these phases.

The Basel manuscript presents evidence for the presence of literature on Antichrist at the council, but also evidence for the cautious approach that some took to this literature. In this manuscript, a German *Tractatus de Entekrist* precedes the *Master of Rhodes Letter* (in Latin). The anonymous, but likely Dominican, author of the *Tractatus* offered a discourse on many points regarding Antichrist and the Last Days. His chapters included explanations of when and where Antichrist would be born, the signs of his coming, what Antichrist's deeds would be, and how he would be defeated. However, in spite of his interest in Antichrist and his inclusion of the *Master of Rhodes Letter*, the author was not actually an advocate of the *Letter*. Rather, he felt that his own information about Antichrist contradicted the *Letter's* claims.

An important point of the discussion in the *Tractatus de Entekrist* was Paul's prediction in his second letter to the Thessalonians that a "discessio," or "falling away" would occur before Antichrist's arrival. 2 Thessalonians 2:3 states, "Let no man deceive you by any means: for that day shall not come, except there come a falling away first, and that man of sin be revealed, the son of perdition."[10] The "man of sin and son of perdition" was commonly understood as Antichrist and the *discessio* had come to be interpreted by medieval exegetes as a time when the Roman Empire's subjects would withdraw their obedience before the Last Days. Late medieval interpreters further understood this passage as predicting that the clergy would fall away from obedience to Rome before the Last Days. For instance, many had viewed the Papal Schism (1378–1417) as the predicted *discessio*. Significantly, the Dominican Vincent Ferrer—whose works were read and discussed at Basel—had perceived the Papal Schism as the *discessio* and evidence of Antichrist's imminent approach. Now, the new struggle between Basel and Eugenius prompted renewed consideration of whether Paul's *discessio* might be at hand.

9 Basel, Universitätsbibliothek, Cod. O I 19, *Tractatus de Entekrist*: fols. 93ra–97va and the *Master of Rhodes Letter*, fols. 97va–98vb. I have not had the opportunity to examine the entire manuscript and there is no catalog description.

10 2 Thessalonians 2:3.

The author of the *Tractatus de Entekrist* explained that the predicted *discessio* would be threefold: there would be a falling away from political obedience to the Roman Empire, a falling away of clerical obedience to Rome, and a falling away of Christians from the true belief. But, in spite of his discourse on the subject, he insisted the *discessio* was not yet at hand. Instead, he concluded his explanation by declaring that, however dreadful the state of the Roman Empire, however much there was schism in the Church, and however much there was a withdrawal of obedience and belief, still the "times in which Antichrist comes are not yet here."[11] Indeed, he repeated this point later in his discussion of the *Master of Rhodes Letter*, which he dismissed point by point. He assured his reader, "the great *discessio* from the Roman Church has not yet occurred, by God's grace." Therefore, in response to such a declaration of Antichrist's birth, "we should remain unmoved, so that we may not be deceived."[12]

The Basel treatise is just one example of conciliarists engaged with the issue of the *discessio* and the *Master of Rhodes Letter*. Evidence for the discussion of Antichrist also appears in the writings of Denis the Carthusian (Denys van Rijkel 1402–1471). Denis was a Carthusian monk in Roermond renowned for his prolific writings on mysticism and theology.[13] Scholars have disagreed about whether Denis was in fact a conciliarist, but his *Letter to the Catholic Princes*—discussed below—strongly suggests that he, like the rest of his order, advocated the conciliarist position. In any case, Denis's writing during the first phase of the Council of Basel reveals two things. The first is that rumours about Antichrist were prevalent even during the council's early years. The second, though, is that in the early years some supporters of the council took a very conservative stance on this issue.

In his *Diologion de fide catholica*, composed in 1432, Denis presented a dialogue between a philosopher and a theologian, in which the theologian schooled the philosopher about the life and times of Antichrist. Denis's comments were mostly conventional, but he did address topical matters such as the *discessio* and contemporary rumours about Antichrist's birth. In this dialogue, Denis's theologian roundly confuted the assertion that Antichrist had already been born.[14] The theologian informed the philosopher, "You should

11 Basel, Universitätsbibliothek, Cod. O I 19, here fols. 93va-93vb.

12 Basel, Universitätsbibliothek, Cod. O I 19, fol. 98vb.

13 On Denis, see Kent Emery, *Dionysii Cartusiensis, Opera Selecta* (Turnhout, 1991); Lundell, *Carthusian Policy and the Council of Basel*, 180–87; and Dennis Martin, 'Carthusians as Public Intellectuals: Cloistered Religious as Advisors to Lay Elites on the Eve of the Protestant Reformation', in Christopher Bellitto and David Flanagan, eds., *Reassessing Reform, A Historical Investigation of Church Renewal* (Washington D.C., 2012), 232–53.

14 Dionysius the Carthusian, *Dialogion de fide catholica*, Liber vi, Art. vii, in *Doctoris Ecstatici Dionysii Cartusiani Opera Omnia*, Vol. 18 (Tournai, 1899), 443.

know that many have been deceived, who were saying that Antichrist would come now or that he will come shortly." He noted, "Even now, in 1432, there are more than a few rumours about the birth of Antichrist." Denis specified the *Master of Rhodes Letter* and the sermons of Vincent of Ferrer as sources for the rumours of Antichrist's birth.[15] The theologian commented, "Truly, a certain letter has been sent from a certain someone, elucidating many miracles on the birth, life and signs of Antichrist now born. Even that famous and learned man called Vincent, in his encyclopaedic discussion of Antichrist, preached publicly that Antichrist was now born." The less cautious philosopher expressed eagerness to "hear that letter" on Antichrist, but the theologian warned, "To trust that letter would seem ill-advised and almost completely ridiculous." He reminded the philosopher (and his readers), "Many are able to fake letters," and advised the philosopher "not to believe lightly, but to commit all to God, and to prepare assiduously for the Last Day."

The theologian and the philosopher also discussed the topic of *discessio*. The theologian explained the idea of the threefold *discessio*, as in the *Tractatus de Entekrist*. He did not consider the possibility that the *discessio* might be happening in his own times, however. Instead the conversation remained abstract. The philosopher commented that Paul said Antichrist would not come unless the falling away of the Roman Empire preceded him, and he marveled that great men had been deceived into thinking that Antichrist had come while the Roman Empire still stood. The theologian corrected him, noting that "what the apostle said about the *discessio* was quite vague." He explained that although no Christian should doubt the words of the Apostles, not every word of scripture should be understood in the same way, and that it was not clear whether the *discessio* would precede the birth of Antichrist or the revealing of Antichrist.[16] Thus, although Denis's treatment of the *discessio* remained abstract, he still made the point that men had mistaken its significance before.

15 On Vincent Ferrer's pronouncements regarding Antichrist, see Roberto Rusconi, *L'attesa della fine: Crisi della società, profezia ed Apocalisse in Italia al tempo del grande scisma d'Occidente* (Roma, 1979), here 228–30. Vincent's most well-known work on Antichrist was a letter he wrote to Benedict XIII in 1412. This is edited in Henri Fages, *Notes et documents de l'Histoire de Saint Vincent Ferrier* (Louvain, 1905). A partial English translation is found in Bernard McGinn, *Visions of the End: Apocalyptic Traditions in the Middle Ages* (New York, 1979, repr. 1998), 256–58. See also the introduction of Laura Ackerman Smoller, *The Saint and the Chopped-Up Baby: The Cult of Vincent Ferrer in Medieval and Early Modern Europe* (Ithaca, 2014), here 136–37.

16 Dionysius the Carthusian, *Dialogion de fide catholica*, Liber vi, Art. vii, in *Doctoris Ecstatici Dionysii Cartusiani Opera Omnia*, Vol. 18 (Tournai, 1899), 443.

Denis, like the author of the *Tractatus de Entekrist*, recognized the eschatological buzz of their time. Both writers considered the topic of Antichrist an important one to address in writing. But both also went out of their way to dismiss the possibility that Antichrist had been born. Nonetheless, these disavowals reveal the prevalence of the *Master of Rhodes Letter*, Vincent Ferrer's sermons, and the general discussion of Antichrist's birth among their contemporaries. The dismissal of rumours of Antichrist seems to have had two motivations. Some supporters of Basel were anxious to combat papalist accusations that the council's resistance to Eugenius represented disobedience and *discessio*. But rumours of *discessio* and Antichrist seemed equally present among the Basel faction. The fact that the *Tractatus de Entekrist* and the *Master of Rhodes Letter* appear in a Basel manuscript indicates the presence of literature on Antichrist at the council. Other examples of interest in the End Times in Basel's first decade can also be found. Nicholas of Cusa discussed the possible approach of the End Times in his *De Concordantia Catholica*, which he dedicated to the council in 1433, although he too dismissed the notion that Antichrist had already arrived.[17] In addition, the Dominican reformer Johannes Nider preached vernacular sermons on the Book of Revelation at Basel during its first decade, indicating widespread interest in the subject.[18] In spite of this evidence, it is not yet clear exactly how rumours of *discessio* and Antichrist played into a program in support of conciliarism in the council's first decade. Once the council entered its second decade, however, the use of apocalyptic language to advocate a conciliarist position became more direct.

2 Phase Two: Hardened Lines 1438–1449

Further evidence of an association between the *Master of Rhodes Letter* and supporters of the Council of Basel appear in two other manuscripts. One copy of the *Letter* is found in a codex now held in the Augsburg University Library, compiled at the Observant Benedictine abbey of Heiligkreuz, in

17 See Paul E. Sigmund's discussion of Nicholas's conciliarism and constitutionalism, 'Nicholas of Cusa on the Constitution of the Church', in Chandler Brooks, Gerald Christianson, Thomas M. Izbicki, eds., *Nicholas of Cusa on Christ and the church: essays in memory of Chandler McCuskey Brooks for the American Cusanus Society* (Leiden, 1996), 127–34.

18 The reform treatise, the *Reformatio Sigismundi*, was also composed in 1439 in or near Basel. Although a very different type of text, the *Reformatio Sigismundi* does contain an eschatological prophecy. See Heinrich Koller, ed., *Reformation Kaiser Siegmunds* (Stuttgart, 1964), and Frances Courtney Kneupper, *The Empire at the End of Time: Identity and Reform in Late Medieval German Prophecy* (Oxford, 2016), 139–40.

Donauwörth, Swabia.[19] This codex is comprised of epistolary material written in the mid-fifteenth century. The *Master of Rhodes Letter* appears alongside several letters from the 1440s regarding the Council of Basel and directly follows a biting satire of those opposing the council (c.1444–1446).[20] This copy of the *Letter* dates Antichrist's birth to 1440, which suggests a connection to the Basel manuscript discussed above and also to the second decade of the council. Given its placement next to documents related to Basel, and especially a pro-Baselian satire, this copy of the *Letter* seems almost certainly to have been circulated in the second decade by someone devoted to the Baselian cause. Another copy of the *Master of Rhodes Letter* appears in an anonymous treatise written by a supporter of Basel, c. 1454 (Phase Three). This treatise is now held in Darmstadt and most likely came from the Cistercian cloister in Cologne.[21] I discuss it below.

The events of Phase Two of the Baselian conflict hardened the lines between papalists and conciliarists. Attempts at rapprochement had failed. The Council of Basel reluctantly but doggedly continued to act in opposition to a reigning pope. The council deposed Eugenius and created its own pope Felix V. Unfortunately for conciliarists, the ensuing rift caused the council to lose support, as many secular leaders chose to remain neutral rather than become embroiled in a new schism.

As opposition grew, pro-Baselian conciliarists became even more likely to interpret their struggle in apocalyptic terms. The recourse to apocalyptic language was also adopted by the papalists. The most famous case is that of Eugenius IV himself, who attacked his rival Felix, referring to him as "Antichrist" and "that first-born son of Satan."[22] Likewise, Juan of Torquemada, the

---

19 Augsburg, Universitätsbibliothek (once Schloss Harburg), Cod. I. 3, 2°, 18, fols. 13r-v. See Karin Schneider, *Deutsche mittelalterliche Handschriften der Universitätsbibliothek Augsburg: Die Signaturengruppen Cod.I.3 und Cod.III.1.* (Wiesbaden, 1988), 60–79.

20 On this poem, see Paul Joachimsohn, 'Spottverse von Basler Konzil', *Neues Archiv der Gesellschaft für Ältere Deutsche Geschichtskunde* 18 (1893), 693–94.

21 The manuscript in question is Hessischen Landes und Hochschulbibliothek Darmstadt, Hs. 528. No published manuscript description exists, but the manuscript most likely comes from the Cistercian Cloister Sion in Cologne. The *Speculum de ultimo antichristo magno et manifesto iam diu in mundo nato* appears on fols. 116r–142r. The *Master of Rhodes Letter* appears at 128va–129ra. A full discussion of this treatise appears in my forthcoming book, *"Future things are hidden from mankind and ought not be known": Contesting Knowledge of the Future in Late Medieval Europe*. I am grateful to Robert E. Lerner for bringing this treatise to my attention.

22 Session 9–23 March 1440 [Monition of the Council of Florence against the antipope Felix V], in Ernst von Birk, et al., eds., *Monumenta conciliorum generalium saeculi decimi quinti*

foremost defender of papal monarchy, referred to the Council of Basel as not merely a schism, but a "*discessio*," thus evoking the language of Paul and the specter of the End Times.[23]

Conciliarists responded in kind. The Carthusian Order emerged as one of the strongest institutions supporting Basel, and several of its members sought to influence the debate through treatises. Three prominent Carthusian reformers and members of the Holy Roman Empire—Bartholomeus of Maastricht, Jacob of Paradise (sometimes erroneously known as Jacob of Jüterbog), and Vincent of Aggsbach—referred to the End Times in their pro-conciliar writings, both during the second decade of Basel and afterwards.[24] All three of these writers took the position that opposition to the council was evidence of the presence of Satan in the world, and implied that the struggle at Basel was a sign of the End Times.

III (Wien, 1892), 480–88 and Georg Hofmann, ed., *Epistolae Pontificiae ad Concilium Florentinum Spectantes*, vol. III: *1440–45* (Roma, 1946), 4–12. See Ursula Gießmann, *Der Letzte Gegenpapast: Felix V: Studien zu Herrschaftspraxis und Legitimationsstrategien (1434–51)* (Böhlau, 2014), 142–44.

23 For instance, in Juan of Torquemada's 1448–1453, *Summa de ecclesia contra impugnatores potestatis Summi Pontificis* Book IV, Par. 1, Cap I. I cite here from the 1561 edition made in Venice, p. 535: "Dico autem cum rebellione, cum et pertinaciter praecepta contemnit, et iudicium eius subire recusat. Sequiter in diffinitione schismatice: ab unitate ecclesiae, scilicet totius, ad differentiam divisionis, sive discessus illiciti ab aliqua particulari hominum congregatione, sive societate: talis enim divisio a tali particulari fraternitate, sive societate non constituit schism, nisi largo modo, sed discessio ab unitate universalis ecclesiae, quae dicitur unitas principalis. Nam unitas particularis aliquorum adinvicem ordinatur ad unitatem ecclesiae, sicut compostio singulorum membrorum in corpore naturali ordinatur ad totius corporis unitatem".

24 Lundell, *Carthusian Policy and the Council of Basel*, 187–235. See Ton Meijknecht, *Bartholomeus van Maastricht, monnik en conciliarist* (Assen, 1982), here 75–114, and William Lundell, 'Bartholomeus van Maastricht on Carthusian Allegiance and Unity during the Basel Schism', in Thomas Burman, Mark Meyerson, and Leah Shopkow, eds., *Religion, Text, and Society in Medieval Spain and Northern Europe* (Toronto, 2002), 250–76. On Jacob of Paradise, see Thomas Wünsch, 'Vom Konziliarismus zur "Devotio Moderna": Die Transformation der Reformidee bei dem polnischen Theologen Jakob von Paradies in den Jahren 1440 bis 1450', in Heribert Müller, ed., *Das Ende des Konziliaren Zeitalters (1440—1450)* (Münich, 2012), 175–96, and Dieter Mertens, *Iacobus Carthusiensis: Untersuchungen zur Rezeption der Werke des Kartäusers Jakob von Paradies (1381–1465)* (Göttingen, 1976). See also Thomas Woelki, 'Die Kartäuser und das Basler Konzil', *Zeitschrift für Kirchengeschichte* 121, (2010), 305–22. The Carthusian reformer and conciliarist Johannes Hagen would also seem a potential source for the connection between apocalypticism and Basel. However, my investigation of his apocalypse commentary from 1453 has yielded no evidence of direct references to Basel or ecumenical councils.

Bartholomeus of Maastricht was a theologian at the University of Heidelberg before he joined the Carthusian Order. He became an important member of the order, serving as prior of the Charterhouse of Roermond (where Denis the Carthusian also resided) beginning in 1438. He emerged as a leader within his order, acting as visitator of the Rhenish province from 1442–1444. He was also a staunch supporter of Basel, and wrote treatises addressed to the princes of the Empire and to his own order encouraging obedience to the council.[25] In 1440 Bartholomeus of Maastricht composed *Tractatus de potestate pape, concilii generalis et ecclesie* for the synod in Cologne, where clergy discussed the schism and the position of the Empire prior to making a recommendation to Friedrich III. In the *Tractatus de potestate pape,* Bartholomeus advocated continued obedience to Basel and condemned anyone who would disrupt the work "already being done by the Holy Spirit at Basel." The goal of this work was to persuade fellow clergymen within the Empire (and ultimately the emperor) to adhere to the Baselian cause. Bartholomeus stated his case—the Council of Basel was called by the Holy Spirit to reform the Church, the popes Martin and later Eugenius had confirmed the Council (as had the authority of the Council of Constance), and Basel was therefore in a legitimate position to judge Eugenius. The council had found Eugenius guilty of heresy and other great and notorious crimes, and hence deposed him.

Having justified the actions of the Council, Bartholomeus turned to a theological discussion of heads and bodies and the relationship between the pope, as acting head, to the rest of the Church, Christ's mystical body. He asserted that literal understandings of heads and bodies would not suffice. It was not the acting head—that is, the pope—who was highest in the Church or in the body of Christ, in the way that a material head would be placed over a material body. Without making any direct accusations, Bartholomeus steered the conversation directly from Christ's body to the body of the "ancient enemy." Speaking of heads, he pointed out that there was a diabolical head as well as a holy one. He stated, "just as our redeemer is one person (in a mystical sense) with an aggregation of good, so is the ancient enemy one person (in a mystical sense) with an accumulation of evil, over which he presides as a head." Bartholomeus added that just as the mystical bridegroom Christ together with his bride was considered one mystical person with one will, likewise Satan and

25 Discussed in Stieber, *Pope Eugenius IV*, p. 86, note 30, pp. 100–101, note 57. See also Lundell, 'Bartholomeus van Maastricht on Carthusian Allegiance'. In 1444, he along with his close associate and fellow conciliarist Johannes Schunde, signed on to the University of Cologne's recommendation in support of Felix V. Bartholomeus also attended the Diet of Nürnberg in that year, where he advocated for Basel and Felix.

the collection of evil ones was called one mystical person with one will, but a will to deformation. He decried, "Oh miserable deformed union, in which a sinner is separated from God the highest good and shaped to the devil!" Again, Bartholomeus never stated it directly, but by moving the conversation from the pope as head and body of the Church to the head and body of Satan, he implied that Eugenius and his followers might as easily be part of the latter as the former.[26]

Bartholomeus also addressed the issue of obedience. He admitted that to suspend obedience from the pope was dangerous to the Church and should be avoided except in cases of absolute necessity.[27] But he declared that the goal of the Church should be to progress in virtue, not vice, and to conform to the eternal laws, not to deform them. In this regard, he asked, "What worse pestilence could there be within the Church of God than to weaken, sicken, kill, and bury the authority of general councils?" Continuing with his metaphor of illness, he asserted, "From this mother pest, a daughter pestilence is conceived—the total disregarding of councils. This is how things now stand in the Church. Its princes do not burn with the fever of charity. They are not even warm. If only the fever burned in them!"[28]

It was at the end of his treatise that Bartholomeus employed apocalyptic imagery—in his parting shot. He fought Paul with Paul—answering accusations of *discessio* with his own recriminations. He left his readers with the assertion that those who would disrupt the legitimate council of Basel acted not from piety, but from wicked love and corruption, as Paul had described in 2 Timothy 3:1–5 when he wrote, "Know this, that in the Last Days perilous times will come. For men will be lovers of themselves… And these will love pleasure rather than God, having the likeness of piety while denying the power of it."[29]

The Carthusian and conciliarist Jacob of Paradise made an even more direct connection in his writings between the dissolution of Basel and apocalyptic events. Jacob was a mystic and a pro-Basel conciliarist. His first career was as a member of the Cistercian Order and professor of theology at the University of Krakow, but he transferred to the Carthusians and resided at the

26 It would be useful to compare this to Thomas Prügl's discussion of Juan of Segovia's conciliarist works, in which Segovia compares the papacy as monarchical head of the Church to Lucifer, head of the angels. Prügl, 'Herbst des Konziliarismus?: Die Spätschriften des Johannes von Segovia', in Müller, ed., *Das Ende des konziliaren Zeitalters*, 153–74.

27 I cite from the edition of Meijknecht, *Bartholomeus van Maastricht,* here p. 102.

28 Meijknecht, *Bartholomeus van Maastricht*, 103.

29 Ibid., 113–14. This passage is cited in Lundell, *Carthusian Policy and the Council of Basel*, 198.

Charterhouse in Erfurt in 1442–1443.[30] Jacob seems to have remained devoted to the conciliarist cause to the bitter end, although his later works reveal a disillusionment with the possibility of institutional reform.[31] In 1441–1442 (during the council's second decade), Jacob wrote a treatise—the *Determinatio basilensis,* known also as the *Determinatio de ecclesia*—in which he considered whether the council or the pope held higher authority in the Church, and determined that the council's authority was superior. This *Determinatio* was a response to Eugenius' 1441 bull *Etsi non dubitemus,* which questioned the validity of *Haec Sancta.*[32]

Years later, in 1449, Jacob composed an *Avisamenta ad papam pro reformation ecclesiae* for Eugenius IV's successor, Nicholas V, in which he demanded that the pope reform the Church and convene regular councils, as stipulated by *Frequens*. In this text, Jacob asserted that if the Church was not reformed by a rightly guided council, the resulting punishment might be the attack of a pagan race. He cautioned, "Just as He set the Persians and Assyrians against the ancient Israelites, so might He set some pagan race against Christendom." Presumably the "pagan race" in question was the Ottoman Turks, as this position—that the Ottomans were God's punishment for the failure of Church reform—appears elsewhere in post-Basel conciliarist writings (see Denis the Carthusian's *Letter to the Catholic Princes* below). Jacob then turned to apocalyptic language, warning that, "Perhaps the amassing of evil deeds by the holy pope, who should be striving for reform, prepares the way for the son of perdition, concerning whom God said to Job: 'Want goes before the face of that one' (Job 41:13), namely of the Antichrist…"[33]

Also in 1449, Jacob composed *De septem statibus ecclesiae in apocalypse mystice descriptis et de auctoritate ecclesiae et de eius reformatione* (*On the seven states of the church in the mystical understanding of the Apocalypse and on the*

30 Here he would have encountered another Carthusian reformer and conciliarist, Johannes Hagen, who wrote commentaries on the Book of Revelation and collected texts related to the Council of Basel. I have not yet found direct evidence that Johannes Hagen referred to the Council of Basel in his analysis of Revelation.

31 See Wünsch, 'Vom Konziliarismus zur "Devotio Moderna"' and Thomas Wünsch, *Konziliarismus und Polen: Personen, Politik, und Programme aus Polen zur Verfassungsfrage der Kirche in der Zeit der mittelalterlichen Reformkonzilien* (Paderborn, 1998).

32 Henryk Anzulewicz, 'Jakob von Paradies, *Determinatio Basiliensis*', in *Polskie traktaty koncyliarystyczne z połowy XV wieku* (*Textus et studia historiam theologiae in Polonia excultae spectantia*), vol. 23 (Warsaw, 1987), 83–115.

33 Cited in Lundell, *Carthusian Policy and the Council of Basel*, p. 225, note 19: "Forte accumulatio malorum sancti papae reformationis assequendae viam parabit filio perditionis, et quo Deus ad Iob loquitur: 'Ante faciem eius praecedat egestas,' scilicet Antichristi…".

authority of the church and its reformation).[34] *De septem statibus* was a commentary on the seven seals of Revelation and their relationship to the current state of the Church. One must keep in mind the significance of the year 1449 in which Jacob chose to comment on Revelation—this was the year that the rump of the Council of Basel finally dissolved, extinguishing every hope for supporters of the council's work. In *De septem statibus*, Jacob combined a discussion of the End Times with his advocacy for reform. He railed against the Church for the greed of its prelates and what he viewed as the failure of discipline. He stated that councils had attempted to carry out necessary reform, but they had encountered the resistance of eminent people, for "the decrees of these councils have been opposed by those of the highest rank, both spiritual and secular." Thus, for Jacob, selfish princes and prelates had opposed, and hence destroyed, Basel. Using an analogy of childbirth, he lamented that this opposition to reform was so forceful "that all the business remains undone and when the time to give birth arrives, the strength to bear the child is not there. The opponents exhibit such barbarity and violence that it is clear that they wish to murder not only the holy offspring—reform—but indeed to destroy also the mother—the authority of general councils and the convoking of such councils."[35]

Jacob also discussed Nebuchadnezzar's dream of the statue made of metals from Daniel 2. This was generally understood by medieval exegetes as a prophecy of the four kingdoms that would last until the End Times, when the last—the Roman Empire—would be crushed. In his own interpretation, Jacob explained that the feet of the statue made of "iron and clay" were reflected in

34 The texts of *Avisamenta ad papam pro reformatione Ecclesiae* and *De septem statibus ecclesiae in apocalypse mystice descriptis et de auctoritate ecclesiae et de eius reformatione* are found in Stanislaw A. Porebski, *Jakub z Paradyza. Opuscula inedita. Wydal, wstepem i notami krytycznymi opat'*, Textus et studia historiam theologiae in Polonia excultae spectantia 5 (Warsaw, 1978). Excerpts of these texts are cited in Lundell, *Carthusian Policy and the Council of Basel.* For a list of manuscripts containing these works see Ludwig Meier, *Die Werke des Erfurter Kartäusers Jakob von Jüterbog in ihrer handschriftlichen Überlieferung* (Münster, 1955), 41, 61. See also Mertens, *Iacobus Carthusiensis.*

35 *De septem statibus*, in Porebski, 'Jakub z Paradyza', 31. Cited in Lundell, *Carthusian Policy and the Council of Basel*, 226: "Et licet quaedam decreta in hunc finem prodierunt ab eisdem conciliis, tamen tanta resistentia altae dignitatis personarum tam spiritualium quam saecularium facta est, ut videmus, quod totum negotium lugemus infectum et cum tempus pariendi advenisset, vires non habuit parturiens. Tanta denique crudelitate debacchati sunt repugnantes, ut solum prolem sanctam, scilicet reformationem necare contendant, set et matrem scilicet auctoritatem conciliorum et eorum convocationem occidant, prout res in prospectu declarat."

his own time, "for humans are now immersed in the clay of carnal pleasure, of appetite, and of greed."[36] Jacob, like Bartholmeus van Maastricht, compared the current state of affairs to that described by Paul in 2 Timothy 3: 2–4, "But know this, that in the Last Days perilous times will come: For men will be lovers of themselves, lovers of money, boasters, proud, blasphemers, disobedient to parents, unthankful, unholy, unloving, unforgiving, slanderers, without self-control, brutal, despisers of good, traitors, headstrong, haughty, lovers of pleasure rather than lovers of God…"[37] He asserted that this list represented the "fifteen sins in which we are now enveloped, for we are fashioned in the form of a foot, which is the last and dirtiest part of a man, for we are them 'in whom history has its fulfilment.'"[38]

Interestingly, while this last statement implied the approach of the "fulfilment of history," Jacob did not assert that the arrival of Antichrist was imminent. He interpreted the seven seals in chapters six and seven of Revelation as referring to the seven stages of Church history, with the sixth containing the reign of Antichrist and the seventh the millennium of peace. For Jacob it was possible for these stages to overlap, and he concluded that he lived in a blended time constituting elements from the fourth and fifth stages. Nevertheless, he implied that the disappointing failure of reform at Basel might prefigure the sixth age. Jacob had also become deeply pessimistic, maintaining that there would be no reform before the Last Days. As he morosely concluded, "The world descends daily into deeper depravity—by the holy disposition of the divine, whose council no one keeps—to the deepest degradation, until the time that the son of perdition should come…."[39]

Thus, in the second phase of Basel conciliarism, conciliarist writers had begun to refer directly to apocalyptic events in their advocacy of the cause. They lambasted prelates—their opponents in the papal party—for sinful living, especially for greed, pride, and lasciviousness. They stressed that this depravity corresponded to prophesied evils anticipating the End, as found in Timothy and Daniel. They bemoaned the failure of reform, and predicted dire and apocalyptic consequences—especially the onslaught of a "pagan race," and the arrival of the "son of perdition," i.e. Antichrist. Jacob of Paradise's later works also exhibited a characteristic of the third phase of Baselian conciliarism: distrust in the efficacy of human attempts at reform.

---

36 Porebski, "Jakub z Paradyza," 361.

37 Ibid., 361–62.

38 Ibid., 361–62. 1 Corinthians 10:11.

39 Ibid., 44. Cited in Lundell, *Carthusian Policy and the Council of Basel*, 231–32.

3 Phase Three—Bitterness, Disappointment, and Recrimination

This pessimism introduces the third phase—support of Basel after its dissolution. The failure of Basel was an enormous disappointment for those who believed in the superiority of the council and hoped for genuine reform. Basel's supporters dealt with their defeat in various ways, but the most radical maintained their advocacy for Basel and the cause of conciliarism well after 1449. Some pro-Basel clerics in the Holy Roman Empire continued to write and to share their thoughts on the subject. The framework of the End Times, already established as an interpretive model within which to view Basel, became even more fitting in the wake of its failure.

Like Jacob of Paradise, Vincent of Aggsbach was another pro-Baselian partisan whose support for conciliarism continued after the council's end. Vincent had been the prior of the Carthusian monastery of Aggsbach in Lower Austria. He was a caustic partisan of Basel, whose acerbic words on the subject eventually led to his removal from the office of prior. This did not deter him from expressing his conciliarist position in a number of personal letters written to his Benedictine contemporary, Johannes Schlitpacher of Weilheim, the Prior of Melk Abbey.[40] In his letters, which continued to advocate conciliarism a decade after the dissolution of Basel, Vincent insisted on the righteousness of a council, asserting that a council could be held without a pope's consent if necessary.[41]

One unique characteristic of Vincent's writing was his willingness to tackle the accusation of "*discessio*" head on. Vincent was aware that the falling away of clerical obedience to Rome was seen as a sign of the End Times. And yet, he openly advocated for such a falling away. In a letter to Schlitpacher written in 1456, Vincent asserted, "Without schism the church cannot be healthy. Schism

---

40 See Dennis Martin, 'Carthusians as Advocates of Women Visionary Reformers', in Julian M. Luxford, ed., *Studies in Carthusian Monasticism in the Late Middle Ages*, (Turnhout, 2008), 142–52. Vincent is also discussed in Stieber, *Pope Eugenius IV*, 101–02, 338–40.

41 Martin, 'Carthusians as Advocates', 144: "In 1456 Vincent was endorsing in letters to Schlitpacher the idea that a council may be held without the pope's consent, recognizing that this might bring about a schism, but insisting that, under certain circumstances, a healing in the Church could not take place without schism. The blame for such a schism would rest not with the council's adherents but with the intransigent Roman curia." Several of these letters are found in Melk Stiftsbibliothek, Cod. 1767. They are published in part in Bernhard Pez and Philibert Hueber, eds., *Codex diplomatico-historico-epistolaris* (vol. 6 of *Thesaurus anecdotorum novissimus*), (Augsburg, 1729), Part III, 327–56. See also the unpublished dissertation of Franz Hubalek, *Auf dem Briefwechsel des Johannis Schlitpacher von Weilheim* (*Der Kodex 1767 der Stiftsbibliothek Melk*) (University of Vienna, 1963).

and falling away should not be desperately feared... neither a general council nor a schism nor a falling away will occur, except that *they* bring it about." Thus, the "falling away" if it was to occur, was not the fault of those attempting to celebrate a council. Instead,

> it is brought about by those, who, in their love of Rome, do not consent to celebrate a council, who when called do not appear (in the hopes of breaking it up), and are hardly willing to heed the church. Regarding such men, who with their deeds have proved themselves heathens, let them fall away. Let them fall away! *They* will bring about schism and falling away, those who will be patiently tolerated for a time, while through dissimulation they are allowed to destroy the vines of my Lord and sow dangerous and damnable errors in the church of God.[42]

Thus, Vincent saw his factional opponents—papalists and members of the Roman curia—as enemies of the Church responsible for the prophesied "falling away" which was to occur in advance of Antichrist.

Some disappointed conciliarists also suggested that the failure of Basel had opened the way for divine punishment in the form of the Ottoman Turks. In 1432 Denis the Carthusian had dismissed the *Master of Rhodes Letter* announcing Antichrist's birth. But in 1454, Denis again took up the topic of Antichrist in a pro-conciliar work composed five years after Basel's conclusion. In this case, the specter of Antichrist appeared in his *Letter to the Catholic Princes*, which he composed in the wake of the fall of Constantinople to inspire the princes in their defense against the Turks. Perhaps because of the intervening events, Denis took a more adversarial stance in his *Letter to the Catholic Princes* than he had in his earlier *Dialogion de fide catholica*. In this *Letter*, Denis,

42 Cited Martin, 'Carthusians as Advocates', p. 144, note 56 from a letter to Schlitpacher, written sometime before Christmas 1456. I have compared this with Melk Stitfsbibliothek, cod. 1767, p. 400: "Sine scismate non erit ecclesie salus, non sunt scisma et discessio multum vehementer timenda tamen persuasum habeam, generale concilium neque scisma neque discessionem facturum, que si fient, necessaria ab illis fient, qui in amor (Roma written above in small letters) habitant, qui vel in concilium celebrandum non consentient, vel vocati ad interessendum non comparebunt, ecclesiamque audire minime parati. Et si tales, qui per facta sua se ethnicos comprobabant, discedant, discedant! Ipsi facient scisma et discessionem, que unque ad tempus tolerabilius sustinebuntur, quam quod sub dissimulacione permittantur vineam Domini demoliri et periculosos imo damnabiles errores in ecclesia Dei seminare." This last was a reference to the the little foxes who destroy the vines in the Song of Solomon 2:15. I have not had the opportunity to review Hubalek's work, but this letter is apparently found in Hubalek, *Auf dem Briefwechsel*, 208–209.

like Vincent of Aggsbach, suggested that his factional opponents—papalist prelates—were enemies of the Church, and that they collectively represented Antichrist. He made this accusation by citing the words of the old firebrand Bernard of Clairvaux, charging prelates with corruption and declaring, "They are called servants of Christ and they serve Antichrist."[43] Denis intimated that the prelates represented the worst tribulation in the Church, and thus a sign of the End. Still citing Bernard, he wrote, "Once it was predicted, and now the time of fulfilment approaches: *Behold for peace I had great bitterness.*" He listed the tribulations of the Church, ending with his own time, "Bitter in the deaths of the martyrs, more bitter in the conflict of the heretics; now most bitter in the ways of those of my household, that is in the abuses and vices of impious Christians."[44] Denis also cited Saint Bridget of Sweden on the danger of corrupt prelates to the Church, noting, "In the *Revelations* of Saint Birgitta one may read about how the Lord Jesus Christ, in the presence of God the father, surrounded by an army of angels…, may yet be conquered by the vicious and scandalous conduct of prelates, princes, and his servants."[45]

Denis did not just accuse prelates of poor conduct. He explicitly stated that one of the major failings of the prelates, which would bring about the "time of fulfilment," was their failure to celebrate a general council. He railed against the evils of the day and the predicted "*discessio*," lamenting that Christians were "falling away" from the faith, that "most care little or nothing about the excommunications and precepts of the highest pontiff," and "obedience has almost totally perished in the church of God."[46] The cause of all this, he explained,

> is especially that the general councils are not celebrated at their appointed time, as was ratified by those councils. What is certain is that the more and greater the evils and dangers that now dwell in the universal church, the greater is the reason—indeed the necessity—to celebrate a general synod without delay, through which so many good things may be done,

43 *Epistola ad principes Catholicos paraenetica de insituendo bello adversus*, in *Doctoris ecstatici D. Dionysii Cartusiani, Opera Omnia*, vol. 36, Articulus XIII, 517. Denis cites here from Bernard of Clairvaux's Sermon 33 on the Song of Songs. See Bernard of Clairvaux, *Sermones super Cantica Canticorum*, vol. 1, in Jean Leclerq et al. eds., *Bernardi, Opera Omnia* (Roma, 1957).

44 *Epistola ad principes Catholicos*, p. 517. The biblical passage is Isaiah 38:17.

45 Ibid., 517.

46 Ibid., 517: "De excommunicationibus et praeceptis summi Pontificis parum aut nihil a multis curatur, et obedientia quasi totaliter perit in Ecclesia Dei."

> that the Lord God may be reconciled to us, that he may show mercy and aid us.[47]

Speaking as Mother Church, he urged, "Come together, my sons, in one place, form a plan, celebrate a holy and general synod and provide for the community and full correction of all errors at every rank, position, and order. Each must turn away from all his wickedness, idleness, and lust. Do not delay, do not ignore this, because a greater danger than you think is at the gates."[48] What was this danger? The Ottomans? The "time of fulfilment"? Denis did not say, but he clearly blamed its approach on prelates and papalists who refused to celebrate regular councils.

I would like to consider one final text which dramatically exploited the apocalyptic implications of Basel's failure in order to place the world on the edge of the End Times. The text is a treatise titled *Speculum de ultimo antichristo magno et manifesto iam diu in mundo nato* (Mirror of the final great Antichrist who is now born and visible in the world), written after the dissolution of Basel in c. 1454 by someone convinced that Antichrist was present in the world. I have not yet been able to identify the author, nor even ascertain to which order he belonged, although he evinced a particular interest in Dominican writers. What is clear, though, is that the author was a partisan of, and likely participant at, Basel. One clue that the author might have been present at Basel is his reliance on Vincent Ferrer's letter on Antichrist to Benedict XIII (1412), as Vincent's works were subjects of interest among the Dominicans at the Council of Basel.[49]

Although the council was over, the author of the *Speculum de ultimo antichristo* had not moved on. Throughout the text, he repeatedly expressed his disappointment with the council's failure, and his continued support for Baselian reform. The author commented positively on Felix V, while expressing

47 Ibid., 517: "Quorum omnium praecipua causa est, quod concilia generalia non celebrantur legitime tempore suo, sicut ab ipsis conciliariis est sancitum. Certumque est, quod quanto nunc plura atque majora mala ac pericula in Ecclesia universali versantur, tanto major est causa, imo necessitas, celebrandi sine dilatione synodum generalem: per quam tot et tanta fierent bona, quod Dominus Deus noster reconciliaretur, misereretur et succurreret nobis, saltem in multis, et multo utique magis quam alias."

48 Ibid., 516: "Convenite, o filii, in unum locum; inite consilium, celebrate synodum sanctam ac generalem, et de communi ac plena emendatione in omni statu, gradu et ordine providete. Convertat se unusquisque ab omni malitia, nequitia et immunditia sua. Nolite differre, nolite dissimulare: quia periculum majus quam creditis in foribus est."

49 On the interest in Vincent of Ferrer at the Council of Basel, see Sigismund Brettle, *San Vicente Ferrer und sein literarischer Nachlass* (Münster, 1924), 2.

pessimism regarding the possibility that humans may accomplish reform. He stated,

> Who can enumerate all of the ways that simony is now committed and even excused under the pretense of piety, for principally this is carried out by those who ought to prohibit and remove and cure such vices, not participate in them. Indeed, avarice, and the errors which have arisen from this, have increased to such a degree, they have come in such long-standing abuse, that it is impossible to get rid of them all through human effort alone. For now they (the sinful prelates) are driven to act in contempt of the universal church, so that they do not wish to hearken, nor do they wish to obey, even the highest pontiff, the former pope Felix v. Because of the current malignity, the reform of the general universal church in head and members, though it would be beneficial to all, may not be effected.[50]

These are themes which had been repeated among Baselian conciliarists. Reform was hindered by prelates who should be leading holy lives, but instead exhibit simony and avarice. The reform attempted by the Council of Basel was obstructed by those who should have supported it. Obedience from the papacy had "fallen away." And the contemporary state of affairs was so wretched that reform was beyond the ability of human agency.

According to this author, reform could only succeed at a later time.[51] His reasoning was that Jesus told the apostles that at the End of Time there would be a defection from charity and faith. Hence in the malignant times in which he found himself, the Church could not be reformed. The reform attempted by the "legitimate council of Basel"—because it occurred during the period of defection from charity and faith—was destined to frustration. Only after Antichrist had ruled and died would there be hope of reform.

These references to Basel were only secondary to the author's expressed intent, which was to examine contemporaneous knowledge of the future and to inform readers about Antichrist. Because of his experience of Basel, the author

---

50 Darmstadt, Hs. 528, fol. 119ra: "Sed quis posset numerare modos quibus symonia iam committitur omnia tamen huiusmodi facta sub specie pietate excusantur, et principaliter fit ab illis qui talia prohibere curare et removere deberent ne fierent, ymmo avaricia et errores qui exinde exorti sunt in tantum creverunt et in tam longum abusum venerunt quod impossibile est omnia illa humanitus extirpare, tum iam eciam aguntur in contemptum universalis ecclesiam quam omnis nolebant audire, nec summo tunc pontifici vero scilicet olim felici pape quinto nolebant obedire ne reformatio generalis universalis ecclesie in capite et in membris sortiretur effectum salutarem."

51 Ibid., fol. 134vb.

wrote as though he had been plunged into the awful realization that Antichrist must have already been born. Thus, while his goal was to write about Antichrist, he referred constantly to Basel. Indeed, he linked the failure of Basel's reform and the birth of Antichrist more explicitly than anyone else we have encountered. He called the papal, anti-conciliarist position heresy, accusing Eugenius of being "like the Hussites in Bohemia." But, he argued, Eugenius was far more dangerous, "for he (Eugenius) says that the Roman pontiff has power over the whole church, and that the general council receives its authority from the pope, and not vice versa."[52] The author concluded that "these heresies and others are signs of the approaching persecution of Antichrist." As further evidence of Antichrist's arrival, he cited the *Master of Rhodes Letter* in full. In his consideration of whether it was possible to know the time of Antichrist's arrival, the author expressed his belief that Antichrist presently walked the earth. He acknowledged that the time of Antichrist's arrival was a great secret, referring to the oft-cited passage in Mark 13:32: "no one knows that hour except the father." Yet, his conclusion, unique as far as I am aware, was that this passage referred to the saints and the Church fathers, who, although illumined by God, did not need to know the hour of Antichrist's arrival. But, he asserted, the situation changed once Antichrist actually arrived. In the present situation, "it is expedient and necessary that men after the birth of Antichrist know that time so that they may safeguard and prepare themselves."[53]

The *Speculum* therefore marks the fullest expression of the apocalyptic thought of the pro-Basel faction, carried through to its logical conclusion. The interpretation posited by the *Speculum*'s author cast Eugenius and his papalist supporters as a tribulation or sign of the approaching End. It also construed the failure of Basel as a sign of the End Times when Christians would abandon their faith and charity. In this context, the letter announcing Antichrist's birth was proof that the author's interpretation of events was correct and the Last Days were at hand.

4 Conclusion

The various examples cited in this essay indicate some of the ways that partisans of Basel within the Holy Roman Empire framed and espoused their conciliarist agenda. It is my assertion that members of the pro-Basel faction shared an apocalyptic discourse, although their employment of this discourse

52 Ibid., fols. 128rb-128va.

53 Darmstadt, Hs. 528, fol. 124vb.

changed over the course of the council. Certain Baselian supporters placed the events of the council in an apocalyptic context, as indicators of troubles that would precede the Last Judgment. Even the most conservative felt obliged to consider the Council within an apocalyptic light, although they did their best to counter insinuations that the rift between the council and papacy represented the *discessio* of 2 Thessalonians. Others embraced the potential for apocalyptic events, circulating news of Antichrist's birth. References to Antichrist's arrival acted both as a goad to reform and as an explanation for the failure of reform. The council was ultimately defeated, but apocalyptic interpretations only became more radical. Some writers perceived a cause and effect relationship between the failure of Basel and the Ottoman conquest of Constantinople. They concluded that the expansion of the Ottomans was a punishment from God for the Church's inability to reform. Still others, such as the author of the *Speculum*, decided that the End Times were truly at hand.

The examples cited here are most likely only the tip of the iceberg. More research into the use of an eschatological framework to promote the conciliarist position during and after Basel is necessary, and this will likely yield more connections. It might then be possible to trace the mechanisms by which conciliarists shared their apocalyptic discourse with each other. This could also be compared with the employment of an apocalyptic discourse among papalists, who made their own claims about the presence of Antichrist. Yet some conclusions may already by drawn. The conjunction of apocalyptic thought and disappointed reform would serve to radicalize a certain sector of pro-Basel partisans. As Basel receded into the past, the provocative combination of apocalyptic thinking and resentment of the papal curia remained. This combination would have long-reaching effects within the Holy Roman Empire. Perhaps most importantly, it had the effect of predisposing certain individuals towards the rejection of Rome in the subsequent events of the Reformation.

Factions in Rome between Papal Wars and International Conflicts (1480–1530)[1]

Maria Antonietta Visceglia

The Guelph and Ghibelline dimension in Roman factions in the fifteenth century was highlighted some years ago by Christine Shaw in her treatment of the more general topic of relations between Roman barons and Renaissance popes.[2] Today, Shaw's studies are still considered very innovative in light of historians' renewed interest in factions and their re-assessment of factions as a crucial category in the political competition of the early modern age. This paper will not go into the question of whether the terms "Guelph" and "Ghibelline" may be applied satisfactorily to the case of Rome.[3] Certainly, the terms were part of the lexicon used by the sources of the period, even though the language describing factions was extremely varied, drawing on a vocabulary of passions. Terms like *partegiani, inimici capitali, inimici coperti, sviscerati amici, devotione* or *setta*, and *briga* recur perhaps more frequently than do "Guelph" and "Ghibelline," which during the modern age took on increasingly negative connotations with no ideological overtones. In the 1520s, "Ghibelline" and "Imperial" were, however, used interchangeably.

In Rome, conflict among factions in the decades straddling the fifteenth and sixteenth centuries revolved around the complex relations between the Orsini and the Colonna, the two most illustrious baronial lineages, because of their deep roots within the city, the prestige that came with being ex-papal families, the extent of their feudal possessions both in the Papal States and in the

1 I use the following abbreviations: ASV: Archivio Segreto Vaticano; ASR: Archivio di Stato di Roma; RIS: Ludovico Antonio Muratori, ed., *Rerum Italicarum Scriptores*, new edition revised, expanded and corrected under the direction of Giosuè Carducci and Vittorio Fiorini (Città di Castello, 1900-); DBI, *Dizionario Biografico degli Italiani, Enciclopedia Treccani* (Roma, 1960-).

2 Christine Shaw, 'The Roman Barons and the Guelf and Ghibelline Factions in the Papal States', in Marco Gentile, ed., *Guelfi e Ghibellini nell'Italia del Rinascimento* (Roma, 2005), 475–94; idem, *The Political Role of the Orsini Family from Sixtus IV to Clement VII. Barons and Factions in the Papal States* (Roma 2007), 100–102; idem, 'The Roman Barons and the Popes', in Marco Gentile and Pierre Savy, eds., *Noblesse et États princiers en Italie et en France au XVIe siècle* (Roma, 2009), 101–24.

3 Franca Allegrezza, *Organizzazione del potere e dinamiche familiari. Gli Orsini dal Duecento agli inizi del Quattrocento* (Roma, 1998), 193; Serena Ferente, *Gli ultimi guelfi Linguaggi e identità politiche in Italia nella seconda metà del Quattrocento* (Roma, 2013), 17.

 | DOI 10.1163/9789004345348_006

kingdom of Naples, and the participation of their *condottieri* in the wars of the period. As we shall see, these lineages were not compact realities but diversely articulated groups riven by internal tensions and conflicts. These tensions were perhaps more serious for the Orsini because of the broader demographic makeup of their lineage. Compared to other cities, factional strife in Rome had some peculiar characteristics that went beyond just violence, even if recurring vendettas and feuds featured regularly in the city chronicles; there was also an institutional dimension to the strife, arising from a political system in which the pope was a sovereign elected by the Sacred College, and therefore in which the great families found it indispensable to have a representative. In the pages that follow, I aim to look closely at the dynamics behind the Roman factions during the early modern age. I identify a change that occurred between the 1480s and the 1530s, at a time when the Italian and European conflicts, in which the papacy acted as a participant, not merely an arbiter, had increased the importance of supralocal events. Moreover, the Protestant schism further complicated matters at the very centre of Catholicism.

1 Papal Wars, Factions, Feuds (1480–1492)

After the events of the Great Schism, the return of the Papal See to Rome coincided with the reconstruction (also in a doctrinal sense) of a strong idea of the papacy, one that was dense with sacred meaning and that renewed links with the imperial heritage of Rome, while also re-asserting the authority of the Vicar of Christ above that of the Ecumenical Council. At the same time, in light of the fact that the fifteenth-century popes had become "Roman" again, they strove with every means to reinforce the temporal Papal States. This latter objective meant establishing control over Rome and the surrounding countryside, and the cities mainly situated along two axes—southwards to Naples and north towards Romagna. In reality, papal capacity to assert itself as a pivotal component in the Italian political system was held back by the popes' incoherent military policy, which saw them engaging not so much in the struggle against the Turk, but as actors in the Italian conflicts, also known as the Papal Wars.[4]

Sixtus IV (1471–1484), the Franciscan Francesco della Rovere, a churchman whose modest family hailed from Liguria, was endowed with an impressive theological culture. He pursued the construction of a curial machine and a

4 David S. Chambers, *Popes, Cardinals and War. The Military Church in Renaissance and Early Modern Europe* (London, 2006).

more structured territorial system in a manner that benefited his relatives. The changes under Sixtus—the reorganization of finances, the proliferation of curial offices by resorting to venality, and the enhancement of the court at the expense of traditional Roman civic liberties (which as late as 1453 had inspired Porcari's "republican" conspiracy) all led to relatively stronger Papal States, but above all resulted in the social ascendency of the pope's own relatives.[5]

In theory at least, two marriages contracted in 1472, one joining Girolamo Riario, the son of the pope's sister Bianca, with Caterina Sforza; the other, Leonardo della Rovere with Giovanna d'Aragona, the illegitimate daughter of King Ferdinand, should have served to raise the Holy See's status as a balancing power in international relations. However, nepotism influenced papal relations with the leading Italian states, which were affected by conflicts within the papal family. Showing equal favour to his family's two branches, the pope bestowed the cardinal's hat on both Pietro Riario, Girolamo's brother, and on Giuliano della Rovere, Leonardo's cousin. Pietro's premature death (1474), followed by that of Leonardo della Rovere a year later, left Girolamo Riario (who in 1473 had become lord of Imola, an important city in Romagna with a long Ghibelline tradition) and Giuliano della Rovere as the most influential nephews, but they were inexorably at odds with each other. The rivalry between Girolamo Riario and Giuliano della Rovere, far from being resolved through family politics, became another variable in Roman factional conflicts, conflicts that were also caught up in the complicated vicissitudes of Italian politics during the closing decades of the fifteenth century. Girolamo Riario fomented the Pazzi conspiracy against the Medici (26 April 1478) with the complicity of Ferdinand of Aragon, and, with the intention of enlarging his own territorial domains in the direction of both Romagna and Naples, he supported Venetian designs on Ferrara and the Adriatic ports while fanning the flames of Orsini hatred for the Colonna. The Colonna di Genazzano had been given the feudal estate of Albe by Ferdinand, who had taken it away from the Orsini.[6] Albe was part of an important complex of territories in Abruzzo that Napoleone and Roberto Orsini (Bracciano) had acquired by fighting for the House of Aragon in the wars that followed the death of Alphonse the Magnanimous (1458). While the Orsini's powerful Neapolitan branches (the princes of Taranto and Salerno), by aligning themselves with the Angevins, headed down a path of

5 On the formation of the curial bureaucracy, Peter Partner, *The Pope's Men. The Papal Civil Service in the Renaissance* (Oxford, 1990). On the Porcari conspiracy, see Anna Modigliani, *Congiurare all'antica. Stefano Porcari, Niccolò V, Roma 1453* (Roma, 2013).

6 Alessandro Serio, *Una gloriosa sconfitta. I Colonna tra papato e impero nella prima età moderna (1431–1530)* (Roma, 2008), 27.

inevitable crisis, the Bracciano line emerged pre-eminent, completing a process of internal hierarchization that would influence subsequent events. The great feudal estate became concentrated in the hands of Gentile Virgilio Orsini, the son of Napoleone (died 1480), because, among other reasons, of the death of his father's brothers. Ultimately Gentile Virgilio was left as the head of the entire extended lineage, and was even recognized as such by the Colonna.[7]

The wound inflicted upon the Orsini by Ferdinand, who had wished to reward the Colonna's military support in the war with Florence, produced immediate after-effects in Rome, unleashing a series of clashes between the two factions. Christine Shaw has argued that "the party allegiances of the Roman baronial families were very firmly fixed",[8] in the sense that the Orsini, Conti and Anguillara were Guelph, while the Colonna, Caetani and Savelli were Ghibelline. Yet while belonging to one or the other camp constituted a mark of identity, this identity did not necessarily apply to every individual or branch of a lineage. Family disputes motivated alliances, perhaps temporary, with an enemy, and the brief respites of peace between flare-ups sometimes led to marriages between members of rival lineages. This even happened between the Colonna and Orsini[9] themselves, and happened repeatedly between the Savelli and the Orsini. Factional identities allowed for a certain degree of flexibility, which meant that they could bend to suit motivations driving individuals or groups. But what made events especially difficult to predict in the case of the Orsini-Colonna conflict was the fact that in Rome these two factions represented an extremely broad swath of families of various ranks and extractions, ranging from the municipal nobility to the *Popolari*. The transversal nature of the factions enabled alliances that, while implying a hierarchical respect for the lead family, interwove the interests and passions of many actors.

The enmity between the Orsini and Colonna intersected with the opposition between the Santacroce and the della Valle and between the Crescenzi and the Margani. The opening shot of Roman factional strife in the 1480s was the assassination of Pietro Margani on 15 September 1480 by Prospero Santacroce, who had recently returned from exile. Margani, a member of a minor family of the Roman nobility engaged in agriculture, stock raising, trade and construction, was related to the della Valle. The latter were the intended targets of Santacroce, who was seeking to avenge the death of his cousin Francesco, murdered

7 Iacopo Gherardi da Volterra, *Il diario romano dal VII settembre 1479 al XII agosto 1484*, E. Carusi, ed., in RIS, t. XXIII/3 (Città di Castello, 1904), 24–25.

8 Shaw, *The Political Role*, 99.

9 Ibidem, 100–02. On the Orsini, see Mori, *L'Archivio Orsini*.

by his own brother-in-law Francesco della Valle.[10] The social profiles of the Santacroce and della Valle families were quite similar, though both were far from wielding the power of the Orsini and the Colonna. In the mid-fifteenth century, the Santacroce drew their wealth from the exploitation of *casali*, from trading companies and money lending. Prospero's uncle, Andrea, had begun a career in the curia and later became a learned consistorial advocate and lawyer of the *Popolo Romano*.[11]

The noble status of the della Valle was more firmly established. Designated *nobiles viri* at the beginning of the fifteenth century, in 1433 the emperor Sigismund had conferred on the della Valle the title of *comes*. The family's social ascent had received a further boost in the mid- fifteenth century, mostly from Paolo, papal archiater and *Conservatore* of Rome during the reign of Oddone Colonna (Martin V), and the husband of Sabella Savelli; and from Nicola, the papal treasurer in Perugia and clerk of the apostolic Chamber who enlarged the family's patrimony through numerous acquisitions.[12] In the next generation Lelio was a consistorial advocate, Pietro auditor of the Rota and bishop of Ascoli, and Filippo archiater of Sixtus IV. The della Valle's close relations with the Colonna did not prevent Callixtus III from employing Lelio as a mediator in the conflict that broke out between the Orsini and Colonna in 1455 (later settled).[13]

It is not known precisely what the state of relations was between the della Valle and the Santacroce in the mid-fifteenth century. It was at this time that a double marriage took place joining Livia di Lelio della Valle with Prospero Santacroce, and Prospero's sister, who was also named Livia, with Francesco della Valle, but these kinships did not prevent the above-mentioned violence. We do know for certain that, in spite of the peace brokered by the pope between Pietro Margani's son and the Santacroce, the feud continued on over the next few years.[14] It later gradually spread to the Orsini and Colonna and became entangled with Italian political events and with the rift within the papal

10 Anna Modigliani, 'Margani, Pietro', DBI, 70 (2008), *ad vocem*. Gherardi da Volterra described Pietro Margani as "related through marriage to the della Valle and belonging to the same faction": *Vallensium affinem et eorum sectam sequentem* (*Il diario*, 44).

11 On Andrea, see Anna Esposito Aliano, 'Famiglia, mercanzia e libri nel testamento di Andrea Santacroce (1471)', in Arnold Esch, ed., *Aspetti della vita economica e culturale a Roma nel Quattrocento* (Roma, 1981), 197–220. In 1470 Prospero was consul of the cloth merchants' guild.

12 ASV, *Archivio delle Valle del Bufalo*, b.55, fasc.20 (*Acquisti fatti da domini della casa della Valle*).

13 ASV, *Archivio delle Valle del Bufalo*, b.34, fasc.1.

14 ASR, *Archivio Santacroce*, 1236 II, fol. 43.

family itself between the Riario and della Rovere branches. In 1482 Roman chroniclers, who were less than objective observers of these conflicts,[15] mentioned a new episode in the private war between the Santacroce and the della Valle. In April of that year, the Santacroce and their supporters launched an assault on the residence of the brothers della Valle. During the attack one of the casualties was Geronimo Colonna, illegitimate son of Antonio (di Genazzano), former prefect of Rome. This event led to an immediate escalation of the conflict.[16]

Recently, Giorgio Chittolini has written on the practice of private war (*bellum particulare* as opposed to *bellum publicum*), comparing Germany, where the *Fehden* were numerous in a context in which the supreme authority—imperial—was elected, with Italy, which was also politically fragmented.[17] Within the extremely diverse political situation in Italy the most fitting comparison with imperial Germany is the ecclesiastical state, which was also governed by an elected sovereign and in which the periods of *interregna* (the Vacant See) were more dramatic than in the imperial Diets. The feuds of 1482–1484, lasting until the year of Sixtus IV's death, must be re-interpreted in light of the contemporary wars on the Italian peninsula and in the context of the approaching Vacant See.

In 1482, after the death of Geronimo Colonna, Pope Sixtus IV punished Giorgio Santacroce and his brother by demolishing their residences in Piazza Giudea in the centre of Rome: "to instil terror both in his family and in all those who were their followers".[18] At the same time, it was clear that in the war between the Kingdom of Naples and the papacy, the Colonna were fighting on the side of the pro-Aragonese coalition (Ferrara, Milan, Florence,

---

15 One of the greatest chroniclers of the age, Iacopo Gherardi was secretary to Cardinal Jacopo Ammannati and later secret chamberlain to Sixtus IV (Stefano Calonaci, 'Gherardi, Jacopo', DBI, 53 (2000), *ad vocem*). Stefano Infessura was *scriba senatus* of the city and one of the Colonna's men (Arnold Esch, 'Infessura Stefano', DBI, 62 (2004), *ad vocem*). Antonio de Vascho was *caporione* of the *rione* Regola, later vice-treasurer to Sixtus IV and treasurer to Innocent VIII, on the side of the Orsini. Sigismondo dei Conti was domestic secretary to Julius II (Roberto Ricciardi, DBI, 28 (1983), *ad vocem*).

16 Stefano Infessura, *Diario della città di Roma*, Oreste Tommasini, ed. (Roma, 1890), 87; Gherardi da Volterra, *Il diario romano*, 93–94; Sigismondo dei Conti da Foligno, *Le storie de' suoi tempi dal 1475 al 1510*, (Roma, 1883), t. I, 134–37.

17 Giorgio Chittolini, 'Private Wars at the End of the Middle Ages: Notes on Italy and Germany in the 15th Century', in Yoshihisa Hattori, ed., *Political Order and Forms of Communication in Medieval and Early Modern Europe* (Rome, 2014), 109–32.

18 Gherardi da Volterra, *Il diario romano*, 94: *ad terrorem tam illius familiae quam omnium eiusdem gentis sequentium.*

Mantua and Urbino). Contemporary observers attributed this choice to the sway of passions—to the envy the Colonna felt over the economic and political preference the pope showed to their rivals.[19] Geronimo Colonna's cousins (of the Genazzano branch)—including the apostolic *protonotarius* Lorenzo and the *condottiero* Fabrizio, who later married Agnese di Montefeltro, the duke of Urbino's daughter (thus bolstering an alliance that already existed between the two families)[20]—barricaded themselves inside the fief of Marino. This *castrum* became an outpost in Latium for the Neapolitan army. As the pro-Orsini chronicler Antonio De Vascho related, in the war with Naples, "the pope's people" made ready to defend Rome and took up positions at the Milvian Bridge. Besides Girolamo Riario, captain-general of the Church, their ranks included Giacomo Conti and the Bracciano, Anguillara, Lamentana, Pitigliano, Monterotondo branches of the Orsini, but also a few Colonna: Giovanni di Palestrina (married to Giustina Orsini); Prospero di Genazzano, brother of the cardinal Giovanni (elevated in 1480); and the bastard Girolamo, who was killed in the feud of 1482.

The presence of a Colonna with the name di Palestrina at the side of the Orsini should come as no surprise. The studies of Andreas Rehberg have shown how Oddone Colonna's ascent to the papacy led to "a colossal displacement of power between these two different lines".[21] The line of Palestrina, which was older and had long predominated, was displaced politically and territorially by the branch to which the pope belonged—the pope assembled on behalf of his family an imposing network of clients composed of families rooted in the city's political and economic life (Astalli, Capranica, Porcari, Mattei, Leni and more). For Prospero however, a member of the dominant line, the motivations for allying with the Orsini were personal, connected to his status as a younger son or perhaps to financial issues. But his was a temporary choice. Prospero quickly reconciled with the other members of the Genazzano branch: "having become the pope's enemy, he proceeded to betray him".[22]

The period after the death of Eugenius IV was one of the moments of greatest tension between the Colonna and papal power. The pope's wrath reverberated

19 Ibidem, 99; Antonio de Vascho, *Il Diario della città di Roma dall'anno 1480 all'anno 1492*, Giuseppe Chiesa, ed., RIS XXIII/3, 88.

20 Caterina Colonna had married Guidantonio da Montefeltro during the pontificate of Martin V.

21 Andreas Rehberg, '*Etsi prudens paterfamilias...pro pace suorum sapienter providet.* Le ripercussioni del nepotismo di Martino V a Roma e nel Lazio', in Maria Chiabò et al., eds., *Alle origini della nuova Roma Martino V (1417–1431)* (Roma, 1992), 225–82 (241). On the Palestrina branch: ASV, Armadio XLIX, 46, *Varia de Columna Familia*, fol. 12r–22r.

22 Vascho, *Diari*, 498.

in the Sacred College with the imprisonment of the pro-Aragonese cardinals Giovanni Colonna and Giovan Battista Savelli. After the defeat of the Neapolitan army, the peace agreement between the pope and Fernando contained a few clauses calling for the return of Albe and Tagliacozzo to the Orsini (the latter was a fief granted by Ferdinand to the Colonna during the war), as well as calling for the marriage between Giangiordano Orsini di Gentile Virgilio and Maria Cecilia, the king's illegitimate daughter. On 26 October 1482, Prospero (with his eldest brother Pier Antonio), Giovanni and Fabrizio Colonna were "arrested, their property confiscated and their houses demolished to the sound of trumpets".[23] Factional wars continued on through the following months and culminated in the events of 1484, which were intertwined with the so-called war of Ferrara, which Sixtus IV—after making peace with Naples—had declared on his former ally Venice, with the aim of "defending" the Este from the designs of the Serenissima. In May of that year, the *protonotarius* Lorenzo Oddone fortified the Colonna "territory", the extensive area of Rome under Colonna control, between the Trevi Fountain and Quirinal Hill (where the Palazzo ai Santi Apostoli stood), and he had his partisans occupy the strategically important Porta Maggiore while the Orsini were arming themselves in their part of the city between Campo dei Fiori and Montegiordano. Just as the Colonna had supported an external power in the previous war with Naples, Paolo Orsini di Lamentana, the illegitimate son of Cardinal Latino Orsini, as related by the pro-Colonna diarist Infessura: "made accommodations with the Venetian *Signoria* who were at that time enemies of the Church".[24] The often-confusing testimony of contemporaries depicts multiple wars which essentially turned on territorial disputes in Latium and control of the Urbs where, in spite of the demographic and military resources of the Orsini and their ancient close relations with the *populares*, the less numerous Colonna had a larger following.

Inside Rome, the epilogue to the long feud appears to have arrived on 30 May 1484 with an attack launched against the Colonna residence in the pope's name by soldiers of Girolamo Riario and partisans of the Orsini, the Crescenzi, the Santacroce and the Conti. The *protonotarius* was captured and, according to Infessura, subjected to ritual humiliation: he was stripped naked and forced to shout "Long live the House of Orsini".[25] Later on 29 June he was beheaded and his remains publicly exposed in the church of Santa Maria di Traspontina. The Colonna houses were looted along with the homes of the

23 Ibid., 501.

24 Infessura, *Diario*, 110.

25 Ibid., 116. Vascho, on the other hand, reports that Virginio Orsini saved Lorenzo Colonna from the wrath of Girolamo Riario (*Diario*, 509).

Mattei and the Margani. Destroying an adversary's home, the physical location of his family, was a serious punishment, both economic and symbolic. Destruction of the della Valle houses proceeded from 31 May to 9 June: "since this family so obstinately and proudly followed the Colonna side against the pope".[26] Interventions by Rome's municipal government are barely mentioned in the sources. The Cesarini made some attempts at mediation, but in the final months of the anti-Colonna crackdown only men of the Orsini faction held the post of *Conservatore*.[27] Under these circumstances, the relationship warmed between the Colonna and the Cardinal della Rovere, whose house provided sanctuary for Paolo Margani, Paolo and Bernardino della Valle and many other members of the Curia aligned with the Colonna.[28] The cardinal's protection of the Colonna aggravated the enmity between the reigning pope's two nephews in the apostolic palace.[29]

The results of the long feud of 1480–1484 were reversed by the expected but feared death of the pope on 12 August: the looting of the Vacant See, as has repeatedly been shown, was full of ritual and symbolic meaning, and represented a continuation of the factional war of the previous two years. The Colonna returned to Rome on 17 August "with all their soldiers and followers",[30] while the Ghibelline cities of Umbria and Abruzzo rose in rebellion. Girolamo Riario was besieging the Colonna fief of Paliano when he was forced to fall back to Rome in order to defend his possessions and his men, and he was captured at the Milvian Bridge. In this climate of violence, the election of Cardinal Giambattista Cybo (Innocent VIII) to the papacy evened the score between Cardinal della Rovere and Girolamo Riario and between the Colonna and the Orsini.[31]

The peace imposed by the new pope was a brief one. Cardinal della Rovere was a "passionate friend"[32] of the newly elected pope and the Colonna. In

---

26 Gherardi da Volterra, *Il diario romano*, 133: *quod ea familia obstinate nimium et contumaciter Columnensium partes contra pontificem sectabatur*; Sigismondo dei Conti da Foligno, *Le storie*, I, 189–94; Paolo Cherubini, 'Tra violenza e crimine di stato: la morte di Lorenzo di Oddone Colonna', in Massimo Miglio et al., eds., *Un pontificato ed una città. Sisto IV (1471–1484)* (Città del Vaticano, 1986), 355–80.

27 Infessura, *Diario*, 138.

28 Ibid., 120, 129.

29 Ibid., 129.

30 Vascho, *Diario*, 514.

31 On the Vacant See of Sixtus IV, see ibidem, 155–70. See also Laurie Nussdorfer, 'The Vacant See: Ritual and Protest in Early Modern Rome', *The Sixteenth Century Journal* 18 (1987), 173–89; Maria Antonietta Visceglia, *Morte e elezione del papa. Norme, riti, conflitti. L'età moderna* (Roma, 2013), 65. On the conclave of 1484, ibidem., 314–17.

32 Vascho, *Diario*, 521: "sviscerato amico".

Rome, the situation became the mirror image of the previous one—papal favour now swung over to the Colonna who, impoverished by the previous feud, occupied Frascati, a estate owned by Gerolamo d'Estouteville, an important member of the opposing faction, while the Savelli attempted to seize Cerveteri, which belonged to the Apostolic Chamber. In the renewed hostility between the pope and the Aragonese king, which had been triggered by the papal rejection of investitures in Benevento, Terracina and Pontecorvo, the barons and Neapolitan cities opposed to the Aragonese (the most important example of this opposition was the dedication of l'Aquila to the Church in October 1485) found support from the pope and Giuliano della Rovere. On the other hand, Gentile Virginio Orsini offered his fief of Vicovaro as a bridgehead for the Neapolitan army, from where they managed to threaten Rome. At the end of the same year, Orsini accepted the appointment to be captain-general of the anti-papal league which united Naples, Milan and Florence. Now it was the turn of Palazzo Orsini in Montegiordano to be sacked and burnt on the orders of Giuliano della Rovere.[33] The tragic situation of these wars in Rome and in Latium only began to improve after a peace agreement was reached in the summer of 1486, partly at the behest of Lorenzo de' Medici. Personally connected to the Orsini through his marriage to Clarice of the Monterotondo branch (10 December 1468), il Magnifico had identified in the Orsini an extended dynasty of *condottieri* who could be employed in the service of the Florentine state. It was no coincidence that in 1486 negotiations began for a new marriage alliance between Piero de' Medici, Lorenzo's son, and Alfonsina Orsini (di Tagliacozzo). Alfonsina's father was the brother of Maddalena Orsini, the mother of Clarice. Clarice travelled personally to Rome in 1487 to negotiate the marriage agreement between her own daughter Maddalena de' Medici and the pope's son Franceschetto Cybo, who in 1491 was invested with the county of Anguillara.[34] Thus we can see that the Medici acted as an important connecting link between the Orsini and the Cybo.

In the two cases I have examined, the mechanisms of factional conflict resemble each other. In both, private enmities, sustained by a desire for vengeance for violent deeds long past, competition for the control of resources and appropriation of fiefs in a period when territorial possessions were relatively fluid, and struggle for domination in the Urbs, all fed into the logic of the conflicts. This logic manifested itself in the plundering of herds and crops, looting, fires, the destruction of houses and homicides. The popes did not appear to

33 Infessura, *Diario*, 189; Sigismondo dei Conti da Foligno, *Le storie*, I, 237–42.

34 Vanna Arrighi, *Clarice Orsini*, DBI, 79 (2013), 633–36; Eadem, *Alfonsina Orsini*, ivi., 615–17; Infessura, *Diario*, 222–23.

have stood above the contending parties, but were instead directly connected with one or other of the coalitions: Sixtus IV on the side of the Orsini, Innocent VIII (at least during the early years of his reign before the shift orchestrated by the Medici) with the Colonna. Over a period of just a few years the battle cry changed from "Orso, Orso! Chiesa, Chiesa!" to "Colonna, Colonna! Chiesa, Chiesa!" Strife between the factions also became entangled with the Papal Wars and with the intricate relationship between segments of the Roman and Neapolitan nobility, the latter always ready to forge new bonds of loyalty in the face of a delegitimized dynasty. In addition, the exceptional power of the Medici in Rome had roots that long preceded the ascent to the papacy of one of that House's members.

Finally, factions, whose members included a cross-section of barons, representatives of municipalities and cardinals, played an undeniable role in the mechanisms of the papal monarchy. Factions were a part of the political system. The violence which resulted from the Vacant See was not a rare episode of disorder generated by a vacuum of power, but rather a show of strength played out beyond the confines of a game being played inside the Sacred College.

2 Roman Factions in the First European Conflicts over Italy (1492–1513)

In a celebrated passage of *The Prince* (XI), Niccolò Macchiavelli, in discussing the state of the papacy in his time, identified an epochal shift away from the scenario in which Italian potentates exploited Roman factions in order to weaken the papacy, to the later situation that began with the reign of Alexander VI, who used the factions to aggrandize his own House rather than the Church. Julius II (Giuliano della Rovere), whose ambitions for a larger and more secure temporal papal state would, in Machiavelli's view, enhance the grandeur of the Church, inherited a situation from Alexander VI in which the Orsini and Colonna factions were weakened, if not altogether tamed. Neither of these popes appointed any members of the Roman nobility to the cardinalship: according to Machiavelli, the factions were fuelled by the ambition of prelates, multiplying episodes of strife and tumult within the city.[35] If, as scholars have suggested, this section of *The Prince* (Chapters I–XI) was written in 1513, then Machiavelli's analysis reflected the climate that was ushered in with the papacy of Leo X, who was elected in March of that year, and with the military victories of the Holy League over the French.

35 Niccolò Machiavelli, *The Prince*, trans. by W.K. Marriott (Chicago, 1990), 16–17.

As borne out by analytical studies, Machiavelli appears to have grasped real elements of the historical situation. The Borgia papacy represented a break. Marco Pellegrini has shown how significant the transformations in the Sacred College were during the reign of Alexander VI. In his nine promotions the Borgia pope created forty-three cardinals, of whom sixteen were Spaniards. With the possible exception of Bernardino Carvajal, none of these Spaniards were creatures of the Spanish monarchy, but rather were relatives of the Borgias and their clients—a "Borgia party" which would later implode after the death of the pope. While Alexander VI was certainly not miserly in bestowing the cardinal's hat on members of the great Italian families, he only promoted two Romans to the cardinalship: Giuliano Cesarini, the brother-in-law of Girolama Borgia, one of his daughters, and Alessandro Farnese, the brother of his beloved mistress Giulia. Moreover, changes in the international situation and the collapse of the Italian political system led the factions to seek ties beyond the Italian princes with the great European monarchies. This was a structural change, consistent with the institutionalization of the figure of cardinal-protector of nations and the growing presence of the European diplomatic network within the papal city.[36] No less important was the link that came to be established between the powers warring over Naples and later over Milan and the *condottieri* of the great Roman families, the latter of whom became confronted with apparently conflicting choices, which were nonetheless consistent with their roles as *condottieri* to princes who were not necessarily their "natural lords". Upon Charles VIII's first descent into Italy (1494), the cousins Prospero and Fabrizio Colonna abandoned Ferdinand of Aragon for the king of France, to whom they pledged their services as commanders (services which were also under the influence of Cardinal Ascanio Maria Sforza),[37] in exchange for a promise of the investitures of Albe and Tagliacozzo. The slogan chanted by the crowd when Charles VIII made his entry into Rome in the company of the "exiled" Cardinal della Rovere was: "Francia! Colonna! Vincula!" The two Colonnas returned to the service of Ferdinand in 1495, obtaining the duchies of Traetto and Fondi in addition to Tagliacozzo. Gentile Virginio Orsini, who ought to have defended Rome against

36 Marco Pellegrini, 'A Turning-Point in the History of the Factional System in the Sacred College. The Power of Pope and Cardinals in the Age of Alexander VI', in Maria Antonietta Visceglia and Gianvittorio Signorotto, eds., *Court and Politics in Papal Rome 1492–1700* (Cambridge, 2002), 8–30. On diplomacy in Rome during the wars of Italy, see Catherine Fletcher, *Diplomacy in Renaissance Rome. The Rise of the Resident Ambassador* (Cambridge, 2015).

37 Sigismondo dei Conti da Foligno, *Le storie*, II, 65–66. On the complex relations between Cardinal Ascanio and the Colonna in 1494, see Marco Pellegrini, *Ascanio Maria Sforza. La parabola politica di un cardinale principe del Rinascimento* (Roma, 2002), vol. II, 534–44.

the French troops, aligned himself with his Medici relatives and granted safe passage to the troops. The pope declared him a rebel and he died in prison in Naples (1497), while the armed men of Vitellozzo Vitelli and the Orsini defeated the papal troops at Soriano. As an epilogue to the dynastic crisis in Naples, a new phase began with the Franco-Spanish agreement to partition the Kingdom (1501). The accord was met with the pope's approval, who considered it to be a league against the Turks and their "accomplices", the Colonna and Savelli, disrupters of the Papal States and hence bandits.[38] In the massacre of Senigallia in January 1503, Cesare Borgia's victims were of the Orsini faction.[39]

But when the Franco-Spanish agreement was followed by war, the Colonna di Genazzano-Paliano chose to throw their lot and that of their family in with the young Spanish monarchy rather than with what appeared to be Europe's leading power, France. Later the Colonna family narrative would represent this decision as having been consistent with their Ghibelline past. But, in fact, during an age of sudden and unforeseeable political changes, it was a decision taken by soldiers, mediated by personal relations with the most celebrated *condottiero* of the age, the Gran Capitano, and susceptible to occasional second thoughts and backtracking, as occurred in the years 1511–1512 and in 1517, when Marco Antonio Colonna entered the service of Francis I. Ultimately, however, their decision proved to be successful and irreversible. These tumultuous events marked a turning point in the history of Roman factions. The Borgia offensive, aimed at reshaping the territorial profile of central Italy, ended by bringing the two rival sides closer together. In 1503, many of the Orsini, with the exception of Giangiordano, sided with the Colonna in support of Spain.[40] A new truce was sanctioned around the time of the Treaty of Blois

---

38 In 1498 the "private" war fought between the Orsini and Colonna for the area around Tagliacozzo ended with the peace of Tivoli (Shaw, *The Political Role*, 108–109). On relations between Alexander VI and the Orsini and Colonna, see Franca Allegrezza, 'Alessandro VI e le famiglie romane di antica nobiltà: gli Orsini, in Maria Chiabò et al., eds., *Roma di fronte all'Europa al tempo di Alessandro VI*, I (Roma, 2001), 330–44; Andreas Reheberg, 'Alessandro VI e i Colonna: motivazioni e strategie nel conflitto tra papa Borgia e il baronato romano', ibidem, 345–86; Serio, *Una gloriosa sconfitta*, 119–43. On papal relations with Naples during the Aragonese dynastic crisis, see Maria Antonietta Visceglia, 'Napoli e la politica internazionale del papato tra la congiura dei baroni e il regno di Ferdinando il Cattolico', in Giuseppe Galasso and Carlos José Hernando Sánchez, eds., *El reino de Nápoles y la Monarquía de España entre agregación y conquista (1485–1535)* (Madrid, 2004), 453–83.

39 According to contemporaries, the pope's decision to "togliere lo stato a Casa Orsina" was already irreversible in 1502 but dissimulated by the accord of Imola(Sebastiano di Branca Tedallini, *Diario romano dal 3 maggio 1485 al 6 giugno 1524*, Paolo Piccolomini, ed., RIS, XXIII/3, 300–01).

40 Ibid., 308.

(September 1504) and another was concluded in May 1509 within the apostolic palace itself.[41]

Julius II's policies engendered a very different situation. Once he was pope, Cardinal della Rovere, the former "passionate friend" of the Colonna and enemy of the Orsini, did not hesitate to weave close marriage alliances with both families. In 1505, his sister's son, Niccolò Franciotti, married Laura Orsini, the daughter of Giulia Farnese; the pope's daughter, Felicia, for whom a marriage had initially been planned with Marco Antonio Colonna, was given as wife to Giangiordano Orsini, Gentile Virgilio's son and widower of Maria Cecilia d'Aragon (1506). But in the same year, Marco Antonio Colonna married Lucrezia Gara, the daughter of the pope's beloved sister Luchina from her second marriage. So Julius launched upon a policy of forging marriage alliances between the papal family and the two great baronial lineages, a policy which Wolfgang Reinhard has identified as significant in the long process of integrating the papal and ancient baronial families.[42]

These marriage alliances did not imply any new cardinals for the two sides, contrary to usual practice. Generous in appointing his own relatives, without delegating power, Julius II created no cardinals from among the Roman baronial families, even after the deaths of Cardinals Giovan Battista Orsini (1503) and Giovanni Colonna (1508). Thus, the Roman factions found themselves deprived of representation in a key decision-making body (notwithstanding the pope's autocratic tendencies), the Sacred College. But the picture of an early papal victory over the factions is misleading. Curial sources and papal propaganda depict the wars the pope waged against Venice for Bologna in order to recover the state of Romagna, and the wars against Ferrara and against France, as aimed at re-establishing law and order by providing an opportunity to perform special rites of pacification within the cities the pope crossed to reach Emilia-Romagna, or as Italian wars waged against the "barbarians".[43]

---

41 Ivan Cloulas, *Giulio II* (Roma, 1993), 125.

42 Wolfgang Reinhard, 'Papal Power and Family Strategy in the Sixteenth and Seventeenth Centuries', in Ronald G. Asch and Adolf M. Birke, eds., *Princes, Patronage, and the Nobility: The Court at the Beginning of the Modern Age, c.1450–1650* (London, 1991), 229–356 (339).

43 Maria Antonietta Visceglia, 'Guerra e riti di pacificazione: le spedizioni di Giulio II a Bologna nelle pagine del cerimoniere del papa (1506–1512)', in Gian Mario Anselmi and Angela de Benedictis, eds., *Città in guerra. Esperienze e riflessioni nel primo '500. Bologna nelle "guerre d'Italia"* (Bologna, 2008), 85–117. On the topic of peace in Julius II's propaganda, see Massimo Rospocher, *Il papa guerriero. Giulio II nello spazio pubblico europeo* (Bologna, 2015), 86–111. On the practices of pacification, see Paolo Broggio and Maria Pia Paoli, *Stringere la pace. Teorie e pratiche della conciliazione nell'Europa moderna sec. XV–XVIII secolo* (Roma, 2011).

In reality, the chief players of these expeditions, which were carried out under dramatic circumstances, were peripheral members of the Roman factions: in Perugia the Baglioni, who were related to the Orsini and part of the Guelph network; and in Bologna the Bentivoglio, whose enemies the Malvezzi and Zambeccari were allies of the Colonna.[44] Venice itself, on whose behalf the Orsini had fought as *condottieri*, did not hesitate to engage them in 1509 and offer Urbino to the Colonna, the possession of which had passed to the pope's nephew Francesco Maria della Rovere after the death of Guidobaldo da Montefeltro.[45]

In the dual war that Julius II waged both militarily and canonically against France (after France's convocation of the schismatic *conciliabulum* of Pisa 16 May 1511), the power of the Colonna grew thanks to the role played by Fabrizio, who served the Spanish as *condottiero*, and because of the close relationship the lineage was able to establish with the Spanish ambassador Jéronimo de Vich (who arrived in Rome in 1507). Among the many misunderstanding the king of Spain had with the pope (still his formal ally) was that the Colonna were his direct contact in the city.

The events of August 1511 must be seen against this backdrop of Julius II's isolation, because of which his critical illness failed to lead to the usual turmoil in expectation of the Vacant See, but rather gave rise to an entirely new situation. A coalition reflecting the moods and passions of life in the city was formed whose aims were not overtly anti-papal. The eminent baronial lineages included in the coalition were the Colonna, led by Fabrizio (also participating was Pompeo, the bishop of Rieti, the real protagonist of the events); the Orsini, headed by Giulio, who pledged their "members and followers"; and the Savelli, the Conti and the deputies of the *Popolo Romano*. Contemporaries described this *pax* of 1511 as a reaction against papal "tyranny" (Francesco Guicciardini), as a protest by the baronial families who had been deprived of a cardinalate because of the "envy" of the pope (Paolo Giovio), and as a defence of the *romanitas* and prerogatives of the Commune (Marco Antonio Altieri). The *pax* was sanctioned by a solemn oath, and demonstrated that the factions could unite in an institutional context that also included the governing council of Rome because they were strong and conscious of their own

---

44 Serio, *Una gloriosa sconfitta*, 162.

45 Ivan Cloulas, *Giulio II*, 171–72; Christine Shaw, *Iulius II: The Warrior Pope* (Oxford, 1993), see Chapters V and VIII. On factional conflict in Rieti (Ghibelline), Spoleto (Guelph) and other towns in Umbria, see Eadem, 'The Roman Barons and the Guelf and Ghibelline Factions in the Papal States', in Marco Gentile, ed., *Guelfi e ghibellini nell'Italia del Rinascimento* (Roma, 2005), 475–93.

powers.[46] Confirmation of this may be seen by how the situation evolved after the pope's unexpected recovery: the voluntary exit of the barons from the city was followed by a papal policy of rapprochement towards them, though this rapprochement was selective (Pompeo Colonna was deposed from his post as bishop of Rieti). After Ravenna (11 April 1512),[47] Julius II was in dire need of the barons' support, and their *entente* with the municipal class appeared to be holding firm, both during the final months of his pontificate and during the Vacant See, which ended a month after his death when the first Medici pope was elected (11 March 1513). This election later ushered in a new phase in the city in which power groups revolved around the Medici-Orsini block. Confronted with this block, the Colonna displayed attitudes of assent and co-operation, but also of opposition when they wished to achieve very concrete aims (for example, control over Urbino, which was handed over in 1516, destined for Lorenzo de' Medici, son of Piero and Alfonsina Orsini, but which the Colonna had their sights set on both before and after this date), and even open antagonism. They became *de facto* agents for the Medicis' great enemies like Francesco Soderini, notwithstanding the latter's membership in the pro-French party,[48] and Alfonso Petrucci.

3 The Origins of the Imperial Party: 1525–1530

The archive of the della Valle-del Bufalo preserves the extraordinary correspondence of members of the della Valle family spanning the period 1409–1829. This correspondence allows us to obtain an inside view of how the alliances of a family located on the middle rungs of the power hierarchy converged with the clientele of the Colonna, with whom the family was intimately linked, and how through the Colonna, they became part of even wider power networks. The della Valle's subordination to the Colonna clearly shows in the formulae used in the letters, especially towards the more eminent members of the Colonna. Agnese di Montefeltro, who managed the Colonna patrimony and family relations during Fabrizio's frequent absences on military campaigns,

46 I refer the reader to Serio, *Una gloriosa sconfitta*, 163–98, who reports the views of Guicciardini, Giovio and Altieri. See also Clara Gennaro, 'La pax romana del 1511', *Archivio della Società Romana di Storia Patria* 90 (1967), 17–60.

47 For a reinterpretation of this event cf. Dante Bolognesi, ed., *1512 La battaglia di Ravenna, L'Italia, l'Europa* (Ravenna, 2014).

48 Kate J.P. Lowe, *Church and Politics in Renaissance Italy: The Life and Career of Cardinal Francesco Soderini (1453–1524)* (Cambridge, 1993).

used a language that was imperious and resolute;[49] and Ascanio, Agnese's son, who belonged to the generation after Fabrizio and Prospero, was referred to as the "commune patrone".[50] Relations between Sciarra Colonna, Ascanio's natural brother, and the della Valle appeared to be less one-sided. Sciarra addresses Fabrizio della Valle, canon of Saint Peter's and San Giovanni, as "brother" and discusses very concrete questions with him: the purchase of harquebuses,[51] refuge to be given to one of his men who "can't go out much publicly"[52] and the protection of exiles to whom he was connected.[53] At the turn of the fifteenth and sixteenth centuries a great resource for the *consorteria* of della Valle and Colonna was Andrea della Valle (son of Filippo and Gerolama Margani) who pursued a brilliant ecclesiastical career under different pontiffs: from subdeacon to bishop of Crotone and Mileto, to regent of the Apostolic Chancellery, to cardinal in the famous promotion of 1517 when Pompeo Colonna and Franciotto Orsini were also invested with the purple. Bishop and later cardinal, Andrea della Valle showed a great capacity to mediate inside the Curia, where he worked to overcome the enmity with the Santacroce. He was also able to mobilize his own extensive family group.

The social profile of some members of the della Valle can help us to understand how the bond between this family and the urban governing class was strengthened. Andrea della Valle's cousins Bernardino and Bernardo de' Cavalieri (di Masciolo and Lucrezia della Valle) were his trusted associates. Bernardino was *provveditore* of the Roman walls and counsellor of the *conservatori*; Bernardo was canon of Santa Maria Maggiore and bishop of Sulmona.[54] After the death of Bernardino (1513), who was married to Lucrezia Altieri, Marco Antonio's sister, the post of counsellor of the *conservatori* went to Bartolomeo della Valle, Andrea's brother and a subcontractor of the Roman customs office. A further marriage alliance was contracted (1518) between the della Valle and the de Cavalieri, involving the marriage of Lelio II to Marzia, Bernardino's daughter. No less interesting were the della Valle's ties of kinship

---

49 ASV, *Archivio Della Valle-Del Bufalo*, b.34, fasc.13, fol. 92r, Agnese di Montefeltro to Lelio della Valle, Castelmareri, 12 October; ibidem, fasc.14, fol.104r, Castelmareri, 10 November.

50 ASV, *Archivio Della Valle-Del Bufalo*, b.34, fasc.20, fol. 212r.

51 Ibidem, fasc.14, fol. 101r, Sciarra Colonna to Fabrizio della Valle, Castello, 12 July 1512.

52 Ibidem, b.35, fasc.1, fol. 8r, Sciarra Colonna to Fabrizio della Valle, Torre, 14 October 1530.

53 Ibidem, fol. 10r., Torre, 29 November 1530).

54 Bernardino was "procurator and administrator" to Andrea, bishop of Crotone: ibidem, b.55, fasc.31 (May 22, 1506); together with Bernardo he looked after Andrea della Valle's interests in Mileto: ibidem, b.34, fasc.3, fol. 49rv, fol. 50r; ibidem, fasc.6, fol. 62–64 and upon his cousin's orders he arranged for the dispatch of some goods to Cardinal Cesarini: ibidem, fasc.4, fol. 54r.

with the Alberini, the Tebaldi[55] and the Porcari, and their "friendship" with Giovan Battista Pontani, *conservatore* of Rome and governor of Rieti and Amelia,[56] which later turned into a marriage alliance between Valerio della Valle and Clelia, Giovan Battista's daughter (1559). In brief, close relations with the della Valle offered to the Colonna many linkages with the municipal governing class to which all the above-mentioned families belonged.

We still need to reconstruct the complex process by which this web of relations, deeply rooted in the city and in the Roman hinterland, came into contact, through the Colonna, with the wider network in Italy and abroad that became the imperial party. We must also remember that the decade that began with the death of Ferdinand the Catholic (1516) and the Medici papacy was one of great uncertainty for all the players on the international stage of the day. Complications following the succession of Charles of Habsburg, which created difficulties for Spanish diplomacy in Rome,[57] Charles V's own doubts about whether to pursue a policy of opposition to France as Ferdinand of Aragon and Maximilian of Hapsburg had done, or follow his Flemish ministers Jean de Sauvage and Guillaume de Croy, Lord of Chièvres in trying to reconcile with the French monarchy, and the about-turns of the Medici popes, all meant that before the military victory of Pavia, the imperial party had acquired no precise physiognomy. As late as 1520, Cardinal Pompeo Colonna, believing himself lightly regarded by the emperor who had not designated him as protector of Spain and had let him know that he preferred Cardinal Medici, was wondering whether he should not serve "another Lord". It was only in the following year that Charles declared reassuringly that "we are very satisfied with cardinal Colonna and the others of the Colonna faction and they will know this from all that will be offered to them".[58] By 1521 many things looked different: at the Diet of Worms (1521) where Chièvres died, the problem of Lutheranism exploded in all its dramatic force, while Francis I had attacked Milan in April of

55 In 1470 Laura della Valle married Marco di Simone de' Tebaldi, the "perpetual chancellor of Rome". Her dowry was 1000 florins (ibidem, b.55, fasc.20, betrothal dated 9 December 1470).

56 Ibidem, b.34, fasc.23, fol. 272r (Silvia de' Pontani to Giovanni Battista de' Pontani, 28 April 1529); fol. 274r (Silvia de' Pontani to Giovanni Battista de' Pontani, 23 June 1529); fol. 276r (Silvia de' Pontani to Giovanni Battista de' Pontani, 8 July 1529).

57 Manuel Rivero Rodríguez, 'Crisis sucesoria en la Corona de Aragón', in José Martínez Millán, ed., *La corte de Carlos V* (Madrid, 2000), 150–66; Alessandro Serio, 'Modi, tempi, uomini della presenza *hispana* a Roma tra la fine del Quattrocento e il primo Cinquecento (1492–1527)', in Francesca Cantù and Maria Antonietta Visceglia, eds., *L'Italia di Carlo V: Guerra, religione e politica nel primo Cinquecento* (Roma, 2003), 433–75.

58 I have taken the quotes from the correspondence of the ambassador in Rome, Juan Manuel with Charles V, cit. in Serio, 'Modi, tempi', 465.

the same year. Vespasiano, Ascanio and Pompeo Colonna with their extensive factions in Naples, Rome and the cities of the Papal States, were indispensable resources for Charles V in the imperial alignment, which in 1522 assumed a new configuration. That year the men who were still associated with the Italian policy of Ferdinand the Catholic were supplanted by aristocrats close to Charles V, like Charles de Lannoy (viceroy of Naples) and the duke of Sessa (ambassador to Rome). In terms of ideology, the old Ghibelline legacy was revamped to fit the political-religious model of the universal monarchy designed by Mercurino da Gattinara.[59] While the imperial project for Italy was taking a clear shape, the attitude of the Medici appeared hesitant and wavering—notwithstanding the emperor's support for Medici Cardinal Giulio against Pompeo Colonna in the conclave of 1523 (the latter added his own votes to his rival's, allowing the election of Clement VII). The new pope, veering away from the alliance his predecessor had made with Charles V, entrenched himself in a policy of neutrality and raised the ideological banner of *libertas Italiae*. To the empire's ideologues (Gattinara, Alfonso de Valdés), Rome looked like the natural seat of a reborn imperial power. With the wound opened by the Lutheran schism, opposing forces that were purely political carried new implications. Church reform and the request for a Council—an eventuality feared by Clement VII because it might lead to his deposition due to his illegitimate birth—became key points in the imperial party's agenda.[60] The party was winning new converts in Rome even in the traditionally Guelph families: a few Orsini aligned themselves with the emperor alongside the Colonna, such as Roberto, a former ally of Pompeo in the events of 1511, and Camillo, who had fought with the imperials at Pavia and later in the 1530s began to keep dangerous company with the Valdensians and make contacts that were frankly heretical.[61]

It is not my aim here to retrace the familiar events leading up to the sack of Rome. I would, however, like to take another look at the della Valle correspondence and see how these events were experienced by the people who lived through them. The attack on the Vatican Palace launched on 20 September 1526 by Pompeo Colonna and his partisans (with the agreement of Hugo de Moncada) was a threatening retaliation against the pope's membership in

59 Carlos Hernando Sánchez considers 1522 to be a crucial year for the formation of the imperial party in Italy: 'Nobleza y diplomacia en la Italia de Carlos V: el duque de Sessa embajador en Roma', in Juan Luis Castellano and Francisco Sánchez-Montes González, eds., *Carlos V Europeísmo y Universalidad*, vol. 3: *Los escenarios del Imperio* (Madrid, 2001), 205–97.

60 Adriano Prosperi, 'Carlo V e i papi del suo tempo', *Archivio storico per le province napoletane* 119 (2001), 239–47.

61 After the sack of Rome, Camillo is thought to have permanently entered the service of the Venetians. On Camillo, Giampiero Brunelli, DBI 79 (2013), *ad vocem*.

the anti-imperial league of Cognac (June 1526), but it was depicted by the Colonna as an act of local rebellion against the tyrannical power of the pope in the name of municipal *libertas*. Clement VII remained isolated during the events.[62] His response, after a phony peace, consisted of sentencing Pompeo for *lèse-majesté* and making war against the Colonna faction. He appointed Vitellio Vitelli and Stefano Colonna di Palestrina (the "pope's soldier")[63] commanders of his troops. The role assumed by Stefano Colonna on behalf of the pope and against the imperials shows how, as in the past, the Colonna di Palestrina made choices that diverged from those of the dominant branch at the time, the Genazzano-Paliano. It is also further confirmation that kinship was not the only criterion that determined the composition of factions, whose membership was also composed of lineages divided into several groupings of unequal power. Cardinal Andrea della Valle was the mediator between two of these groupings, while Lelio was Ascanio's lieutenant. Lelio wrote his brother Fabrizio asking him to confirm his unwavering loyalty to Hugo di Moncada and Pompeo Colonna, but not to mention this to Cardinal della Valle: "do not say a word to the most reverend about what I am writing to you, that I submit to the lordship of Pompeo Colonna as my patron".[64] The entire war correspondence reveals that the coordinators of the operations of 1526–1527 were Moncada and

62 On the pope's isolation, see *I Ricordi di Marcello Alberini,* in Domenico Orano, ed., *Il sacco di Roma nel 1527*, I (Roma, 1901), 224–26; the datary Giberti also wrote that the pope: "sperava che almeno li Gentilhuomini Romani chi per la disonestà della casa [Colonna], chi per amore e l'honore di sua Santità e della Sede Apostolica, chi per interesse della Patria, e suo proprio si muovesse a pigliar l'armi et diffenderla, li mancò, et non fu mai huomo che si movesse" ("hoped that at least the gentleman Romani either because of the dishonesty of the House [Colonna] or out of love and for honour of the His Holiness and the Apostolic See or in the interest of the fatherland and their own interests, would be moved to take arms and defend him, but there was not—there wasn't a single man who made a move"), ASV, *Fondo Pio,* 53, from datary to Sanga and Gambara, fol. 12v–24r (fol. 13r), 20 September 1526. Giberti continued, showing an awareness of the political logic of conflict: "[l'imperatore] non harà da insuperbirsi tanto […] per vedere che così come il cognato ha perso l'Ungheria, il fratello perderà ancora l'Austria et poi comincierà a toccar la Sicilia et Regno di Napoli et altri stati suoi" (ibidem, fol. 18r). ("[the emperor] should not become so proud […] seeing that just as his brother-in-law has lost Hungary, his brother will yet lose Austria and then it will be the turn of Sicily and the Kingdom of Naples and his other states").

63 This was the expression used by Marcello Alberini (*I Ricordi*, 265). On the sentence against Pompeo see ASV, Armadio XLIX, 46, fol. 388r–425r.

64 "Et al reverendissimo non dirrete una parola sopra de ciò de questo ch'io ve scrivo, che me rimetto alli commandamenti de Sua Signoria [Pompeo Colonna] como mio patrone" (Lelio to Fabrizio della Valle, Avezzano, November 8, 1526, in Pierpaolo Piergentili and Gianni Venditti, eds., *Scorribande, lanzichenecchi e soldati ai tempi del sacco di Roma.*

Ascanio and Pompeo Colonna, who answered directly to Caesar, and that the clash was a peripheral conflict in a European war in which Rome was the objective. Whether it was a planned or inevitable event, the occupation of Rome by the imperial army (6 May 1527–17 February 1528), which some contemporaries saw as presaged by omens and signs, exposed both the pope's weakness and the imperial party's fragility. The impotence of the Roman imperial party in front of the sacrilegious looting, which they themselves fell victim to, was stigmatized in the accounts of the tragic event that have come down to us. They tell us precisely who in 1527–1528 was considered imperial. "Cardinals and partisans of Caesar" were Giovanni Piccolomini, Andrea della Valle, Alessandro Cesarini, Ferdinando Pozzetti and Cristoforo Numai. The latter two cardinals had come over to the imperial side only recently. The Florentine Pozzetti, the former commissary of the revenues from the sale of indulgences for the construction of Saint Peter's, was connected with the Medici popes' financial machine. The Franciscan Numai had been confessor to Luisa di Savoia and as late as the conclave of 1523 he was numbered among the pro-French cardinals, though his family was Ghibelline from Romagna.[65] Like Ponzetti, he had been commissary for the construction of Saint Peter's during the first Medici papacy and, in addition, he was a member of the commission that Clement VII set up in 1523 to look into the effects of Luther's preaching. These two cardinals, likely because of the offices they had held in the past, were subject to vicious rituals of inversion: "Ponzetti dressed as a Lutheran was forced with kicks and punches to visit the most frequented places", and the cardinal of Ara Coeli (Numai) was carried around dressed in papal vestments but on a bier in a symbolic funeral of the papacy.[66] Families that were closely connected to the Colonna like the Massimi, the Jacobacci and the Altieri, lodged Spanish and German soldiers in their palaces, though this did not spare them from having to make large payments of money.[67]

What was the consequence of these events in the reconstruction of power groupings within the city of Rome? For the Colonna, the consolidation that came with Pompeo's appointment as lieutenant-general in the Kingdom of Naples and Ascanio's as governor of Abruzzo, made up for the difficulties that no doubt beset their relationship with the city, highlighted in Marcello

---

Papato e Colonna in un inedito epistolario dall'Archivio Della Valle-Del Bufalo (Roma, 2009), 136–37).

65 Casanova, 'La riorganizzazione del potere urbano: le fazioni e le famiglie', in *1512 La battaglia di Ravenna*, 255–73.

66 ASR, *Archivio Santacroce*, H 222, fol. 157v–158r.

67 Ibid., fol.156v–157r.

Alberini's diary when it refers to the municipal class's crisis of trust in the powerful family.[68] But is it still possible to speak of a Colonna faction in the troubled years that followed the death of Vespasiano in 1528, during a period marked by strife within the lineage itself, while conflicts no less serious were tearing the Orsinis apart? What role did the Italian imperial party assume in the difficult reconciliation between the pope and Charles V and in the debate that raged over who had been responsible for the sack, which was either put down to the emperor's "impiety" or explained as God's punishment for the deplorable state of the Church and its clergy? The presence, as yet little studied, of the Spanish ambassador Miguel Mai, a Catalan and refined Erasmian, who was harshly critical of the temporal power of the pope and arrived in Rome in 1528, was certainly crucial.[69] Three years later Juan de Valdés also arrived in Rome.[70] The imperial party's consolidation in those years in Italy was marked by a strong demand for Church reform and, as recent studies have shown, some of its members harboured anti-papal sentiments.[71] But above all, during the period that began with Charles V's coronation in Bologna—which coincided with the deployment of a programme of *restitutio ad pristinum* of imperial authority in Italy based on the values of the devotion and friendship of the Italian princes for Charles V—the factions in Rome seemed to be playing at a higher level in the court and inside the Sacred College, the latter of which was permeated by a broad international presence. This does not mean that control of territory and resources at a local level did not continue to be important objectives, but, on a European scale, careers under the multinational Habsburg monarchy were also desirable and important. It is likely that the ancient dichotomy between the Orsini and Colonna as it existed in the late Middle Ages lost its central importance in the political struggle, and that the conflict between the two lineages was played out on other levels, symbolic and otherwise. But these are hypotheses for another history that has yet to be written.

68 Alberini, *I Ricordi*, 256–57, 278–83.

69 Pere Molas Ribalta, *Familia i política al segle XVI catalá* (Barcelona, 1990).

70 Massimo Firpo, 'Il sacco di Roma del 1527 tra profezia, propaganda politica e riforma religiosa', in *Dal sacco di Roma all'Inquisizione. Studi su Juan de Valdés e la Riforma italiana* (Alessandria, 1998), 7–60.

71 Stefania Pastore, 'Una Spagna anti-papale. Gli anni italiani di Diego Hurtado de Mendoza', *Roma moderna e contemporanea* XV (2007), 63–94; Elena Bonora, *Aspettando l'imperatore. Principi italiani tra il papa e Carlo V* (Torino, 2014).

The Prince and the Factions: Rebellion and Political Propaganda in Sixteenth-Century Geneva*

Mathieu Caesar

During the first decades of the sixteenth century, political life in Geneva was marked by the growth of two rival factions.[1] On one side were the *Eidguenots*, who desired an alliance with the Swiss cities of Fribourg, Bern and Solothurn; on the other were the *Mammelus*, who opposed this initiative. In this context, the Eidguenots negotiated two alliance treaties called *bourgeoisie* or *combourgeoisie* with Fribourg, in 1519, and with Bern and Fribourg in 1526. This rapprochement provoked an intervention from both the bishop and the duke of Savoy, Charles II, who considered the combourgeoisies to be illegal and the Eidguenots to be rebels.

From an urban perspective, the rivalry between the Eidguenots and Mammelus was a factional struggle similar to those experienced by many other cities. But, seen from the bishop's and the duke of Savoy's perspective, this conflict was sedition by one of the parties, a rebellion against the legitimate authority. The Eidguenots' actions were certainly not a classical armed uprising. Violence and street fighting were part of Geneva's political life, but its political struggles also took the form of a protracted conflict fought through legal argument, diplomatic negotiations, treaties and propaganda. This paper aims to analyse the political beliefs of the two factions involved in this conflict, as well as how each party explained its position, and the way the princely powers responded to them.

* Abbreviations: AEG: Archives d'État de Genève; ASTo: Archivio di Stato di Torino; AEG, PC: Procès criminels, series 1 à 3; EA: *Amtliche Sammlung der ältern eidgenössischen Abschiede 1245–1798*, 22 vols. (Luzern, 1839–1890); DHS: *Dictionnaire historique de la Suisse* (online: http://www.hls-dhs-dss.ch/); RC: *Registres du Conseil de Genève (1409–1536)*, 13 vols. (Geneva, 1900–1940); SDGE: Émile Rivoire and Victor Van Berchem, eds., *Les sources du droit du canton de Genève*, 2 vols. (Aarau, 1927–1934).

1 For a brief overview of this period, see Mathieu Caesar, *Histoire de Genève. La cité des évêques* (Neuchâtel, 2014), 128–147 and William Monter, *Calvin's Geneva* (New York, 1967), 64–93.

 | DOI 10.1163/9789004345348_007

1 Turning Swiss: The Combourgeoisie with Bern and Fribourg (1519–1526)

The possibility of an alliance with Fribourg became a matter of public political debate at the beginning of 1519. On 7 January, as a first step towards an alliance, eighty-five Genevans were admitted (individually) as burghers of Fribourg.[2] One month later, Besançon Hugues, one of the leaders of the Eidguenots, presented a draft of the treaty before the city's General Council for approval, explaining that Fribourg wished to grant the bourgeoisie to the entire Commune, not only to specific individuals. No text of this draft is conserved. At that stage, negotiations were still ongoing; we know their general substance only through the minutes of the Genevan General Council on 6 February which reported Hugues's speech to the council.[3] In this speech, he defined the alliance as a "friendship and bourgeoisie". Hugues explained that the treaty reserved the bishop's rights and his jurisdiction, the city's franchises, and finally, that no tribute was necessary to conclude the alliance.[4]

Although some members opposed the combourgeoisie, the majority of the council accepted Fribourg's offer. In a letter sent to Fribourg's authorities, the Genevans affirmed their willingness to be "good burghers and true friends".[5] The letter also suggested that the alliance could be extended to the city of Solothurn.[6] However, the reaction of the bishop and the duke effectively scuttled the agreement. The duke entered Geneva with his army, and during the month of April, he forced the General Council to renounce the

2 List in *RC* 8, 690, n.1.

3 *RC* 8, 289–91. The Council gathered in order to elect new mayors, and the speech given by Besançon Hugues, who had been one of the mayors in 1518, was given in the normal course of the Council's business.

4 The short-lived alliance with Fribourg in 1519 as well as the combourgeoisie of 1526 constituted a very common type of treaty formed in the southern part of the Empire. The terms "friendship" or "combourgeoisie" were commonly used to define an urban alliance involving two or more cities. For a more detailed description of the Swiss context, see Andreas Wurgler, 'Combourgeoisie', in *DHS*, URL: http://www.hls-dhs-dss.ch/textes/f/F9829.php, version of 03/08/2005 and Claude Cuendet, *Les traités de combourgeoisie en pays romands, et entre ceux-ci et les villes de Berne et Fribourg: (XIIIe au XVIe siècle)* (Lausanne, 1979). For another broader perspective, see Laurence Buchholzer, Olivier Richard, eds., *Ligues urbaines et espace à la fin du Moyen Âge. Städtebünde und Raum im Spätmittelalter* (Strasbourg, 2012).

5 *RC* 8, 291–93: "bons borgois [sic] et vrays amys".

6 Solothurn's role during these years has not been studied. The fact that the combourgeoisie of 1526 was concluded only with Bern and Fribourg has partially obscured Solothurn's position in the Genevan affair.

combourgeoisie. A few months later, in August, the bishop and duke dismissed the city's four mayors (*syndics*) and its governing Council and called new elections. Their main purpose was to impose a new government controlled by the Sabaudian faction, the Mammelus. From August 1519 until February 1526 when the Eidguenots regained power, Geneva's municipal institutions were dominated by the Mammelus.[7]

By September 1525, growing tension within the city had led to the flight of the most prominent Eidguenots. About twenty Eidguenots left the city, finding refuge in Fribourg.[8] Among them were the leaders of the faction: Besançon Hugues, Ami Porral, Jean Philippe, Thomas Vandel and the Baud brothers. In Fribourg, the Eidguenots met several times with the municipal authorities of Fribourg, Bern and Solothurn and managed to convince Fribourg and Bern to agree to a new combourgeoisie. As in 1519, the alliance was approved by the General Council (25 February 1526), with the duke and the bishop again arguing that the treaty was illegal. This time, however, their efforts to prevent the combourgeoisie were unsuccessful and the treaty went into force.

During the fourteenth and fifteenth centuries, the relationship between Geneva and the House of Savoy was quite complex. Even though the city was not juridically subject to the authority of the dukes, it regularly paid gifts to Charles II, who was considered the protector of the city. The Burgundian Wars, however, resulted in a loss in prestige and power of the dukes of Savoy, who were increasingly threatened by both the nearby French kingdom and the Swiss Confederates (mainly the cities of Bern and Fribourg) in their northeastern territories.[9] Fribourg and Bern were now significant political partners, and a Genevan alliance with them was a realistic possibility. There was historical precedent for this—in 1477, at end of the Burgundian Wars, the bishop had concluded the first combourgeoisie with Bern and Fribourg (that lasted until his death in 1482) in order to enhance the security of Geneva.[10] In light of this, the treaty of 1526 may be seen as a further step in the rapprochement between Geneva and the Swiss Confederacy, motivated on Geneva's side by the need to ensure the city's peace and protection.[11]

---

7 On the princely policy, see below, point 3: 'The Prince and the Factions: A Complex Relationship'.

8 Cf. *RC* 10, 106, n.1.

9 For a detailed study of medieval Geneva, see Mathieu Caesar, *Le pouvoir en ville. Gestion urbaine et pratiques politiques à Genève (fin XIIIe-début XVIe siècles)* (Turnhout, 2011).

10 *SDGE*, vol. 2, 47–52.

11 The Eidguenots concluded the combourgeoisie in order "to maintain the goods that God gave us, in rights, rest and good peace" (*SDGE*, vol. 2, 237 : "desmourer aulz biens que Dieu nous haz donné en droitz, repos et bonne paix"). The challenges of urban peace and

The Eidguenots' agenda was not unusual in the context of the period. In fact, at the end of the fifteenth century and in the first decades of the sixteenth century, many cities in southern Germany and at the western borders of the Empire sought, and sometimes concluded, alliances with the Swiss Confederation or with some of its cities. Turning Swiss, as Thomas Brady has shown, was one of the main political options of this period.[12] In the immediate years before the Genevan attempt of 1519, Mulhouse had concluded an alliance with the XIII Cantons (1515) and Besançon had concluded a combourgeoisie with Bern, Fribourg and Solothurn (1518). Rottweil allied with the VIII Cantons some months after the abortive Genevan agreement, in April 1519. The neighbouring city of Lausanne signed a combourgeoisie with Bern and Fribourg in 1525, and Constance established a combourgeoisie (strictly connected with its fight for the Reformed faith) with Zurich in 1527 and with Bern in 1528.

Rapid changes on the geopolitical scene in the first decades of the sixteenth century—both regionally and Europe-wide—often generated a temptation on the part of many cities to evade their lawful sovereign, which was especially true for border towns.[13] Geneva was not the only city which attempted to escape the Sabaudian princely power and which experienced harsh factional struggles as a result. Within the Duchy of Savoy, the best-documented case was that of Mondovì, demographically the most important city in the Italian part of the principality. The elites of Mondovì were divided over political issues, and the ducal power intervened against one of the two factions it regarded as being guilty of rebellion and treason. To ducal jurists, the struggle between the two parties assumed the contours of a conspiracy which culminated in 1532 with trials against Mondovì's Ghibellines, who were convicted of plotting to surrender the city to the duke of Mantua.[14]

Unlike the case of Geneva, Italian factional struggles were often connected with endemic family feuds. In Mondovì, one of the protagonists informed the duke that the hatred between local parties was a "hereditary and incurable" evil.[15] However, and without underestimating the role of family hatreds

---

protection were often an essential motivation for entering into a combourgeoisie (see *DHS*, 'Combourgeosie').

12 Thomas A. Brady, *Turning Swiss. Cities and Empire, 1450–1550* (Cambridge, 1985).

13 See Marco Bellabarba, *La giustizia nell'Italia moderna XVI–XVIII secolo* (Rome, 2008), 45–46.

14 The trial, not yet studied, is conserved: ASTo, Corte, Paesi, Città di Mondovì, mazzo 1, fascicolo 27. Concerning factionalism in Mondovì, see also below.

15 ASTo, Materie politiche per rapporto all'interno, Protocolli dei notai, Serie rossa, n° 147, fol. 196v. Characterizing factions as an illness in the body politic was common in the political language of fifteenth and sixteenth century Italy. Cf. Serena Ferente, *Gli*

in certain local contexts, the cases of Geneva and Mondovì both suggest that the factional struggles of this era cannot be understood solely as the result of private feuds or personal interests.[16] These disagreements concerned crucial political choices regarding how best to preserve the common good and ensure municipal survival and freedom. In Geneva, at the beginning of the sixteenth century, Bern and Fribourg were, for some citizens, a reasonable alternative to the authority of the duke of Savoy. In Mondovì, the duke of Mantua became a possible option to counter Sabaudian power. In both cases, the anti-Sabaudian choice led to factional struggles and direct challenges to the bishop's and duke's authority.

2 Urban Factionalism: Shaping the Enemy

The traditional Genevan historiography—now dated and seen as flawed by a certain teleological view of events from a "nationalist" perspective—understood the Eidguenots' struggle as a fight to defend civic liberties.[17] The leaders of the party have been described as "fathers of the combourgeoisie" and "martyrs for urban liberties".[18] The two Genevan factions have also often been depicted as socially homogeneous but clearly shaped by their struggles for two

---

ultimi Guelfi. Linguaggi e identità politiche in Italia nella seconda metà del Quattrocento (Rome, 2013), 242–45.

16 For the Flemish situation, cf. Jonas Braekevelt *et al.*, 'The politics of factional conflict in late medieval Flanders', *Historical Research*, 85/227 (2012), 26.

17 James A. Galiffe, *Matériaux pour l'histoire de Genève*, 2 vols. (Geneva, 1829–1830); James A. Galiffe, 'Bezanson Hugues : libérateur de Genève', *Mémoires et documents publiés par la Société d'histoire et d'archéologie de Genève* 11 (1859), 196–524; Victor Van Berchem, 'Amé Lévrier: à l'occasion du 4e centenaire de sa mort (13 mars 1524)', *Étrennes genevoises* (1925), 5–37 ; Charles Borgeaud, 'Philibert Berthelier, Bezanson Hugues, pères de la combourgeoisie de Genève avec Fribourg et Berne', *Étrennes genevoises* (1927), 18–45; Henri Naef, *Fribourg au secours de Genève : 1525–1526* (Fribourg, 1927); Victor Van Berchem, 'La mort de Berthelier', *Étrennes genevoises* (1928), 28–64; Henri Naef, 'Bezanson Hugues, son ascendance et sa postérité, ses amis fribourgeois (notes et documents inédits)', *Bulletin de la Société d'histoire et d'archéologie de Genève*, 5 (1934), 335–573; Henri Naef, *Les origines de la Réforme à Genève*, 2 vols. (Genève, 1936–1968) and Henri Naef, 'L'occupation militaire de Genève et la combourgeoisie manquée de 1519', *Revue d'histoire ecclésiastique suisse*, 52 (1958), 48–86. It is important to remember that this interpretation was a consequence of the fact that in the nineteenth century Geneva became a member of the Swiss Confederation. The early sixteenth century Eidguenots were later seen as the city's forefathers.

18 For instance, Galiffe, *Matériaux pour l'histoire de Genève*, vol. 1, 21; Borgeaud, 'Philibert Berthelier, Bezanson Hugues'; and Galiffe. *Notices généalogiques*, vol. 1, 15.

different and conflicting political ideals: the Eidguenots advocating for a free city allied with the Swiss and the Mammelus for a city subject to the duke of Savoy. However, as I intend to show, this view derived predominantly from the Eidguenots' own propaganda and from the first chronicle of the city written (in 1563) by the Eidguenot François Bonivard.[19]

The events of the years preceding the first attempt to enter into a treaty with Fribourg, and the precise content of the discussions with the municipal authority of the city on the Sarine, are still unclear. That some Genevan burghers, like Philibert Berthelier, were actively seeking support from the Confederates was well-known. Already in August of 1517, the Venetian chronicler and politician, Marin Sanudo, recorded in his diaries hearsay attesting that Geneva and Constance wished to become Swiss cantons.[20] The usual explanation given by the traditional Genevan historiography is that an alliance was an answer to the increasing political aggressiveness of and attempts to conquer the city by the duke of Savoy, as well as problems with the vidomne, a Sabaudian officer involved in administering the city's judicial system.

In fact, the idea that the duke was oppressing Genevan citizens was a key point made by Eidguenot propaganda. In order to convince Fribourg and Bern to accept them as combourgeois, they portrayed Charles II as a tyrant who inflicted many hardships on the Genevans. The trial and the execution of Philibert Berthelier in 1519, also a burgher of Fribourg, played a central role in the Eidguenots' argument.[21] On 1st March 1519, when asked by the Swiss Diet to explain why they accepted Geneva as combourgeois, Fribourg's ambassadors stated that injustices had pushed the Eidguenots to look for "friendship and bourgeoisie" with the city.[22] In 1525–1526, again the Eidguenots stressed the "cruelties" the duke had committed against them. In October of 1525, Bern, Fribourg and Solothurn were informed by their ambassadors in Geneva about the way Charles II had "martyrized and given the rope to many poor burghers without reason" and "tyrannized many others".[23] On 10 January 1526, Besançon Hugues, speaking to the ambassadors of Bern and Fribourg, begged them to "listen to the grievances of the poor Genevan burghers and [hear] of

19 François Bonivard, *Chroniques de Genève*, ed. Micheline Tripet, 3 vol. (Geneva, 2001–2014).
20 *Diarii di Marino Sanuto*, vol. 24, (Venice, 1889), col. 566: "si voleno far cantoni di Sguizzari".
21 On this trial, see Galiffe, *Matérieaux pour l'histoire de Genève*, vol. 2, 93–154.
22 RC 8, 297.
23 RC 10, 562–65: "martirizé et donné la corde a pluseurs pouvres bourgoys sans cause"; "tiranniser plusieurs autres".

the violence and cruelties that the duke of Savoy inflicted upon them".[24] One month later Hugues pleaded again for the Swiss to grant Geneva the combourgeois since this was, he said, "the strongest security, and the best, and most lasting we could have".[25]

Despite the arguments used by the Eidguenots to push the negotiations between the cities forward, for many months Bern and Solothurn remained sceptical. The negotiations of autumn 1525 did not convince Solothurn, which perceived the persecutions and "cruelties" of which the Eidguenots spoke to be an exaggeration. Solothurn wrote to Bern that its ambassador in Geneva had reported a less serious situation within the city than was being portrayed by the Eidguenots. Solothurn also suggested that Fribourg was willing to tolerate the Eidguenots because of their hatred for Charles II.[26] Bern's ruling elite was also aware of the fact that the Eidguenots were carrying out an intense and misleading propaganda campaign. On October 23, the municipal authorities wrote to their subject communities in the Oberland, warning them that some rebellious Genevans were falsely accusing the duke of Savoy; since they were nothing more than ordinary troublemakers, they should not be trusted.

Despite the cities' doubts, however, the Eidguenots' propaganda was effective. On 9 February, anxious officials from Bern wrote to Fribourg when an armed troop from Gessenay (a mountain region south of Bern) marched towards Geneva to aid the Eidguenots, potentially triggering a war against the House of Savoy.[27] It is difficult to know exactly what the Eidguenots were saying about the duke to convince the people of Gessenay to take up arms, but they probably used similar arguments to those they employed in communicating with the municipal authorities of the Swiss cities. It is also noteworthy that the Offischer family, living in Geneva but originating from the region of Gessenay, was probably a central source of the anti-duke propaganda.[28] We must also remember that the turmoil caused by the Peasants' War reached Bern and its territories in April and May 1525. It is not completely impossible that the Genevans used this conflict and its reverberations to achieve a more

24 RC 10, 582: "...antandre les plaints des povres bourgeois de Genève et des viollences et cruaultés que leur hont estés faytes par Monseigneur le duc de Savoye".

25 RC 10, 584: "la plus grande seurté et la meillieur et plus durable que pourrions avoer".

26 Letter cited in Naef, *Fribourg au secours*, 60. In December 1525, Fribourg was still trying to obtain 15,000 golden crowns (as stipulated in 1519) from the duke of Savoy (*ibid.*, 87).

27 On the affair see EA, IV/1a, 786–87, and Naef, *Fribourg au secours*, 65–66, 184 and 230–31.

28 Blanca Baechler, *Petit Conseil de Genève (1460–1540). Étude prosopographique d'une élite dirigeante dans une période de crise politique et religieuse*, vol. 2 (Geneva, 1995) 519–20, and RC 10, 106, n. 1.

successful propaganda against a prince whom they could easily portray as a tyrant persecuting and disregarding the liberties of poor burghers.[29]

In some respects it is difficult to really understand the situation within the city at this time and to know whether the Eidguenots were exaggerating their situation.[30] During negotiations and diplomatic meetings, one side would often accuse the other of dishonesty to discredit its enemy. On 10 January 1526, at the beginning of his speech in front of the Swiss ambassadors, Besançon Hugues was forced to defend himself against this type of accusation.[31] And when, some weeks later, he presented the treaty to the General Council of Geneva, which he translated and summarized—the treaty was written in German—he felt the need to swear to the authenticity of its contents.[32] This kind of justification was not only a rhetorical device, a sort of *captatio benevolentiae*, but was evidence of a real problem: the need of the speaker to prove his trustworthiness to his audience. Thus, it is important to underline how negotiations over alliances presented not only a puzzling legal problem in the context of a political climate in which a certain degree of legal uncertainty existed—the negotiations also involved the parties fighting against sometimes exaggerated or false portrayals of them or of the facts by their opponents.

During the main trial against the principal Mammelus in 1527, the two factions were described as homogeneous groups with clear political ideas. According to the articles of accusation, the Mammelus wanted the duke of Savoy to be the supreme lord of the city, while the Eidguenots endorsed the combourgeoisie and refused to recognize Charles II as the lord of the city.[33] The Mammelus were accused of having helped the duke with his plans to conquer the city and having supported him in his attempt to become the imperial vicar

29 The peasants were attached to their privileges and charters and firmly held that the duty of governors was to protect their subjects and their subjects' rights. See Hans von Rütte, 'Paysans, guerre des (1525)', in *DHS*; Edgar Bonjour, *Die Bauernbewegungen des Jahres 1525 im Staate Bern* (Bern, 1923); and Conrad André Beerli, *Le peintre poète Nicolas Manuel et l'évolution sociale de son temps* (Geneva, 1953), 249–50. A similar situation occurred again in 1535 when peasants from Bern wanted to rescue Geneva from the Sabaudian threat. Cf. Catherine Santschi, 'Les mandements changent de maîtres', in Matthieu De La Corbière, Martine Piguet et Catherine Santschi, eds., *Terres et châteaux des évêques de Genève. Les mandements de Jussy, Peney et Thiez des origines au début du XVIIe siècle* (Geneva, 2001), 360–71.

30 The same problem exists for scholars studying the actions of the Peneysans and the associated troubles during 1534–1536. Cf. Santschi, 'Les mandements', 335.

31 *RC* 10, 583.

32 *RC* 10, 205.

33 AEG, PC, 1ère série, nº 228bis, p. 228.

and supreme lord of the city by disseminating dishonest propaganda.[34] The Mammelus were also charged with having helped the duke conduct his unjust trials and executions of Blanchet, Navis and Berthelier in order to subject the entire city to them and to the duke.[35] Eventually, forty-seven members of the Mammelus faction were condemned to death (in absentia) on account of their "conspiracy, sedition and treason, both against the person of our very reverend and respected lord and prince [the bishop] and his authority and jurisdiction, against the franchises and liberty of the city, and in the same way against the citizens, burghers and inhabitants of this city of Geneva."[36]

A similar description was adopted by François Bonivard in his chronicle:

> The duke's partisans called the Fribourg's burghers *les Eiguenot*, which they [the Eidguenots] did not consider as an insult, but as a great honour, because the others they called them *Eidgenossen*, which is the German name of the Swiss and means 'allies' or 'sworn in'. The duke's partisans corrupted this epithet partly to make fun of their enemies, partly because they did not understand German, saying '*les Eiguenot*'. And the Eidguenots (among those who did not know German) called themselves by this epithet, and their children went out yelling: *Vivent les Eiguenot*. And they called the others *Mammeluz*, from the name of the Cairo Sultan's soldiers who are all renegade Christians and slaves of the Sultan, because they denied their rural freedom. Whence came this faction and partiality which has always been called 'Eidgnoss' and 'Mammelucz'.[37]

34 Ibid., p. 225.

35 Ibid., p. 231 and 234. On these trials, see also Galiffe, *Matériaux pour l'histoire*, vol. 2, 93–154 and 166–211.

36 Ibid., p. 258: "conspiracions, sedycions et trahisons […] tam contre laz persone de nostre tresreverand et redoubté signieur et prynce que son auctorité, juridicions, les franchyse et lyberté de laz cité et parelliemant aut citoyens, bourgoys et habitans de cete cité de Genesve".

37 Bonivard, *Chroniques de Genève*, vol. 2, 136–37: "Les ducaux havoient imposé aux bourgeoiz de Fryburg les Eiguenot, ce que eux ne prenoient pas à injure. Mais pour grandt honeur, car les autres les cuidoient nomer *Eidgnossen*, qu'est le nom appellattif en alleman des Souysses et signiffie allié ou assermenté. […] lequel nom ce[s] ducaux corrompoient en partie par moquerie de leurz adversaires, en partie pour non entendre l'alleman disant les Eiguenot. Et eux mesmes (de ceux, dy je, qui ne sçavoient pas l'alleman) se nomoient ainsy et alloient leurz enfantz mesmes criantz: *Vivent les Eiguenot*. Et appeloient les autres Mammeluz du nom des soldatz du soudan ou sultan du Caire qui sont touz chrestiens regniez et esclaves dudict sultan, pource qu'ilz havoient regniee la liberté paysanne. D'où sordit ceste faction et partialité que c'est tousjours appelee des Eidgnoss et des Mammelucz…".

The reality, however, was more complex because the two factions were less well-defined than Bonivard's narrative of the Mammelus' trials suggests. Presenting the opposing faction as a cohesive group with well-defined political ideas was the aim of factional propaganda. It is clear, however, that some joined the factions simply for practical reasons, without necessarily endorsing the group's political goals.[38] In addition, the allegation that the Mammelus' main political goal was for the city to become part of the duchy of Savoy is questionable at the very least. Jean Balard, an important member of the ruling elite, wrote in his journal that in September 1525, one of the Mammelus' mayors told the Sabaudian ambassadors that "we do not owe any obligation to the emperor, even less to his vicar".[39] In describing the dissenters' position at the 1526 General Council during which the combourgeoisie with Bern and Fribourg was approved, Bonivard stated that some Mammelus expressed their desire for "no other protection nor alliance than those coming from God, Saint Peter and their bishop and prince".[40] Like the Eidguenots, the Mammelus declared their attachment to Genevan liberties and franchises.

It is thus clear that in studying factions and their beliefs, one must consider that the nature and characteristics of a faction were partially a construction of its opponent's propaganda. Public riots and verbal insults certainly played a role in this construction as well, and the labels given to the two parties became, in fact, an important component of the political discourse used to shape the enemy. As Bonivard wrote, the labels 'Mammelus' and 'Eidguenots' began as sobriquets (even if the Eidguenots "did not consider [the name 'Eidguenots'] as an insult"), not as names chosen by the factions themselves. Official documents such as letters and minutes of the councils, very rarely used these labels for identifying the two groups. Letters written in 1525–1526 during negotiations over the combourgeoisie never mentioned the names of the two factions. The Eidguenots, for instance, were always referred to as the "fugitives" or "those of Geneva".[41]

38 Cf. the case of Bastien Grangier: Caesar, *Histoire de Genève*, 143–44.

39 Jean-Jacques Chaponnière, ed., 'Journal du Syndic Jean Balard ou relation des événements qui se sont passés à Genève de 1525 à 1531', *Mémoires et documents publiés par la Société d'histoire et d'archéologie de Genève* 10 (1854), 14: "Nous ne debvons point de recognoissance a lampereur et encoures moins a son vicayre". This claim is most likely supported by the Golden Bull. The imperial vicar is the duke of Savoy. On the vicariate and on the Golden Bull, see below point 3 'The Prince and the Factions: A Complex Relationship'.

40 Bonivard, *Chroniques de Genève*, vol. 2, 83: "autre protection ni alliance que celle de Dieu, saint Pierre et leur evesque et prince".

41 Cf. Bern to the duke (*RC* 10, 573 and 587), the Sabaudian ambassadors to the Swiss (*RC* 10, 579 and 588–89), the bishop to a Sabaudian officer (*RC* 10, 578) and the Mammelus to the Swiss (*RC* 10, 593).

The two terms were not the official names of the factions; rather, they were intended as insults used mainly during riots or arguments. In 1520, Robert Vandel, an important member of the ruling elite, suggested that in order to pacify the city, use of the terms Mammelus and Eidguenots should be prohibited.[42] On 15 July 1527, the General Council forbade the factions from insulting each other with these names.[43]

Especially after February 1526, when the Eidguenots regained power and achieved ratification of the new combourgeoisie with Bern and Fribourg, the name "Mammelus" became synonymous with treason. The effects of this fact were made worse because during this period, as the sources clearly show, many Genevans experienced more or less violent confrontations with the duke's partisans or with Genevan Mammelus.[44] For example, on 13 April 1526, Jean de Foys, a Genevan burgher, was attacked while traveling to Geneva by three masked knights shouting the phrase "treacherous Eidguenot".[45]

For the Mammelus, regarding their opponents as traitors was a direct consequence of their political ideas. The combourgeoisie was an act of treason against the lord of the city. To the Mammelus, not only had the treaty been concluded without the bishop's approval, but it also violated the rights of the duke. In 1519, the Mammelus clearly supported the intervention of the bishop and duke approved by the General Council on 3 September. Like the bishop and the duke, the Mammelus supported the measures taken at that time (the mayor's dismissal and Berthelier's trial) as being necessary for the eradication of factionalism. The Mammelus also stated that most of the citizens did not want the combourgeoisie not because they "despised it, but because those

42 RC 8, 461.

43 RC 10, 425. Similar measures can be found elsewhere within the duchy of Savoy, both in ducal codes (*e.g.*, in the law codes of 1403 and 1559) and urban legislation (*e.g.*, Cuneo 1407 and Mondovì 1516), punishing the use of the terms "Guelph" and "Ghibelline". Cf. Gian Carlo Buraggi, 'Gli statuti di Amedeo VIII di Savoia del 31 luglio 1403', *Memorie dell'Accademia delle scienze di Torino. Classe di scienze morali, storiche e filologiche* 70, no. 2 (1940), 10–11; Felice Amato Duboin, *Raccolta per ordine di materie delle leggi, cioè editti, patenti, manifesti, ecc. emanate negli Stati di terraferma sino all'8 dicembre 1798 dai sovrani della Real Casa di Savoja*, t. 6, vol. 8, libro 5 (Torino, 1830), 1–3; Paolo Grillo, 'L'éta sabauda', in *Storia di Cuneo e del suo territorio 1198–1799*, Rinaldo Comba, ed. (Savigliano, 2002), 136–37; and ASTO, Materie politiche per rapporto all'interno, Protocolli dei notai, Serie rossa, n° 149, fol. 6r.

44 Three other recorded incidents took place in April 1526 (ASTO, Paesi, Genève, cat. 1, paq. 12, no 6), one in 1527 (RC 10, 348) and one in 1529 (RC 11, 600).

45 ASTO, Paesi, Genève, cat. 1, paq. 12, no 6: "Donons dessus se treytre Exquenox!".

bourgeoisies must not be done without the consent of their lord".[46] In the case of the second combourgeoisie in 1526, the Mammelus once again asserted its unlawfulness because it was concluded without the bishop's consent.[47] They also underlined the general atmosphere of intimidation and violence present during the negotiations of the General Council which approved it.[48]

3 The Prince and the Factions: A Complex Relationship

The first attempt at forming a bourgeoisie with Fribourg in 1519 was immediately contested by both the bishop and the duke of Savoy, who turned to the Swiss Diet. Charles II of Savoy invoked previous treaties he had signed with some of the Swiss cantons and reminded them that according to these documents, neither of the contracting parties could receive the other party's subjects as bourgeois nor take them under its protection. For their part, Fribourg's and Geneva's municipal authorities argued that such claims were legally unfounded because their citizens could not be considered subjects of the duke.[49] The Diet gathered for the first time in Bern on 21 February and then on 17 March in Zurich, and asked Fribourg to renounce the combourgeoisie.[50]

Although Geneva's negotiations with Fribourg stipulated that the bishop's privileges and his jurisdiction should be preserved, it was unclear if Fribourg's citizens had the power to conclude a combourgeoisie with Geneva's burghers. It is also possible that ducal opposition to the combourgeoisie was prompted

46 AEG, Bourgeosie A2, fol. 9v: "…n'a pas esté mesprisant icelle, mes pour ce que telle generalité de borgoysie ne se doibt fere par les subgectz sans le consentement de leur seignieur" (instructions for the Mammelus ambassadors sent to the Diet in Solothurn in October 1519).

47 In fact, Pierre de La Baume had an ambiguous attitude towards the combourgeoisie, changing his mind many times. See Louis Binz, Jean Emery, Catherine Santschi, *Le diocèse de Genève. L'archidiocèse de Vienne en Dauphiné*, Bern, 1980 (*Helvetia Sacra* I/3), 113–14.

48 Cf. the letter written by the Mammelus (20 March 1526) to the Swiss Diet, edited in *RC* 10, 592–94. About the violence that took place within the city after the ratification of the combourgeoisie, see also the memoir the Mammelus sent to Charles II (26 September 1526, edited in *RC* 10, 603–06) and Naef, *Fribourg au secours*, 259.

49 Cf. the account by Fribourg's and Bern's ambassadors before Geneva's General Council on 1st March (*RC* 8, 296–98). The duke concluded a treaty (27 August 1512) with the cities of Zurich, Bern, Lucerne, Zug, Basel Fribourg, Solothurn and Schaffhausen (edited in *EA* III/2, 1348–1351), and previously one with Bern, Fribourg and Solothurn in 1509 (19 and 22 March: *EA* III/2, 1323–1327). The 1509 treaty was followed by an agreement (3 December 1517: *EA* IV/1, 3) which Fribourg refused to join (see *RC* 9, 481).

50 *EA*, III/2, 1137, letter *m* and 1143–1144.

by the fact that, on 15 October 1503, emperor Maximilian I granted the title of imperial vicariate to the duke of Savoy, a privilege previously given to (but later withdrawn from) the House of Savoy in 1365 by emperor Charles IV. The vicariate stipulated that anyone holding imperial fiefs in the duchy was required to take an oath to the duke as vicar of the emperor. The act also provided that the duke would exercise "the jurisdiction, lordship, sovereign rights and sovereignty" of the emperor and that he could prosecute crimes and also enact statutes to deter crime.[51] Maximilian I reconfirmed the vicariate with two acts dated 5 August and 7 November 1518.[52] At first glance, the legal implications seem clear: the bishop, as an imperial prince, had to swear an oath to the duke of Savoy because the vicariate abrogated the privilege of imperial immediacy, or so thought the duke's jurists. In fact, the significance of the vicariate was subject to different interpretations.[53] In particular, the status of Geneva's citizens (*bourgeois*) immediately appeared unclear: did they remain subjects of the bishop, or did the vicariate grant sovereignty over them to the duke of Savoy?

The decision of the Swiss Diet—forcing Geneva and Fribourg to renounce the alliance—demonstrates how Charles II's claims to apply the vicariate to Geneva were not entirely unfounded or at least not easy to refute.[54] Beyond the argumentation of the parties involved, it must be emphasized that the situation was juridically complex, and the legal uncertainty offered the parties substantial room to manoeuvre. It is thus less important to assess the legitimacy or illegitimacy of the ducal rights in retrospect than to grasp contemporary perceptions of the Sabaudian authority. Even when faced with an inherently unstable situation, a portion of Geneva's elite considered the duke's claims to be completely legitimate and believed it would be prudent to assent to his demands. In short, contrary to the traditional historiography, the duke was not necessarily seen as a tyrant, at least not by all of the city's elite.

---

51 The privilege granted by Charles IV in 1365 is published in *SDGE*, vol. 1, 170–72. The privilege of 1503 (ASTo, Corte, Diplomi imperiali, mazzo 9, nº 5) is edited in Samuel Guichenon, *Histoire généalogique de la royale maison de Savoie*, vol. 4: *Deuxième partie* (Turin, 1780), 468–62.

52 ASTo, Corte, Diplomi imperiali, mazzo 10, nº 6 e nº 7. The vicariate was later confirmed on several occasions by emperor Charles V (cf. *RC* 11, 583–85).

53 The precise value of the vicariate was also a matter of dispute between the duke and the imperial court. Cf. Giovanni Tabacco, *Lo Stato sabaudo nel sacro romano impero* (Torino, 1939), 59–66.

54 Other reasons for the Diet's decision must be taken into account as well: the suspicion of some Cantons towards Bern western expansionism and a desire to avoid war with the House of Savoy.

The vicariate also appears to have been the central argument in the unsuccessful attempt to prevent the second combourgeoisie in 1526.[55] With respect to this combourgeoisie, Charles II obtained support from both the pope and the emperor. The pope addressed two briefs (dated 29 October 1525) to the Commune and to the bishop, enjoining them to recognize the duke of Savoy as imperial vicar and labelling the citizens opposing Charles II rebels.[56] Emperor Charles V did the same, requesting (on 28 April 1526) that the combourgeoisie be invalidated.[57] It is clear that during this period the Eidguenots never tried to contest the validity of the vicariate itself;[58] instead, they argued that Geneva had obtained complete autonomy from the emperor and that the only recognized lord of the city was the bishop. Their position was that the vicariate was simply not applicable to Geneva. The city's independence was supported by the so-called Golden Bull, a document fabricated around the 1480s.[59] Nineteenth-century historians demonstrated that this document was falsified; however, in 1525–1526, the Golden Bull was considered valid and served as a powerful political weapon. On 9 December 1525, the officials of Bern informed Charles II that Genevans had presented "one Bull by the emperor Frederick which shows that sole authority over Geneva was given to the bishop of Geneva".[60] On 10 January 1526, in arguing against the Sabaudian legists, the Eidguenots claimed that Geneva was "only subjected to Monseigneur of Geneva, our good bishop and lord, and not to any other person".[61] To the Eidguenots, the vicariate was a serious threat to the city's independence, and the only way to refute it was to declare the city independent from the emperor's authority.

In the immediate wake of the Diet's decision in 1519, the Eidguenots and Fribourg continued their attempts to achieve the combourgeoisie. This defiance provided the duke of Savoy with a good reason to intervene. Charles II

55 Claude Cuendet, *Les traités de combourgeoisie en pays romands, et entre ceux-ci et les villes de Berne et Fribourg: (XIIIe au XVIe siècle)* (Lausanne, 1979), 21–25, and Naef, *Fribourg au secours de Genève*.

56 Naef, *Fribourg au secours*, 100–101. The Brief to the Commune is edited in *Quellen zur Schweizer Geschichte*, t. 21, 314–17.

57 Cf. RC 10, 601.

58 The Genevan "nationalist" historiography, unaware of the new vicariate granted in 1503, looked at the validity of the Sabaudian claims with suspicion. Cf. Naef, *Fribourg au secours*, 56, and 100–103.

59 Cf. Caesar, *Le pouvoir en ville*, 71–72.

60 Edited in RC 10, 574: "une bulle de l'empereur Friderich contenant la superiorité de Genesve ester donnee a l'esvesque de Genesve."

61 Edited in RC 10, 583: "seullemant subjecte à Monseigneur de Geneve, nostre bon eveque et seigneur, et non à aultre".

entered the city with some seven to eight thousand armed men, and summoned a General Council (11 April), during which the attempt to form an alliance with Fribourg was finally broken.[62] At this moment, the vicariate did not grant the duke his desired sovereignty, but it did give him an opportunity to present himself as a good prince attempting to bring peace to the city and to eradicate factionalism. In fact, the official deed of renunciation acknowledged the decision of the Zurich Diet and recognized the duke as "very excellent prince and our very reverend lord, Monseigneur the duke of Savoy, prince and perpetual vicar of the Holy Empire".[63]

On 27 August 1519, the city's four *syndics* (at least two of whom were committed Eidguenots[64]) were deposed by the bishop and the duke, the latter acting as arbitrator and mediator at the request of the citizens and the bishop. Four Mammelus were "elected" to replace them, while the duke, pursuant to his authority, chose six additional councillors. Charles II also enacted new statutes, including a reform of the mayoral election process.[65] The two princes justified their actions by arguing that the previous election had been illegal and that reform was needed to end the factional struggles. Charles II's political moves were accompanied by the above-mentioned trial and execution of an Eidguenot leader, Philibert Berthelier, accused of sedition and conspiracy against the bishop.[66]

Again, it is less important to establish the credibility of the princes' allegations and the legitimacy of Berthelier's trial than to be aware that peace within the city was an important value for all parties involved. The existence of factionalism, because it was seen as harmful to the city, became a justification for both princely and municipal policies. In 1525, Fribourg and especially Bern were reluctant to agree to a new combourgeoisie. The Eidguenots were obliged to convince the Swiss that the combourgeoisie was not in violation of

---

62 Naef, 'L'occupation militaire'.

63 Edited in *RC* 8, 317–18, n. 3: "tres excellent prince et nostre tres redoubté seigneur, Monseigneur le duc de Savoye, prince et vicaire perpetual du sainct empire". Charles II had already invoked his title of imperial vicar in 1517 in order to arbitrate the dispute between the bourgeois of Lausanne and their bishop. Cf. *Les sources du droit du canton de Vaud*, ed. Danièle Anex-Cabanis and Jean-François Poudret, vol. B/I. *Droits seigneuriaux et franchises. Lausanne et les terres épiscopales* (Aarau, 1977), 393–97 and Jean-François Poudret, *La Maison de Savoie évincée de Lausanne par Messieurs de Berne* (Lausanne, 1962), 103–15.

64 One of them, Étienne de la Mare, negotiated the combourgeoisie of 1519 with Fribourg.

65 See the act of deposition made by the bishop *RC* 8, 345–51, and the new statutes in *SDGE*, vol. 2, 212–17. The power of enacting new statutes was granted by the vicariate, cf. *supra*.

66 Van Berchem, 'La mort de Berthelier', *Étrennes genevoises* (1928), 28–64.

the bishop's rights and that the majority of Genevans wanted it.[67] Bern and Fribourg, like the bishop and the duke, did not want to be perceived within Geneva as the cause of the factional struggles and in fact worked to mitigate the conflicts. On 12 March 1526, eight ambassadors from the two Swiss cities were ordered to witness the oath of the entire Commune in favour of the combourgeoisie. Standing in front of the General Council, they asked Geneva's citizens, and in particular the Eidguenots, to pardon their fellow citizens who opposed the alliance. Commenting on the opposition, the ambassadors recalled that "there is never such beautiful wheat that doesn't have some waste".[68]

The ducal policy adopted in the Genevan affair was not limited to that city; the duke adopted similar methods in other cities under his dominion. For instance, in Cuneo and Mondovì, where factional struggles were also acute, the duke of Savoy promoted reforms of the municipal statutes, in particular concerning the process for electing mayors.[69] Further study is still necessary, but it is clear that this political tactic was carefully planned and carried out.

At the beginning of the sixteenth century, intellectuals from the Duchy of Savoy reflected upon the nature of factions and their place within principalities.[70] Claude de Seyssel (ca. 1450–1520), especially in the last chapter of the fifth part of his famous *Monarchie de France*,[71] explicitly addressed the problem of factions.[72] In line with many other juridical and theological treatises of his

67 Cited in Naef, *Fribourg au secours*, 174.

68 *RC* 10, p. 218: "n'est jamais sil beau bled qui n'ait toujours quelques ordures". Possible reference to the parable of the weeds (Mt 13, 24–30).

69 For Cuneo Grillo, 'L'éta sabauda', 168–70. About factional struggles in Mondovì, see Giancarlo Comino, 'I Ferrero a Mondovì nel Quattrocento e nel Cinquecento: strategie economiche e lotte politiche tra Medioevo e prima età moderna', in *Nobiltà e Stato in Piemonte. I Ferrero d'Ormea, atti del convegno, Torino-Mondovì, 3–5 ottobre 2001*, Andrea Merlotti, ed. (Torino, 2003), 121–35; Giancarlo Comino, 'Al timone di "una città inquieta": il governatore sabaudo nel Piemonte di antico regime e in particolare a Mondovì', in *Il palazzo del Governatore a Mondovì Piazza. Un cantiere tra operatività e conoscenza*, Fulcheri Gemma, ed., (Mondovì, 2012), 63–69.

70 See Giovanni Rossi, '*...partialitas in civitate est tanquam vermis in caseo...*: il giudizio (negativo) sulle fazioni politiche in Giovanni Nevizzano (1490 ca–1540)', in Marco Gentile, ed., *Guelfi e Ghibellini nell'Italia del Rinascimento*, (Rome, 2005), 79–108.

71 The *Monarchie* was written in 1515 and first printed in Paris in 1519. For the text of the *Monarchie*, see Claude de Seyssel, *La Monarchie de France*, ed. Renzo Ragghianti (Paris, 2012). On Claude de Seyssel, see Claudio Caviglia, *Claudio di Seyssel (1450–1520). La vita nella storia de' suoi tempi*, (Torino, 1928) and Rebecca Ard Boone, *War, domination, and the monarchy of France: Claude de Seyssel and the language of politics in the Renaissance* (Leiden, 2007).

72 Claude de Seyssel, *La Monarchie*, 177–80, entitled "*Comme l'on se doibt gouverner es pais qui vivent en partialite*".

time, Seyssel's work argued that princes must try to eliminate factions.[73] According to Seyssel, if factions cannot be eliminated, the prince must at least prevent them from operating openly.[74]

In the second part of this short chapter, however, Seyssel took a very pragmatic approach which was a departure from most contemporary works. He stated that if it was impossible to eradicate factions, the duke could support one of them, according to his interests. Seyssel was certainly aware that this was an unusual position and concluded somewhat defensively, "so all good princes and politicians have done, and [this] is not contrary to divine law".[75] Seyssel also provided some concrete examples of what it meant to support a faction; the prince must, for example, select people from the preferred faction for offices or dignities.[76] This unusual advice regarding urban factionalism was probably strongly connected with Seyssel's own political experiences. In 1496, Seyssel participated, as ducal commissioner, in one of the numerous attempts to pacify the factions in the episcopal city of Mondovì. Unfortunately, Seyssel's commission promulgated a few short-lived statutes which did not prevent continuing violence. Notably, one measure taken by Seyssel was a prohibition on using party names—a way to ensure that factions "*ne se monstrent point descouvrement*."[77]

During the last years of his life, Seyssel was involved with the political struggles in Geneva as a counsellor of Charles II. In a letter concerning the two factions dated 15 June 1519, Seyssel advised him to "...use both your and Monseigneur of Geneva's [i.e. the bishop's] grace towards them in general, especially to all those who will behave humbly and whom we can trust; as for the others, who will be more suspect [to us], it will be necessary to limit their authority, if possible remove them from the city, and prevent them from going to the land of the [Swiss] Leagues, and especially to Fribourg."[78] Those who could

73 Ibidem, 178: "tacher par tous les moiens qu'il peut d'esteindre lesdites parcialitez".

74 Ibidem, 178 : "doibt à tout le moings garder que telles parcialitez ne se monstrent point descouvrement".

75 Ibidem, 180: "Ainsi ont faict tous bons princes et policiens et ne repugne à la loy divine".

76 Ibidem, 178: "en preferant les gens d'icelle en offices, dignitez, charges et proffiz".

77 Caviglia, *Claudio di Seyssel*, 45–46. This measure was enacted again in 1516 with statutes that forbade saying "Tu es Guelfus" and "Tu es Gibellinus" (cf. ASTO, Materie politiche per rapporto all'interno, Protocolli dei notai, Serie rossa, nº 149, fol. 6r).

78 Letter edited in Caviglia, *Claudio di Seyssel*, 638: "...user tant vous que monseigneur de Genesue, de bonté envers eulx en general et encores en particulier envers tous ceulx qui viendront a humilite et desquelz l'on pourra prendre fiances; et des aultres qui seront plus suspectz s'en assurer le mieulx qu'on pourra et les oster de la s'il est possible et garder qu'ilz n'aillent poinct au quartier des Ligues, surtout à Fribourg." The term Leagues ("Ligues") was commonly used in French to refer to the Swiss at that time.

be trusted in this case were the Mammelus, the party favourable to the duke. The "more suspect" individuals were obviously the leaders of the Eidguenots. Seyssel's advice was clear: if possible, they had to be removed from the political scene.

The election of new mayors and the statutes of September 1519 were proof that the duke and his court chose to follow Seyssel's suggestions. Charles II's decisions exhibit all the ambiguity and complexity encompassed in the ducal policy towards factions. In the period around 1500, most politico-theological treatises considered factions harmful and discouraged princes from exacerbating urban struggles by utilizing factions for their own purposes.[79] In reality, princes often had to compromise with urban societies, and they did not hesitate to use factions for this purpose.[80] In 1520, the Venetian ambassador Gian Giacomo Caroldo reported that the duke of Savoy, although a Guelph (supporting the French king), supported Ghibelline families (in favour of the Empire) whenever this was useful for achieving his goals.[81] In Geneva, Charles II presented himself as a peacemaker dedicated to eradicating factionalism. But in 1519, the elimination of factional struggles meant removing the most prominent members of one of the competing factions, the Eidguenots, who were judged to be in rebellion. This policy, however, while increasing ducal power in Geneva, failed to resolve the factional conflicts within the city. The factional struggles lasted for years after 1519, becoming further complicated by religious turmoil beginning in the 1530s, and only ended after 1555 when Calvin and his faction finally took control of the city.[82]

79 Cf. Rossi, '*...partialitas in civitate*', 97–99.

80 Cf. Ferente, *Gli ultimi Guelfi*, 231–32.

81 Cf. Eugenio Albèri, *Relazioni degli ambasciatori veneti al Senato*, vol. II (Florence, 1858), 325.

82 On factional struggles after the Reformation, especially during 1540–1555, see William G. Naphy, *Calvin and the consolidation of the Genevan Reformation* (Manchester, 1994).

Not Only Blood: Factions on the Venetian *Terraferma* during the Early Modern Period*

Andrea Savio

Medieval Vicenza had a small population and its governing noble elites were prone to infighting; for these reasons, it was not one of northern Italy's major cities. The city sat at the heart of the Veneto region, and as a result it was an appetising target for powerful neighbouring lords and was forced to defend itself repeatedly against attack. This situation continued until 1404 when it became one of the first cities to submit voluntarily to the Most Serene Republic of Venice, becoming known as the *primogenito* (firstborn).[1]

In the sixteenth century, Vicenza was described by Leandro Alberti in his *Descrittione di tutta Italia,* as a city blessed "with a great abundance of wealth" inhabited by "men [...] of lively mind, of great courage and most predisposed to the arts, arms and trade".[2] By the mid-1500s, it was home to between 30,000 and 32,000 people, possibly making it larger than Padua.[3] Another of the city's distinguishing traits was its governing noble class, praised by the Marche scholar Giovanbattista Dragonzino da Fano in the 1530s for its "pure lineage" and "ancient and noble Vicentine blood".[4]

Vicenza was also one of Italy's earliest manufacturing towns, with its thriving wool and silk industry. Both sectors drove the city's international trade, which was mainly with Lyon until 1572. From then until the Thirty Years' War, its main trading partners were Anvers, the German-speaking canton of Switzerland, and England. Vicenza also boasted a range of international merchant businesses run by the city's wealthy noble families, many of which employed the renowned architect Andrea Palladio.[5]

* I would like to thank the University of Padua for granting me the research funds that made the writing of this article possible. Abbreviations used: Archivio di Stato, Venezia = ASV.

1 James Grubb, *Firstborn of Venice* (Baltimore, 1988).

2 Leandro Battista Alberti, *Descrittione di tutta Italia* (Venice, 1551), 383.

3 Walter Panciera, 'Vicenza. L'età moderna (1516–1813)', in Giuseppe Gullino, ed., *Storia di Vicenza* (Verona, 2014), 137–40.

4 Giovanbattista Dragonzino, *Nobiltà di Vicenza* (Vicenza, 1525; *ristampa anastatica* Vicenza, 1981), 23.

5 Luca Molà, *The Silk Industry of Renaissance Venice* (Baltimore, 2000); Francesco Maria Vianello, 'Cloths for Peasants and the Poor: Wool Manufactures in Vicenza Countryside (1570–1700)',

 | DOI 10.1163/9789004345348_008

Upper Vicenza was home to the Republic of Venice's largest mining district. The apogee of the local silver mining industry was between the 1480s and 1520s, when the area experienced an influx of Bavarian labourers. After this period, crisis struck local mining and production ground to a halt. Between 1573 and 1575, attempts were made to reopen some of the silver mines in Tretto di Schio, and although the attempts ultimately failed, they were "important for other reasons in that gunpowder was used to mine silver for the first time in mining history".[6]

Regarding politics, the Republic of Venice used the local bureaucracy to insinuate itself into the Mainland's governing classes, a pragmatic move that brought its influence to the suburbs of many cities.[7] Venice's subject cities enjoyed a high degree of autonomy, with contemporary political language reinforcing this approach; for example, Venice had no objection to the Commune of Vicenza choosing to call itself *respublica*. Vicenza was also free to award citizenship, use its own units of measure and hold its own festivities.[8]

---

in Giovanni Luigi Fontana and Gérard Gayot, eds., *Wool: Products and Markets (13th–20th Century)* (Padua, 2004), 411–17; Francesco Maria Vianello, 'Rural Manufactures and Pattern of Economic Specialization: Cases from the Venetian Mainland', in Paola Lanaro, ed., *At the Center of the Old World. Trade and Manufacturing in Venice and Venetian Mainland (1400–1800)* (Toronto, 2006), 347–61; Edoardo Demo, 'Industry and Production in the Venetian *Terraferma* (15th-18th Centuries)', in Eric R. Dursteler, ed., *A Companion to Venetian History, 1400–1797* (Leiden, 2013), 291–318; Edoardo Demo, 'New Products and Technological Innovation in the Silk Industry of Vicenza in the Fifteenth and Sixteenth Centuries', in Karel Davids and Bert De Munck, eds., *Innovation and Creativity in Late Medieval and Early Modern European Cities* (Farnham, 2014), 81–93. On Palladio, see Guido Beltramini and Howard Burns, eds., Palladio (London, 2008).

6 Raffaello Vergani, 'Gli inizi dell'uso della polvere da sparo nell'attività mineraria: il caso veneziano', *Studi veneziani*, nuova serie 3 (1979), 104–15; idem, 'L'argento veneto: mito e realtà nei secoli XV–XVI', *Ricerche Storiche*, anno XIV n. 1 (January–April 1984), 143–61.

7 On the Mainland, see Angelo Ventura, *Nobiltà e popolo nella società veneta del '400 e '500* (Bari, 1964); Matteo Melchiorre, *Conoscere per governare. Le relazioni dei Sindici inquisitori e il Dominio veneziano in Terraferma (1543–1626)* (Udine, 2013); Michael Knapton, 'The Terraferma State', in Eric R. Dursteler, ed., *A Companion to Venetian History, 1400–1797* (Leiden, 2013), 85–124; Michael Knapton, John E. Law, Alison A. Smith, eds., *Venice and the Veneto during the Renaissance: the Legacy of Benjamin Kohl* (Florence, 2014).

8 James Grubb, 'Elite Citizens', in John Martin and Dennis Romano, eds., *Venice Reconsidered. The History and Civilization of an Italian City-State, 1297–1797* (Baltimore, 2000), 339–64. On Republicanism, see Edward Muir, 'Was There Republicanism in the Renaissance Republics? Venice after Agnadello', in John Martin and Dennis Romano, eds., *Venice Reconsidered. The History and Civilization of an Italian City-State, 1297–1797* (Baltimore, 2000), 137–267; Filippo De Vivo, 'Rhetoric and government in sixteenth-century Venice: some paradoxes',

Under Venice, Vicenza's political institutions were independent, with the only exceptions being its two *rettori*, namely the Venetian patricians elected by the Republic's greater council as representatives to its subject cities. One was the *podestà*, who was in charge of administration and justice, and the other was the *capitano*, in charge of military affairs. Vicenza's main institution was the greater council, comprising 500 members, but it also had a minor council of 150 members and an assembly of forty councillors. Vicenza's main executive powers were entrusted to eight *deputati ad utilia*, the city's highest-ranking politicians, aristocrats elected by the greater council. A key role in city life was also played by the *consolato*, a court open to jurists from the city's nobility that had the power to impose the death sentence and, from 1545, to exile certain criminals from Venetian territory. Vicenza's (and Verona's) aristocracy used the *consolato* to deal with local disputes, putting it in competition with Venice's judges. The *consolato* also ensured that Vicenza enjoyed much greater autonomy than any of Venice's other subject cities. Vicenza had twelve *consoli*: four jurists who presided over the city's civil courts plus eight "lay" members, all of whom were aristocrats elected by the city's greater council.[9]

1 The Rise of Vicenza's Factions: The Nobility's Hired Thugs

The city of Vicenza was a theatre of violence throughout the 1500s, as well as during much of the 1600s. At one stage, several gangs numbered more than one hundred people. Violence broke out across the Italian peninsula, mainly in areas where the local *clientela* (private armies) had been disbanded in the 1400s, but Vicenza was the backdrop for some of the period's worst brutalities. The rise of these gangs was gradual in the cities of Venetian Lombardy, especially in Brescia and Bergamo, which were experiencing conditions similar to Vicenza in the mid-to-late 1500s. In Vicenza, however, the violence erupted more suddenly than in other Mainland cities because of small private armies which sprang up in the surrounding countryside. The first signs that these private

The Italianist, 27 (2007) special issue, Jill Kraye and Laura Lepschy, eds., *Caro Vitto: Essays in Memory of Vittore Branca*, 188–205.

9 Claudio Povolo, 'Crimine e giustizia a Vicenza. Secoli XVI–XVII. Fonti e problematiche per l'approfondimento di una ricerca sui rapporti politico-giudiziari tra Venezia e la Terraferma', in Amelio Tagliaferri, ed., *Venezia e la Terraferma attraverso le relazioni dei Rettori* (Milano, 1981), 411–32; Gaetano Cozzi, 'Ambiente veneziano, ambiente veneto. Governanti e governati nel Dominio di qua dal Mincio nei secoli XV–XVIII', in Gaetano Cozzi, ed., *Ambiente veneziano, ambiente veneto. Saggi su politica, società, cultura nella Repubblica di Venezia in età moderna* (Venezia, 1997), 291–352.

armies were affecting affairs within the aristocracy began to appear in the 1520s and 1530s.

Today, we know that the absence of its own standing army forced Venice to look to the local nobility to levy and train local militias as quickly as possible, especially in border areas where outbreaks of war were frequent. Venice, still licking its wounds after its defeat at the Battle of Agnadello, sought increasing numbers of recruits from rural areas in general, which made up the "the grassroots cells of the State's complex military system, the men who administered it, both in war as in peace".[10]

From the 1520s, Vicenza's nobles began to surround themselves with their poorest relatives and the most skilled fighters from local farming communities. At the same time, the number of men that Vicenza provided for the Venetian army was halved, a move that demobilised large numbers of trained soldiers. According to accounts by Vicenza's *rettori*, it had been the norm for the nobility to enlist a restricted number of armed men, with Vicenza's young nobles often escorted by two or three armed guards. From the 1530s, however, the number of armed guards soared, a situation caused partly by local events—between 1527 and 1531 a horde of rogues from the mountainous area on Venice's borders descended upon Vicenza in the wake of a major economic crisis. During that period, criminals and low-cost retainers were willing to work as guards for anyone who would provide them a decent living, and men from the countryside became soldiers for the aristocracy out of financial and social need.

Although Venice was quick to make contact with the local aristocracy, it was slow to bolster relations once cities had been subjected to its authority, a failure that the Holy Roman Emperor used to his advantage. A visit by Charles V to the Vicenza area in October 1532 revived the military and imperial sentiments of local families, and the highest representatives of Vicenza's most influential houses, including the Trissino, Valmarana and Gualdo, went to pay their respects. From then on, many aristocrats campaigned more fervently for even greater autonomy from Venice, and their actions may explain why conditions in Vicenza took a bloody turn for the worse.[11]

---

10 Matteo Di Tullio, *La ricchezza delle comunità. Guerra, risorse, cooperazione nella Geradadda del Cinquecento* (Venezia, 2011), 19. On the Venetian army, see John Rigby Hale and Michael Edward Mallett, *The Military Organization of a Renaissance State. Venice c. 1400 to 1617* (Cambridge, 1983).

11 One example is the relations between Rome's factions and the Holy Roman Empire, which have been researched the most extensively, see Maria Antonietta Visceglia, '«Farsi imperiale»: faide familiari e identità politiche a Roma nel primo Cinquecento', in Francesca Cantù and Maria Antonietta Visceglia, eds., *L'Italia di Carlo V. Guerra, religione*

Until the late 1530s, the violence was restricted to fighting between individual nobles and between noble families, but from the 1540s gangs from several houses were largely responsible. Between 1500 and 1520, the causes of violence were financial and economic rather than ideological, and the violence itself was directed at the Thiene family. Beginning in the 1530s, however, the aristocratic lineages pooled their forces to fight the Trissino and Capra families. The scholar Giangiorgio Trissino neatly summed up the clashes in Vicenza in the 1520s and 1530s: "The da Porto and Thiene against Giovanni da Trissino; the Thiene against the Capra; the da Roma against the Godi; Davide Loschi against Francesco Capra; Marcantonio di Thiene against the Velo; Marco Thiene against the Angaran; the Branzo against the Monza".[12] Before the 1530s, the Trissino, Valmarana, Gualdo and Capra were Vicenza's only strongly pro-Empire families; the Thiene and da Porto were pro-Venetian. Loyalties, however, were not always clear-cut.

When the violence in the city escalated in 1537 and 1538, Vicenza's *podestà* issued a decree that forbade citizens to bear unauthorised arms. The citizens, however, managed to circumvent the measure, and the *podestà* was forced to petition the Council of Ten, Venice's supreme court, for advice on what actions to take to prevent further violence.[13]

In June 1539, on the basis of letters from Vicenza's two *rettori*, the chief councillors on the Council of Ten described Vicenza as "a city split in two": on one side was the oligarch party led by the da Porto and Thiene families, and on the other the recently ennobled families. The chief councillors ordered "the five main leaders" of the largest, most troublesome groups from each faction to be summoned to Venice. Venice also ruled that nobles could have no more than four retainers in their entourage as they walked the city. That summer, the *podestà* was insulted publicly by a mob that had probably been incited by the anti-oligarch faction, and from that time murders increased "from day to day".[14]

---

e politica nel primo Cinquecento (Roma, 2003), 477–508; Elena Bonora, *Aspettando l'imperatore. Principi italiani tra il papa e Carlo V* (Torino, 2014).

12 Bernardo Morsolin, *Giangiorgio Trissino. Monografia di un letterato nel secolo XVI* (Firenze, 1894), 99–100.

13 ASV, *Lettere rettori, Consiglio di dieci, Capi, Vicenza*, b. 223, n. 215, 7 January 1538.

14 Amelio Tagliaferri, ed., *Relazioni dei Rettori veneti in Terraferma. Podestaria e Capitanato di Vicenza* (Milano, 1976), vol. VII, 20: "among their citizens is a certain discord that is serious to say the least". On the factions, see Hendrik Spruyt, *The Sovereign State and Its Competitors: An Analysis of Systems Change* (Princeton, 1996), 130–50; Marco Gentile, ed., *Guelfi e ghibellini nell'Italia del Rinascimento*, (Roma 2005); Marco Gentile, 'Factions and Parties: Problems and Perspectives', in Andrea Gamberini and Isabella Lazzarini, eds., *The Italian*

In spring 1540, the city descended into bloody chaos as the two factions clashed: on one side were the Thiene and da Porto families, on the other were almost all of the city's other families, led by Marco Trissino. On 20 April, the *podestà*, concerned by the "hatred and rancour that burn among the citizens", foresaw an imminent outbreak of fighting between the families—"for all have raised arms with an enormous number of retainers"—and he attempted to confiscate the weapons of both the retainers and their masters. Unfortunately, the officials he sent to carry out his orders returned empty-handed. Immediately afterwards, Marco Trissino's brother Achille went to see the *podestà* on the pretext of speaking with him, but instead threatened him in his chamber "with colourful language full of fire and of scandal".[15]

Until then much of the violence occurred in order to avenge family honour, and the Venetian authorities were forced to intervene frequently. From 1541, however, the two factions fought for control of the main city councils, transforming physical violence into institutional conflict.

2 Venice Reforms Vicenza's Council of One Hundred

Spring 1541 was one of the periods of the greatest institutional tension in the history of Vicenza, and it involved the city's most influential families. On 24 March 1541, city council elections were held, but riots interfered with the vote count and almost all of the incumbent councillors were re-elected. The aristocratic group, which included the Thiene and da Porto families, had always held a majority, and saw this majority increase slightly after the elections. In early April, some members of the recently ennobled aristocracy who opposed the Thiene, travelled to Venice to protest against the oligarch group's attempts to maintain power and to ask Venice to intervene. In a bid to settle the differences, representatives of all of the squabbling families were summoned to Venice on 25 April 1541. As the risk of civil war began to loom larger, Venice was forced to dissolve all of the main city councils. The intervention of the Council

Renaissance State (Cambridge, 2012), 304–22; Serena Ferente, *Gli ultimi guelfi. Linguaggi e identità politiche in Italia nella seconda metà del Quattrocento* (Roma, 2013).

15 ASV, *Lettere rettori, Consiglio di dieci, Capi, Vicenza*, b. 223, n. 224, 20 April 1540. The membership of the two groups was composed as follows: on one side were the Counts Porto of the branch of the magnifico collaterale and the brothers Counts Marco Antonio and Adriano Thiene; on the other were Achille Trissino, Marco Trissino and his brothers, Giovanni Battista Monza, Giacomo Valmarana, Girolamo Godi, Bernardino Velo, Bartolamio Pagliarino and Ottaviano Garzadori.

of Ten, which imposed a peace agreement on all the parties involved, bore testimony to the complexity of Vicenza's political crisis. In June 1541, Venice intervened again by introducing a reform of Vicenza's Council of One Hundred. In accordance with proposals put forward by the *rettori*, the composition of the entire council was changed to include representatives from all of Vicenza's oldest and most important families, with the new council including the Scroffa, Almerico, da Monte and Magrè families. Members of the da Schio, da Roma and Trento families were included among the *consoli*. The reform also introduced the *contumacia*, a compulsory rotation of council members designed to extend power to a wider range of families. Although the new council comprised families who were highly critical of the da Porto and Thiene, it did not include the Monza and Valmarana,[16] who were believed to have been responsible for the circumstances leading to the dissolution of the previous council.

On 17 July 1541, the Thiene family were forced to sign a peace agreement with their rivals (the Capra, Nievo, Velo and Garzadori) before the Council of Ten. On the surface, it appeared that the central power in Venice had acted forcefully against the Thiene, but it had actually left some institutions untouched, thus allowing the incumbent governing class to retain its power until the late 1550s. Beginning in 1542, the oligarch faction, composed of the Thiene and da Porto, Vicenza's oldest and most powerful families, re-established its grip on power, trampling Venice's reform. This faction had managed to survive the 1541 crisis and to re-assert its hold over the city's institutions.

Before 1539, none of Vicenza's families were organised into factions; after this time, however, two rival political groups sprang up: an elitist faction which included the pro-Venetian da Porto and pro-French Thiene; and a pro-Holy Roman Empire, pro-Spanish faction, which originally included the houses of Valmarana, Monza, Godi and Gualdo, but was later joined by the Capra and Trissino, as well as the newly ennobled families. This latter faction sought greater international prestige in terms of titles or careers for their children at the Spanish court. Both factions were represented in the city's institutions, including civic offices and city councils, and each voted to ensure that its men captured influential positions. Vicenza's factions were mainly bound by lineage, i.e. all branches of kinship. Lineage was used as a synonym for "house" and included the cadet branches of a family, but was also extended to non-related families and individuals who, during the course of the 1500s, acted to strengthen ties with blood members by providing support and friendship.

16 Andrea Savio, *Strategie nobiliari. La famiglia Godi fra Vicenza e l'Europa (1480–1588)*, PhD thesis, XXV cycle, tutor Alessandro Pastore, Università degli Studi di Verona, 2013, 67–68.

During the 1540s, membership in these factions was unstable, with the secondary branches of some houses shuttling between gangs until the end of the 1500s, with a number even switching to rival factions. On rare occasions, the sons of impoverished minor aristocrats, usually the cadets, or sons who had clashed with their fathers, also switched to rival factions.

Political clashes inside the council always mirrored physical clashes outside it, with tensions peaking in the summer of 1541, the late 1570s, and the early 1590s. Between 1546 and 1554, the *deputati ad utilia* were granted greater and more extensive powers, but it was only in 1558 that the anti-oligarch faction, led by the Capra family, managed to enforce Venice's 1541 reform, after which this group recruited new blood for the city councils and ended the domination of the da Porto and Thiene. From then on, the decline of Vicenza's two oldest families was irreversible, despite a 1567 law known as the *legge serrata* (lockout law), which saw the da Porto family attempt to prevent additional families from assuming enhanced power in local councils, and a 1593 reform that increased the number of council members to 150.[17]

3 A Bloody Noon on 3 July 1548

Between 1541 and 1543, a veneer of peace descended on the city, although this truce was briefly broken by younger faction members on both sides, probably because their own families had excluded them from the list of council candidates. In March 1542, the sons of the da Porto and Thiene families clashed with their counterparts from the Valmarana and Velo families. Worried that Venice would intervene again and realising that they might permanently lose their seats on the council, the heads of the families called the young rebels to order and peace returned anew.[18]

This peace, however, was short-lived. In 1543, a spate of killings once again broke out across the city. On 7 November 1543, the *podestà* Bernardo Venier, anxious about this turn of events, wrote in his report to Venice that "the number of crimes [...] rises [...] higher each day". He feared that the clashes would worsen come spring during the elections of councillors, who were in

---

17 Claudio Povolo, *L'intrigo dell'onore. Poteri e istituzioni nella Repubblica di Venezia tra Cinque e Seicento* (Verona, 1997), 284–85; idem, *Furore. Elaborazione di un'emozione nella seconda metà del Cinquecento* (Verona, 2015).

18 ASV, *Lettere rettori, Consiglio di Dieci, Capi, Vicenza*, b. 223, nn. 245–246, 6 marzo 1542; Paola Lanaro, *Un'oligarchia urbana nel Cinquecento veneto. Istituzioni, economia, società* (Torino, 1992), 37–82.

theory chosen for being "the oldest, most noble and most prudent of the city's gentlemen".[19] Venice intervened once again, and again a relative peace fell over the city between 1544 and July 1548. The situation in the countryside was, however, still unstable—a number of country nobles were robbed and a few even murdered—but the city's aristocracy was untouched by this fresh outbreak of violence. Although banditry and lawlessness were to blame for these attacks, noble bandits enjoyed the protection of faction members with positions in the city's judiciary. Behind some of these attacks were Galeazzo and Leonardo da Roma, two vicious, unscrupulous nobles who had set up a small gang in 1543, but their crimes did not affect the city's aristocracy directly until 1548. The gang had been involved in scuffles with the retainers of some nobles, who had even managed to have the two da Porto tried in Venice, but they were acquitted by the Supreme Court of Forty,[20] probably due to the influence of the da Porto family's Venetian contacts. The actions of the da Porto gang would, however, soon plumb new depths. At noon on 3 July 1548, probably to avenge family honour, the gang carried out some of the most ruthless murders in the history of Vicenza's aristocracy. In broad daylight, Galeazzo and Leonardo da Roma, together with Giuseppe Almerico, broke into the Valmarana family residence in the Vicenza city centre and murdered the three young brothers Tommaso, Niccolò and Alberto Valmarana. They then rushed to the home of the Monza family and murdered the jurist Giovan Battista Monza.[21]

The bloody revenge of 1548 was the first in a string of vendetta attacks carried out by a small number of Vicenza's aristocratic families. After the 1548 murders, Venice clamped down on violence in the city generally and managed to prevent its spread to the rest of the city's noble classes, with the result that for a period of time after the murders, no nobles outside the warring factions were killed. The violence, however, only affected a small minority of the city's

19 ASV, *Miscellanea codici*, b. 125, pezzo 36, seconda parte, vol. 20.

20 Enrico Niccolini, *3 luglio 1548. Mezzogiorno di sangue a Vicenza* (Vicenza, 1985), 26–27.

21 On vendetta in Northern Italy, see Edward Muir, *Mad Blood Stirring: Vendetta and Factions in Friuli during the Renaissance* (Baltimore, 1993); Furio Bianco, '*Mihi vindictam*: aristocratic clans and rural communities in a feud in Friuli in the late Fifteenth and early Sixteenth centuries', in Trevor Dean and Kate J.P. Lowe, eds., *Crime, Society and the Law in Renaissance Italy* (Cambridge, 1994), 249–73; Marco Gentile, 'La vendetta di sangue come rituale. Qualche osservazione sulla Lombardia fra Quattro e Cinquecento', in Francesco Salvestrini, Gian Maria Varanini, Anna Zangarini, eds., *La morte e i suoi riti in Italia tra Medioevo e prima Età moderna* (Firenze, 2007), 209–41; Dennis Romano, 'The Limits of Kinship: Family Politics, Vendetta, and the State in Fifteenth-Century Venice', in Michael Knapton, John E. Law, Alison A. Smith, eds., *Venice and the Veneto during the Renaissance: the Legacy of Benjamin Kohl* (Florence, 2014), 87–102.

nobility, and thus the authority of its most powerful families was never called into question. Swept along by the emotionally charged situation after the attacks, the *rettori* decreed that anyone daring to draw or touch weapons in public would immediately lose a hand. For some time, it seemed that the decree had worked, as the murder rate fell, with people choosing to brawl or fight with clubs instead. The *deputati ad utilia*, however, probably pressured by their rebellious younger relations, demanded that the *sindaci inquisitori*, Venetian officials who heard appeals against the decisions of the *rettori* in subject cities, revoke the punishment as they claimed it was dishonourable for the nobility.[22]

The decline of the Thiene and da Porto families began when they were unable to prevent their younger family members from breaking the 1541–1543 truce. Negotiating truces, which was the chief method of settling disputes, was always a complex process which encouraged both sides to seek a mutually beneficial agreement. Ironically, truces were often a pretext for legitimising fresh violence, as they required observance of unwritten social regulations and rules of etiquette. Truces, which were often imposed from the outside, had long been considered essential for re-establishing public order, but they began to lose their effectiveness by the mid-1500s. From then on, negotiations failed to ensure that squabbling factions co-existed peacefully, although the rise of the Capra and Valmarana families during this period brought greater peace and security to the city's institutions.

4 Political Factions and Religious Factions

The Protestant Reformation gained a foothold in Europe during the first half of the 1500s and then spread across the continent. Various forms of religious dissent reached Vicenza, with the majority of its dissenters becoming Calvinists (although there were also some Anabaptists and Lutherans). In 1542, a secret, mysterious Vicenza reform church was founded and in the 1560s a large group of Calvinists, supported by the Thiene and da Porto families, established an open presence in the city.[23] Prior to this, during the 1530s, Spanish Catholic influences had been introduced into Vicenza. The hallmarks of these influences were the radical spirituality and fervent religious charity practised by

22 ASV, *Lettere rettori, Consiglio di Dieci, Capi, Vicenza*, b. 224, nn. 40–46.

23 Aldo Stella, 'Le minoranze religiose', in Franco Barbieri and Paolo Preto, eds., *Storia di Vicenza. L'età della Repubblica Veneta (1404–1797)*, III/1, (Vicenza, 1989), 201; Achille Olivieri, 'Alessandro Trissino e il movimento calvinista vicentino del Cinquecento', in *Rivista di Storia della Chiesa in Italia*, 21 (1967), 54–117.

the Barnabites, the Angelic Sisters of Saint Paul, and the Valmarana, Godi and Gualdo families. These three families supported the founding of these orders and funded them for decades.

The Angelic Sisters of Saint Paul was founded by Father Antonio Maria Zaccaria in Milan around 1530 and began its work in the city's rough suburbs. The Sisters lived in communities, had no hierarchy, and were generally women estranged from their wealthy families. Pope Paul III authorised the Angelic Sisters to establish convents in January 1535, but exempted them from cloister life so that they could carry out works of apostolate. By papal edict the following July, the pope established an equivalent order for monks, the Barnabites. When Antonio Maria Zaccaria died in 1539, Sister Paola Antonia Negri, referred to by her followers as "divine mother and mistress" on account of her mystic powers and great charisma, took over as head of the order. The reputation of Sister Negri—"one of the most controversial religious female figures in the first half of the 1500s"[24]—had been greatly enhanced before Zaccaria's death by their July 1537 trip to Vicenza at the summons of the bishop's delegate to the city.

The strict rules of the Angelic Sisters and the Barnabites had attracted the attention of Cardinal Niccolò Ridolfi and of *madonna* Maddalena Valmarana (the eventual donor of the Sisters' convent in Vicenza),[25] both of whom had asked the two orders for help with reforming local religious orders. After her successful trip to Vicenza, Sister Negri was summoned to Verona by the local bishop Gian Matteo Giberti in 1542, and later visited Padua and Venice,[26] where she founded other communities of the Angelic Sisters. This charismatic woman attracted much attention and many converts, the majority of them noblewomen, proof that a fresh religious message was in great demand.

Sister Negri received a warm welcome in Vicenza, especially from the women of two of the city's most powerful families, the Valmarana and the Godi, who together led Vicenza's Spanish faction.[27] Maddalena Valmarana was quick

24 Gabriella Zarri, *Le sante vive: profezie di corte e devozione femminile tra '400 e '500* (Torino, 1990), 99 and Prudence Renée Baernstein, 'Vita pubblica, vita familiare, e memoria storica nel monastero di San Paolo a Milano', in Gianna Pomata and Gabriella Zarri, eds., *I monasteri femminili come centri di cultura fra Rinascimento e Barocco* (Roma, 2005), 297–312.

25 Elena Bonora, *I conflitti della Controriforma. Santità e obbedienza nell'esperienza religiosa dei primi barnabiti* (Firenze, 1998), 417.

26 Adriano Prosperi, *Tra evangelismo e controriforma: G.M. Giberti (1495–1543)* (Roma, 1969), 280–81 and 313 and, about Ridolfi, 305.

27 Howard Burns, '*Da naturale inclinatione guidato*: il primo decennio di attività di Palladio architetto', in Arnaldo Bruschi, ed., *Storia dell'architettura italiana. Il primo Cinquecento* (Milano, 2002), 388. Also see Francesco Barbarano de Mironi, *Historia Ecclesiastica della Città, Territorio, e Diocese di Vicenza* (Vicenza, 1760), vol. IV, 235. The title "Knight of Saint

to offer Negri the monastery and church of Saint Mary Magdalene for use by the order of Saint Paul the Apostle in Milan. This highly generous donation was followed by equally generous offers from other wealthy members of House Valmarana, and both the Barnabites and the Angelic Sisters enjoyed widespread support among Vicenza's Spanish faction.

In February 1551, when Sister Negri was at the apex of her prestige and popularity, Venice decreed that the Barnabites and Angelic Sisters of Saint Paul were to be expelled from Venetian territory.[28] This decree sparked an inquest in Rome, which resulted in Sister Negri being confined to a convent in Milan and the Barnabites and Angelic Sisters being separated, with the latter being cloistered. The Roman Inquisition cloistered Sister Negri on 7 July 1552, and she died in 1555. Her supporters among Vicenza's noblewomen were also confined to cloisters.

The real motivations behind Venice's decree are still not clear, but they may not have been entirely religious. It was alleged that Sister Negri was so charismatic that she had, on behalf of the governor of Milan, tricked Venetian nobles into revealing political secrets to her.[29] Later, rumours circulated that the decree was due to Venice's alleged fear that the numerous Spanish priests with close ties to the Barnabites and Angelic Sisters were acting as spies.[30] Indeed, the Venetian authorities believed that the Barnabites were eliciting political information from nobles during confession.

It seems reasonable to conclude that there were links between Spain and the Angelic Sisters because Gabrio Casati and Domenico Sauli, two prominent pro-Spanish politicians in Milan, leapt to Sister Negri's defence. A few years later, Casati became the head of Spanish policy in Italy and was appointed regent

---

James" was awarded in the 1500s by the King of Spain to only two of Vicenza's families: the Valmarana and the Gualdo.

28 Daniele Santarelli, *Il papato di Paolo IV nella crisi politico-religiosa del Cinquecento: le relazioni con la Repubblica di Venezia e l'atteggiamento nei confronti di Carlo V e Filippo II* (Roma, 2008).

29 'Besozzi Giovanni Pietro' Adriano Prosperi, ed., in *Dizionario Biografico degli Italiani* (Roma, 1967), vol. 9, 680–84: "Besozzo, in a dispatch sent to Carlo Borromeo on 19 October 1579, says that the accusations included political espionage on behalf of the governor of Milan". For more on Milanese espionage in Venetian territory, see Paolo Preto, *I servizi segreti di Venezia. Spionaggio e controspionaggio ai tempi della Serenissima* (Milano, 2010), 123.

30 Elena Bonora, *I conflitti della Controriforma. Santità e obbedienza nell'esperienza religiosa dei primi barnabiti* (Firenze, 1998), 502. An original study regarding the multiple implications of secret information can be found in Filippo de Vivo, *Information and Communication in Venice: Rethinking Early Modern Politics* (Oxford, 2007).

of the Supreme Council of Italy, as well as President of the Milan Senate, where he served from 1565 until his death. Sauli was a Genoan noble, a patron of the arts and a benefactor, as well as a jurist and a diplomat, who had moved to Milan in the 1520s after serving as the papal ambassador to the court of Charles V. We know that Sauli, who had contacts in Vicenza in the 1530s, followed the events surrounding the Barnabites because his second-eldest son, Alessandro, had joined the order (after first serving as a page at the court of Charles V in the early 1550s) and earned a reputation as a great preacher. Alessandro Sauli later became confessor to cardinals Carlo Borromeo and Niccolò Sfondrati, the future Pope Gregory XIV.

The demise of the Barnabites and the Angelic Sisters caused great dismay in Vicenza, but the recently founded order of Spanish Jesuits was quick to mop up the support of families, such as the Valmarana, who had radical Catholic sympathies. The Imperial government may well have rewarded the Valmarana family's faith in Sister Negri, initially in 1540 when Charles V awarded the Valmarana the title of Counts Palatine, and later by accepting the Valmarana children as pages at Charles's court, which gave the family access to invaluable political contacts.

Vicenza was just one of many cities where the Reformation affected the relations between factions. It is unknown whether these factions became more entrenched in response to opposing religious opinions following the fighting of the 1540s, but they did play a key role in bolstering certain political groups, as the Spanish faction was led by the hard-line Catholic Valmarana family. Very little is known about their Protestant rivals due to a lack of primary sources. Furthermore, historical studies have overlooked Protestantism as a whole to focus mainly on individual Protestants with strong links to religious and political circles in Switzerland and France. Indeed, many of these individuals moved to France.

5 Conclusion

This article recounts events that were part of the wider backdrop of relations between Vicenza's factions, and the scenario that emerges from these glimpses of aristocratic life in Vicenza raises a series of political, social and cultural issues.

First, it appears that the Valmarana, Gualdo and Godi families, i.e. the main representatives of the Spanish faction, plus other Mainland nobles, slackened their ties with Venice over a twenty-year period by sending their children to serve as pages at Europe's courts in a bid to seek power and influence elsewhere. This and similar actions, however, risked openly offending Venice and exposed the family members remaining at home to threats and reprisals. This is why many houses, once they realised they did not stand to benefit from positions outside Venetian territory, renewed their support for Venice.

Part of Vicenza's governing class managed to find positions of favour at foreign courts despite holding secondary positions within the Republic of Venice. Their reasons for reaching out to foreign courts lay as much in their legitimate desire for personal and family ambition and for international standing and prestige, as it did in their widespread frustrations with the difficulties of climbing to the top of the civil and military ladder within Venice's subject cities.[31] Because of the difficulty of interacting and collaborating with Venice's governing class, many aristocrats found it simpler and more rewarding to do business with foreign powers.

In Venice's subject cities, power groups were often divided into two factions: one with sympathies for Spain and the Holy Roman Empire, and the other for Venice. Their rivalry often led to feuds and violence that resulted in intervention by the Venetian judiciary and State, often at the highest levels.[32] Against this backdrop, Italian and European courts were often safe havens for members of Vicenza's nobility mired in bloody local disputes. Faction members received protection from foreign ambassadors, as was the case with Vicenza's Spanish faction, which was helped by the Spanish ambassador to Venice on a number of occasions.[33] From 1572, documents used the term "faction" with increasing frequency, and from 1576 the obsolete medieval terms "Guelf" and "Ghibelline" were revived to describe the rival groups. Faction members almost certainly used these labels to establish international relations with the upper echelons of European society; for instance, the Spanish ambassador to Venice regarded Vicenza's Ghibelline movement to be supporters of his country's policies.

---

31 Claudio Donati, 'The Profession of Arms and the Nobility in Spanish Italy: Some Considerations', in Thomas James Dandelet and John A. Marino, eds., *Spain in Italy. Politics, Society, and Religion 1500–1700* (Leiden, 2007), 299–324.

32 James Grubb, *La Famiglia, la Roba e la Religione nel Rinascimento. Il caso veneto* (Vicenza, 1999), 245–86.

33 Enrico Basaglia, 'Il banditismo nei rapporti di Venezia con gli stati confinanti', in Gherardo Ortalli, ed., *Bande armate, banditi, banditismo e repressione di giustizia negli stati europei di antico regime* (Roma, 1986), 423–40; Peter Laven, 'Banditry and lawlessness on the Venetian Terraferma in the late *Cinquecento*', in Trevor Dean and Kate J.P. Lowe, eds., *Crime, Society and the Law in Renaissance Italy* (Cambridge, 1994), 221–48; Jonathan Walker, 'Bravi and Venetian Nobles, *c.*1550–1650', *Studi veneziani* 26 (1998), 85–113; Sergio Lavarda, 'Banditry and Social Identity in the Republic of Venice. Ludovico da Porto, his Family and his Property (1567–1640)', *Crime, Histoire et Société* 11/1 (2007), 2–24.

This political division also influenced institutional protocol, e.g. when foreign royalty visited Vicenza, the faction supporting the visitor would typically be allowed to pay its respects before the rival group could do so, as happened in the case of Emmanuel Philibert of Savoy in 1566. The Guelfs and the Ghibellines were Italy's two opposing political factions between the twelfth and fourteenth centuries. The former supported the Pope and the latter the Holy Roman Empire. In sixteenth-century Veneto, it appears the term "Ghibelline" was used to mean both supporters of Spain and the Empire.

The second issue regards the repeated high-profile honour attacks, mainly vendettas, especially in Brescia and Vicenza.[34] Although the aristocratic houses kept most of the attacks in check, by the 1570s the houses had become unable to settle their disputes by mutual agreement, partly due to measures introduced by Venice. From then on, groups rarely switched sides, and the composition of the two factions remained unchanged for much of the 1600s, with the Capra and Valmarana families on one side and the da Porto family on the other. A document dated 15 March 1577 affords a clearer insight into the members of Vicenza's warring groups: the Capra faction, which controlled the main magistrate positions (the *consolato* and *deputati ad utilia*) and had amassed huge stores of political patronage throughout the town and countryside, had also come to include "the Pogliana, Garzadori, Godi, Monza, and others; to the extent that each of their dependents is highly advantaged; he who is not among these dependents is unlikely to win justice in keeping with the crimes committed".[35] This quote demonstrates the negative consequences of the struggle between the factions, but there was also a positive side—it was owing to the factions that talks took place between Vicenza's institutional leaders and Venice beginning in the 1570s. Although Venice did not formally recognise these factions, it did recognise the authority of the most important positions on the city councils and, consequently, the authority of the people who held them.

34 Cf. Stephen D. Bowd, *Venice's most loyal city: civic identity in Renaissance Brescia* (Cambridge, 2010).

35 ASV, Collegio, Risposte di fuori, fol. 331, 15 marzo 1577.

A Temperate Factionalism: Political Life in Amiens at the End of the Wars of Religion*

Olivia Carpi

At the end of 1584, after a respite of nine years, France became embroiled in a new civil war. After the death of his brother the duke of Anjou (10 June 1584), King Henri III was without a male descendant and the Catholics were facing what for the vast majority of them was a frightening prospect: Henri of Bourbon, king of Navarre and Henri III's cousin, but also a Protestant and leader of the rebel Huguenot party, had become the presumptive heir. As a consequence, a portion of the French nobility and some bourgeois in Paris and other cities in the kingdom formed a Catholic League, also called the "Holy Union" (the name preferred by its adherents), promoted by Henri de Lorraine, the duke of Guise, and supported by Philip II, king of Spain. The League's aims were made public in a manifesto issued on 31 March 1585: to force the king to resume war against the 'heretics', deprive Navarre from his claims to the throne, and also to thoroughly reform the state, which the Leaguers condemned for its fiscal rapacity and authoritarian tendencies.

Confronted by political and military pressure, Henri III reluctantly promulgated the Treaty of Nemours (18 July 1585), prohibiting the reformed religion and annulling any rights to the throne claimed by Navarre and his cousin, the prince of Condé. These concessions were, however, not enough to satisfy the most uncompromising Catholics. Their suspicion, even hostility, to the king, explains the insurrection in Paris of 12 May 1588 known as the Day of the Barricades. Henri III was forced to flee Paris, which was left under the control of the Leaguers, and to sign the Edict of Union in Rouen (17 July), in which he confirmed the decisions taken three years earlier for the defence of the Catholic religion and also convoked the Estates-General. Henri III hoped to regain control during the meeting of representatives from the three orders of the kingdom; however, he had to confront the numerous Leaguers attending the Estates who were determined to force him take decisions he considered an attack on his sovereignty.

In an attempt to squelch the League—which he wrongly believed to be led solely by Guise—Henri III ordered the assassination of the duke and his

* Abbreviations: ACA: Archives communales d'Amiens antérieures à 1790; BnF: Bibliothèque Nationale de France.

 | DOI 10.1163/9789004345348_009

brother, the cardinal of Guise (both of which occurred on 23 and 24 December 1588), and the arrest of the League's principal leaders. Yet, this "coup de majesté" failed to strengthen Henri III's control and provoked a radicalisation of many cities controlled by the League, cities against which he and his successor Henri IV fought for the next decade.[1] In his *Déclaration contre les villes rebelles* of May 1589, Henri III discussed the "faction of the League", identifying the inhabitants "who diverted and separated the people from the obedience they owe" to their king, adding that the people "have been seduced by the scheming of those who would disrupt the public peace". The king described the faction as members of a "heinous conspiracy" who, under cover of "our holy religion", "daily try to lure to them and their party the other inhabitants", exerting on them "every sort of cruelty".[2] Two years earlier, during spring 1587, in a letter by the duke of Nevers (governor of Picardy) to the king, the membership of this party was identified as "the gentlemen of the Guise". The duke's letter recounted how the members of this party had attracted to them many "satellites", through "false rumours" and "money deposited with many persons whom they desire to make, by this means, obliged and well-disposed to them".[3]

It was at the time of the Holy Union (1585–1598) that the terms "faction" and "party" acquired a pejorative meaning. In contemporary French dictionaries, a "faction" is defined as "a group which engages in a subversive activity in order that its interests prevail" and is a synonym for "plot", "conspiracy", "intrigue" and "sedition". The first negative connotations of the term date back to the fourteenth century, but it was only during the 1580s in which it definitively acquired the sense of an association of plotters, or a group of political troublemakers.[4]

---

1 Olivia Carpi, *Les guerres de religion. Un conflit franco-français* (Paris, 2012).

2 *Declaration du roy contre les villes rebelles...*, à Tours, chez Jamet Mettayer, 1589, fol. 3: "(...) Nous avons recherché par tous les moyens à nous possible de reduire et remettre par la douceur tous nos subjectz en l'obeissance qu'ilz nous doivent, de laquelle plusieurs ayant esté seduitcz par les artifices et fausses impressions d'aucuns rebelles et perturbateurs du repos public et le nostre se sont distraicts et separez (...). Et s'efforcent journellement par toutes sortes d'artificieuses inventions d'attirer à eux et à leur party nos autres subjects et serviteurs qu'ils cognoissent avoir encores engravé en l'ame l'honneur l'affection et fidélité qu'ils doivent à leur Roy et Prince naturel, exerçant envers ceux qui ne veulent aderer toutes sortes de cruautez et inhumanitez (...) faire une telle punition et si exemplaire de ceux qui ont esmeu et soustiennent cette execrable conjuration".

3 BnF, Mss. Fr. 3634, fol. 117.

4 Nicolas Offenstadt, 'Guerre civile et espace public à la fin du Moyen Âge. La lutte des Armagnacs et des Bourguignons', in Laurent Bourquin and Philippe Hamon, eds., *La politisation. Conflits et construction du politique depuis le Moyen Âge* (Rennes, 2010), 111–29; Loïc Cazaux,

The negative connotations of the term "faction" were not merely a problem of semantics—the negative meanings have long been a leitmotiv in the historiography of the League, which was moulded by the royalist version of events, a narrative which denounced the Catholic princes and their followers as conspirators who had sold out to foreigners, and were driven only by their ambitions, and who concealed their true purpose under a guise of piety and patriotism.[5]

During the 1980s and 1990s, when study of the League was being renewed, historians doubted the factional dimension of the movement. Élie Barnavi refused to treat the Parisian Sixteen as a "faction", arguing that "a faction is a handful of people sharing similar social origins, with limited political goals, pushing to replace people in power but never the Power in itself. Hence, a skimpy ideology, built in haste around the main idea of a return to a Golden Age".[6]

Wolfgang Kaiser has depicted the factional struggles in Marseille during the 1580s and 1590s as "political struggles led by rival groups of the ruling elite, which leaned horizontally on economic and familial relations and vertically on fidelity and obligations owed by socially inferior groups. These conflicts aimed at seizing political power and gaining command of the economy, with the ultimate goal of hegemony. The Wars of Religion brought a new element to these disputes: the religious problem".[7] This politically-centered view concurs

---

'Les lendemains de la Praguerie. Révolte et comportement politique à la fin de la guerre de Cent ans', in François Pernot and Valérie Tourelle, eds., *Les lendemains de guerre. Les hommes, l'espace et le récit, l'économie et le politique. Actes du colloque de l'Université de Cergy-Pontoise (2008)*, Bruxelles, 2010, 365–74.

5 Jean-Marie Constant, 'La Ligue vue par les historiens du XVIe siècle à la fin du XXe siècle', in idem, *La Ligue* (Paris, 1996), 467–75; Penzi Marco, '*Damnatio memoriae*: la Ligue catholique française e la storiografia, tra politiques, rivoluzionari, mistici e liberali', *Quaderni storici* 118, (2005), 236–84.

6 Élie Barnavi, 'La Ligue parisienne (1585–1594); ancêtre des partis totalitaires modernes?' *French Historical Studies* XI, (1979), 31: "une faction, c'est une poignée d'hommes aux origines sociales semblables, aux buts politiques limités, à la rigueur remplacement des titulaires du pouvoir, jamais du Pouvoir lui-même. De là aussi une idéologie squelettique, bâtie à la hâte autour de quelques idées force de retour à l'âge d'or".

7 Wolfgang Kaiser, *Marseille au temps des troubles. Morphologie sociale et luttes de factions (1559–1596)* (Paris, 1992), 166–67: "des luttes politiques menées par des groupes concurrents de l'élite politique, qui s'appuyaient horizontalement sur des relations économiques et familiales et verticalement sur des liens de fidélité et d'obligations avec des groupes socialement inférieurs. Ces conflits avaient pour finalité de s'emparer du pouvoir politique et d'accéder aux commandes de la vie économique, d'atteindre ou de briser une hégémonie. Les guerres de Religion apportèrent un élément nouveau dans ce jeu: la question religieuse".

with the interpretation proposed by René Pillorget in 1972 for a later period of the factional struggles in Marseille, and was then confirmed by William Beik's study on the minority of Louis XIV. Beik saw factionalism as an endemic feature of aristocratic society in the French Midi during the first half of the seventeenth century, caused by weaknesses in the monarchy, which was unable to balance the interests of local elites.[8]

We can question the applicability of this explanatory model to all the cities in France because the model was forged from the very specific cases of Paris and the southern cities of the kingdom. This is the reason that this study is based on the northern cities of the kingdom of France, particularly Amiens. What exactly was the nature of factionalism in Amiens? Can we grasp its nature and functioning by a comparative analysis of royalist sources, which condemned it, and municipal sources? The latter have been often neglected, although they provide an understanding of factionalism from within the context of the practices of and issues facing local governments.

We will attempt to demonstrate how, contrary to the traditional picture, the Leaguers were neither "political tools" in the hands of more powerful rulers, nor unscrupulous people motivated only by their lust for power and social preeminence. The bourgeois of the League were inspired by political and religious convictions, and their civic republicanism should not be reduced to an unsophisticated form of anti-absolutism; certainly, the Leaguers believed that their actions provided a service to the "public good".

1 A Factional Profile

The factionalism of Amiens' League can be studied through a rich mine of sources, about which some precautionary comments are in order. The numerous letters and memoirs received by Henri III "de bonne part" (i.e. from noblemen and bourgeois of the city or from agents and informers) between May and October 1588 allow us to judge the conduct of the bourgeois Leaguers at the crucial moment when they took control of the city and instituted changes in the city's government. The problem is that it is difficult to counterbalance these allegations of royal agents or informers with witnesses from the League. The Leaguers were little prone to expressing themselves about their actions. When they did, it was often a posteriori and not without unease, "like defeated

8 René Pillorget, 'Luttes de factions et intérêts économiques à Marseille de 1598 à 1618', *Annales ESC*, 27e année, no 3 (1972), 730; William H. Beik, 'Urban factions and the Social Order during the Minority of Louis XIV', *French Historical Studies* 15, no 1 (1987), 36–67.

people, pleading for the defeated".[9] Even when Leaguer voices were expressed, they were not private reflections, but rather speeches in the context of exercising political office, and historians have tended to attribute little importance to these speeches, judging them as too conventional and stereotyped. The reality is, however, that their language, despite being formulated in a strongly rhetorical style, provides evidence of a real political culture.[10] Thus it is necessary to decrypt the conduct of these bourgeois partisans of the League by putting it in its proper context, as determined by institutional, sociological, ideological and other factors.

In their correspondence, the king and his "good servants" depicted Amiens' Leaguers as a "faction" engendered by the "complicity" of "many notable persons and common people", a "confederation" of "relatives and allies", "partners and friends", "neighbours" or "pensioners", which "frequently communicated" among themselves, and held "secret conventicles" during the night in order to "discuss State affairs" and to mock the king. They are also described as "unreasonable" people, whose "pertinacity" could be compared to that of heretics who refuse to abjure their error; "boisterous" persons driven only by "their passions and particular affections", who had been seduced by "those (princes) who are moved more by ambitions than by affection for the good of homeland", or even as "bad French" and "good Spaniards". According to these descriptions there was nothing more redoubtable than the initiatives of these "mutineers", whose goal was to "usurp the temporal authority of the city", using "lies" and "ruses and machination", "conspiring with weapons and open assemblies" and hounding those opposing them with "rage and fury".[11]

This royalist version, which obscures the significance of the League and tries to deprive it of any legitimacy, should be nuanced by noting that the League was a "Guisard movement" which did not act autonomously.[12] Despite this, Amiens' Leaguers were accused by their detractors of acting in concert with the Paris Sixteen "to open the city gates to those who would have subjugated

9 Maurice Rousset, 'Bulletin critique sur *L'Histoire de la Ligue* de Charles Valois', *Revue d'Histoire de l'Église de France* 6, no 33 (1920), 506; Fabrice Micaleff, 'Comment la bonne Ligue sauva la monarchie. 1593 selon Nicolas Lefèvre de Lezeau', *Les Dossiers du Grihl*, online November 29, 2011, http://dossiers grihl.revues.org/4708.

10 Hilary J. Bernstein, *Between Crown and Community. Politics and Civic Culture in XVIth Century Poitiers* (Ithaca, 2004).

11 BnF, Mss. Fr. 3411, fol. 65–68, 94–96, 108–114, 119–120, 133–134, 138–142.

12 Michel Cassan, *Le temps des guerres de Religion. Le cas du Limousin*, Paris, 1996, p. 274; François Caillou, 'L'essor et l'échec de la Ligue à Tours (1576–1588)', *Annales de Bretagne et des pays de l'Ouest* 114, no 4 (2008), 50–51.

it".[13] Such was the supposed purpose of an "armed assembly" which took place on the night of 16 May 1588. This assembly occurred the day after the arrival of a certain Gigault, who, according to rumours, "had run from Paris to Amiens" in order to warn Amiens' Leaguers that the king had left the capital and that in Paris "people were yelling 'vive Guise' and that everything that was done was by the authority of the said Guise".[14] According to these rumours, that night Charles of Lorraine, the duke of Aumale, a cousin and ally of the duke of Guise, and Aumale's lieutenant, *sieur* de Saveuse, had taken a stand in the abbey of Saint-Jean, in Amiens' faubourgs, with "an enormous number of soldiers, ready to enter the city".[15]

The records of Amiens' *échevinage* confirm that a tumult occurred.[16] The duke of Aumale had coveted the government of Picardy since 1585, but Henri III had refused to grant him authority over this strategic region, given its border with the Spanish Netherlands and its ports useful for attacking England and Scotland.[17] Indeed, Aumale multiplied his "enterprises against some of the cities and places of this government",[18] managing to capture Corbie, Pont-Rémy, Le Crotoy, Montreuil and Doullens, the latter only thirty kilometres from Amiens, the capital, which was Aumale's main objective. Aware that taking Amiens, considered impregnable, was beyond his capabilities, Aumale tried, in vain, to circumvent the mayor in 1585 and 1587 and, in order to incite the inhabitants to insurrection, he spread the rumour that the king was about to install a garrison and build a citadel in Amiens.[19]

The bourgeois of Amiens were not willing to renounce the exemption Louis XI had granted in 1470–1471 from the presence of a military governor, a citadel and a garrison. During the fall of 1587 the *échevins* politely refused the offer of military assistance made by the *sieurs* of Piennes and Crèvecœur; in May 1588, they defiantly barred the *sieur* d'Estrées and his military escort from the city, and they also refused to allow the *sieur* de Saisseval, acting on behalf of Épernon, to take arms from the city's arsenal for his use. They were certainly not willing to give up the city to Aumale.[20]

---

13 BnF, Mss. Fr. 3411, fol. 119: "ouvrir les portes de la ville à tels qu'ils auraient entrepris de l'assujettir".

14 Ibid., fol. 65.

15 Ibid., fol. 68: "infinité de soldats, prêts à entrer dans la ville".

16 Archives Communales d'Amiens antérieures à 1790 (ACA), BB 48, fol. 131 et 133.

17 Constant, 'La Ligue vue par les historiens', 123.

18 ACA, BB 47, fol. 5v, 9, 18v.

19 Ibid., BB 47, fol. 13 v; BB 48, 19, 26v, 31, 53, 59.

20 Ibid., BB 48, fol. 18, 21, 26v, 130v, 131, 133.

Both before and after the existence of the League, Amiens' municipal authorities refused to give up military control of the city despite threats. After Paris had submitted to Henri IV, the duke of Mayenne insisted on putting a garrison in Amiens, but this only accelerated the city's submission to the new king (9 August 1594). Similarly, the *échevins* refused several times the king's offer of Swiss soldiers to protect the city from the Spaniards occupying Doullens (who later conquered Amiens, on 11 March 1597).[21] The city's rejection of every form of indenture to princes may in general be explained by the bourgeois' deep-rooted attachment to its "droits, franchises et libertés". However, at no time, even when they threatened to destroy the city (as did the duke of Mayenne in 1594), did the Catholic princes succeed in subjugating the *échevinage*, largely made up of Leaguers. The *échevins'* stubborn attachment to the city's liberties is best illustrated by their refusal to free the duchess of Longueville until 1592. The duchess, who was the daughter of the duke of Nevers and the wife of the Provincial Governor, could have been exchanged for the young duke of Guise or other leaders of the League being held by the king.[22]

The city's preoccupation with political autonomy affected relations between the *échevinage* and the Sixteen in Paris, which, according to Élie Barnavi, sought bonds of loyalty from other League cities similar to the bonds between patron and client.[23] Undeniably, Amiens' municipality had established and maintained close relations with the leaders of the Paris League, and a formal union had been concluded between the two cities in June 1588 in order to defend their common interests before the king in the meeting of the Estates-General.[24] This solidarity weakened rapidly after the rupture with the king, insofar as each city faced different priorities to ensure its survival.[25] The formal alliance never implied real collaboration between the *échevinage* and the Paris League, even less subjugation by Paris, as was asserted only by royalist historians such as Palma Cayet and Jacques Auguste de Thou.[26]

A client-patron relationship usually exists between people of unequal rank, more so than between political institutions. The question of client-patron relationships among Leaguers arises concerning whether there were any Leaguers

21 Olivia Carpi, *Une république imaginaire. Amiens pendant les troubles de religion* (Paris, 2005), 182–83; 203–06, 224.

22 Ibid., p. 127, 132–34, 171–74; 206–207.

23 Élie Barnavi, 'Centralisation ou fédéralisme? Les relations entre Paris et les villes à l'époque de la Ligue (1585–1594)', *Revue Historique* CCLIX, (1978), 337.

24 BnF, Mss. Fr. 3411, fol. 56, 69–70, 71.

25 Carpi, *Une république imaginaire*, 162–64.

26 Barnavi, 'Centralisation ou fédéralisme?' 339.

among those the royalists called les "espagnolisés", who were considered traitors to the French king and were suspected of being in the service of the king of Spain. Even though Philip II officially went to war with France only on January 17, 1595, he had prior to this date been giving military and financial support to the League for the purpose of defending Catholicism and also in support of his hegemonic ambitions. However, among the Amiens Leaguers (as identified by sources dating to spring 1588), only three could in fact be suspected of links with the Catholic king. Proof of these links is slight and must be inferred from the fact that these three individuals fled to Brussels after Amiens' submission to the king in 1594, where they received financial assistance from the Spanish crown. Only one Amiens Leaguer, the *maieur* of the city, actually served Philip II during the Spanish occupation of 1597 by offering the obedience of Amiens to the Catholic King.[27] In fact, Hispanophilia was less a fact of political allegiance than the fruit of an "integral Catholicism" and of "Christians without State", involving those who were neither satisfied with the temporal laws of the kingdom of France, nor with a strictly Tridentine and Gallican reform of the Church. Thus a handful of these unsatisfied Catholics decided to exile themselves and enter into the service of Philip II as soldiers or spies.[28]

According to royalist sources, in 1588 some Amiens Leaguers were clients of the Guises; for example, Nicolas de Nibat, described as "agent of the affairs of the sieur d'Aumale and *bailli* in his land of Picardy", Antoine de Berny: "seeking servants for the duke of Guise throughout Picardy", and Nicolas Leroy: "warder of the League, usually in touch with the *sieur* de Saveuse".[29] Actually, only Nicolas de Nibat, collector for the *baronnie* de Boves, a few kilometres from Amiens, appears to have been an agent of Aumale.[30] As for those who are normally considered to have been leaders of the Amiens League, like the general lieutenant of the *bailliage* Vincent Leroy and the bishop Geoffroy de La Marthonie, we should not consider them as creatures of the Lorraines simply because the bishop was in contact with the cardinal of Guise, archbishop of Reims, during a provincial synod in 1583, or because both Leroy and La Marthonie met the duke of Guise in Blois as members of the Estates. Certainly, these contacts led to their arrest immediately after the execution of the princes, but they were

27 Carpi, *Une république imaginaire*, 226.

28 Robert Descimon and José Javier Ruiz Ibáñez, *Les ligueurs de l'exil. Le refuge catholique français après 1594* (Seyssel, 2005), 7, 35, 47.

29 BnF, Mss. Fr. 3411, fol. 138v, 139v.

30 Stuart Carroll, 'The Guise Affinity and Popular Protest during the Wars of Religion', *French History* 9, no 2 (1995), 147.

freed, in contrast to other more prominent Leaguers, like La Chapelle-Marteau, head of the municipality of Paris.[31]

Some similar remarks can be made about the nature of the bonds among the Amiens Leaguers of 1588. According to the royalist sources, François Bigant was in debt to the bishop for his brother's benefice of canonry; Le Scellier was a "creature" of Nibat, who managed to have him elected to the office of royal *prévôt* in 1587; Jean Postel was governor of the bishop; and Jacques Normant was a Leaguer because of his brother-in-law Le Scellier. Also, Annette Finley-Croswhite has demonstrated that Nibat was married to a sister of Vincent Leroy, who was the godfather of Bigant's daughter.[32] However, the same sources show that Robert Fournel was a "good servant of the king, even though the majority of his most prominent relatives within the city were great Leaguers", and that Philippe Matissart was also a servant of the king, even while a "mate and great friend" to Bigant.[33] Annette Finley-Croswhite has also remarked that many citizens of Amiens had family bonds with people of the other party, a fact confirmed by Mack P. Holt concerning the Leaguers of Dijon.[34] Therefore we have to recognize that to raise connexions among persons of any kind or nature is not enough to conclude that there was a network forming the basis of a political party.[35]

This analysis of the social dimensions of factionalism in Amiens allows us to correct another interpretation of the urban League as a creature of class antagonism between bourgeois at a lower level, blocked in their ascent, and members of a class concerned with preserving its privileges.[36] On the list of the twenty-four *échevins* elected in 1588, compiled for the king by an informer, twelve are said to be Leaguers, seven royalists, and four plus the *maieur* (the head of the municipal government) considered "variable" (one of the *échevins* had died while serving his office). Of the twelve Leaguers, two were *bourgeois rentiers*, three royal officers, three merchants and four jurists. Moreover, among these twelve Leaguer *échevins*, three had previously been elected *maieurs*, two

31 Ibid., p. 150; Carpi, *Une république imaginaire*, 133.

32 Annette Finley-Croswhite, *Henry IV and the Towns* (Cambridge, 1999), 29–33.

33 BnF, Mss. Fr. 3411, fol. 138–142.

34 Finley-Croswhite, *Henry IV*, 33–37; Mack P. Holt, 'Les réseaux d'autorité et de pouvoir à l'Hôtel de ville et au Parlement de Dijon entre 1580 et 1630', *Annales de Bourgogne* 85, no 1 (2013), 19–35.

35 Robert Descimon, 'Compte-rendu critique de l'ouvrage d'A. Finley-Croswhite', *Annales ESC* 56, no 2 (2001), 545.

36 Holt, 'Les réseaux d'autorité', 20–22; Olivia Carpi, 'Élites citadines et sédition en France à l'époque des troubles de religion', in Philippe Depreux, ed., *Révolte et Statut social de l'Antiquité tardive aux temps modernes* (Münich, 2008), 255–71.

had been royal *prévôts* and eight had already been *échevins*. Only four of them were, in 1588, serving their first mandate as *échevins*. Finally, the most prominent Leaguers received the most votes to become *échevins* in 1588.[37] It is clear that, as in Dijon, Rouen, Angers, Rennes, Nantes, and Troyes, the Leaguers of Amiens were not outsiders, neither from a social nor a political point of view.[38] It was thus not a desire for a place within the city oligarchy, no matter the cost, that stimulated their partisanship. It can be asked whether in fact ideas played a role in uniting these men and inspiring them to take unconventional trajectories in order to triumph.

2 The Force of Convictions

Amiens' royalist party invoked the violence of the Leaguers' politics as a way to deny them the status of "good Christian Catholics, loyal French, jealous of the city's ancient glory, and of its security and that of the rest of its inhabitants".[39] The royalist documentation also relates how, once the news about the Paris barricades was known, the Leaguers had spread a rumour about "their resolution to cut the throats of all those not of their party".[40] Although nothing similar ever happened, the rumour was effective. The two most prominent Amiens royalists, Robert Coureux and Antoine Bernard, both *échevins*, decided to leave the city, a flight which was also motivated by a military display that took place during the night of 15 May 1588. By mobilizing many of the inhabitants, including some of the religious people, the Leaguers were trying to push the *maieur* to adopt policies in favour of their party. In May 1588, the Leaguers were not a majority within the *échevinage*, and the *maieur* was the only person legally authorized to take decisions such as summoning a council of inhabitants or enacting ordinances. Moreover, knowing that decisions concerning the entire community should be taken by consensus, the Leaguer *échevins* sought to obtain it by accusing their opponents of trying "to betray the city and massacre it through policies and Huguenots", thus depriving the opponents of popular

37 BnF, Mss. Fr. 3411, fol. 138–142.

38 Holt, 'Les réseaux d'autorité'; Philippe Benedict, *Rouen during the Wars of Religion* (Cambridge, 1981), 182–83; Robert Harding, 'Revolution and Reform in the Holy League: Angers, Rennes, Nantes', *Journal of Modern History*, no 53 (1981), 379–416; Penny Roberts, *A City in Conflict. Troyes during the French Wars of Religion* (Manchester, 1986), 176.

39 BnF, Mss. Fr. 3411, fol. 109: "bons chrétiens catholiques, fidèles françois, jaloux de l'antique gloire de la ville et de la seureté et repos de leurs cohabitants".

40 Ibid., fol. 65: "leur résolution de copper la gorge à tous ceulx qui n'estoient de leur party".

support. The Leaguers also resorted to intimidation during public debates, by interrupting or hailing the *maieur*, changing the usual order of the speeches, or "yelling loudly 'the church, the church! Nothing, nothing!'" in order to overwhelm those who dared to contradict them.[41]

Although the demonstration of 15 May did not lead to any physical confrontation, the "tumult" and the Leaguers' strategy to "become stronger within the public council" was successful.[42] On 16 May, the *maieur* declared that henceforth the *sieur* d'Estrée, the lieutenant of the Provincial Governor, and his military escort were no more allowed to remain in the city. On 17 May, the inhabitants who "had previously practised the supposedly reformed Religion" were disarmed and expelled from the city guard, and the permission previously granted to the *sieur* de Saisseval (at the service of Épernon) to take seventy-one lances from the city arsenal was revoked. On 19 May after examining a request presented by the king's procurator in the *bailliage*, the fiscal procurator and four city councillors, all of them Leaguers, the *maieur* ordained a meeting for the following day. Two hundred of the most prominent inhabitants of the city, the bishop, deputies of the cathedral chapter canons and parish priests, were asked to solemnly swear the Holy Union oath and "to use their means and lives for the honour and service of God, the conservation of his holy religion catholic, apostolic and roman, the extirpation of the heretics, the service and obedience owed to the most Christian and catholic king, and the conservation of the privileges, franchises and liberties of the inhabitants". This ordinance was ratified by the nineteen *échevins* present (of whom twelve were Leaguers), against three royalists (Coureux and Bernard being absent), and on 20 May, the citizens' assembly took the Union oath. On 24 May, the Union was extended to the inhabitants of Abbeville.

On 10 June, the organisation of the municipal militia was reformed. There were to be twenty-one companies of bourgeois, made up of eight groups of one hundred men, called *portiers*. These companies were commanded by captains elected by their members, if necessary for life. The captains were able to impose fines on any defaulting men in their companies, a sanction that was traditionally within the *maieur*'s sole competence as the head of militia. The majority of these captains were Leaguers, and this way the League assumed military control of the town.

On 13 June, a council was gathered to allow the *échevinage* to describe its grievances to the king, which was also attended by members of the clergy and

41 Ibid., fol. 65, 67, 68, 102, 112, 114: "trahir la ville et la massacrer par les politiques et Huguenots"; "criant à haute voix l'église, l'église, rien, rien".

42 Ibid., fol. 95, 108, 114.

some royal officers. Finally, on July 3, an alliance was concluded with Paris for the purpose of formulating "common complaints and protestations" to the king.[43]

The Leaguers definitively strengthened their position with the municipal election on 28 and 29 October 1588. Only four of those elected, the mayor included, were not Leaguers.[44] These elections occurred in a very tense climate. At many crossroads, "placards directed against the honour of many people" were posted, and various schemes were employed to affect the election outcome. On the election day, although the covered market where the vote took place was heavily guarded, a tumult broke out during the *maieur*'s election. The crowd's yells, "nothing, nothing, continued", obliging the *bailli* to take the special step of extending the term of *maieur* Collemont.[45] In fact, on the election day, the *échevinage* had received a letter from the king asking that they elect a *maieur* of "old and ancient tradition". We also know that Collemont had been ennobled by Henri III on 4 September.[46]

Moreover, an anonymous memoir found in Henri III's papers stated that for the *maieur*'s election it was necessary to control some of the Leaguers and their vote. The memoir also stated that if the "person elected is on the side of the eight or nine stubborn" Leaguers, "there will be no other means to oppose him, if not by tumult and the crowd's cry demanding another one more to its liking". And, the document stated, that if among the three candidates for the *mairie* there were two Leaguers, it would be necessary "to influence the head of the gates and their *comportiers*, so that the ballots bear the names we choose".[47] The Leaguers were thus not the only side using underhanded tactics to gain power.

The records of the *échevinage* debates implicate the royalists in the affair *de la Saint Honoré*. On 17 May 1588, a search of the house of Robert Coureux found

---

43 ACA, BB 48, fol. 130v, 131, 134–139, 142, 150v–153v, 154, 158v, 159, 166, 172, 174, 178 : "qui ont faict cy devant exercice de la Religion Prétendue Réformée"; "emploier leurs moiens et vies pour l'honneur et service de Dieu, conservation de sa saincte religion catholique apostolique et romaine, extirpation des hereticques, pour le service et obéissance deue au roy très chrétien et catholique, pour la conservation des privilèges franchises et libertez des habitants"; "plaintes et remontrances communes".

44 Carpi, *Une république imaginaire*, 131.

45 ACA, BB 49, fol. 22, 29, 30, 33; BnF, Mss. Fr. 3411, fol. 123.

46 Ibid., fol. 30v; BN, Mss. Fr. 3411, fol. 121.

47 BnF, Mss. Fr. 3411, fol. 133–134: "l'élection tombe du costé des huit ou neuf obstinés"; "il n'y aura pas grand moien de s'opposer à celui qu'ils porteront, si ce n'est par un tumulte et cri du peuple qui en demande un autre plus à son gré"; "pratiquer les chefs de portes et leurs comportiers afin que leurs bulletins portent les noms de ceux qu'on aura choisis".

fifteen spears from the *Hôtel de ville*, but the presence of these arms could have been explained by Coureux's office of master of the artillery. During the night of 15 May, Bernard's house was also searched, but nothing more than his personal weapons was found. Nevertheless, Coureux and Bernard were put on trial. Coureux was accused of having asked five members of the crossbowman company to help him in case of sedition. Gaspard Fouache, another *échevin*, was also implicated in the affair, and with Bernard and Coureux, was banned from the traditional municipal banquet of the Assumption. The ban against Gaspard was lifted on 24 May, and on 27 May he resumed his role as *échevin*. Between 28 May and 2 June, four of Coureux's presumed accomplices were released, and on 14 July, Coureux appeared before the *échevinage* and by mutual agreement the affair was set aside.[48]

Even though the city's treatment of the royalists cannot be described as a witch-hunt, the records of the *échevinage* debates characterise the royalists as "factious" and members of a "conspiracy" against the city.[49] Were these accusations only a means for the Leaguer *échevins* to reduce their opponents to political impotence? An in-depth analysis of the sources reveals that the municipal authorities actually believed that the king and his servants were trying to forcibly introduce a garrison into the city. Even though the king denied this intention in two letters (16 and 22 May),[50] treating the accusations as the "fabrications" of his enemies, the city's concerns were not completely groundless. Five Picards noblemen and their *compagnie d'ordonnance* (i.e. a military unit of several hundred men) were deployed in Picardy at the king's request during June, officially in order to "relieve the country from the oppression" it was suffering from military threats.[51] On 27 May, the *échevinage* received letters from the King announcing the arrival of one of those noblemen, the duke of Halluin, supposedly "to visit the city in order to know its condition and exhort everyone to the devotion and affection owed to the king". The *échevins* replied that the duke would not be granted permission to enter the city. On 29 May, a rumour spread that Saisseval, "who was of the party of the duke of Épernon", was trying to enter the city as he had previously tried to do two weeks earlier. In response, measures to reinforce the city's security were taken.[52] Also, Henri III—who knew that the Spaniards, helped by Aumale, wanted to use Picardy's ports for the Invincible Armada—appointed Épernon as governor of Boulogne

48 ACA, BB 48, fol. 131, 141v–142, 143, 145v, 148, 164, 182v; BnF, Mss. Fr. 3411, fol. 68.
49 ACA, BB 48, fol. 135, 137, 138v, 140v, 134v, 139, 141 156v.
50 Ibid., fol. 139v, 140, 168v, 169v, 175v–177, 179v–180.
51 BnF, Mss. Fr. 3411, fol. 73.
52 ACA, BB 48, fol. 142v, 146.

to protect the region. Between 4 and 12 May, Aumale put the city under siege. That the Amiénois were afraid and suspicious of any military presence is not surprising.[53] Undeniably, the propaganda that was spread in the region by the Leaguers about the possibility that Amiens could fall into the hands of Navarre thanks to Épernon, contributed to the fear which pushed Amiens' bourgeois to the same "movement of urban self-defence" which took place in Paris during the Day of the Barricades.[54]

The same thing happened in Grenoble, when on 29 September, 1589 the city refused to recognize Henri IV, fearing that it would be placed under the authority of the duke of Lesdiguières, the leader of the Dauphinois Huguenots. Although the fear of losing "its soul", "its prosperity" and "its privileges" played a decisive role in the shift towards dissent from the king in these town, these were not the only explanation for the religious and political commitment of the Leaguer citizens.[55] For the Amiens' Leaguers this choice exposed them to the king's unhappiness and the animosity of their opponents. The decision of the Amiens Leaguers to risk these consequences was possibly the result of a precise conception (which was profoundly anchored in their spirit) of the city as a unique religious, political and social body.[56]

In their public speeches, the Leaguers presented themselves as being completely devoted to "the religion, the state and the public good", a commitment which was expressed on three levels: the kingdom, the province and the city.[57] In their relations with the king, this devotion was translated into the promise of "obedient fidelity", provided that the king fulfilled his own duties by "uprooting the heretics" and protecting "the true religion", by reforming the government, and especially by "publishing and observing the Council of Trent".

The Parisian leaders of the League pushed Amiens to present joint requests during the Estates-General, so that "begged by all his cities at the same time, His Majesty will listen more gladly". Henri III did not appreciate this initiative,

53 Alain Lottin, ed., *Histoire de Boulogne-sur-Mer* (Villeneuve d'Ascq, 2014), 131–32; ACA, BB 48, fol. 140.

54 ACA, BB 48, fol. 134–135; Nicolas Leroux, *Les guerres de Religion* (Paris, 2009), p. 253; Constant, 'La Ligue vue par les historiens', 145, 147.

55 Stéphane Gal, 'Peurs urbaines et engagements politico-religieux au XVIe siècle: l'exemple de la Ligue grenobloise', *Histoire, Économie et Société*, 20e année, no 1 (2001), 3–21; Benedict, *Rouen during the Wars of Religion*, 178–79.

56 ACA, BB 48, fol. 175v, 178v-180; Robert Descimon, 'Le corps de ville et le système cérémoniel parisien au début de l'âge modern', in Marc Boone and Maarten Prak, ed., *Statuts individuels, statuts corporatifs et statuts judiciaires dans les villes européennes* (Louvain, 1996), 73–128.

57 BnF, Mss. Fr. 3411, fol. 69–70; ACA, BB 48, fol. 135, 137, 152, 158v, 170.

even if the Amiens Leaguers did not pretend, in contrast to the Paris Leaguers, to strive for "the common good of Christendom and the restoration of the State". Amiens' Leaguers simply stated their desire to act "for the good of the country", asking for lower taxation and a reduction in the number of officers. In fact, apart from subscribing to a common League platform, which was far from ever being realized, the Amiens Leaguers were mostly concerned about their city, particularly with safeguarding "its precious and important privileges and liberties". More concretely, the Amiénois expected that the sovereign "would not permit that the strength and government of the city depend from another authority than that of the *maieur*" and that the king would "leave to the inhabitants their customary freedom to elect the *maieur*, the *échevins* and the officers of the city".[58]

On the one hand, the municipal authorities' concern for the common good involved looking after the "repose" and "the peace and tranquillity" of the citizens by taking necessary security measures. On the other hand, the city rulers also needed to find a solution to the "schism, divisions, partialities and differences" in the city, with the (utopian?) hope of establishing a "concord", a true "union" among the citizens, who should "mutually recognize themselves and unite through a holy, perpetual, and indissoluble bond, all speak the same language, and all think and strive together in their common work".[59]

Coercive or extraordinary measures were sometimes used to achieve these objectives. Thus, in May 1588, support of the Union became mandatory, at risk of banishment. Twenty-six years earlier, during the fall of 1562, while the city was riven by confessional fractures and under the threat of a Huguenot coup de main following the insurrection led by the prince of Condé, a "catholic phalanx"—made up of the bishop and some clerics, royal officers, lawyers, merchants and *bourgeois rentiers*—forced the king to replace the *maieur* and the royal *prévôt*, who were suspected of colluding with the Huguenots. Later this group secured the arbitrary nomination of ten new *échevins*, all "good Catholics". The infraction of the municipal constitution was justified by the

58 BnF, Mss. Fr. 3411, fol. 69–70; ACA, BB 48, fol. 134, 135, 137, 140v, 144v, 152, 154, 159–163v, 175v: "suppliée de toutes ses villes en mesme temps, Sa Majesté preste plus volontiers l'oreille"; "bien commun de la chrestienté et à la restauration de l'estat"; "ne permettre que la force et gouvernement d'icelle dépendent d'autre authorité que monsieur le maieur"; "laisser les habitants en leur liberté accoustumée d'élire les maieur eschevins et officiers d'icelle ville".

59 ACA, BB 48, fol. 134, 135, 137, 140v, 144, 150, 154, 134, 176v: "scisme divisions partialitez et différances"; "s'entrecognoissent les uns les aultres se unissent par saincte perpétuelle et indissoluble tresson, parlent tous un mesme langage, pensent et mettent la main à l'œuvre de mesmes les ungs que les autres".

seriousness of the situation and was accompanied by a challenge to the Edict of Toleration (January 1562): Protestant worship was declared illegal in Amiens and in other cities of Picardy. At the same time, a confession of the Catholic faith and an obligation to participate in religious services was imposed on all the inhabitants, on pain of possible banishment.[60]

This aspiration to unity, even if compelled, was not simply the fruit of a mystical exaltation, but was rooted in a civic spirit still very much alive during the "calamitous times" of civil war, a spirit which reminded the municipal authorities of their role as "father of the people", elected by their fellow citizens in order "to anticipate their evil, and procure their salvation".[61] The Leaguers ruling the city were not alone in having this awareness and acting on it. In Amiens, as in Dijon and Rouen, efforts to stabilize and unite the community were continuous, both during and after this critical period. Urban municipalities adopted policies exalting civic identity, pairing it with and completing Catholic confessionalization.[62]

However, even if the Leaguer *échevins* of these cities "resembled very much their royalist counterparts from a social point of view, and in their political ideas and religious commitments as well", a distinction can be observed in their methods of promoting the faith. These "zealots" were less capable of moderation and political compromise than the "Catholic-Navarrais".[63] A sharp divergence in methods of governance also distinguished them from their more conservative colleagues. Under the pressure of urgency or necessity, the Leaguers did not hesitate to "innovate" for the good of the "republic".

---

60 Carpi, *Une république imaginaire*, 77–80 and 'L' « esprit de la Ligue » dans le Nord de la France en 1588', in Véronique Castagnet et al., eds., *Les affrontements religieux en Europe* (Villeneuve-d'Ascq, 2008), 103–116.

61 Ibid., fol. 134, 135, 163v; Claire Dolan, 'Des images en action: cité, pouvoir municipal et crises pendant les guerres de Religion à Aix-en-Provence', in Laurier Turgeon, ed., *Les productions symboliques du pouvoir* (Québec, 1990), 65–86; François-Joseph Ruggiu, 'Pour une étude de l'engagement civique au XVIIIe siècle', *Histoire urbaine*, no 2 (2007), 145–64: "ces temps calamiteux"; "pères du people", "préveoir leur mal, procurer leur salut".

62 Stéphane Gal, 'Entre loyalisme et rébellion: les assemblées générales de la ville de Grenoble (1588–1598)', *Revue d'Histoire Moderne et Contemporaine*, no 49/3 (2002), 7–25; Carpi, 'Des vertus de l'oligarchie: la municipalité amiénoise au XVIe siècle', in Laurent Coste, ed., *Liens de sang, liens de pouvoir* (Rennes, 2010), 189–211; idem, 'Identité civique et sortie de guerre. Le cas d'Amiens au lendemain des guerres de Religion', *Revue du Nord*, Hors-série, no 30, (2014), 249–66 et idem, 'Élites citadines et sortie de guerre civile en France. Les cas des anciennes villes ligueuses', in Laurent Coste and Sylvie Guillaume, eds., *Élites et crises du XVIe au XXIe siècle. Europe et Outre-mer* (Paris, 2014), 363–75.

63 Holt, 'Les réseaux d'autorité', 22; Michel Cassan, 'Laïcs, Ligue et réforme catholique à Limoges', *Histoire, Économie et Société*, 10e année, no 2 (1991), 167.

The reform of the bourgeois militia, necessary because of its dysfunctions and the "eminent danger" weighing upon the city, provoked many reactions. The Leaguers were accused of changing the "ancient order" without the king's approval and of being willing to "keep the whole city subjugated". The Leaguer *échevins* replied that they were not the only ones to use "practices and instigations" with the king or other bourgeois, and that they were not attacking the municipal constitution. They believed that they were acting within the prerogatives allowed by the king and saw as their only goal the "conservation and splendour of the city", a preoccupation that to them legitimised changing traditional practices.[64]

3 Conclusion

We conclude that the events in Amiens during 1588 cannot fully be described as "factional struggles". The concept of "factionalism", not in the disputed anthropological sense of this term, but in the meaning given by Anglo-Saxon political culture, better characterizes Amiens during this period.[65] Indeed, the behaviour of the Amiens Leaguers is not characteristic of an archaic society, in which socially-defined groups organized into alliances and kinships clashed, often violently, in order to acquire or conserve a monopoly over material and symbolic resources. On the contrary, a real modernity may be observed through the activity of a group which was more or less organized, built around a few charismatic people, and whose members shared common convictions. The Leaguers sometimes used unorthodox methods, not simply to provoke change within the ruling elite, but to propose an alternative political program which would at the same time not undermine the entire political structure.

Unlike a minority of radical Parisian Leaguers—who have been considered advocates of a totalitarian policy for the purpose of establishing a new, more egalitarian, order—the provincial Leaguers were not revolutionary, separatist or democratic; even though they withheld obedience from the legitimate

64 Carpi, 'La milice comme instrument de reconstruction identitaire de la communauté citadine à Amiens dans le premier tiers du XVIIe siècle', in Serge Brunet and José Javier Ruiz Ibáñez, eds., *Les milices dans la première modernité* (Rennes, 2015), 21–34 ; ACA, BB 48, fol. 135, 141; BnF, Mss. Fr. 3411, fol. 91–92, 98.

65 James Boissevain, 'Factions, Parties and Politics in a Maltese Village', *American Anthropologist*, no 66/6 (1964), 1275–87; Robert J. Alexander, 'Splinter Groups in American Radical Politics', *Social Research* 20, no 3 (1953), 282–310.

sovereign,[66] they were chiefly moved by a "civic republicanism", which must be understood foremost as a defence of fundamental liberties and adherence to a political ethic combining Augustinianism and Humanism. This was an ethos based on a principle of charity, not only in its Christian meaning, but also aimed (within an oligarchic and unanimous system) at improving the lives of citizens who would have been keenly aware of their rights and obligations.[67]

66 Roland Mousnier, *Les hiérarchies sociales de 1450 à nos jours* (Paris, 1969); Élie Barnavi, *Le Parti de Dieu* (Louvain, 1980).

67 Carpi, 'Henri Drouot et la notion de république : réflexion sur l'expérience politique des villes ligueuses du nord-est de la France', *Annales de Bourgogne*, no 87/4 and 88/1 (2015), 83–100.

The Imperial Court during the Thirty Years War: A Battleground for Factions?[1]

Rubén González Cuerva and Luis Tercero Casado

To some extent, the Thirty Years' War began as a challenge to the authority of the House of Austria. This crisis of power was immediately felt at the imperial court. At the time war broke out, marking the severe economic and political weakness of Ferdinand II (1619–1637), his three main allies, the duke of Bavaria, the Spanish king and the pope, held very influential positions at the Viennese court. The contemporary Protestant propaganda and traditional German historiography since Schiller have blamed the emperor for is incapacity to carry out a national policy. The argument of the propaganda and the historiography has been that Ferdinand II was controlled by foreign interests, working as a pawn of the great plans of Catholic imposition and Spanish hegemony. In this view, nuncios and especially Spanish ambassadors bribed the ministers of Ferdinand II and Ferdinand III (1637–1657) as a means to control imperial policy-making. It is true that the Viennese high courtiers who had crucial roles as chief advisers maintained fluid contacts with other Catholic courts. Notwithstanding this, however, the real mechanics of decision-making were more complex. In addition to the constraints imposed by foreign policy, these courtiers acted from other more powerful familial, spiritual, and regional constraints. Consequently, while operating under the general label of a Catholic or Spanish faction, they built dynamic groupings whose nature and means of self-preservation will be analysed here.

1 Myth and Debate on a Spanish Faction

The Thirty Years' War presented a substantial challenge to the authority and legitimacy of three consecutive emperors: Matthias (1612–1619), Ferdinand II (1619–1637) and Ferdinand III (1637–1657). Their Protestant opponents were

1 Abbreviations: Add. Mss. (Additional Manuscripts), AGS (Archivo General de Simancas), AHN (Archivo Histórico Nacional), ASFi (Archivio di Stato di Firenze), Barb. Lat. (Barberiniani Latini), BAV (Biblioteca Apostolica Vaticana), BL (British Library), E (Estado), MP (Mediceo del Principato), SN (Sección Nobleza). This research has been made possible by the MCA FP7-MC-IEF 328536.

 | DOI 10.1163/9789004345348_010

not integrated into the court system and therefore did not constitute a dissenting court faction. For this reason, and in contrast to the situation of the French Wars of Religion, the imperial court remained a comparatively peaceful island in a fiercely divided world. However, the outbreak of war brought an intolerant response from the court: the relatively tolerant atmosphere around Matthias rapidly vanished after the Defenestration of Prague (23 May 1618), and Cardinal Klesl, Matthias's powerful favourite and an advocate for a peaceful agreement to resolve the Bohemian crisis, summarily fell from grace on 20 July 1618 and was imprisoned. This decisive action was the result of a consensual intrigue between the future Ferdinand II, his favourite Hans Ulrich von Eggenberg, Archduke Maximilian, and the Spanish ambassador, the count of Oñate.[2] By showing initiative in this way, Ferdinand II exposed the decadence of senile Matthias's regime, and delivered a clear message: only committed Catholics were acceptable in his entourage and there was no room for any explicit challenge to the new dynastic-confessional turn.

Ferdinand II's court has traditionally been depicted as a tool for furthering Spanish and papal forces which were attempting to impose an imperialist and radical Catholic agenda, even despite the slow emergence of a German alternative which favoured a policy of supporting and encouraging pacts. According to Friedrich Schiller's influential *History of the Thirty Years War* (1792), the Spanish branch of the Habsburgs was able to keep the Austrian family dependent, and to some extent to dictate their policy goals owing to its military strength and American gold. According to this view, Emperor Rudolf II's policy was inspired by the Jesuits and the Spaniards, and Matthias was carefully watched by Spain and Rome. The view of Ferdinand II was even worse, who was described as the Spaniards' and Rome's "slave". Therefore, it follows that if Ferdinand III paved the way for the Peace of Westphalia it was in part due to his weak attachment to these influences. According to Schiller, Spanish ambassadors acted as "incendiaries and assassins" and hoped to determine the chief decisions of imperial policy. However, according to Schiller's interpretation, the Spaniards did not influence matters through the funding of a courtier party, but rather by improperly influencing individual ministers. Schiller did not attribute any significance to the debates among imperial ministers; rather, they were seen as a disorganised group eager to be bribed, at least by Wallenstein or the Spaniards.[3]

---

2 Rubén González Cuerva, *Baltasar de Zúñiga. Una encrucijada de la Monarquía hispana (1561–1622)* (Madrid, 2012), 392.

3 Friedrich Schiller, *Geschichte des dreissigjährigen Kriegs* (Frankfurt, 1792), 90, 111, 395.

The first consistent identification of factions in the imperial court in German historiography appears after 1848. Eduard Vehse's forty-eight-volume *History of the German Courts Since the Reformation* described the entourage of Ferdinand II as the arena of two contending forces: the German Party represented by the emperor's favourite Eggenberg and generalissimo Wallenstein versus the Italian Party of military men and courtiers allied with the Spaniards and the Jesuits.[4]

In addition, in the second half of the nineteenth century the authoritative versions of Venetian reports and nunciature correspondence from their representatives in Vienna were published. These sources recorded the events in detail, in contrast to the sparse contemporary German documents, and reinforced the evidence for the existence of factions in the imperial court. Both the Venetian and papal representatives in Vienna spoke of the existence of a powerful "Spanish Party".[5] This label of a Spanish Party was popularised in the 1960s by Marxist historians such as Polisensky and Trevor-Roper, who depicted it as an imperialist, counter-reformative and aristocratic reaction to the Protestant-capitalist path to modernity. This image still pervades a good amount of current literature, especially in the Anglophone world.[6]

As may be imagined, the reality was far more complex. First, the Italian sources that are available merit further criticism because of their hostile bias towards the dynastic entente between both branches of the Habsburgs, which Venetian and papal representatives regarded as menacing. These representatives explained their relative isolation at the Viennese court as a consequence of the organised opposition of leading courtiers against them. In addition, the

---

4 Carl Eduard Vehse, *Geschichte der deutschen Höfe seit der Reformation*, Section 2: *Geschichte des österreichischen Hofs und Adels und der österreichischen Diplomatie* (Hamburg, 1852), vol. III, 30–34, 120, 264–65 and vol. IV, 13–16, 42.

5 Nuncio Carafa, 'Relatione della Corte Imperiale', 1621, BAV, Barb. Lat., 6929, fols. 86v-87r; Nuncio Rocci to Cardinal Francesco Barberini, Vienna, 19 April 1631, in Rotraud Becker, ed., *Nuntiaturen des Giovanni Battista Pallotto und des Ciriaco Rocci (1630–1631)*, Nuntiaturberichte aus Deutschland IV/4 (Tübingen, 2009), 462; 'Relatione di S. Renier Zen Cav. Pro. [et] S. Anzolo Contarini Cav. ritornati ambasciadori estraordinari all'Imperatore', Venice, 18 February 1637, in Joseph Fiedler, ed., *Die Relationen der Botschafter Venedigs über Deutschland und Österreich im siebzehnten Jahrhundert* (Wien, 1866), vol. I, 197–98.

6 Robert J.W. Evans, *Rudolf II and His World. A Study in Intellectual History 1576–1612* (Oxford, 1973), 50–51, 69–72; Peter H. Wilson, *The Thirty Years War: Europe's Tragedy*, (Cambridge MA, 2009), 126–27; Joseph F. Patrouch, *Queen's Apprentice. Archduchess Elizabeth, Empress Maria, the Habsburgs, and the Holy Roman Empire, 1554–1569* (Leiden, 2010), 23, 33; Sally Metzler, *Bartholomeus Spranger: Splendor and Eroticism in Imperial Prague* (New York, 2014), 153; Robert Bireley, *Ferdinand II, Counter-Reformation Emperor, 1578–1637* (Cambridge, 2014), 224–25, 292.

Italian observers were members of a political culture that tended to see divergences of opinion as evidence of contending and organised factions. At the papal court of Rome, the conflict between Guelphs and Ghibellines evolved throughout the sixteenth century, as did the opposition between the families Orsini and Colonna and, at a European level, between the French and the Spaniards. To declare oneself "Spagnolo" in Rome or Venice had a local, factional, meaning and carried implications of international alliances. Italian diplomats translated these national categories to the Austrian courtiers without further reflection.[7]

The picture that emerges from Spanish sources is coloured very differently. Iberian statesmen did not acknowledge having organised a court party and, in contrast with their omnipotent reputation as described by other observers, they lamented the difficulties they faced in getting their proposals heard. They especially complained about the fact that, although many courtiers declared themselves to be servants of the Spanish king, their actions did not bear this out.[8] Regardless of whether they exaggerated their difficulties or whether it was a case of their expectations being exceedingly high, the Spaniards did not think that the imperial court was divided into national influences but rather into clienteles of powerful ministers. The accounts of Spanish statesmen held that after the fall of Cardinal Klesl in July 1618, two contending bands of ministers dominated the court, one led by Leonhard Helfried von Meggau and the other by Johann Eusebius Khuen.[9] This alleged arrangement did not last long because Matthias died soon thereafter (March 1619), and then Ferdinand II's favourite, Eggenberg, struggled to gain control over the court with the support of Spanish ambassador Oñate.[10] Eggenberg was regarded as Ferdinand II's most influential adviser, and he succeeded in maintaining the court's balance

7 For the evolution from the Ghibelline to the Spanish faction in Rome, see Alessandro Serio, '*Nationes* hispanas y facción española en Roma durante la primera Edad Moderna', in Carlos J. Hernando, ed., *Roma y España un crisol de la cultura europea en la Edad Moderna* (Madrid, 2007), 241–48; Miles Pattenden, 'Rome as a "Spanish Avignon"?' in Piers Baker-Bates and Miles Pattenden, eds., *The Spanish Presence in Sixteenth-Century Italy: Images of Iberia* (Aldershot, 2015), 65–84. In Venice, the influential adviser Paolo Sarpi forged this vision of a global entente of *papalini* and *spagnoli* at the beginning of the seventeenth century. Webster G. Tarpley, *Paolo Sarpi, his networks, Venice and the coming of the Thirty Years' War*, unpublished PhD thesis (Washington DC, 2009), 1–4, 16, 51–54, 192–94, 203.

8 Count of Castañeda to Philip IV, Vienna, 22 October 1633, AGS, E, 2414, no. 112.

9 Meggau and Khuen were 'cabezas de dos facciones q. aora goviernan la corte' ['the heads of two factions which are currently governing the court']. Count of Oñate to Philip III, Vienna, 24 September 1618, AHN, E, 1638, s. fol.

10 According to the imperial ambassador in Madrid, Khevenhüller, Eggenberg had formed a league ('bando') with the counsellors Preiner and Harrach against Khuen. The Spanish

of power until the beginning of the 1630s. By 1630, according to the Spanish representatives, the most important future threat to Spanish interests was a group led by the baron Christoph Simon von Thun, the former tutor and High Steward of Ferdinand II's heir, the future Ferdinand III.[11] At the same time, from Madrid, Philip IV and his favourite, the count-duke of Olivares, distinguished Viennese courtiers as being "Austrians" (loyal servants of the emperor and the dynasty) or "Imperials", who were described as autonomous, mistrustful, and close to the duke of Bavaria.[12] This is the only example of a nationally based picture of the imperial court from Spanish sources. This unusual viewpoint from the Spanish can be explained by the context of radical polarisation caused by the exigencies of war.

Having surveyed the available sources, scholars have long discussed how best to categorize the networks present at the imperial court during the War as well as their relative political power. According to the classical view of Jean Bérenger, it was only after 1648 that there were two contending parties with different political priorities: the Spanish party and the German (or Bavarian) party. Until then, according to Bérenger, the imperial court was composed only by the powerful clienteles of favourites linked with a member of the dynasty: Eggenberg with Ferdinand II and Trauttmansdorff with Ferdinand III. Ivo Cerman has rightly criticised this approach because it overstates the ability of foreign policy choices to reveal divisions within the court.[13] Following an actor-centred perspective, it can be shown that clashes of national interests were not at the centre of court discussions, and that several layers of affinities and groupings coexisted in addition to national identity. As a result of this fact, courtiers were able to switch roles and allegiances.[14] While it is true that the parties did not exist in a pure and continuous form, and that the image of two

ambassador in Vienna, Oñate, was also supporting them. Count of Benavente to Philip III, Madrid, 17 July 1619, AGS, E, 2504, fols. 130–31.

11 Quintín Aldea Vaquero, *España y Europa en el siglo XVII. Correspondencia de Saavedra Fajardo* (Madrid, 1986), vol. II, XXVII–XXIX, LXX–LXXII.

12 Philip IV to the duke of Guastalla, Madrid, 15 September 1631, in Heinrich Günter, *Die Habsburger-Liga 1625–1635. Briefe und Akten aus dem General-Archiv zu Simancas* (Berlin, 1908), 304.

13 Jean Bérenger, 'La Cour impériale de Léopold Ier: partis, clans et clientèles', in Klaus Malettke and Chantal Grell, eds., *Hofgesellschaft und Höflinge an europäischen Fürstenhöfen in der Frühen Neuzeit (15.–18. Jh.)* (Münster, 2001), 262–66; Ivo Cerman, '"Kabal", "Parthey", "Faction" am Hofe Kaiser Leopolds I', in Werner Paravicini and Jan Hirschbiegel, eds., *Der Fall des Günstlings. Hofparteien in Europa vom 13. bis zum 17. Jahrhundert* (Ostfildern, 2004), 235–47.

14 Hillard von Thiessen, 'Switching Roles in Negotiation: Levels of Diplomatic Communication between Pope Paul V Borghese (1605–1621) and the Ambassadors of Philip III', in

defined blocks is oversimplified, an understanding of the more nuanced patterns discussed below also rules out a conclusion that the court was simply a chaotic vortex.[15]

2 The Labyrinths of the Imperial Court: Structures of Access among Elites and Households

2.1 *Ferdinand II (1619–1637)*

Contrary to Hubert Ehalt's attempts to fit the seventeenth-century Viennese court into the scheme of a Versailles-style absolutist court, current research tends to analyse the Viennese court primarily as a space of communication in which processes of negotiation and cooperation were more important than the simple imposition of the ruler's will.[16] It is acknowledged that, at least until the eighteenth century, the imperial court represented only half of the Austrian and Habsburg system of power. In contrast with the progressive concentration of power in the courts of Paris and Madrid, in Vienna a diarchy of emperor and regional Estates (*Kaiser und Stände*) persisted.[17] However, after his victory in the Battle of White Mountain in 1620, Ferdinand II's power dramatically increased, and the imperial court became the key decision-making centre in Central Europe for managing the Thirty Years' War and for confessional initiatives. In addition, the confiscation of rebel nobles' properties permitted Ferdinand II to reward his allies. As a result, after 1620 the imperial court became more attractive to elites and a new radical Catholic court aristocracy began to consolidate.[18]

Stefano Andretta et al., eds., *Paroles de négociateurs: l'entretien dans la pratique diplomatique de la fin du Moyen Âge à la fin du XIXe siècle* (Rome, 2010), 151–72.

15 Jeroen Duindam, *Vienna and Versailles: the Courts of Europe's dynastic Rivals, 1550–1780* (Cambridge, 2003), 248–58. The mixture of political and confessional visions, private interests and foreign interferences as factors in imperial decision-making were identified in Pekka Suvanto, *Wallenstein und seine Anhänger am Wiener Hof zur Zeit des zweiten Generalats 1631–1634* (Helsinki, 1963), 21.

16 Hubert Christian Ehalt, *Ausdrucksformen absolutistischer Herrschaft: der Wiener Hof im 17. und 18. Jahrhundert* (München, 1980); Mark Hengerer, *Kaiserhof und Adel in der Mitte des 17. Jahrhunderts. Eine Kommunikationsgeschichte der Macht in der Vormoderne* (Konstanz, 2004).

17 Petr Mat'a and Thomas Winkelbauer, eds., *Die Habsburgermonarchie 1620 bis 1740. Leistungen und Grenzen des Absolutismusparadigmas* (Stuttgart, 2006).

18 Ehalt, *Ausdrucksformen absolutistischer Herrschaft*, 30–31; Mark Hengerer, 'Court and Communication: Integrating the Nobility at the Imperial Court (1620–65)', *The Court Historian* 5 (2000), 223–29.

In court society, the politics of access were crucial in enabling communications, inasmuch as only those who were able to access the emperor could hope to influence his decisions and gain his favour.[19] Access was quite relevant generally in the context of the imperial court, which followed the rigid Burgundian ceremonial rules, and even more relevant to Ferdinand II, whose cautious character led him to rely heavily on the advice of his counsellors, and whose moral scruples made his confessors and clergymen extremely influential.[20]

The Viennese ceremonial model was to a large extent established under the rule of Ferdinand I in the second third of the sixteenth century.[21] Court observers have noted that beginning in this period, four chief officials of the emperor's household enjoyed a significant ability to access and influence him. These officials were the High Steward (*Oberstshofmeister*), the Lord Chamberlain (*Oberstkämmerer*), the Master of the Horse (*Oberststallmeister*), and the Court Marshall (*Oberstmarschall*). At a lower echelon, the chamberlains were also influential.[22] The main body advising the emperor in State decision-making was the Privy Council (*Geheime Rat*). The High Steward was the legal director of this council, and its members were the four top officials of the imperial household, the chancellor of Bohemia, the imperial vice-chancellor, and those individuals specifically invited by the emperor. During most of Ferdinand II's rule, the director of the Privy Council was not, as customary, his High Steward but rather his Lord Chamberlain and undisputed favourite, the Prince of Eggenberg. This grouping of servants and ministers held the key to influencing the emperor's decisions and priorities.[23] Within this more or less public circle, the imperial confessor and preachers were among the most influential individuals

19 Carl Schmitt, *Gespräch über die Macht und den Zugang zum Machthaber* (Pfullingen, 1954), 15–16; Dries Raeymaekers, *One Foot in the Palace. The Habsburg Court of Brussels and the Politics of Access in the Reign of Albert and Isabella, 1598–1621* (Leuven, 2013), 193–230.

20 Nuncio Carafa, 'Relatione della Corte Imperiale', 1621, BAV, Barb. Lat., 6929, fols. 80r-81v; Ronald Asch, 'The Princely Court and Political Space in Early Modern Europe', in Beat Kümin, ed., *Political Space in Pre-industrial Europe* (Aldershot, 2013), 44.

21 Jakob Wührer, 'Ein teilausgebautes Haus ohne Fundament? Zum Forschungsstand des frühneuzeitlichen Wiener Hofes am Beispiel der Organisationsgeschichte', *Mitteilungen des Instituts für Österreichische Geschichtsforschung* 117 (2009), 23–50.

22 Heinz Noflatscher, 'Regiment aus der Kammer? Einflußreiche Kleingruppen am Hof Rudolfs II', in Paravicini and Hirschbiegel, *Der Fall des Günstlings*, 209–34.

23 Henry Frederick Schwarz, *The Imperial Privy Council in the 17th Century* (Cambridge, Mass., 1943), 85; Mark Hengerer, '*Ab omnibus amatus et aestimatus*: kaiserliche Günstlinge und ihre Gräber im 17. Jahrhundert', in Arne Karsten, ed., *Das Grabmal des Günstlings* (Berlin, 2011), 140–48.

in the emperor's household. Ferdinand II was assisted by Jesuit confessors, as was the tradition in the Styrian branch of the House of Austria: Martin Becan until 1624 and then William Lamormaini, a prominent unofficial figure and at times a rival of Eggenberg for the role of leading adviser.[24] Lastly, representatives of the most important foreign powers, in particular the pope's nuncios and representatives of the king of Spain and the Republic of Venice, also had a place in the order of courtiers. They were entitled to attend the imperial chapel, and while there they enjoyed privileged moments for communicating with the imperial courtiers.[25]

Beyond his household, the familial entourage of the emperor occupied a central political space—the empress and the archdukes enjoyed special rights of access and domestic situations in which they could interact with Ferdinand II. In a dynastic-courtier order, the households of the emperor's relatives were the only legitimate power bases which were mostly beyond his control. Their household structures allowed the empress and the archdukes to become alternative court patrons. During the decade of the 1630s there were three important households.

The first important household was that of Empress Eleonora Gonzaga (I) (1598–1655), who became the second wife of Ferdinand II in 1622. She did not play an active role in policy-making except concerning issues related to her native Duchy of Mantua, especially during the harsh War of the Mantuan Succession (1628–1631), when she allied with the imperial confessor Lamormaini against the interventionist line of the Spanish faction.[26] The second household was that of Ferdinand II's eldest son, the future Emperor Ferdinand III, who became king of Hungary in 1625. Many dynastic servants who were not part of the clientele of Ferdinand II's favourite, Eggenberg, found space in the entourage of Ferdinand III, including Thun and Trauttmansdorff. Finally, the household of Ferdinand III's wife, the Spanish *infanta* Maria Anna of Austria, was constituted in 1631. Maria Anna's intention to become a court patron was fairly obvious. Her brother, the Spanish King Philip IV, instructed her to become "my greatest ambassadress" in Vienna, notwithstanding his counsellors' scruples.

24 Robert Bireley, *The Jesuits and the Thirty Years War: Kings, Courts, and Confessors* (Cambridge, 2003), 37–41, 56–62, 82–114.

25 Martin Scheutz, '... *hinter Ihrer Käyserlichen Majestät der Päbstliche Nuncius, Königl. Spanischer und Venetianischer Abgesandter*. Fronleichnamsprozessionen im frühneuzeitlichen Wien', in Richard Bösel et al., eds., *Kaiserhof—Papsthof (16.–18. Jahrhundert)* (Wien, 2006), 173–205.

26 Marquis of Aytona to Philip IV, Vienna, 23 August 1628, BL, Add. Mss. 28474, fols. 68r–72v; Consultation of the Council of State, Madrid, 16 July 1629, AGS, E, 2329, no. 63, fol. 6r.

Moreover, she was given large sums of Spanish money to increase her power and to make her more visible in the Viennese court.[27]

2.2 *Ferdinand III (1637–1648)*

Ferdinand II's efforts to bind the nobility to the court soon began to bear fruit and entered its consolidation phase during his son's rule. The Viennese nobility's multi-ethnic character and growing numbers presented particular challenges that increasingly prompted emperors to use Burgundian protocol as a key instrument of courtly order. The ceremonial dimension undoubtedly demonstrated the particular relevance of courtly culture at the Viennese court.[28] Within this framework, access to the monarch, governed by ceremonial guidelines, took on unprecedented importance during Ferdinand III's reign.[29]

From his rise to the throne in 1637, Ferdinand III sought to stress these regulations and thereby put his personal stamp on his government. In this context, the imperial Privy Council was called upon to play a special role. Only those individuals summoned by the sovereign could have the prerogative of attending his deliberations. Because of this, it was hardly surprising how easily the emperor's trusted *Obersthofmeister* Maximilian von Trauttmansdorff increased his power in Ferdinand III's court. With his appointment as Head of the Privy Council in 1639, the influential minister saw his position of High Steward, which under Ferdinand II had been stripped of its rightful function in the Privy Council, regain its former status.[30]

Höbelt has recently stressed the observation of his contemporaries that the emperor intended to rule with a certain "Spanish" style.[31] Although it is true that Trauttmansdorff's possession of both the highest courtly rank and the presidency of the main decision-making organ provided him with durable levers of authority, his scope of action was far more limited than that of Olivares or Cardinal Richelieu. His authority was based on personal chemistry with the monarch and preserved by his own intuition as to what might constitute an abuse of his advisory powers. In fact, a key factor that distinguished

27 Instructions of Philip IV for his sister Maria Anna, 1630, in Aldea Vaquero, *España y Europa en el siglo XVII*, vol. I, 316–17; Andrea Sommer-Mathis, 'Ein *pícaro* und spanisches Theater am Wiener Hof zur Zeit des Dreißigjährigen Krieges', in Andreas Weigl, ed., *Wien im Dreißigjährigen Krieg: Bevölkerung, Gesellschaft, Kultur, Konfession* (Köln, 2001), 651–91.

28 John H. Elliott, 'Europa después de la paz de Westfalia', *Pedralbes* 19 (1999), 131–46 (here 141).

29 Duindam, *Vienna and Versailles*, 199; Hengerer, *Kaiserhof*, 281ff.

30 The importance of the office of High Steward declined after Eggenberg's death. Schwarz, *The Imperial Privy Council*, 133.

31 Lothar Höbelt, *Ferdinand III. Friedenskaiser wider Willen* (Graz, 2008), 112.

Trauttmansdorff's exercise of power from most of his predecessors was his use of patronage mechanisms devoid of direct personal benefit to him. This presented a deliberate mirroring of the monarchs' practices: just as the emperors sought to reward the loyalty of highly ranked courtiers in order to strengthen their own authority, Trauttmansdorff intended to reproduce this behaviour as the dispenser of favours within his clientele networks in order to consolidate kinship or friendship bonds.[32] Within the courtly "labyrinth" of access to the monarch, the minister knew very well how to take advantage of available filtering tools.

As was the case with Ferdinand II, the diverse households that coexisted parallel to Ferdinand III's imperial court boasted prerogatives of access. These key structures gained special momentum during the 1640s. In particular, until her death in 1646 Empress Maria Anna was actively involved in imperial politics as the emperor's informal adviser. She was a strong focus of influence and patronage for pro-Spanish clients in Vienna. This ascendancy increasingly eclipsed the influence of her husband's stepmother, Empress Dowager Eleonora (I). But this did not mean that Eleonora was bereft of close contacts at court. From a very early stage, she had shown an inclination towards the emperor's brother, Archduke Leopold Wilhelm. Their affinity was now reinforced by a conscious realization that they had become "second fiddles" to the imperial couple.[33] Both continued to exert considerable influence at court by attracting an important clientele that, given their common sponsorship interests, established an overwhelming presence in Vienna, particularly in relation to Italian culture. Nevertheless, Eleonora saw her political influence as a courtly broker seriously decline after Ferdinand II's death.[34] This was not the case for Leopold Wilhelm. The archduke gathered around him those who were disaffected with Trauttmansdorff and provided them with an alternative broker. Indeed, the archduke's clique would have much to say during and after Leopold I's election as "King of the Romans" in 1658.[35]

---

32 Brigitte Lernet, *Maximilian von Trauttmansdorff: Hofmann und Patron im 17. Jahrhundert*, unpublished PhD thesis (Vienna, 2004), 138–62.

33 Renate Schreiber, *'ein galeria nach meinem humor'. Erzherzog Leopold Wilhelm* (Vienna, 2004), 20.

34 Sommer-Mathis, 'Ein *pícaro*'; Renate Schreiber, '"Gnedigster Herr und vilgeliebter Herr Brueder…". Private Briefe von Erzherzog Leopold Wilhelm an und über Kaiser Ferdinand III.', *Frühneuzeit-Info* 18/1 (2007), 39–43; Mark Hengerer, *Kaiser Ferdinand III. (1608–1657): eine Biographie* (Vienna, 2012), 128.

35 Höbelt, *Ferdinand III.*, 154; Luis Tercero Casado, 'A Fluctuating Ascendancy: The "Spanish Party" at the Imperial Court of Vienna (1631–1659)', in Rubén González Cuerva and

3 Ferdinand II (1619–1637): The Emperor and the Alternative Patrons

The arrival of Maria Anna symbolised both the reinforced alliance between Ferdinand II and Philip IV and the renaissance of Spanish patronage in Vienna. The emperor was the main, although not the only, patron and dispenser of privileges. Even though decision-making was in the hands of Ferdinand II, the pope, the Spanish king, the duke of Bavaria, and generalissimo Wallenstein were capable of influencing court dynamics and decisions and were more or less beyond his control. The Spanish king, as master of the Order of the Golden Fleece, could induct Ferdinand II's courtiers into the Order as knights at will. The status of these individuals inducted into the Order was automatically enhanced in imperial court ceremonies, and they held the unique privilege of being equals of the emperor, who was also a knight of the Order.[36]

Despite the ephemeral nature of court factions, Spanish patronage had been a long-term factor in imperial politics since the division of the House of Austria into two branches in 1556. Successive emperors tolerated it, sometimes reluctantly, as an inevitable consequence of their weaker powers of patronage. Moments of open mistrust were rare: they mainly occurred between 1598 and 1611, as Rudolf II became more paranoid and increasingly determined to expel the Spanish clients in his entourage as being allegedly unreliable advisers. Despite these efforts, Rudolf II's inconstant and negligent character permitted Spanish ambassadors to further infiltrate the imperial household, and the court regulations of 1611 were in part intended to lessen the uncontrolled powers of Spanish patronage. Normally, the dynamic was more cooperative: emperors asked many favours from the Spanish king, not for themselves but in order to reward imperial servants. These favours consisted not only of traditional pensions and other payments, but also social capital. The Spanish king was able to spend more than the emperor on gratifying individuals with knighthoods, Italian titles, and Golden Fleeces. For Viennese court society, which was undergoing a process of consolidation, the favour of the Spanish king offered the legitimating stamp of traditional Catholic aristocracy.[37]

Valentina Caldari, eds., *The Secret Mechanisms of Courts: Factions in Early Modern Europe*, Librosdelacorte.es, Monográfico 2, Año 7 (2015), 39–53.

36 Pere Molas i Ribalta, 'Austria en la orden del Toisón de Oro, siglos XVI–XVII', *Pedralbes* 26 (2006), 123–52; Pavel Marek, *La embajada española en la corte imperial (1558–1641). Figuras de los embajadores y estrategias clientelares* (Praga, 2013), 175–83.

37 Thomas Fellner and Heinrich Kretschmayr, *Die österreichische Zentralverwaltung*, vol. I/2 (Vienna, 1907), 371–75; Karin J. MacHardy, *War, Religion and Court Patronage in Habsburg*

The enormous challenge of the Thirty Years' War meant that in the decade of the 1620s, Spanish patronage in Vienna reached its peak both in terms of expenditures and of a deliberate royal strategy to secure the king's interests in the Empire. However, the Spanish hope of attracting every single relevant actor in the imperial court through the payment of pensions was impracticable. Spanish ambassadors complained bitterly about their lack of financial resources because unrewarded courtiers often felt dishonoured and might become potential enemies. The ambassadors pleaded to be allowed the more feasible strategy of rewarding individual services in lieu of guaranteeing payments for life.[38]

The most important change in Spanish management of the court was the arrival of *infanta* Maria Anna of Austria as the bride of the future King Ferdinand III in 1631. In contrast to the diplomats, Maria Anna could act not only as a broker but also as a legitimate patron. In addition, she was able to create—and gain access to—additional levels of courtly political communications. Maria Anna was expected to sway her husband Ferdinand III to the Spanish positions and to at least obtain the neutrality of Empress Eleonora.[39] Until the arrival of Maria Anna, the main channel of communication with and influence over the emperor was provided by his favourite, Eggenberg, who was also the chief interlocutor with the imperial ambassador in Madrid, Franz Christoph von Khevenhüller. Reliance on Eggenberg was nearly absolute, but he was an elderly and tired man by this time and Spanish ministers wanted to prepare for his departure by guaranteeing a new imperial favourite who would favour Spanish interests.[40] The Spanish ministers did not wish to support a faction within the court, but rather to multiply interlocutors and channels of communication. Philip IV preferred that the opponents of his policy should be persuaded, not defeated, but between 1629 and 1631 his ambassadors worked unsuccessfully to win the support of Empress Eleonora, imperial confessor Lamormaini, Trauttmansdorff and Thun. Philip IV desired a consensual Viennese court under his aegis, but he did not succeed.[41] As for the pope, he did not attempt to replicate such a complex and costly patronage. Until the

---

Austria: The Social and Cultural Dimensions of Political Interaction, 1521–1622 (Houndmills, 2003), 4–7, 15–18, 125–33, 151–64.

38 Marquis of Aytona to Philip IV, Vienna, 6 September 1624, BL, Add. Mss. 28473, fol. 79v; Marek, *La embajada española*, 130–140, 164–168.

39 Aldea Vaquero, *España y Europa en el siglo XVII*, vol. II, XX.

40 Philip IV to the Count of Monterrey, Madrid, 6 September 1632, AGS, E, 2458, no. 151, in Günter, *Die Habsburger-Liga 1625–1635*, 341–42.

41 Consultation of the Council of State, Madrid, 7 September 1631, AGS, E, 2332, no. 66.

reign of Ferdinand II, the militant Catholic agenda had not been fulfilled at the imperial court despite the frequent cooperation and shared goals of Spanish and papal agents. Because of this cooperation, belief in the existence of a solid Catholic party and a close alliance between the papacy and the Spanish Monarchy became commonplace in the Empire. Notwithstanding, their roads began to separate irrevocably after 1621 due to disagreements over the Palatinate question and the anti-Habsburg policy of Pope Urban VIII. After that, the nuncios protested that the promises Ferdinand II had made to them in private audiences were subsequently not implemented because the ministers of the Privy Council were clients of the Spanish king and had consequently denied their support.[42]

The weapons of the Holy See for gaining a share in imperial decision-making did not consist of an extensive network of ministers but rather of a few efficient clergymen. The nuncios played the card of appealing to Ferdinand II's moral scruples to convince him, among other delicate issues, to award Frederick V of the Palatinate's electoral title to the duke of Bavaria.[43] Their instruments were friars who were highly esteemed by Ferdinand II, such as the Capuchin Jacinto da Casale and the Carmelite Domingo de Jesús María, as well as the emperor's Jesuit confessors, Becan and Lamormaini. The latter acquired so much influence over Ferdinand II that he became increasingly autonomous from and deaf to the nuncio Carafa's strategies.[44] The clergymen had to maintain a delicate balance: they presented their admonitions as disinterested and pious, while the ministers considered only their material implications. At the same time, the clergymen were always at risk of invading a political sphere beyond their duties, and Ferdinand II at times rejected their messages as intrusive.[45]

---

42 Nuncio Carafa to Cardinal Ludovisi, Vienna, 14, 21, and 28 August 1621, BAV, Barb. lat., 6946, fols. 13–16. In general, see Irene Fosi and Alexander Koller, eds., *Papato e Impero nel pontificato di Urbano VIII (1623–1644)* (Città del Vaticano, 2013).

43 The Calvinist Frederick V, Elector Palatine, led the Bohemian rebellion against Ferdinand II in 1619. After Frederick V was defeated at the Battle of White Mountain (November 1620), he was deprived of all his titles, including the privilege of being among the seven imperial princes who elected the emperor. The electoral title was awarded to the loyal Catholic Maximilian I of Bavaria in 1623. Brennan C. Pursell, *The Winter King: Frederick V of the Palatinate and the Coming of the Thirty Years' War* (Aldershot, 2003), 185–87.

44 For Giacinto da Casale, see Nuncio Carafa to Cardinal Ludovisi, Vienna, 4 September 1621, BAV, Barb. lat., 6946, fols. 20–2. For Domingo de Jesús María, see Silvano Giordano, *Domenico di Gesù Maria, Ruzola (1559–1630): un carmelitano scalzo tra politica e riforma nella chiesa posttridentina* (Roma, 1991), 187–91.

45 Niccolò Sacchetti to Andrea Cioli, Vienna, 30 August 1631, ASFi, MP, 4385, s. fol.; Robert Bireley, *Religion and Politics in the Age of the Counterreformation: Emperor Ferdinand II,*

In addition to the two great powers of the Catholic world, Duke Maximilian of Bavaria (1597–1651) played a very important role in the policy of Ferdinand II, as leader of the Catholic League and as Ferdinand's greatest ally within the Empire, at least in the first decade of the Thirty Years' War. In contrast to the pope and the king of Spain, Maximilian of Bavaria had a long-standing direct relationship with his cousin Ferdinand II. They had shared childhood experiences and met personally several times during their adulthood: the nuncio believed that Maximilian I was the only person capable of convincing Ferdinand II to take important decisions.[46] In contrast with the prominence of Maximilian I's direct contacts and his frank correspondence with the emperor, his permanent agent in the court at Vienna, Johann Stückl, occupied a weak ceremonial position. Bavaria did not follow the Spanish model of a powerful fixed representation because Maximilian I preferred to maintain fluid contacts at court through special emissaries. Among them were the aforementioned friars Jacinto da Casale and Domingo de Jesús María.[47] Maximilian I enjoyed two assets for the successful advancement of his interests at the imperial court: nearly unconditional papal support, as Bavaria had become the Holy See's chief ally beyond the Alps, and the alignment of his interests with a few imperial ministers, including Zollern, Meggau and Trauttmansdorff.[48] Trauttmansdorff was the second most prestigious member of the Privy Council after Eggenberg, but the imperial favourite did not allow him to expand his political influence. Trauttmansdorff responded with an attempt to build his own political space by refusing Spanish patronage and approaching the duke of Bavaria as an alternative protector.[49] The close alliance between Ferdinand II and Maximilian I was desirable for Spanish representatives as long as Bavaria did not stray from Spanish objectives. In the event of conflict, the ministers of Philip IV were certain they would be opposed by a Bavarian party. It is true that Emperor Maximilian II (1564–1576) employed ministers linked to Albert

William Lamormaini, S.J., and the Formation of Imperial Policy (Chapel Hill, NC, 1981), 178–81.

46 Bireley, *Ferdinand II*, 11–13, 109–11, 151–56, 224.

47 For the Bavarian agents, see Istvan Hiller, 'Gli Ambasciatori della Cappella. Riflessioni sulla perdita del potere', *Nova Corvina* 11 (2003), 8–14. For the friars, Nuncio Carafa to Cardinal Ludovisi, Regensburg, 14 December 1622, BAV, Barb. lat., 6946, fol. 161.

48 For the papal support of Bavaria, see Nuncio Rocci to Cardinal Francesco Barberini, Regensburg, 9 September 1630, in Becker, *Nuntiaturen des Giovanni Battista Pallotto*, 271–274. On the ties of Zollern and Meggau to Maximilian I, see Niccolò Sacchetti to Andrea Cioli, Vienna, 8 March 1631, ASFi, MP, 4385, s. fol.

49 Count of Castro to Philip IV, Vienna, 4 April and 1 August 1629, AGS, E, 2329, no. 171 and 142.

V of Bavaria to counterbalance Spanish influence and to ease the alliance with Munich.[50] Continuing fear of a Bavarian connection endured in the Spanish ministers, but it does not appear that an extensive Bavarian network of patronage existed during the reign of Ferdinand II.

The last court patron to be mentioned is the polemical Albrecht von Wallenstein, generalissimo of the imperial army. Offering his services to Ferdinand II as *condottiero*, Wallenstein rose dramatically to power, becoming a prince of the Empire and one of the richest men in Central Europe before his assassination in 1634. Suvanto and Lutz among others have extensively analysed how Wallenstein built his network of partisans at the imperial court. He was a part of Eggenberg's extended family relations thanks to both men marrying into the Harrach family. In addition, Wallenstein was surrounded by military men he had promoted (such as Collalto) and was backed by the Spanish king.[51]

Wallenstein held the dubious honour of being the most divisive figure at the imperial court. In the eyes of many, his tremendous military successes were counterbalanced by his ambition and ruthless methods. Supporting or opposing Wallenstein was the main polarising factor at the court between 1626 and 1634 and this polarisation tested the solidity and durability of existing clienteles and factions. Because Wallenstein possessed the economic capital needed to reward his courtier supporters, his enemies continually accused him of bribing imperial ministers to advance his position.[52]

A micropolitical approach shows the weak explanatory power of simple labels when analysing the issues surrounding Wallenstein. For example, the "Spaniards", which are often thought of as a unified entity, have traditionally been characterized as the fiercest opponents of Wallenstein and the chief instigators of his murder. In reality, there was no such united Spanish strategy: in Madrid King Philip IV and his favourite Olivares consistently supported Wallenstein as an associate of Eggenberg even in the explosive final phase of 1633–1634. In that moment, the clash between Wallenstein and the future Ferdinand III for control of the imperial army reached a peak, and there was

---

50 Maximilian Lanzinner, 'Geheime Räte und Berater Kaiser Maximilians II (1564–1576)', *Mitteilungen des Instituts für österreichische Geschichtsforschung* 102 (1994), 298, 301, 309–11.

51 Suvanto, *Wallenstein und seine Anhänger am Wiener Hof*, 24–32; Georg Lutz, 'Wallenstein, Ferdinand II. und der Wiener Hof', *Quellen und Forschungen aus italienischen Archiven und Bibliotheken* 48 (1968), 207–43.

52 Schiller, *Geschichte des dreissigjährigen Kriegs*, 145. The boundaries between patronage and corruption tended to be unclear: in this case, Wallenstein's extreme wealth, unconcealed use of his money and dubious role as generalissimo favoured the accusations of an illegitimate use of patronage.

a serious risk of escalating factional struggles through the collision of two divided armies, one led by Ferdinand III and the other by Wallenstein. Philip IV did not hesitate to take the side of Wallenstein against his own brother-in-law Ferdinand III. In Vienna, the triumphant Spanish group around Diego de Quiroga, confessor of Maria Anna of Austria, pursued an alliance with Wallenstein, while the Spanish ambassadors Oñate and Castañeda and their allies opposed him. Oñate was ultimately accused of taking part in the conspiracy against Wallenstein. At the same time the murder was being carried out, Philip IV was debating whether or not to reward Wallenstein by giving him the important Italian city of Bari. Such radical contrasts between the positions of the different Spanish representatives was not exceptional but somehow encouraged: blowing hot and cold broadened the scope of Spanish diplomacy and its ability to negotiate with the disparate actors of court society.[53]

4 Ferdinand III (1637–1648): The *Kaiserhof* as an Arena of Factions?

Few personalities in Habsburg court history have generated such highly polarised views as Trauttmansdorff. Ferdinand III's first councillor was often branded by contemporaries and historians as a member of the Spanish faction.[54] The opposite view has also been asserted,[55] with some historians going so far as to define him as the co-leader of the "pro-Bavarian" party.[56] According to Spanish sources, Philip IV's ministers never acknowledged that he supported the king's

53 Consultation of the Council of State, Madrid, 24 December 1630, AGS, E, 2331, no. 112; Aldea Vaquero, *España y Europa en el siglo XVII*, vol. II, LXX–LXIII; vol. III/2, 508–510; Suvanto, *Wallenstein und seine Anhänger am Wiener Hof*, 357.

54 Observation of the papal nuncio in 1639, cited in Hengerer, *Kaiser Ferdinand III.*, 424 (n. 57); Höbelt, *Ferdinand III.*, 117–118; Pavel Marek, 'La diplomacia española y la papal en la Corte Imperial de Fernando II', *Studia Historica* 30 (2008), 109–44.

55 The Venetian ambassador in Madrid went so far as to state that Trauttmansdorff held 'avversione alla casa di Spagna ed alla nazion spagnuola.' ['aversion to the House of Spain and to the Spanish Nation.'] 'Relazione di Spagna di Girolamo Giustinian, ambasciatore a Filippo IV dall'anno 1643 al 1649', in Nicolò Barozzi and Guglielmo Berchet, eds., *Relazioni degli stati europei lette al Senato dagli ambasciatori veneti nel secolo decimosettimo, Serie I, 'Spagna,'* II (Venice, 1860), 182; José Alcalá-Zamora y Queipo de Llano, 'La Monarquía Hispánica y Westfalia', in Bernardo García García, ed., *350 años de la Paz de Westfalia. 1648–1998. Del antagonismo a la integración en Europa* (Madrid, 1999), 21–32 (here 29).

56 Mecenseffy, *Im Dienste dreier Habsburger. Leben und Wirken des Fürsten Johann Weikhard Auersperg (1615–1677)* (Vienna, 1938), 364.

interests; on the contrary, he was seen by these ministers as "anti-Spanish".[57] These contradictory and overly simplistic conceptions certainly need to be refuted. In fact, Trauttmansdorff was a figure who was "above" factions, a canny prime minister who avoided showing a special affinity for any particular group.[58] Because he had a strong rapport with the emperor, who placed full confidence in him, he did not need to align himself with any particular court party. As long as the Spanish-imperial military alliance produced good results, he guaranteed Spanish ascendancy at court. But after the imperial defeat of 1645 in the fields of Jankov, Trauttmansdorff was pragmatic enough to go against his master's preferences so as to ensure the emperor's survival and pave the way to the peace—even at the cost of separation from Spain. He also behaved judiciously with regards to Bavarian politics. Trauttmansdorff attempted to maintain a balance in imperial relations with both veiled rivals and was neither a "Spaniard" nor a "Bavarian". His chief aim was his master's dynastic policy—and the safeguarding of his throne.

If the Austrian Habsburgs continued to pay heed to the Spanish court's designs, it was certainly due to the emperor's own desire to enhance relations with Philip IV. He even appeared to some as the "head" of the Spanish faction.[59] Long before assuming the *Reichskrone* in 1637, Ferdinand III had decided to step out of his father's shadow by exerting his own Spanish-oriented policy. Thus, the assumption that his rise brought about a substantial reduction of Spanish ascendancy at the imperial court can only be rejected. Even less sustainable is the theory that the emperor intended to "neutralise" the faction's influence.[60] Rather than constituting an "anti-Spanish" move, the changes within the Privy Council responded to the sovereign's own method of ruling; that is, with Trauttmansdorff exerting control over most State affairs.

As has been shown, a central role within the new courtly structure was granted to Maria Anna, but also to her confessor, Diego de Quiroga, both of whom had a *carte blanche* to access the emperor. As a recognized interlocutor of Spanish interests at the imperial court, Quiroga's status as an influential clergyman gave him an authority that earned him control of the Spanish

57 John H. Elliott, *El conde duque de Olivares. El político en una época de decadencia* (Barcelona, 2004), 597–98.

58 This characterization of Trauttmansdorff has also been adopted by Duindam, *Vienna and Versailles*, 243, and Thea Lindquist, *The Politics of Diplomacy: The Palatinate and Anglo-Imperial Relations in the Thirty Years' War*, unpublished PhD thesis (Madison, 2001), 72.

59 Hengerer, *Kaiser Ferdinand III.*, 101.

60 Lernet, *Maximilian von Trauttmansdorff*, 69–71.

embassy's affairs,[61] which made him more powerful than Philip IV's envoys.[62] Quiroga's far-reaching scope of action was further reinforced by the empress's influential Spanish retinue and his collaboration with the Spanish ambassadors and their officials.[63] Maria Anna's case was different. Her position as a dynastic member granted her influence far above that of mere network members, as she was motivated by family solidarity rather than a clientele relationship. Her importance and the confessor's extensive experience in diplomatic missions made them a formidable combination, and as a team they exerted influence in favour of a stronger link between the two lines of the House of Austria.[64]

The political crisis that arose from the Imperial-French peace negotiations in 1645 put an end to the almost trouble-free dominance of the Spanish faction.[65] This moment became a turning point that brought the emperor to a more serious position at the negotiating table of Westphalia. A year later, the premature death of Maria Anna came as a harsh blow to both courts. This misfortune eroded Spanish influence at the imperial court in the long-term, not least due to the departure from Vienna of her influential entourage. In addition, the long-lasting conflict between the Spanish Monarchy and France was leaving the embassy coffers devoid of financial resources to grease the patronage network's machinery or to bribe recalcitrant councillors. This shortage of financial means, indeed, undermined the effective functioning of measures taken to exert Spanish pressure.[66]

Beginning in 1646 the Spanish ambassador was the duke of Terranova, whose erratic performance set him against the majority of the court while harming Spanish interests.[67] In the absence of fruitful diplomatic means, the most successful instruments for shoring up relations between Madrid and Vienna during this period originated from the empress's clique. Before her death in 1646, Maria Anna, counting on the secret connivance of her brother, had

61 This took place during the interim period following the dismissal of ambassador Marquis of Cadereyta. Hildegard Ernst, *Madrid und Wien 1632–1637. Politik und Finanzen in den Beziehungen zwischen Philipp IV. und Ferdinand II.* (Münster, 1991), 281.

62 Bireley, *Religion and Politics*, 161.

63 Marek, *La embajada española*, 134–35.

64 Ernst, *Madrid und Wien*, ch. 2, and Hengerer, *Kaiser Ferdinand III*. 91–92, 130–31.

65 Grete Mecenseffy, *Habsburger im 17. Jahrhundert. die Beziehungen der Höfe von Wien und Madrid während des Dreißigjährigen Krieges* (Vienna, 1955), 85.

66 Count of Lumiares to Count of Peñaranda, Vienna, n.d. (around October 1648), AHN-SN, Frías, C.54, D.1, fols. 277–281; Ibidem, 6 January 1649, AHN-SN, Frías, C.56, D.1, fols. 754–62.

67 Count of Lumiares to Count of Peñaranda, Vienna, 10 June 1648, AHN-SN, Frías, C.50, D.2, fols. 50–56; Ibidem, 23 September 1648, AHN-SN, Frías, C.49, D.1, fols. 37–40.

taken the initiative of supporting not only Crown Prince Baltasar Carlos's marriage with her daughter Mariana,[68] but also a second marriage between her son Ferdinand (IV) and *infanta* Maria Theresa. Baltasar Carlos's unexpected death in 1646 put a sudden end to this plan. While the death of the prince did not pose an obstacle to proceeding with a marriage alliance, this time between Philip IV and his niece Mariana, the completion of this union represented only a hopeless illusion of an alleged dynastic renaissance—as Westphalia would later demonstrate. In addition, Quiroga's return to Spain in 1648 not only left the king's interests bereft of its main driver but revealed a decline in Spanish power at court—in favour of Bavarian interests, or more accurately, Bavarian pressure.

During the last phase of the war, the duke of Bavaria did not need to support or deploy a proper network of influence in Vienna. His most effective weapon for achieving his goals remained military blackmail; i.e., the threat of withholding military support from the emperor. In any case, the appointment in 1637 of Count Ferdinand Siegmund Kurz—brother of elector Maximilian's *Oberhofmeister*—as imperial vice-chancellor (*Reichsvizekanzler*) decisively reinforced the pro-Bavarian party within the imperial court. In 1640 Kurz was also chosen to attend meetings of the Privy Council, where he could count on Trauttmansdorff's support. The Spaniards were very wary about Kurz's influence, not only upon imperial matters, but also concerning issues related to the Austrian Hereditary Lands. Although it might have been an exaggeration to brand him the obvious "head" of Bavarian support in Vienna,[69] diplomats saw him as such. Indeed, an unambiguous implication cannot be denied, considering his performance during the years just before and after the Peace of Westphalia.[70] In reality, Kurz advocated a continued understanding with Maximilian as long as it did not put the emperor's own goals at risk. On that basis, Kurz provided support to the Spanish cause whenever the circumstances required it.

In 1645, the defeat at Jankov forced Maximilian to increase his pressure upon the emperor. The most effective tool he had was not the pro-Bavarian network but rather the aforementioned strategy of depriving the emperor of any military assistance if he did not enter into negotiations with France. Kurz also played his part by urging the emperor to demand that Spain waive its

68 Mecenseffy, *Habsburger im 17. Jahrhundert*, 79–80, and Idem, 'Philipp IV. von Spanien und seine Heirat mit Maria Anna von Österreich', in *Historische Studien. A.F. Pribram zum 70. Geburtstag dargebracht* (Vienna, 1929), 41–70 (here 48).

69 Schwarz, *The Imperial Privy Council*, 261.

70 Consultation of the Council of State, Madrid, 28 May 1648, AGS, E, 2352.

rights over French-occupied Alsace.[71] From that moment onwards, the Spanish faction came under increasing pressure. When the Swedes crossed the border of Bohemia in 1647, this pressure became unbearable. The elector seized the chance to negotiate peace with more vigour,[72] and managed to channel the discontent of the imperial states into forcing Vienna to yield before France and Sweden. Bavarian pressure thus led directly to the exchange of signatures in Münster and Osnabrück.

5 Conclusions

In conclusion, we can assert that the power dynamics at the imperial court cannot be summarised either as a bilateral factional opposition or as a chaotic vortex. Viennese court society was composed of several layers of clienteles and loyalties whose consistency was tested at critical decisional crossroads. The available sources clearly document the alignments of courtiers and their lobbying strategies used to influence decision-making. Thus, in addition to the internal logic of households and councils, "alternative patronage"; i.e., protection by more than one ruler, was an extremely important dynamic.

In the case of the Spanish king, his *protégées* constituted a heterogeneous collection of individuals rather than a like-minded group. In the reign of Ferdinand II, this "Spanish faction" was more visible thanks to its relationship with the clientele of the imperial favourite Eggenberg. He was labelled the head of a Spanish faction, but he received neither a pension nor a title apart from Knight of the Golden Fleece—he simply used his privileged access to Spanish patronage to reward his own clients.[73] A double game was established in which both sides used the other. Concerning Spanish influence, the natural successor of Eggenberg during Ferdinand III's rule was not a minister but the Spanish empress Maria Anna. From the perspective of the factions, Empress Maria Anna possessed an undeniable and timely magnetism as both patron and broker due to her obvious importance for the emperor. Her authority to access the monarch was far above the other courtly households, but these also played a meaningful role in the assignment and distribution of influence at the imperial court, and, more importantly, as a breeding ground for clienteles. Due to her lofty role, Maria Anna was, like Trauttmansdorff, above factional struggle. Trauttmansdorff's

71 Hengerer, *Kaiser Ferdinand III.*, 236.

72 Karsten Ruppert, *Die kaiserliche Politik auf dem Westfälischen Friedenskongreß (1643–1648)* (Münster, 1979), 314.

73 Nuncio Carafa, 'Relatione della Corte Imperiale', 1621, BAV, Barb. Lat., 6929, fol. 85.

ambiguous political stance was misunderstood and confused contemporaries and historians alike. In reality, he had a remarkable ability to stand above factions. Instead, he favoured maintaining a balance between Spanish and Bavarian influences at the imperial court—the most significant ascendancies during Ferdinand III's rule.

The automatic assumption that these evident political ascendancies existed as organised factions has proved to be unclear and problematic. In an Aristotelian conception of order in which polities were envisaged as bodies, factions meant an undesired tumour. The Spanish king was powerful enough to factionalise the Viennese court but too weak to treat it as a protectorate, and the need to reward courtiers was proof of a relative defeat for Philip IV, as well as being a severe economic blow. The Spanish king fought to keep under his vigilance the different routes of direct communication with both Ferdinand II and Ferdinand III. Empress Maria Anna played a crucial role of mediation, but dynastic solidarity was not enough to control the two emperors in light of the more immediate constraints of war.

By contrast, neither the pope during the 1620s nor the duke of Bavaria during the 1640s needed to build a strong network of patronage in Vienna to further their interests. Popes Gregory XV and Urban VIII resorted to spiritual threats to gain the allegiance of pious Ferdinand II to their position. For his part, Maximilian I of Bavaria preferred more direct means: an intimidating strategy aimed at separating the emperor from his natural ally, Spain, subjecting him to Cardinal Mazarin's terms. The emperors clearly understood that their immediate and pressing interests were not dynastic ententes but German consensus. Ferdinand III's stance, resulting in his separate peace at Westphalia in 1648, entailed a transformation of the factional struggle at the imperial court. Without the constraints of the Thirty Years' War, the dichotomy between "Spanish" and "Bavarian" factions ceased to be the dominant reality, leaving the way open for other courtly showdowns to evolve out of the succession to the throne of Ferdinand III.

Divide and Rule? Rival Factions and Prussian State Management in Eighteenth-Century Neuchâtel

Nadir Weber

In November 1707, King Frederick I of Prussia formally took over possession of the Principality of Neuchâtel. The event came as a shock to the French crown. For more than two hundred years, the small territory located between France and the Swiss Confederacy had been ruled by *princes du sang* of the house of Orléans-Longueville. Strong political and commercial bonds between Neuchâtel and the French monarchy had been established during this period. Not at all inclined to accept the decision of the local estates of Neuchâtel to recognize the Prussian claims of succession as legitimate in the middle of the War of the Spanish Succession, Louis XIV immediately declared the borders closed to all commercial traffic, and sent the *maréchal* de Villars to Franche-Comté to prepare an invasion of the Principality. However, the snowy mountains separating France from Neuchâtel and the troops that had been deployed by the Protestant Republic of Bern to secure its allied territory made these plans too risky. In spring 1708, a neutrality agreement was negotiated, and in the treaty of Utrecht of 1713, the French king formally accepted the Prussian succession.[1]

This might have been the end of the story of Neuchâtel's transition from French to Prussian rule. But as was true so often in the *ancien régime*, the situation was not as simple as the legal mandates and treaties would suggest. In fact, Frederick I of Prussia had already discreetly entered the political scene in Neuchâtel years before the death of the previous French sovereign, the duchesse de Nemours, and despite the Principality's formal status after 1707, members of the French court nobility as well as French representatives in Switzerland maintained contacts with clients in the Principality. As in other comparable cases such as the Swiss cantons, the Roman nobility, or the courts of medium-sized powers, "factions", "parties", "cliques" and "cabals", as these

1 For the events, see Adrian Bachmann, *Die preussische Sukzession in Neuchâtel. Ein ständisches Verfahren um die Landesherrschaft im Spannungsfeld zwischen Recht und Utilitarismus (1694–1715)* (Zürich, 1993), esp. 388–436. I use the following abbreviations for archival sources: AAE (Archives des Affaires Étrangères, Paris-La Courneuve); AdSM (Archives départementales de Seine-et-Marne, Dammarie-les-Lys); AEN (Archives de l'État de Neuchâtel, Neuchâtel); AN (Archives Nationales, site de Paris); GStAPK (Geheimes Staatsarchiv Preussischer Kulturbesitz, Berlin-Dahlem). I would like to thank Samuel Weber (Bern) for comments that greatly improved the manuscript.

 | DOI 10.1163/9789004345348_011

networks were mostly referred to by their enemies, blurred clear distinctions between domestic and foreign relations.[2] They at least temporarily split social groupings such as court nobilities and local elites, and linked various actors of different status and origin through personal ties and common goals. As this article will argue, the political and economic history of the Principality of Neuchâtel in the eighteenth century was decisively shaped by the fact that alternatives to Prussian patronage and rule continued to exist and had beneficiaries and supporters within the local elite.[3]

By analysing factional networks instead of proposing a dichotomous opposition between central court and local estates, this case study aims at contributing to the reconstruction of the heterogeneous and fragile, but also flexible and cooperative, character of the eighteenth century Prussian

2 Several works of (primarily German-language) historiography have recently studied the effects of trans-territorial ties of patronage and protection on both diplomacy and internal power structures, following, especially, the pioneering works of Wolfgang Reinhard. For the Roman case, where the main European powers competed for influence over the elections of the Pope, see the paradigmatic case study of Hillard von Thiessen, *Diplomatie und Patronage. Die spanisch-römischen Beziehungen im Pontifikat Pauls V. Borghese 1605–1621 in akteurszentrierter Perspektive* (Epfendorf, 2010). For the Swiss cantons, where the many relationships with foreign powers heavily influenced the compositions of the local elites, see Andreas Affolter, *Verhandeln mit Republiken. Die französisch-eidgenössischen Beziehungen im frühen 18. Jahrhundert* (Köln, Weimar, Wien, 2017). For the influence of personal trans-territorial networks on the foreign relations of mid-sized German courts, see Tilman Haug, *Ungleiche Aussenbeziehungen und grenzüberschreitende Patronage. Die französische Krone und die geistlichen Kurfürsten (1648–1679)* (Köln, Weimar, Wien, 2015), and Sébastien Schick, *Des liaisons avantageuses. Action des ministres, liens de dépendance et diplomatie anglaise dans le Saint-Empire romain germanique (années 1720–1750)* (PhD thesis, Université Paris I Panthéon-Sorbonne, Ludwigs-Maximilians Universität München, 2015, in preparation for publication). At large courts, the action of factions was mainly focussed on the patronage (offices, titles, pensions) of the sovereign. On the structure and language of factionalism at the French court—besides the "classical" studies of Roger Mettam and Emmanuel Le Roy Ladurie and the overviews by Jeroen Duindam—see esp. Leonhard Horowski, *Die Belagerung des Thrones. Machtstrukturen und Karrieremechanismen am Hof von Frankreich 1661–1789* (Ostfildern, 2012). On the language of factionalism at the emperor's court, see Ivo Cerman, *"'Kabal", "Parthey", "Faction" am Hofe Kaiser Leopolds I.'*, Jan Hirschbiegel, Werner Paravincini, eds., *Der Fall des Günstlings. Hofparteien in Europa vom 13. bis zum 17. Jahrhundert* (Ostfildern, 2004), 235–47.

3 This article is largely based on my study of the role of the Principality of Neuchâtel within the context of the eighteenth-century Prussian monarchy and its foreign relations. See Nadir Weber, *Lokale Interessen und grosse Strategie. Das Fürstentum Neuchâtel und die politischen Beziehungen der Könige von Preussen (1707–1806)* (Köln, Weimar, Wien, 2015).

monarchy, an interpretation that has recently begun to replace the traditional view of a centralized, absolutist military state.[4] While the effects of factionalism have been described with respect to the very top of the central government and portions of the royal armies, systematic studies on informal networks at the Prussian court and comparative approaches to the crown's handling of factions within territories of the composite monarchy still appear to be rare.[5] With the goal of avoiding overhasty generalizations on the basis of a specific case, this article will suggest that analysis of the trans-territorial networks of local elites may be a promising key to understanding the functioning of state management within a system characterized by territorial fragmentation.[6]

As a first step, we will see that factionalism, both in the Principality and at the French court, played a decisive role in the process of decision-making of the local estates in 1707 and in the formation of a French faction in the first years of Prussian rule. In the second part, the factional struggles in Neuchâtel in the period 1723–1727 will be analysed in more detail. We will see that these struggles seemed to offer a chance to strengthen royal authority at first, but soon spun out of Berlin's control. In the third part, we will inquire into the continuity, long-term goals and evolving influence of the French faction in Neuchâtel in the following decades. I will argue that despite the fact that the Principality remained under Prussian rule until 1806, the continuing presence of local magistrates with strong ties to France significantly influenced the balance of power between subjects and ruler, as well as shaping foreign relations.

---

4 For the new perspective, see esp. the comprehensive handbook of Karin Friedrich, *Brandenburg-Prussia, 1466–1806. The Rise of a Composite State* (Basingstoke, 2012), and the articles in Bernd Sösemann, Gregor Vogt-Spira, eds., *Friedrich der Grosse in Europa. Geschichte einer wechselvollen Beziehung*, 2 vols. (Stuttgart, 2012).

5 For the approach to factionalism at the highest levels of the monarchy, see, e.g., Brendan Simms, *The Impact of Napoleon. Prussian High Politics, Foreign Policy and the Crisis of the Executive, 1797–1806* (Cambridge, 1997); for factionalism's effect on the army: Benjamin Marschke, *Absolutely Pietist. Patronage, Factionalism, and State-Building in the Early Eighteenth-Century Prussian Army Chaplaincy* (Tübingen, 2005); for the court: Frank Göse, 'Der "unpolitische Hof"? Zum Verhältnis von Hof und Zentralbehörden in friderizianischer Zeit', *Friederisiko. Friedrich der Grosse. Die Essays* (München, 2012), 87–97.

6 The expression "state management" is inspired by a view that sees early modern rule as "a form of business" which consisted of an exchange of political, social and economic resources between the crown and local power elites. See Robert Descimon, 'Power Elites and the Prince: The State as Enterprise', Wolfgang Reinhard, ed., *Power Elites and State Building* (Oxford, 1996), 101–21, 110.

1 Parties and Decision-Making: Factionalism and the Prussian Succession

The succession in Neuchâtel had been a contested issue long before the Princess Marie d'Orléans, duchesse de Nemours, died on 16 June 1707.[7] After the death of Henri II d'Orléans, duc de Longueville, who ruled over Neuchâtel from 1618 to 1663, the Principality had gradually entered a period of political instability. When the last member of the dynasty, the abbé Jean-Louis d'Orléans, who had lived in a cloister due to a mental handicap, died in 1694, François-Louis de Bourbon, prince de Conti, and Marie d'Orléans, duchesse de Nemours, both claimed their rights of succession. Because the territory was considered a *principauté souveraine*, independent from imperial or French jurisdiction, it was the *Trois-États* (a sort of representative body of the Principality composed of delegates from the local nobility, the bourgeoisie of the city of Neuchâtel, and officeholders of the Principality) which was in charge of the decision over the succession. Having considered the memoirs and genealogies of the pretenders, the *Trois-États* finally declared Marie de Nemours *princesse souveraine*, but the succession was contested by the losing party. After having been declared the legitimate heir of the abbé d'Orléans by the *parlement* of Paris—an institution whose jurisdiction had been objected to by his opponent—the prince de Conti, backed by French diplomacy, travelled to Neuchâtel in 1699 to take possession of the territory. However, local resistance proved to be stronger than expected, especially because it was supported by the Republic of Bern, which, as the most ancient and powerful Swiss ally of the Principality's corporations, aimed at restricting the influence of the expansionist monarchy of Louis XIV.[8]

7 For a description of the following events, see Bachmann, *Die preussische Sukzession in Neuchâtel*, 14–46.

8 The Republic of Bern, which covered almost a third of the ancient Swiss Confederacy, had continuously renewed its alliances (*traités de combourgeoisie* or *Burgrechtsvertsäge*) with the sovereigns and local corporations of the Principality since the fifteenth century. Besides military support, the alliances also implied arbitration rights in case of disputes between the sovereigns of Neuchâtel and their subjects, which guaranteed the Republic's strong influence on matters relating to the Principality. In the seventeenth century, the alliances often served the subjects of the Principality by counterbalancing the influence of their French (and Catholic) princes. In the eighteenth century, however, the Republic tended to support the Prussian rule, which brought many strategic advantages, including a direct alliance with a major Protestant power (and its patronage resources) and a continuing strong influence in Neuchâtel due to the distant sovereign's dependence on their military support. For Bernese-Prussian relations in the eighteenth century, see the detailed study of Rudolf Witschi, *Friedrich der Grosse und Bern* (Bern, 1926). For Neuchâtel's relationship to the Swiss cantons

Thus, the prince was called back to the French court and the project ended in failure. Marie d'Orléans, even if disgraced by the Sun King because of her resistance to the royal will in this affair, remained the sovereign of Neuchâtel until her death in 1707.

Disputes over the succession among members of the French high nobility led to the formation of factions within the Principality's local elite. After her investiture in 1694, the duchesse de Nemours discharged supporters of the prince de Conti from their offices and replaced them with her own followers. Important figures such as Georges de Montmollin or Daniel de Pury fell into disgrace, which was extended to their sons who were also excluded from offices. Others, most importantly members of the Chambrier family, were rewarded with key positions in the *Conseil d'État*, the local government of the Principality, and were called the "*princes de sang de Neuchâtel*" by the princess in a mélange of irony and flattery.[9] Meanwhile, the "*Contistes*", as they were called, remained in contact with the pretender and mobilized family members, friends, and clients to support a regime change. In response, the "*Nemouristes*" assembled their networks to demonstrate the loyalty of the subjects to their sovereign when, in 1699, the prince made a renewed attempt to secure power. Later, however, when it became clear that the prince, who was 40 years younger than the childless duchesse de Nemours, appeared to have a stronger legal and political basis for a looming succession battle, the *Nemouristes* and others who could not expect to be rewarded should Conti be successful, were forced to look for alternative pretenders. The Protestant German elector Frederick of Brandenburg

(among which the cantons of Lucerne, Solothurn and Fribourg were allied to Neuchâtel, but remained absent in the first decades of Prussian rule), see Léon Montandon et al., *Neuchâtel et la Suisse* (Neuchâtel, 1969).

9 This information can be found in a later memoir, which, like the other unpublished writings in the same volume, describes the composition of Neuchâtel's elite at the time of the Prussian Succession in detail. See François-Louis de Pesmes, Seigneur de Saint-Saphorin, *Mémoires sur la Souveraineté de Neufchâtel et de Valangin* [1708] (GStAPK, 1. HA, Rep. 64, IV. Neufchâtel, 1. Generalia, I, Convol. XXIX), p. 17. The *Conseil d'État* of Neuchâtel was composed of about ten (under French rule) or over twenty (under Prussian rule) *conseillers d'État*, all of whom were members of the local patriciate and in most cases occupied additional jurisdictional or administrative offices in the Principality. The *conseillers* were formally nominated by the prince and assisted his or her direct representative, the governor, in ruling the Principality. De facto, no political decision could be implemented without the approval and support of the majority of the *Conseil d'État*, which therefore formed a sort of local government. For the history of this institution, see the detailed study of Rémy Scheurer, Louis-Edouard Roulet, and Jean Courvoisier, *Histoire du Conseil d'Etat neuchâtelois. Des origines à 1945* (Neuchâtel, 1987).

gained more and more popularity among that group, especially after his coronation as king of Prussia in 1701. Thus, a "Prussian" party, supported by diplomats of the powers who were allied in coalition against Louis XIV and by some influential Bernese magistrates, and with considerable financial backing from Berlin, began to take shape.

When in the summer of 1707 the process of succession got underway, the supporters of the Prussian king were still in the minority. In addition to the prince de Conti, other prominent members of the French court nobility including the comte de Matignon, the duchesse de Lesdiguières (represented by the duc de Villeroy), the marquise de Mailly, and Louise-Léontine de Bourbon-Soissons, who had been the favourite of the late princess, claimed their rights of succession and gained supporters within the Principality. Together they would have constituted a clear "French" majority within the *Conseil d'État* and within the *Conseil de ville* de Neuchâtel, which sent four of the twelve judges to the *Trois-États*.[10] Still, as the French agent François Bouret warned the crown in a memoir dated 5 August 1707, if the French faction did not settle on one candidate either by agreement or by order of the king, the Prussian party would win.[11] Things were further complicated by the fact that Bouret himself was suspected by the other pretenders of defending the prince de Conti's interests. Louis XIV remained neutral, while the influences of his rival ministers, Torcy and Chamillart, neutralized each another.[12] After the most promising candidate, Conti, left the Principality under protest in early September, and despite the pretenders' assertions to serve only the king and the state, the situation turned even more sour for the French cause: increasing numbers of local partisans of French pretenders were switching over to the Prussian party, at least in some cases with the consent of their patrons. The French diplomacy's strategic goal of securing continuation of French rule in Neuchâtel was thus undermined by factionalism at the court, short-term personal interests, and the agonistic culture of honour within the high nobility.

This division between the French forces smoothed the way to Prussian rule. Far too late, in October 1707, King Louis XIV sent his ambassador Puyzieulx to

10 Cf. Bachmann, *Die preussische Sukzession in Neuchâtel*, 290–93.

11 François Bouret, *Mémoire sur l'état présent de Neuchâtel*, 5 August 1707 (AAE, CP Neuchâtel, vol. 5, fol. 15–17v), fol. 15v.

12 For the rivalries at the French court at the time of the Neuchâtel succession, see the description by Louis de Rouvroy, duc de Saint-Simon, *Mémoires. Additions au Journal de Dangeau*, ed. by Yves Coirault, 8 vols. (Paris, 1983–1988), vol. 2, 987–91. Torcy and Chamillart were part of rival factions at the French court; see the detailed analysis in Emmanuel Le Roy Ladurie, *Saint-Simon ou le système de la Cour* (Paris, 1997), 181–235, esp. 195.

Neuchâtel and had the *parlement* of the Franche-Comté declare the French king sovereign of Neuchâtel (as successor of the ancient Burgundian overlords), a step that would turn out to be counterproductive, as it confirmed fears of an impending integration of the highly privileged Principality into the French monarchy. Meanwhile, the Prussian representative, Metternich, and his agents managed to gain the trust and support of a clear majority of the judges and institutional actors in the territory by guaranteeing and even extending the privileges of the local corporations in the *articles généraux*,[13] promising financial and honorary rewards to individuals and corporations, and pledging strong military support in case of an emergency. After the *Trois-États* declared its judgment, only the two small Catholic communities of Le Landeron and Cressier refused at first to take the oath to the Protestant king, while the *Conseil d'État* and the privileged corporations all declared their fidelity and signalled their will to cooperate with the new regime.

However, the interest of the high-ranking French pretenders in the border Principality did not end with the Prussian succession. After plans to invade Neuchâtel had been abandoned, Conti and Matignon attempted, with the aid of their partisans, to enlist the diplomatic support of the French crown to reverse the decision by the *Trois-États*. Aware of the precarious situation, Metternich was anxious not only to reward the Prussian king's supporters, but also to integrate key figures who had supported his opponents into the new political system. François de Chambrier, *conseiller d'État*, *maire* of Neuchâtel, and a faithful partisan of Matignon, was left in his offices. Samuel de Pury, who had been a leading figure in the Conti campaign but who had switched allegiance after the latter's retreat, was even rewarded with a pension, nobilitated and promoted to the *Conseil d'État* in 1709.[14] Despite these measures, some of the ancient *Contistes*—among them Samuel de Pury— remained in contact with the house of their patron (who died in 1709), waiting for a turnaround after the formal recognition of Prussian rule by the

---

13 The *articles généraux* were negotiated and signed by Metternich before the final decision of the *Trois-États* on 3 November 1707 and ratified by the Prussian king shortly after the succession. They thus represented a de facto precondition for the Prussian rule and were, especially in the following decades, interpreted as a sort of political contract guaranteeing extensive privileges to the inhabitants and corporations of the Principality. For the content and the significance of the *articles généraux*, see Bachmann, *Die preussische Sukzession in Neuchâtel*, 223–40.

14 For a discussion of the promotions see Weber, *Lokale Interessen und grosse Strategie*, 85–96.

French crown in 1713.[15] Other pretenders, such as the house of Mailly-Nesle, continued pressing their claims,[16] and from time to time, influential *princes du sang* such as the duc d'Orléans and the duc de Bourbon, as we will see, rediscovered their interest in becoming a sovereign *prince étranger* of Neuchâtel.

The continued contacts between members of the French court nobility and the elite of Neuchâtel were facilitated and strengthened by the ongoing mercenary services the inhabitants of the Principality offered to France—the Prussian sovereign had had to formally guarantee the right to offer mercenary services in the *articles généraux*. Many local patricians served as officers in the Swiss regiments of the French king, where they fostered friendships or family ties with "French" families of the Swiss cantons. Being a *Contiste* could facilitate one's career in French regiments, especially after Louis Armand de Bourbon, prince de Conti, became *lieutenant général des armées du roi* in 1719. Furthermore, the many traders and bankers from Neuchâtel who were active in Paris also benefited from the *crédit* of court nobles. Thus, even when the chances for a change of regime in Neuchâtel were slim, there were still significant circumstances that could bind members of the Principality's elite to the French court. The Perregaux family, who were active in both mercenary services and banking and secured a special pension from the French king, kept up regular correspondence with the French embassy in Solothurn throughout the eighteenth century.[17] This correspondence and frequent journeys to Solothurn not only served as a channel for informal political communications between the authorities of Neuchâtel and the French crown, but also facilitated the maintenance and coordination of a network of members of the local elite with "no drop of blood that is not French".[18]

---

15 In 1717–1719 for instance, when the outlook seemed favourable, zealous partisans of the prince de Conti travelled between Neuchâtel and Paris and mobilized supporters within the Principality. The project, however, did not succeed, not least because of the lack of money. See the documentation in AN, K 547–50.

16 See Armand Du Pasquier, 'Les prétentions de la maison de Mailly-Nesle sur Neuchâtel au XVIIIe siècle', *Musée neuchâtelois* (1921), 10–206.

17 On the Perregaux, see Philippe Henry, 'Patriciat neuchâtelois, traditions familiales et service étranger. Les Perregaux à la fin du XVIIIe siècle', in Norbert Furrer et al., eds., *Gente ferocissima. Solddienst und Gesellschaft in der Schweiz (15.-19. Jahrhundert)* (Zürich, 1997), 137–48; Weber, *Lokale Interessen und grosse Strategie*, 160–67 and 362–70.

18 See Perregaux's formulation in a petition to the French court 'à protéger mon neveu dans sa juste prétention, et de vous rapeller qu'il est d'une famille où il n-y-a goute de sang qu'il ne soit françois'. [François-Frédéric Perregaux] to François de Tott, 3 June 1767 (AAE, CP Suisse, vol. 274).

The Prussian court therefore faced the challenge of an influential network of French-oriented patricians, even within the local government. However, this network could not openly act as a "French party", at least when a member of the network held an office in the Principality and was therefore obliged by oath to serve only the interests of the sovereign. And as in other contexts, the network was not a stable, formally organized unity, but rather a group of actors who shared some interests and who could potentially mobilize relatives and friends, if collective action was required. Nevertheless, the French faction was a group to be reckoned with given the distance between Berlin and Neuchâtel and the difficulties of military intervention in the case of a rebellion. The Berlin court wanted to decrease local support for the return of French rule, but sought to achieve this goal by dealing with the local elite carefully, which usually meant leaving administration of the Principality in the hands of those elites and strictly observing their guaranteed privileges. Consequently, fiscal revenue remained extremely low, and Neuchâtel was exempt from Prussian military recruitment drives. Thus the informal trans-territorial relations of a portion of the Principality's elite turned out to be a powerful instrument for the subjects as a whole in their relations with the sovereign.

Not satisfied with this situation, the Prussian ministers looked for possibilities to strengthen the authority of the sovereign in the distant territory. At the beginning of the 1720s, growing tensions between the two privileged bourgeoisies of Neuchâtel and Valangin, in combination with the dissatisfaction of some patrician families with the distribution of offices and friendly diplomatic relations with the French crown, seemed to open up a new window of opportunity for the Prussian king.

2 Balancing Powers: The Prussian Crown and Factional Struggles in 1723–1727

On 16 June 1724, the Prussian commissioner Friedrich Konrad von Strünckede arrived in Neuchâtel with a royal order to investigate local troubles and to look for opportunities to improve revenues for the crown.[19] In the preceding years, the bourgeoisie of Valangin had sent two deputations to the Prussian court to register their grievances about the policy of the *Conseil d'État* which, among other things, had sought to ban the importation of red wine from Burgundy

19 For the following events, see Wolfgang Stribrny, *Die Könige von Preussen als Fürsten von Neuenburg-Neuchâtel (1707–1848). Geschichte einer Personalunion* (Berlin, 1998), 49–54, and Weber, *Lokale Interessen und grosse Strategie*, 466–80.

and to keep the local dignitaries of Valangin away from the government affairs of the Principality. Although the court had ruled in their favour, conflict simmered on. When the *conseiller d'État*, Jean Henri de Montmollin, was sent to Berlin to inform the court about the situation in autumn 1723, an anonymous letter from the Principality claimed that Montmollin was not the appropriate man for this task, but was instead part of the problem. According to the letter, there were "two families who give cause for jealousy among the others. The distance of His Majesty is regretted by many, and the governor who turns himself over to the Chambrier and to the Montmollin is the cause for all these decisions."[20] In Berlin, the two powerful families, Chambrier and Montmollin, had, until that moment, been seen as pillars of the Prussian regime. But shortly after his arrival, Strünckede reached the same conclusion as the anonymous letter writer, and advised the court to reduce the families' influence by strengthening the bourgeoisie of Valangin and their rivals within the patriciate of Neuchâtel.

The Prussian court, or, more precisely, the leading state minister Heinrich Rüdiger von Ilgen, who directed the foreign affairs of the Prussian crown as well as the affairs of the Principality, followed Strünckede's advice. The commissioner was ordered to "cut the wings" of the two leading families and to "balance" their influence by promoting other suitable candidates for offices. With the aid of the loyal Valanginois, these actions would allow the crown to make a "perfect state".[21] As a consequence of this policy, three new *conseillers d'État* had already been nominated by the autumn of 1724, and three more from families who had not previously been represented were successfully put forward by Strünckede the following year. In addition, important offices of the local justices were assigned to the bourgeois of Valangin. At the same time, the promotion of an already-designated member of the Chambrier family was postponed. In June 1725, tensions began to escalate when Strünckede suspended François de Chambrier from his offices as *conseiller d'État* and *maire* of Neuchâtel after a verbal argument. The bourgeoisie of Neuchâtel protested against these violations of their privileges and sent deputies to the neighbouring Republic of

20 '[...] deux familles qui donnent de la jalousie aux autres. L'éloignement de sa Majesté fait peine à plusieurs et le gouverneur se livrant comme il a fait aux Chambriers et aux Montmollins, donne lieu à toutes ces résolutions'. Anonymous, *Avis désintéressé sur la source des désordres de Neufchâtel*, October 1723 (GStAPK, 1.HA, Rep. 64, IV, I, convol. XLI, [vol. 2], fol. 46–47r).

21 'Ihnen die Flügel auff alle Weise beschneiden'; 'balanciren'; 'vollkommenen Staat machen'. The king (countersigned by Ilgen and Knyphausen) to Strünckede, Berlin, 6 February 1725 (GStAPK, Rep. 64, IV, I, convol. XLIII, fol. 30–33v).

Bern in order to secure protection. In this situation, the Prussian court recalled the commissioner, who left Neuchâtel in September.

The Berlin ministers continued, however, to pursue Strünckede's *divide et impera* strategy. This confrontational course seemed to pose no risk because of the crown's friendly relations with the French court. "We can now insist with much more liberty and consequence on Your Royal Majesty's authority in this land", reported Ilgen to the King, "because Your Majesty stands in good terms with France, and the disloyal subjects in Neuchâtel will not be heard there."[22] Strünckede had returned to Berlin and his report led the court to entrust important tasks to people within Strünckede's trusted network in Neuchâtel, tasks such as negotiating a new salt treaty with France, and corresponding directly to the court on events in the Principality without being required to inform their colleagues in the *Conseil d'État*. It was hoped that a more heterogeneous composition of the local government and the vigilance of the correspondents would rein in tendencies towards self-empowerment among the dominant families, enabling the court to strengthen its authority.

However, a closer look at the composition of Strünckede's network in Neuchâtel reveals a surprising fact: its closeness to France. At least three of the six new *conseillers d'État* in 1724–25 came from families with a continuing tradition of providing mercenary services to France (Abram de Pury), or had been in direct contact with French ambassadors, ministers and pretenders (Jean-Pierre Brun d'Oleyres, David de Tribolet) after 1707.[23] Furthermore, Strünckede was in regular contact with Charles-François Bergeon and Jean-Jacques de Merveilleux, two busy characters who had frequently travelled between Paris and Neuchâtel during recent years. In Paris, Bergeon and Merveilleux had been in regular contact with members of the high nobility having an interest in Neuchâtel, such as the duc de Luynes, the regent duc d'Orléans, and the duc de Bourbon. Having been informed about their activities by the Prussian resident at the French court, the Neuchâtelois Jean de Chambrier, the Berlin court had

22 'Man kann jetziger Zeit über Eurer Königl: Maÿ: Authorität in selbigem Lande so viel freÿer und nachdrücklicher halten, weil Eure Königl: Maÿ: mit Frankreich wohl stehen, und die untreuen Leute zu Neufchatel daselbst kein Gehör finden werden.' Ilgen an den König, Berlin, 18. December 1725 (GStAPK, I. HA, Rep. 64, IV, I, convol. XLIII, [vol. 2], fol. 356–359r, fol. 359r). With the handwritten remark 'guth' (good) by Frederick William I.

23 The cases of François Charles de Guy, who was a cousin of Charles-François Bergeon, and François Antoine de Rougemont, whose sons became bankers in London and Paris, also imply their proximity to the French faction, but less clearly. A contrasting figure is Simon Chevalier, who had served the Prussian armies before the Succession and may be seen as an actor with a strong orientation to the sovereign.

demanded and obtained their expulsion from France in late 1723.[24] Now, however, they were supported by Strünckede and formally rehabilitated by a royal rescript to the *Conseil d'État*. In January 1727, Merveilleux was even sent to the French court to negotiate a salt treaty—and possibly to replace the Prussian resident Chambrier. The potential effects of these measures seem paradoxical. Did the Prussian court aim to consolidate its authority with the aid of local actors who were sympathetic to France?

Shortly before Strünckede's arrival in Neuchâtel, some well-informed observers had assumed that there was another, secret goal behind the commissioner's mission: to prepare the ground for a cession of the Principality to the new French prime minister, Louis IV Henri de Bourbon, prince de Condé, known as the duc de Bourbon.[25] Although the details are beyond the scope of this article, there is strong evidence to suggest that this scenario was contemplated in Berlin by state minister Ilgen—Strünckede's father-in-law—as a contingency plan in case the confrontational strategy in Neuchâtel failed. Had the Principality indeed changed hands, this could have been very lucrative for Ilgen, who already received money from France: contemporaries estimated Ilgen's possible reward to be worth about 100,000 guilders.[26] What is certain is that there had been secret negotiations about a cession between the French and Prussian courts involving the duc d'Orléans in 1723, which were later renewed by the duc de Bourbon and the French envoy to Berlin, Rottembourg.[27] King Frederick William I was actually inclined to cede the small and distant Principality to France, but had insisted that he would do this only in exchange for another territory and not for money. This may be the reason why the king was possibly not fully informed about Strünckede's soundings in Bern and in

---

24 On their activities, culminating in the unsuccessful attempt of Louis de Mailly-Nesle in 1734, see Weber, *Lokale Interessen und grosse Strategie*, 370–82, esp. 378–79.

25 In May 1724, when Strünckede was in Bern, the Bernese senator Isaak Steiger asked the commissioner directly if the rumour was true without receiving any clear answer, a fact which he reported to his friend Brun d'Oleyres. Isaak Steiger to Jean-Pierre Brun d'Oleyres, Bern, 14 June 1724 (Archives de Chambrier, Cormondrèche, vol. CX) and the earlier letters dated 6 April, 23 April, and 11 June 1724.

26 See [Abram de Pury], *Mémoires de Samuel Pury* (AEN, Fonds Pury, V 7b), 184. On the secret French pensions for Ilgen, see Jörg Ulbert, 'Der Leiter der preussischen Aussenpolitik Heinrich Rüdiger von Ilgen (1654–1728) als Informant der französischen Diplomatie. Anwerbung—Bezahlung—Gegenleistung', in Sven Externbrink, Jörg Ulbert, eds., *Formen internationaler Beziehungen in der Frühen Neuzeit. Frankreich und das Alte Reich im europäischen Staatensystem. Festschrift für Klaus Malettke zum 65. Geburtstag* (Berlin, 2001), 274–96.

27 See Weber, *Lokale Interessen und grosse Strategie*, 340–45.

the Principality, and why there is no direct evidence of these in Strünckede's official correspondence with the court. In any case, Bergeon and Merveilleux, who, as mentioned, had already been in contact with the duc de Bourbon in Paris, seemed to be the perfect intermediaries in the negotiations between the commissioner, the French court, and the local elite in Neuchâtel.

The project failed for several reasons. First, in December 1725, the Republic of Bern, an ancient ally of Neuchâtel which viewed itself as a kind of guarantor or protector of its constitution, wrote a letter to the king of Prussia in which it revoked the alienability of the Principality, and thus expressed its opposition to a possible cession to a French pretender—a step that forced the Prussian court to formally deny the secret negotiations. Second, on 11 June 1726, the duc de Bourbon received a *lettre de cachet* requesting him to leave the court, which meant that he lost the influential position that had enabled him to use French diplomatic channels for the negotiation. And third, in March 1727, Ilgen was forced by royal decision to hand over direction of Neuchâtel's affairs to his colleague, state minister Knyphausen. Knyphausen immediately abandoned the previous course by denying Strünckede's confidants access to the court, re-establishing the discharged officers, and promoting new *conseillers d'État* who belonged to or were on good terms with the Chambrier and Montmollin families, in order to "balance" the influence of the new faction in the local government.[28]

The first and the third of these three factors can be seen as effects of the factional rivalries in Neuchâtel. The origins of the first factor, the diplomatic intercession of the Republic of Bern, can be found in a network which had close connections to the French ambassador in Solothurn, the marquis d'Avaray.[29] Théophile Perregaux, who regularly wrote letters to the embassy and who had just been forced to move from Valangin to Neuchâtel after having been denounced as a pensioner of the French king by the *maîtres-bourgeois*,[30] expressed his distrust of the activities of Bergeon and Merveilleux in the Principality. As he reported to Solothurn, Jean-Pierre Brun d'Oleyres, another man, as we have seen, with connections to France, had informed him about

28 'Balanciret'. Knyphausen to the king, Berlin, 29 July 1727 (GStAPK, 1. HA, Rep. 64, IV, 5. Bediente, vol. 1719–1728).

29 On d'Avaray's network in Switzerland, see the detailed analysis by Affolter, *Verhandeln mit Republiken*, and on factionalism in the Swiss Republics, the chapter by Andreas Würgler in this volume.

30 Maîtres-bourgeois and Conseil de Valangin to the king, Valangin, 30 June 1723 (GStAPK, 1. HA, Rep. 64, IV, I, Convol. XLI, [vol. 1], fol. 319–328r).

a conversation with Bergeon. The latter had apparently told d'Oleyres that Strünckede's mission had a "more considerable goal" than the official instructions suggested, without, however, offering more precise information.[31] As they were obviously not part of the game, Perregaux and Brun d'Oleyres warned the ambassador about the negotiations, which were not going through his channel, and offered their own, more promising services to mediate a French acquisition of the Principality.[32] By withholding the certificate signed by the king which promoted Brun d'Oleyres to the *Conseil d'État*, Strünckede certainly missed the chance to alienate the highly connected magistrate. Apparently frustrated by Strünckede's activities, Brun d'Oleyres wrote a memoir in which he summarized the reasons why Neuchâtel could not be legally alienated and handed it to his friend, the Bernese Counselor Isaak Steiger. The paper would later serve as the basis for Bern's diplomatic intervention.[33] Thus, not unlike the situation in 1707, plans to (re)-establish French rule in Neuchâtel failed because of rivalries within the "French" faction.

In the case of Ilgen's dismissal and the end of the divide-and-rule strategy, it was, unsurprisingly, actors with close connections to the Chambrier-Montmollin network who brought about the reversal at the Prussian court. These actors, however, had entered the scene in disguise—as Protestant clergymen. The *compagnie des pasteurs*, one of the local corporations that enjoyed special privileges guaranteed in the *articles généraux*, sent a deputation to Berlin in 1726. Despite attempts by the *maître-bourgeois* of Valangin and Strünckede's confidants to denounce the three clergymen as representatives of the "*clique Chambreline*",[34] they were received by King Frederick William I himself and

---

31 'Objet plus considérable'. See the memoir written by Théophile Perregaux to the embassy, 11. 6. 1725 (AdSM, 164 J 105, 1 Mi 3435/2; now integrated in the inventory AAE, PA-AP 460, Papiers d'Avaray).

32 Brun d'Oleyres wrote a memoir in which he proposed an alternative way to secure Neuchâtel for the duc de Bourbon, but when the letter finally reached the French court via Solothurn, it did not produce any results. See AAE, CP Neuchâtel, vol. 9, fol. 286–291r, and the correspondence from March to December 1725 in AdSM, 164 J 105, 1 Mi 3435/2.

33 See the correspondance between Brun d'Oleyres and Steiger in Archives de Chambrier, vol. CX, esp. the letters from Steiger 3 November 1724, 7 December 1724, and 15 January 1725. Steiger was also in informal contact with the French embassy (via Perregaux), but refused to accept a French pension. See Affolter, *Verhandeln mit Republiken*, 200.

34 On the deputation of the *compagnie des pasteurs*, see James Paris, 'La députation de la vénérable classe à Berlin en 1726', *Musée neuchâtelois* XLVIII (1911), 187–268, 236 (letter of *commissaire* L'Epée to Strünckede, Valangin, 12. 8. 1726). As a matter of fact, the doyen of the *compagnie*, the famous theologian Jean-Frédéric Ostervald, was a cousin of the discharged *maire* François de Chambrier, and David Vattel, one of the three deputies (and

soon gained his confidence. During their one-year stay at the court, they not only obtained guarantees of the privileges of their corporation, but also letters that confirmed their nominations as *chapelains et ministres de la cour*, the nobilitation of their families, and the right to correspond directly with the court. Most importantly, however, they directly influenced the royal decision to remove Ilgen from involvement in Neuchâtel's affairs—the decision was written in the king's own hand on the back side of a petition from one of the clergymen.[35] From March 1727 until their return to Neuchâtel in September, the three clergymen advised Knyphausen about matters involving the Principality, which resulted in a return to the cautious approach of the years before the mission of the scheming commissioner. Finally, a royal rescript officially declared the factional struggles to be at an end, ordering the *conseillers* "to dispense peace and tranquillity within the state [...], and avoid anything that could excite the spirit of cabal and division between you."[36]

3 Between Cooperation and Rebellion: The Persistence of the French Faction

What followed was a period of relative tranquillity, but the French faction in the local government was still present and in contact with the embassy in Solothurn. In 1732, a group of three *conseillers d'État*—Samuel de Pury, Jean-Pierre Brun d'Oleyres and Josué Gaudot—even offered their services to the French ambassador marquis de Bonnac to negotiate a cession of the Principality to France by the Prussian king.[37] However, this project soon petered out, and when the French pretender Louis III de Mailly, marquis de Nesle, made an daring journey to the Franco-Neuchâtelois frontier in order to provoke a revolution

father of the international legal scholar Emer de Vattel), was a brother-in-law of *chancelier* Montmollin.

35 Cf. GStAPK, 1. HA, Rep. 64, IV, I, Convol. XLVI, fol. 539 (dated 14 March 1727).

36 'Enfin nous vous ordonnons très expressément [...] de faire régner la paix et la tranquillité dans l'État [...] et éviter tout ce qui pourrait exciter l'esprit de cabale et division au milieu de vous.' The king (Knyphausen) to the governor and *Conseil d'État*, 22 July 1727, quoted after Paris, 'La députation de la vénérable classe à Berlin en 1726', 265.

37 Cf. the account by the Bernese agent Kaspar von Muralt to ambassador Bonnac, 11 November 1732 (AAE, CP Neuchâtel Suppl., Vol. 2, fol. 267). For the context, see Jean Courvoisier, 'Essai sur les projets de cession de Neuchâtel à la France entre 1707 et 1789', *Schweizerische Zeitschrift für Geschichte* 9 (1959), 145–67, esp. 151–56.

in the Principality, nobody in the *Conseil d'État* was inclined to follow his call.[38] Facilitated by friendly relations between the kings from the late 1730s onwards and by the cautious, deliberative administration of the Prussian ministers, tensions between the corporations became rare and factionalism within the local government even seemed to disappear. In 1748, one of the few critics of this harmonious cooperation wrote the following (shortly before being nominated himself to the *Conseil d'État*): "This council [i.e., the *Conseil d'État*] is but one family, together with almost all the heads of jurisdictions of the State."[39]

One may ask if there was still such thing as a French party within the elites of Neuchâtel if the former opponents of the Prussian regime had become perfectly integrated into the governing system. I would argue that a French-aligned network, grouped around some key figures (Perregaux, Pury, Brun d'Oleyres) and their families, persisted, but did not openly act as a faction during this period. The reason for this inactivity may be found, first, in the fact that a good portion of its goals—establishing good relations with France and securing local privileges such as the unrestricted ability to offer mercenary services to foreign powers—had been fulfilled. Second, the network's former primary goal, regime change, was, at least temporarily, out of reach for geopolitical reasons, and ceased to be an urgent issue for both the network and the French crown.

With the outbreak of the Seven Years' War, however, the situation changed dramatically. After the battle of Rossbach (5 November 1757), in which several hundred Neuchâtelois had fought for the French king against their own sovereign, King Frederick II challenged the right of the inhabitants of the Principality to enter the military service of foreign powers, resulting in strong—and ultimately successful—opposition by the local corporations, and especially by the city of Neuchâtel. In the following years, the Principality was rattled by repeated episodes of political unrest that culminated in the *troubles de Neuchâtel* in 1766–1768, one of the most serious rebellions against royal authority during Frederick II's reign as the Prussian monarch.[40] Although it is not possible here

38 Mailly-Nesle had hoped that in the political context of the Polish War of Succession, the French king—who had had a liaison with Mailly-Nesle's daughter Louise Julie—would support his project. However, the opposite was true and Mailly-Nesle was immediately recalled to the court. On the episode, see Du Pasquier, 'Les prétentions de la maison de Mailly-Nesle', esp. 89–99 and 124–34.

39 '[…] ce Conseil ne faisant qu'une même famille avec presque tous les chefs de jurisdictions de l'État'. Jean-Henri Andrié to king Frederick II, Berlin, 10 June 1748 (GStAPK, 1. HA, Rep. 64, IV, I, vol. LII).

40 See Wolfgang Stribrny, 'Die Neuenburger Wirren—Friedrichs des Grossen schwerster innenpolitischer Konflikt', in Jürgen Ziechmann, ed., *Fridericianische Miniaturen*, vol. 2 (Bremen, 1991), 133–46.

to discuss these events in detail, it is noteworthy that the most prominent leaders of the revolts were part of the French faction. In the mercenary controversy, of course, their interests were directly concerned. But the *conseillers* Abram and David de Pury were also among the first to protest publicly against a new system of taxation in the autumn of 1766. After being discharged from their offices, they mobilized their network in the city. Quickly, the *bourgeoisie de Neuchâtel* asserted protests against violations of privileges and convened the representative assembly of the *corps et communautés de l'État* to confront the prince and his representatives. It was the unattractive scenario of the Principality's imminent reduction to a Prussian province without rights that enabled the French-aligned leaders of the opposition to mobilize a broader popular resistance against the new tax system and other attempts to reform the *status quo*. The leaders of the protest sought French support through the channel of François-Frédéric Perregaux. It is thus not surprising that, when writing about these events some years later, the Neuchâtelois, Prussian diplomat and later governor of Neuchâtel, Jean-Pierre de Chambrier d'Oleyres, attributed the troubles to the actions of a "*cabale française*", with Abram de Pury as "*chef de parti*", at least for actions taken in public.[41]

During the course of the conflict, the opposition leaders' goal became clear—secession of the Principality from the Prussian monarchy and its transformation into a republic under French protection. This transformation, for which smaller Swiss Republics such as Solothurn and Fribourg served as a model, would have guaranteed local autonomy and good terms with France, and simultaneously secured the domination of the French faction within the local elites. These efforts to change the regime were supported by a French agent sent to Neuchâtel, François de Tott, who travelled between Neuchâtel, Bern and Solothurn to gain support for the secession project (and a possible future return to French rule).[42] After a letter arrived in Bern from the French

41 'C'est alors que la cabale française donna de la constistence à ces intrigues. Le colonel Pury étoit devenu chef de parti mais c'étoit pour l'action extérieure, et il n'avoit point tout le secret de la cabale dont il étoit le coopérateur [...]'. *Journal de Jean-Pierre Chambrier d'Oleyres* (Extracts, unpublished manuscript in Archives de Chambrier, Cormondrèche), 122.

42 See Ferenc Tóth, 'La mission secrète du baron de Tott à Neuchâtel en 1767', *Revue historique neuchâteloise*, 2003, 133–59; Weber, *Lokale Interessen und grosse Strategie*, 522–33. In fact, the broader popular resistance would presumably have tended to a rather democratic or mixed system as embodied by the Rousseau-inspired opposition in the parallel unrest in Geneva. However, the French crown made clear that they would only support an aristocratic republic. In 1768, the leading figure Abram de Pury wrote a memoir in which he elaborated how Neuchâtel's secession from the Prussian king could be mediated.

foreign minister, the duc de Choiseul, in April 1768, which finally seemed to formally declare French protection for Neuchâtel, the rebellion culminated in the assassination of the Prussian king's advocate, Claude Gaudot. Shortly thereafter, however, the city of Neuchâtel was subdued by the military forces of Bern and the three Catholic allies (*Burgrechtsorte* or *cantons combourgeois*)—Lucerne, Solothurn, and Fribourg—who acted at the request of Robert Scipio von Lentulus, the Prussian general and king's agent, while French diplomacy remained passive. Despite the fact that putting an end to the undesirable relationship with the Prussian king would have perfectly fit the "grand strategy" of the duc de Choiseul, a direct conflict with the most important Protestant canton of Bern or even with Prussia, a major European power, presented a disproportionate risk for the French crown.

Neuchâtel thus remained a Prussian possession. The return to the *status quo ante* was facilitated by the moderate course of Lentulus, who was named governor of the Principality. Even the leading figures of the revolt were quick to recognize the advantages of the situation. After the corporations' privileges were once again guaranteed, the discharged officers reinstated, and stable, distant rule from Berlin was re-established, the inhabitants of the border territory had access to multiple sources of protection for their political and commercial interests, describing themselves as Prussians, Swiss or French according to their needs in a particular situation, as one observer would later describe.[43] In the negotiations over the inclusion of the Principality into the new Franco-Swiss alliance of 1777, faithful servants of the prince and members of the French faction worked hand-in-hand to secure the support of both courts.[44] The interests of the two factions merged more or less completely during the French Revolution and in its aftermath. After the outbreak of the War of the First Coalition and the dissolution of the Swiss regiments in 1792, the former servants of the French crown sought to weather the storm of foreign threats and domestic revolutionary movements by strengthening their commitment to the distant ruler in Berlin. It was not because of the presence of a French faction within the elite, but because of a formal treaty between King

---

See Jules Jeanjaquet, 'Un projet d'émancipation de Neuchâtel en 1768', *Musée neuchâtelois* (1902), 202–10.

43 See the memoir of Augustino Angelini to the French Directoire in January, ed. in Armand Du Pasquier, 'Un mémoire sur la réunion de Neuchâtel à la République française', *Musée neuchâtelois* 48 (1911), 155–229, esp. 161, 169–70.

44 On these negotiations, see Philippe Gern, 'Essai sur l'indigénat helvétique de la principauté de Neuchâtel, XVIIIe siècle', *Musée neuchâtelois* 3 (1966), 153–65, and Weber, *Lokale Interessen und grosse Strategie*, 382–423.

Frederick William III and Emperor Napoleon in 1806, that the Principality of Neuchâtel was finally returned to French rule—if only for eight years.[45]

4 Conclusion

The history of the "first" period of Prussian rule over Neuchâtel from 1707 to 1806 is the history of a successful failure. Measured by analytical models which describe the Brandenburg-Prussian style of government as a "coercive-intensive mode" of state-building,[46] the small Principality which supplied neither large tax revenues nor recruits to the crown, seems to have been more an appendage of a rising European power than an integral part of its political success. Apart from the difficulties of communicating with a far-off political centre and the absence of a military garrison, the presence of a local elite with socio-political and commercial ties to France was unquestionably one of the main factors which prevented the monarchy from taking a firmer grip on the Principality's resources. Reforms to increase the crown's fiscal revenues were either not undertaken or were swiftly abandoned as threats of a French-backed rebellion mounted.

On the other hand, the Principality supplied useful resources to the Prussian kings other than money and recruits. For instance, a significant number of Neuchâtelois entered the diplomatic service of the crown, among them figures such as Jean de Chambrier and David-Alphonse de Sandoz-Rollin, both of whom served as Prussian representatives in Paris for many years.[47] The French ties possessed by members of the bourgeois elite of Neuchâtel were part of the social capital of these diplomats, facilitating their access to information and multiplying avenues for negotiation, and for this reason these men were highly useful to the Prussian crown. The same is true for Prussia's relations to the Swiss Confederacy that were mediated through existing family relations and political alliances, combined with the shared experiences of magistrates in Neuchâtel to facilitate access to the ruling elites of the cantons. Thus, the

45 See Jean Courvoisier, *Le Maréchal Berthier et sa Principauté de Neuchâtel, 1806–1814* (Neuchâtel, 1959), 9–29.

46 Charles Tilly, *Coercion, Capital, and European States, AD 990–1990* (Cambridge, Mass., 1990), 30.

47 Concerning the diplomats who were part of the Neuchâtelois-Prussian success story, see also Nadir Weber, 'La principauté de Neuchâtel et la diplomatie prussienne: un croisement fructueux', in Elisabeth Crettaz-Stürzel, Chantal Lafontant Vallotton, eds., *Sa Majesté en Suisse. Neuchâtel et ses princes prussiens* (Neuchâtel, 2013), 106–13.

trans-territorial ties of the Neuchâtelois not only produced factionalism and opposition, but also helped to widen and strengthen the political network of Prussia when it was a rising European power.

In the long run, common interests prevailed over factionalism within the Principality's elite. Most of the members of the French faction did not wish Neuchâtel to be directly integrated into the Kingdom of France because this scenario would have limited their local autonomy and endangered their privileged standing between several protectors. At the same time, most of the servants of the Prussian king were not interested in subjecting Neuchâtel to the intensified state-building processes often employed by the monarchy. To be sure, collaboration among the local elites limited the Prussian king's prospects of strengthening his rule to such a degree that, at the end of the eighteenth century, contemporary observers such as John Adams saw Neuchâtel as a kind of "monarchical republic".[48] The results of the factional struggles in the 1720s had shown that a divide-and-rule strategy was inadequate to manage the distant territory. But by integrating the different local forces into the governmental system and allowing questions of administration and nomination for offices to remain de facto in the hands of a self-regulating elite, the Prussian court could finally profit from the resources of the Principality while expending a minimum in costs to administer and maintain it. The political successes of the eighteenth-century Prussian monarchy depended upon both its successful organizational efforts to generate and extract significant resources from the central territories and its flexibility in dealing with elites in peripheral but useful "border territories" such as the Principality of Neuchâtel.

48 Adams also put England and Poland into this category. See John Adams, 'A Defence of the Constitutions of Government of the United States of America' (1778), *The Works of John Adams*, vol. IV, Boston 1851, 374–79. For other contemporary views of the constitution of Neuchâtel see Philippe Henry, 'Libertés neuchâteloises et liberté suisse. Regards étrangers sur les institutions de la principauté de Neuchâtel au XVIIIe siècle', in Philippe Henry, ed., *Des chartes de franchises à la nouvelle Constitution. Une histoire des institutions neuchâteloises* (Neuchâtel, 2002), 143–67.

Factions and Parties in Early Modern Swiss Conflicts

Andreas Würgler

1 "The Worm in the Cheese": "Factions" in Early Modern Legal and Political Discourse

"We put first as a general maxim that factions and parties are dangerous, and threaten the well-being, of all kinds of commonwealths". This statement by Jean Bodin (1529–1596) might well have been an expression of early modern European common sense about the nature of factions and parties. He continues in his famous "Six Books of the Commonwealth", printed in 1576: "But if factions and seditions are dangerous to monarchies, they are even more so to popular states and to aristocracies. Monarchs can preserve their authority, either by impartially composing quarrels, or in alliance with one of the parties by bringing the other to reason, or by destroying it altogether. But if the people in a popular state are divided, there is no sovereign to appeal to, any more than there is when the governing class in an aristocracy splits up into cliques". According to Bodin, the partition of the body politic into rival groups threatens public peace, especially in a "popular state", because such a state's "sovereignty is vested in the very people who are divided, and the magistrates are nothing more than their subjects".[1]

Bodin's view represents the mainstream early modern attitude towards the phenomenon of factions. They were considered evil because they were often the first step to sedition, rebellion and even civil war. The Italian legal historian Mario Sbriccoli (1941–2005) reconstructed the semantics of the terms used by medieval and early modern jurists and political writers dealing with any form of disobedience that could be called *crimen laesae maiestatis*. According to the German jurist Philipp Andreas Oldenburg (c. 1620–1678), cited by Sbriccoli, "Factions and tumults gave birth to sedition which are the mothers of civil wars".[2] Oldenburg also cited Baldus de Ubaldis (1327–1400): "Partiality in the

1 Quotations from Jean Bodin, *The Six Books of the Commonwealth*, abridged and trans. by M.J. Tooley (Oxford, 1955), Book IV, Chapter 7, accessible online at: http://www.constitution.org/bodin/bodin_.htm [12 August 2015].

2 "Ex factionibus et tumultibus nonnumquam nascuntur et proveniunt seditiones quae matres sunt bellorum civilium", Oldenbourg (1675), quoted in Mario Sbriccoli, *Crimen laesae*

 | DOI 10.1163/9789004345348_012

state is like the worm in the cheese: as the cheese vanishes, the worm gets fat", and Andreas Barbatia (1399–1482): "Discord in the state is an open door for intruding enemies".[3]

But this is only one side of the coin. Sbriccoli insisted on the other side; namely, that the Roman law tradition acknowledged the double character of *factio, seditio and discordia.* If a State was ruled by a tyrant, the nobles or citizens had the right or even the duty to disobey and organise resistance. One of Sbriccoli's sources, the German jurist Konrad Braun (c. 1495–1563), put it in 1550 as follows: "Faction is a division among the multitude produced by competition to prevail over others. Factions can be divided between lawful and unlawful according to their justifications. Therefore we have good and bad factions, although at the beginning the term had a positive meaning". And Braun later on: "If we can assemble our friends to defend our properties, we can even more assemble to defend the political community by connecting the good persons and to protect the political community. For the same reason the faction is right and lawful when it organises good citizens to expel tyranny from the community—if this cannot be done by other, more suitable means".[4]

Roman law tended to see factions as resulting from organised dissent. From the rulers' point of view organised dissent tended to disobedience, and disobedience was the basis of all sorts of *crimen laesae maiestatis*, from faction to conspiracy to rebellion and civil war. The only case of "legitimate" dissent was resistance to tyranny, a situation which permitted the nobles or citizens

---

maiestatis. Il problema del reato politico alle soglie della scienza penalistica moderna (Milan, 1974), 300.

3 "Partialitatem in civitate esse tanquam vermen in caseo: sicut enim his caseum exedit, ipse pinguescit"; "discordiam in civitate esse portam patentem ad introducendos inimicos", quoted in Sbriccoli, *Crimen laesae maiestatis*, 278.

4 Konrad Braun [Conradus Brunus], *De seditionibus libri sex, rationibus et exempliss ex omni doctrinarum et Authorum genere locupletati* (Mainz, 1550), 64: "Factio est divisio multitudinis alicuius per aemulationem, in diversa studia, cum inter ipsos alij alija priores esse volunt. Quod & honestis ex causis, & ex inhonestis fieri potest. Unde & factio in bonam & in malam partem accipitur, ac initio quidem factio honestum vocabulum erat". And later, 64–65: "Quod si enim ad defensionem rerum nostrarum amicos congregare possumus, quanto magis pro defensione Reipublicae, bonis inter se societatem inire, & adversos improbos cives Rempublicam tueri licebit: sicut & iusta est factio, quae ob id inter bonos cives coalita est, ut Tyranni ex Reipublicae ericiantur, qui nulla alioqui ratione commode expelli possunt". Cf. Sbriccoli, *Crimen laesae maiestatis*, 282; Fabrizio Del Vera, 'Quietis publicae perturbatio: Revolts in the Political and Legal Treatises of the Sixteenth and Seventeenth Centuries', in Malte Griesse, ed., *From Mutual Observation to Propaganda War. Premodern Revolts in Their Transnational Representations* (Bielefeld, 2014), 305.

to form factions. Bodin's theory, however, did not recognise this case of "legitimate" resistance.[5]

According to the legendary narrative of the founding of the Swiss Confederacy, it was William Tell who, by killing the "tyrant" Habsburg bailiff Gessler, gave birth to the confederation of the three cantons, which sealed their alliance with an oath, a tale celebrated by Friedrich Schiller's (1759–1805) classic play "William Tell" (1804). The German dramatist Schiller, who had never been to Switzerland, adapted the legend from regional Swiss narratives documented since the 1470s. This story of the Swiss conspiracy against the noble Habsburg "tyrants" fits very well into the patterns of legal resistance provided for in Roman law.[6] Even if the tale has little to do with historical realities, it became an important touchstone for late medieval, early modern and even twentieth century justifications for Swiss independence. But the events described were not generally discussed in terms of "faction".

If factions were, according to Bodin, most likely to occur in popular states and aristocracies, the Swiss Confederacy and its member cantons, constituted as popular ("democratic") or "aristocratic" republics, should have provided a promising field for the study of factional conflicts. However, even if references to "party politics" at the Swiss Diet or in the cantons' councils are quite frequent in Swiss historiography, there are only a few recent detailed studies dedicated to the phenomenon of factions. These focus on factions in the con text of rebellions[7] or on factional strife in the rural, "popular" cantons.[8]

---

5 Wolfgang Reinhard, *Geschichte der Staatsgewalt. Eine vergleichende Verfassungsgeschichte Europas von den Anfängen bis zur Gegenwart* (Munich, 1999), 112–13; Thomas Maissen, *Die Geburt der Republic. Staatsverständnis und Repräsentation in der frühneuzeitlichen Eidgenossenschaft* (Göttingen, 2006), 47–60.

6 Cf. Peter Blickle, 'Friede und Verfassung. Voraussetzungen und Folgen der Eidgenossenschaft von 1291', in Hansjakob Achermann, Josef Brülisauer, Peter Hoppe, eds., *Innerschweiz und frühe Eidgenossenschaft*, (Olten, 1991), vol. 1, 13–202, 24–36; Guy P. Marchal, 'Wilhelm Tells Geburt', in Guy P. Marchal, *Schweizer Gebrauchsgeschichte* (Basel, 2007), 283–303; Thomas Maissen, *Schweizer Heldengeschichten—und was dahintersteckt* (Baden, 2015), 53–78.

7 Rudolf Braun, *Das ausgehende Ancien Régime in der Schweiz* (Göttingen, 1984), 256–309; Andreas Suter, *"Troublen" im Fürstbistum Basel (1726–1740). Eine Fallstudie zum bäuerlichen Widerstand im 18. Jahrhundert* (Göttingen, 1985); Andreas Würgler, *Unruhen und Öffentlichkeit. Städtische und ländliche Protestbewegungen im 18. Jahrhundert* (Tübingen, 1995); Martin Merki-Vollenweider, *Unruhige Untertanen. Die Rebellion der Luzerner Bauern im Zweiten Villmergerkrieg (1712)* (Luzern, 1995); Niklaus Landolt, *Untertanenrevolten und Widerstand auf der Basler Landschaft im sechzehnten und siebzehnten Jahrhundert* (Liestal, 1996).

8 Fabian Brändle, *Demokratie und Charisma. Fünf Landsgemeindekonflikte im 18. Jahrhundert* (Zurich, 2005); Kaspar Michel, 'Regieren und Verwalten', in Historischer Verein des Kantons Schwyz, ed., *Geschichte des Kantons Schwyz* (Zurich, 2012), vol. 3, 9–67.

The phenomenon of political "parties" has recently been discussed in terms of clientelism[9] and corruption.[10]

In what follows I shall analyse the different types and forms of "factions" or "parties" that appeared in the early modern Swiss Confederacy.[11] Sections two and three describe episodic factions suppressed by "aristocratic" as well as "democratic" governments which characterised them as disturbances or rebellions. The fourth section discusses permanent factions among the governing elites in the Confederacy as well as within single cantons in connection with foreign relations, the latter a phenomenon which contributed to the structure of political life in early modern Switzerland, and which has traditionally been seen as a kind of "party" struggle. The fifth section discusses actors' options in choosing participation in a faction. The conclusion addresses the question of why factionalism was perceived as being a pernicious evil but nevertheless inevitable, and compares early modern factions to contemporary political parties.

---

9 Ulrich Pfister, 'Politischer Klientelismus in der Schweiz', *Schweizerische Zeitschrift für Geschichte* 42 (1992), 28–68; Daniel Schläppi, '"In allem übrigen werden sich die Gesandten zu verhalten wissen". Akteure in der eidgenössischen Aussenpolitik des 17. Jahrhunderts. Strukturen, Ziele und Strategien am Beispiel der Familie Zurlauben von Zug', *Der Geschichtsfreund* 151 (1998), 5–90; Simon Teuscher, *Bekannte—Klienten—Verwandte. Soziabilität und Politik in der Stadt Bern um 1500* (Cologne, 1998); Christian Windler, '"Ohne Geld keine Schweizer". Pensionen und Söldnerrekrutierungen an den eidgenössischen Patronagemärkten', in Hillard von Thiessen, Christian Windler, eds., *Nähe in der Ferne. Personale Verflechtung in den Aussenbeziehungen der Frühen Neuzeit* (Berlin, 2005), 105–33; Carlo Steiner, 'Informelle Netzwerke in der Aussenpolitik der eidgenössischen Orte. Das labile Kräfteverhältnis in der Beziehung zwischen dem Zuger Solddienstunternehmer Beat II. Zurlauben und dem französischen Ambassador Jean de la Barde', *Argovia* 122 (2010), 45–65; Philippe Rogger, *Geld, Krieg und Macht. Pensionsherren, Söldner und eidgenössische Politik in den Mailänderkriegen 1494–1516* (Baden, 2015).

10 Valentin Groebner, *Gefährliche Geschenke: Ritual, Politik und die Sprache der Korruption in der Eidgenossenschaft im späten Mittelalter und am Beginn der Neuzeit*, Constance, 2000; Andreas Suter, 'Korruption oder Patronage? Aussenbeziehungen zwischen Frankreich und der Alten Eidgenossenschaft als Beispiel (16.-18. Jahrhundert)', *Zeitschrift für Historische Forschung* 37 (2010), 187–218.

11 For general background, cf. Andreas Würgler, '"The League of the Discordant Members" or How the Old Swiss Confederation Operated and How it managed to Survive for so long', in André Holenstein, Thomas Maissen, and Maarten Prak, eds., *The Republican Alternative. The Netherlands and Switzerland compared* (Amsterdam, 2008), 29–50; *Historisches Lexikon der Schweiz* 13 vols. (Basel, 2002–2014) [open access to all 36, 000 articles (without illustrations) of the *e-HLS* in German, French, and Italian versions, www.hls-dhs-dss.ch].

2 "Rebels" and "Obedients"? Faction as Sedition

The "communal basis" (David Sabean) of early modern rural revolts in Europe has been noted in the research since the 1970s.[12] Yves-Marie Bercé stated that in seventeenth-century southwestern France the most frequent mode of community organization was the unanimous village.[13] Village communities shaped everyday agricultural life by organizing forms of collective production, religious life through common worship within the parish, and local political life through election and control of communal officers in communal assemblies. For these reasons, communal institutions offered structure which could be used to organise resistance, and it should not be surprising that Swiss revolts followed this pattern of the "communalistic" (Peter Blickle) structure.[14] Two case studies of rural revolts illustrate these findings, but at the same time point to the fact that rebel movements lost their unanimity during conflicts that lasted longer than a decade. Both studies relate to factionalism within rebel movements, but without explicitly using the term.[15]

The first of these case studies involves a rebellion of the valley of Toggenburg against its lord, the prince-abbot of St. Gallen, which occurred from

12 Yves-Marie Bercé, *Histoire des croquants. Etude des soulèvements populaires au XVIIe siècle au sud-ouest de la France*, 2 vols. (Geneva, 1974), vol. 1, 185–226; and more clearly in the abbreviated version, Yves-Marie Bercé, *Histoire des croquants* (Paris, 1986), 385; David Sabean, 'The Communal Basis of Pre-1800 Peasant Uprisings in Western Europe', *Comparative Politics* 8 (1976), 355–64; Peter Bierbrauer, 'Bäuerliche Revolten im Alten Reich. Ein Forschungsbericht', in Peter Blickle, ed., *Aufruhr und Empörung? Studien zum bäuerlichen Widerstand im Alten Reich* (Munich, 1980), 1–68; Peter Blickle, *Unruhen in der ständischen Gesellschaft 1300–1800* (Munich, ^{3}2012 [1988]), 5.

13 Bercé, *Histoire des croquants*, vol. 2, 683.

14 In general: Peter Blickle, *Kommunalismus. Skizzen einer gesellschaftlichen Organisationsform*, 2 vols. (Munich, 2000), vol. 2, 85–99.

15 Peter Blickle, 'Bäuerliche Rebellionen im Fürststift St. Gallen', in Peter Blickle, ed., *Aufruhr und Empörung? Studien zum bäuerlichen Widerstand im Alten Reich* (Munich, 1980), 215–95; Suter, *Troublen*. More recent articles referring to the term 'faction': Sandro Guzzi-Heeb, 'Ribelli innovativi. Conflitti sociali nella Confederazione svizzera (XVII–XVIII secolo)', *Studi storici* 48 (2007), 383–408; Sandro Guzzi-Heeb, 'Revolte und soziale Netzwerke. Mechanismen der politischen Mobilisierung in einem alpinen Tal des 18. Jahrhunderts', *Geschichte und Gesellschaft* 36 (2010), 497–522. Rebellions in territories adjacent to Switzerland have been studied from the perspective of faction: David Martin Luebke, 'Factions and Communities in Early Modern Central Europe', *Central European History* 25, no. 3 (1992), 281–301; David Martin Luebke, *His Majesty's Rebels. Communities, Factions, and Rural Revolt in the Black Forest, 1725–1745* (Ithaca, 1997); Martin Zürn, *"Ir aigen libertet". Waldburg, Habsburg und der bäuerliche Widerstand an der oberen Donau* (Tübingen, 1998).

1701–1712. Peter Blickle identified the emergence in the valley, in the early eighteenth century, of two rival groups with different aims and tactics as an early manifestation of political parties in the context of the representative or proto-parliamentary system of the "Landschaft".[16] The Landschaft was the corporation used by communes to communicate with their lords.[17] The valley of Toggenburg had exhibited a tradition of resistance going back to the fifteenth century, but in the sixteenth and seventeenth centuries, confessional differences provided fresh grounds for division.[18] The prince-abbot of St. Gallen ruled over a territory roughly composed of two parts: the entirely Catholic "princely lands" and the mixed valley of Toggenburg where two-thirds of the population had adopted the reform in the sixteenth century. By the time of the revolt, however, which reached its height from 1704 to 1707 and again in 1734, the confessional antagonism was less important than political issues. The revolt was squelched by military interventions, but before that the abbot had managed to divide the rebels along confessional lines based on the rebels' own introduction of a policy of free exercise of the Reformed confession (alongside the "official" Catholic confession).[19] The Landschaft and the revolt itself were limited to the Toggenburg valley. Thus, on the territorial level, only one of the two parts of the abbots' possessions was involved in the revolt, but Blickle did not consider this division to be the product of "faction" because the princely lands and the Toggenburg valley did not share a common political organization (Landschaft), and therefore could not split from each other.[20] Within the valley, however, the rebel peasants were divided according to the classical dichotomy between radical and moderate. The opposing parties emerged because of differences about how far to go in opposition to the abbot, and were called "parties" rather than "factions" by historians, and called "hard" and "soft"

16 Blickle, 'Rebellionen', 290–91. Cf. for the eighteenth century Val de Bagnes in Valais, Guzzi-Heeb, 'Ribelli', 297.

17 Peter Blickle, *Landschaften im Alten Reich. Die staatliche Funktion des Gemeinen Mannes in Oberdeutschland* (Munich, 1973).

18 E.g., the assassination of the abbot's bailiff Hans Ledergerw by Reformed conspirators in 1621, cf. Bruno Z'Graggen, *Tyrannenmord im Toggenburg. Fürstäbtische Herrschaft und protestantischer Widerstand um 1600* (Zurich, 1999).

19 Blickle, 'Rebellionen'; Würgler, *Unruhen*; Andreas Würgler, 'Formen der Konfliktlösung im Vergleich. Unruhen in Schwaben und in der Schweiz (1650–1800)', in Wolfgang Wüst, ed., *Mitregieren und Herrschaftsteilung in der Frühen Neuzeit* (Erlangen, 2016), 147–69. For the seventeenth century, cf. Z'Graggen, *Tyrannenmord*, 230–45. This issue can be followed in the Dutch revue *Mercure Historique et Politique* 42 (1707), 546–48, 623–24; 44 (1708), 505–07; 45 (1708), 624–30; 46 (1709), 280–81, 522–31 and so on.

20 Blickle, 'Rebellionen', 237.

by their contemporaries.[21] The "radicals" or "hard" referred to their "reformist" rivals as "soft" or "wigs" ("Perücken").[22] The political difference between the radicals and moderates lay both in their goals and the means chosen to achieve those goals. The radicals were ready to use violence if necessary so that the valley of Toggenburg could become a free republic—hopefully the fourteenth canton of the Swiss Confederacy—just as Appenzell, a former subject territory of the same abbot of St. Gallen, had managed to emancipate itself to become the thirteenth canton of the Confederacy in 1513. The moderates, however, would have been satisfied to see their economic grievances redressed and their local autonomy preserved; they were generally closer to the prince-abbot's administration and therefore called "wigs".

The second case study relates to the revolt against the prince-bishop of Basel (1705–1740). This revolt was directed against the lord's plans to centralise the administration of his many different districts. To do this, he introduced new taxes and issued orders without, after 1707, consulting the representative assembly of the Estates ("Landstände", "Etats du pays"). The complex structure of the prince-bishopric, an exclave of the Holy Roman Empire between France and the Swiss cantons, made the subjects' resistance quite heterogeneous. Whereas some of the Reformed southern districts profited from the powerful support of the Reformed canton of Bern in resisting the prince-bishop's attempts to centralize and strengthen his rule, the northern, Catholic districts could not rely on Swiss support, but instead relied on the imperial courts. For his part, the prince asked the help of the Catholic Swiss cantons, but they could not assist him because the Reformed canton of Bern refused the transit of Catholic troops. As a subject of the Emperor, the prince appealed to the imperial courts and, in 1739, he entered into an alliance with the king of France, who provided troops to crush the revolt in 1740.[23] Andreas Suter limited his case study to the rebellion of the northern districts from 1726 to 1740. He underlined the importance of communal structures for the organization and mobilization of resistance, but at the same time he insisted on the fact that the communes' apparent unity in rebellion was quite often the product of rhetoric and coercion within the villages and not their "natural" condition.[24]

21 Cf. Alfred Mantel, *Über die Veranlassung des Zwölfer- oder zweiten Villmergerkrieges. Die Toggenburgerwirren in den Jahren 1706–1712* (Zurich, 1909), 133; Ulrich Im Hof, 'Ancien Régime', in *Handbuch der Schweizer Geschichte*, vol. 2 (Zurich, 1977) 673–784, 697.

22 Johann Hässig, *Die Anfänge des Toggenburger- oder Zweiten Villmergerkrieges 1698–1706* (Basel, 1903), 138–40, 188; cf. Blickle, 'Rebellionen', 252–53; Würgler, *Unruhen*, 55–56.

23 Würgler, *Unruhen*, 70–78.

24 Suter, *Troublen*, 368–72; 238–339 for the general causes of this revolt.

Suter presented this sometimes artificial unity in great detail at the commune and district levels, but again without using the term “faction”. At the level of the commune, he showed that opponents of the rebellion were coerced by attacks on their houses, fields, fences and other belongings, or even subjected to bodily aggressions.[25] The same was true at the district level: if some of the village communities were not willing to follow the majority decision in the Landschaft (the assembly of the district’s village communities) they might be “visited” by armed bands from villages belonging to the majority. Usually the simple “visit” was sufficiently threatening for the minority villages to change their minds.[26] One might add the territory as a third level of possible dissent from the rebellion. The districts had formerly attended assemblies of the Estates and they resumed this tradition during the revolt. At the territorial level, however, there was no consensus about the strategy of resistance, as shown above: the southern districts preferred a quick and positive solution with the support of the canton of Bern to a risky revolt with no assistance from external powers.[27] We may conclude that the difference between these options was not to “rebel” or “obey”, but rather how best to preserve local autonomy and opportunities against the expansion of the lordship’s or the state’s centralising power.[28]

If we leave the two case studies and take a look at the greatest social conflict of the period, the Swiss Peasants’ War in 1653, we discover similar phenomena. At the communal level, there were no major problems integrating individuals into the resistance, according to Andreas Suter’s comprehensive study of this event.[29] The situation was very different at the district level. The peasants’ protest movement succeeded in integrating all the districts only in the canton of Lucerne. In the canton of Bern, only the districts bordering on Lucerne joined the revolt, whereas those in the Bernese Alps negotiated separately with the government, and the peasant militia of the canton’s French-speaking districts actually helped the government crush the uprising. By promising military support via their militia, the alpine districts obtained substantial concessions to their economic demands. Once these concessions were granted by contract (which was, surprisingly, respected by the government), the alpine militia

25 Ibidem, 117–20, 198–222.

26 Ibidem, 141–47.

27 Roger Ballmer, *Les Etats du pays ou les assemblées d’états dans l’ancien Évêché de Bâle* (Delémont, 1985); Würgler, *Unruhen*, 70–78.

28 This point supports Luebke, *Rebels*, 2–5, 22.

29 Andreas Suter, *Der schweizerische Bauernkrieg von 1653. Politische Sozialgeschichte—Sozialgeschichte eines politischen Ereignisses* (Tübingen, 1997), 501. On p. 225–26, though, he presents some evidence of dissent in a few communities.

went back home without being required to ally with the government against their peasant fellows, and in fact, in those alpine districts that had decided not to take part in the revolt, there were small groups of young men who went to support the rebels on their own.[30]

For the sixteenth century, there is some evidence that a tax revolt in the rural areas of Basel in the 1590s was not unanimously supported, but the documentation is too sketchy to discern the emergence of two factions.[31] The same goes for the conflicts concerning pensions during the Italian wars (1494–1516), in which divisions between individuals, communes and districts seem to have existed.[32] There is a lack of evidence of factions in the short-lived protests in Bern and Lucerne in 1513 and in Zurich in 1516, which may be because well-established factions were simply absent during these protests. This might also be due to the fluid and quickly changing character of factions in general. If factions did not become decisive for the course of a revolt, they had little chance to be documented, given the low level of literacy among rural communes. This absence of documentation would also have been true for internal conflicts in the cantons' capital cities, because council protocols only provided for documenting actual decisions, not discussions.

3 The "Hard" and the "Soft": Factions in the Popular Cantons

Social conflicts in the form of factions were common in those rural cantons of the Swiss Confederacy that were organised as popular or "democratic" regimes. This early modern version of "democracy" consisted in the fact that, depending on the canton and the century, all men above fourteen or sixteen years possessing the so-called "Landrecht"—a sort of "citizenship" in the country—had the right to participate in the general assembly ("Landsgemeinde"). The Landsgemeinde was regarded as the "sovereign" according to John Bodin's definition of that term,[33] and therefore legitimated to elect the "Landammann" (chief magistrate) and all other officers (responsible for finance, military and so on), and to make new or abolish old laws by majority decision. Given this constitutional setting, this general assembly served as the main arena for negotiating power relations in the popular cantons. The typical conflict that arose in these

30 Peter Bierbrauer, *Freiheit und Gemeinde im Berner Oberland 1300–1700* (Bern, 1991), 357–62.

31 Landolt, *Untertanenrevolten*, 442.

32 Rogger, *Geld*, 66–67, 168–69, 340–41.

33 This was also the explicit argument of an early eighteenth century "rebel" in Schwyz, quoted by Brändle, *Demokratie*, 325.

cantons, especially in Schwyz, Zug and Appenzell,[34] was popular resistance against the process of aristocratisation that allowed a few rich families to monopolise political benefits and opportunities; for example, privileged access to the mercenary market.

Historiography formerly referred to these conflicts as "party struggles". Both contemporaries and the historiography usually identified the two opposing parties as the "hard", i.e., the opposition, and the "soft", i.e., the ruling group of families. There is some evidence that such quarrels in the canton of Schwyz dated back to at least the mid-sixteenth century, but the absence of sources prevents detailed research.[35] The term "faction" is sometimes used by historians as a synonym for "party" in these situations, but without conceptualizing the difference in these terms.[36] In his most recent and most detailed analysis of five such conflicts in the eighteenth century, Fabian Brändle refuses to employ the label of "faction". To explain this type of conflict, he prefers the model of a charismatic leader usually from a non-ruling family who was able to voice the "hidden transcript" of popular grievances.[37]

For eighteenth-century conflicts in the popular cantons, it is not possible to identify the exact social composition of two opposing factions. This is partly due to the fact that the inhabitants of these cantons did not pay direct taxes, and so there are no tax records which could support a socioeconomic analysis. Nevertheless, one might say that regional rather than social factors were primarily responsible for an individual's choice of faction. Usually the ruling families were located in the geographical centre—in the main valley or in the

34 In the two other democratic cantons, Uri and Glarus, the setting of the conflict was slightly different, cf. Urs Kälin, *Die Urner Magistratenfamilien. Herrschaft, ökonomische Lage und Lebensstil einer ländlichen Oberschicht, 1700–1850* (Zurich, 1991), and Markus René Wick, 'Der Glarner "Landhandel". Strukturgeschichtliche und konfliktsoziologische Hypothesen zum Glarner Konfessionsgegensatz', *Jahrbuch des Historischen Verein des Kantons Glarus* 69 (1982), 49–240.

35 Michel, 'Regieren', 37–51; Brändle, *Demokratie*, 111–18.

36 Randolph C. Head, *Early Modern Democracy in the Grisons. Social Order and Political Language in a Swiss Mountain Canton 1470–1620* (Cambridge, 1995), 121–24, 141; Würgler, *Unruhen*, 198; François Walter, *Histoire de la Suisse*, vol. 2, (Neuchâtel, 2009), 110; André Holenstein, 'Händel—Schiedsgerichte—Vermittlungen. Konflikte und Konfliktlösungen in der alten Schweiz', in Peter Rauscher, Martin Scheutz, eds., *Die Stimme der ewigen Verlierer? Aufstände, Revolten und Revolutionen in den österreichischen Ländern (ca. 1450–1815)* (Vienna, 2013), 387–413, 407.

37 Brändle, *Demokratie*, 322, referring to Pierre Felder, 'Ansätze zu einer Typologie der politischen Unruhen im schweizerischen Ancien Régime 1712–1789', *Schweizerische Zeitschrift für Geschichte* 26 (1976), 324–89, 340–47; Braun, *Ancien Régime*, 272–76.

vicinity of the most important village of the popular canton—whereas the opposition tended to be stronger in the periphery. The great numbers of innkeepers, schoolteachers, barbers and priests supporting or even leading the opposition is noteworthy.[38] Though the factions were called "hard" or "soft" there is no evidence of identifying emblems or a specific dress code for the factions in Appenzell, Schwyz and Zug.[39]

These conflicts broke out into the open occasionally, mostly triggered by mistrust towards elites. The popular opposition advocated for "more democratic" rules for elections and especially for more transparency in public finances and in the ruling elites' role in the mercenary market. The latter point links these internal conflicts with international diplomatic affairs and explains why the French, Spanish or imperial ambassadors or the pope's nuncio were very likely to be involved in these struggles. This cast of characters allows us to look at these conflicts from another perspective.

4 The "French" and the "Spanish": Factions and Foreign Politics

In addition to temporary factions connected to peasant revolts and anti-aristocratic conflicts in rural cantons, we can also observe permanent factions and parties in the Confederacy. These resulted from foreign relations and occurred in both rural and urban cantons. The Swiss cantons did not act as a belligerent party in any European wars during the entire early modern period (1516/1536–1798). The large number of Swiss soldiers who did participate in warfare did so as mercenaries paid by European powers. The mercenary system was organised by treaties involving all or some of the cantons and various belligerent European powers. These treaties fixed the terms of access to the Swiss mercenary market, thus establishing a political monopoly. The most important treaties were negotiated with the French king in 1516 and 1521 by all the cantons except Zurich (which joined in 1614) and Bern (which signed in 1521, left in 1529 and joined again 1584). They were renewed several times, the last renewal occurring in 1777.[40] In exchange for the right to recruit soldiers within the Confederacy, the French crown granted Swiss merchants commercial privileges such as the elimination of taxes on Swiss exports to France and imports of salt and grain into Switzerland. Furthermore, the French crown paid considerable

38 Brändle, *Demokratie*, 331.

39 Ibidem, 332.

40 Andreas Würgler, 'Symbiose ungleicher Partner. Die französisch-eidgenössische Allianz 1516–1798/1815', *Jahrbuch für Europäische Geschichte* 12 (2011), 53–75.

sums, called official pensions, to the cantons' treasuries on an annual basis. Additionally, the French paid huge sums of money in private or secret pensions to important politicians who the crown considered able to facilitate decisions necessary to the mercenary recruitment process by the cantonal councils, the assemblies, and the federal Diet. Because the Catholic cantons entered into similar treaties with the duke of Savoy (1560), the pope (1665), and, far more importantly, with Milan-Spain (1587), and the Reformed cantons Zurich and Bern with the margrave of Baden (1612), Venice (1615, 1706) and the Dutch Republic (1712/1748), the European powers became direct competitors in the Swiss mercenary market.[41]

Because the cantons had established certain political monopolies with respect to the (legal) mercenary market, the diplomatic representatives of warring European powers attempted to tie Swiss politicians to their causes by providing them with precious resources: private pensions, salt, titles, jobs, information and so on. As a result, two or more client networks linked to different foreign powers emerged in most of the cantons. If it was quite common that single members of elite families received private pensions from more than one foreign power during the sixteenth century, this seems to have become rather rare during the seventeenth and especially the eighteenth centuries: by that time, the Swiss clients generally had to choose a single patron—either France or Habsburg Spain in the seventeenth century and either France or Habsburg Austria in the eighteenth century.[42] Some families, however, managed to secure patrons in both the French and the Spanish factions.[43] This was

---

41 Andreas Würgler, 'Eidgenossenschaft', in *Historisches Lexikon der Schweiz* vol. 4 (Basel, 2005), 114–21; André Holenstein, *Mitten in Europa. Verflechtung und Abgrenzung in der Schweizer Geschichte* (Baden, 2014), 115–24.

42 Rudolf Bolzern, *Spanien, Mailand und die katholische Eidgenossenschaft. Militärische, wirtschaftliche und politische Beziehungen zur Zeit des Gesandten Alfonso Casati (1594–1621)* (Luzern, 1982); Groebner, *Geschenke*; Andreas Würgler, *Die Tagsatzung der Eidgenossen. Politik, Kommunikation und Symbolik einer repräsentativen Institution im europäischen Kontext* (Epfendorft, 2013), 485–90; for Schwyz: Nathalie Büsser, 'Militärunternehmertum, Aussenbeziehungen und fremdes Geld', in Historischer Verein des Kantons Schwyz, ed., *Geschichte des Kantons Schwyz* (Zurich, 2012), vol. 3, 69–127, 80–84; Rogger, *Geld*, 153–207; for Zug: Schläppi, 'Akteure', 31–36. For the role of salt, Urs Kälin, 'Salz, Sold und Pensionen. Zum Einfluss Frankreichs auf die politische Struktur der innerschweizer Landsgemeindedemokratien im 18. Jahrhundert', *Der Geschichtsfreund* 149 (1996), 105–24; Windler, 'Ohne Geld', 126–30.

43 E.g. the Pfyffer of Lucerne, Windler, 'Ohne Geld', 116–21, and the Reding of Schwyz during the eighteenth century, Josef Wiget, 'Der Stand Schwyz im 18. Jahrhundert', in Historischer Verein des Kantons Schwyz, ed., *Geschichte des Kantons Schwyz* (Zurich, 2012), vol.

of great advantage to these families because one or more of the foreign powers was quite often in arrears with its payments. The absence of French pensions during the religious wars spurred the alliance with Milan-Spain in 1587, and Spanish arrears around 1600 facilitated a renewal of the French alliance in 1602.

Foreign relations became an issue in many factional conflicts beginning in the late fifteenth and early sixteenth centuries.[44] One type of conflict between subjects and rulers concerned proper competence to sign, renew or modify alliances with European powers. Rural subjects of the city cantons repeatedly asserted their right to participate in decision-making on foreign affairs (Bern 1513, 1531, 1653; Solothurn 1513, 1653; Lucerne 1513, 1653; Zurich 1516, 1531; Basel 1525, 1653) as did the non-ruling urban factions (Lucerne 1651–1653; Basel 1691; Bern 1710, 1744, 1749; Zurich 1713, 1734, 1777; Fribourg 1781–1784).[45] Sometimes rural subjects openly claimed their share of foreign pensions as well (Bern, Solothurn, Lucerne and Zurich in the period 1513–1516).[46] Factions within city elites often competed for election to the councils in order to gain access to the secret pensions. Only rarely did this competition lead to open conflicts; conspiracies or secret arrangements were more common,[47] and not only when the rivalry concerned pensions.[48] In the popular cantons, factional rivalries might cause popular uprisings, as discussed in section three. On occasion, these popular uprisings blended with permanent factional conflicts, as for instance in Zug 1728–1735 and 1764–1768[49] and in Schwyz 1763–1767,[50] but in

4, 9–43, 29. The same goes for the for the von Mont family in the Grisons, linked with the Spanish as well as the Venetian faction, Head, *Early Modern Democracy*, 141.

44 Cf. Teuscher, *Bekannte*, 144–55 (Bern); Würgler, *Tagsatzung*, 343–44, 362–63, 544–45 (Zurich, Bern, Lucerne); Rogger, *Geld*, 301–08 (Zurich, Bern, Lucerne).

45 Würgler, *Unruhen*; Würgler, 'Soziale Konflikte', in *Historisches Lexikon der Schweiz*, vol. 11 (Basel, 2012), 647–49. Cf. Holenstein, 'Händel'.

46 Rogger, *Geld*, 55–118.

47 For Basel 1521, Groebner, *Geschenke*, 210–17; for Lucerne 1559–1569 and Bern up to the 1620s, see Windler, 'Ohne Geld', 116–19, 126–30; for early modern Bern see Andreas Würgler, 'Zwischen Verfahren und Ritual. Entscheidungsfindung und politische Integration in der Stadtrepublik Bern in der Frühen Neuzeit', in Rudolf Schlögl, ed., *Interaktion und Herrschaft. Die Politik der frühneuzeitlichen Stadt* (Constance, 2004), 63–91, 66–75.

48 E.g., when it was a problem of public finances (Schaffhouse 1689), or of the distribution of power between the large and small councils (Basel 1691, Bern 1682, 1710), Würgler, *Unruhen*, 46–52, 99–101.

49 Brändle, *Demokratie*, 165–210; Renato Morosoli, Kaspar Michel, 'Harten- und Lindenhandel', in *Historisches Lexikon der Schweiz*, vol. 6 (Basel, 2007), 111–13.

50 Brändle, *Demokratie*, 243–80; Wiget, 'Stand', 27–34.

most cases the leading families managed to keep their disputes secret. Some of these aristocratic families, such as the Reding in Schwyz and the Zurlauben in Zug, were loyal clients of the French crown for centuries. The same goes for the Büeler of Schwyz and the Fleckenstein of Lucerne with respect to Spain, even if Spanish (and Savoy) money apparently stopped coming in after the War of the Spanish Succession (1701–1714).[51] These factions or parties, in contrast to the rebel factions discussed above, were more formed by family ties, client networks and professional or confessional opportunities than by political or ideological conviction.[52]

With respect to these factions, Swiss historiography again preferred the term "party" or "party struggles" to the more rarely used term "faction", even if contemporary sources used both terms. Most recently, these forms of conducting foreign relations have been described in terms of "patron-client" relations.[53]

The studies which have identified this political mercenary system as "patron-client" relations implicitly suggest that this situation was commonly accepted and even "natural". But research from other perspectives has emphasised a contemporary discourse from the late fifteenth to the late eighteenth centuries which used the term "corruption" to describe this system. Contemporary discomfort with pensions is mirrored in the (ultimately failed) attempts to control or even eliminate many kinds of pensions,[54] and in countless attempts to introduce more transparency in their payment.[55] There was a lively early modern discussion about what was "corrupt" and what was not in this regard.[56]

51 Büsser, 'Militärunternehmertum', 90; Markus Lischer, 'Fleckenstein', in *Historisches Lexikon der Schweiz*, vol. 4 (Basel, 2005), 550–52.

52 Schläppi, 'Akteure', 64–74; Büsser, 'Militärunternehmertum', 80–88.

53 Pfister, 'Klientelismus'; Schläppi, 'Akteure', 26–31; Windler, 'Ohne Geld', 108–09; Andreas Würgler, 'Verflechtung und Verfahren. Individuelle und kollektive Akteure in den Aussenbeziehungen der Alten Eidgenossenschaft', in Hillard von Thiessen, Christian Windler, eds., *Akteure der Aussenbeziehungen. Netzwerke und Interkulturalität im historischen Wandel* (Cologne, 2010), 82–85; Büsser, 'Militärunternehmertum', 85–88.

54 Martin Körner, 'Zur eidgenössischen Solddienst- und Pensionendebatte', in Norbert Furrer et al., eds., *Gente ferocissima. Mercenariat et société en Suisse (XVe–XIXe siècle)* (Lausanne, 1997), 193–203; Würgler, 'Verflechtung', 79–93; Würgler, *Tagsatzung*, 298, 485–87, 605–06; Rogger, *Geld*, 152–207.

55 Groebner, *Geschenke*, 37–49; Büsser, 'Militärunternehmertum', 100–03.

56 Groebner, *Geschenke*, 129–54; Würgler, 'Verflechtung', 85–92; Suter, 'Korruption', 200–11.

5 Choosing a Faction?

Why did factions and parties occur? Not every dissent within various groups making up a political entity (community, canton, confederation) resulted in the presence of factions. In the case of short-term seditions or revolts, the emergence of factions was the result of the minority's inability or unwillingness to accept crucial majority decisions.[57] In the case of permanent factions there seemed to exist a latent consent to tolerate factions in order to improve opportunities in the mercenary markets. But all mono-causal explanations of factions referring exclusively to geography (centre-periphery model), economics (forms of production, wealth), social structure (status), kinship (family and godparents), clientelism (patron-client relations) or confession (Catholic-Protestant) have proved to be too simple.[58] Each of these factors doubtlessly helped to shape factions, but none of them alone is able to explain why certain individuals, communities, districts or Estates chose one or another faction. In confessional or confessionalised conflicts, though, an individual's or group's unfettered choice of a faction was limited in the sense that Catholics were not likely to join the Reformed faction and vice versa. But factions involving members of both confessions existed, as the cases of Toggenburg and the Swiss Peasants' War showed. With respect to the latter, in 1653 the subjects of two Catholic cantons (Lucerne and Solothurn) and the subjects of two Reformed cantons (Bern and Basel) joined together to stage the greatest and most ambitious revolt in early modern Switzerland, called a "revolution" by contemporaries.[59]

It is possible to distinguish the importance of these various factors in shaping certain types of factions. First, we have seen in the Toggenburg and prince-bishopric of Basel cases that the division of a territory often followed district borderlines, and the division of a district occurred between communities.

57 For the problem presented by majority decisions, cf. Olivier Christin, *Vox populi. Une histoire du vote avant le suffrage universel* (Paris, 2014), 45–46.

58 Opting for economics (in his polemic against Luebke): Herman Rebel, 'What do the Peasants Want Now? Realists and Fundamentalists in Swiss and South German Rural Politics, 1650–1750', *Central European History* 34, no. 3 (2001), 313–56, and the reply: David M. Luebke, 'Symbols, Serfdom, and Peasant Factions', ibidem 357–82, esp. 374–78. For the other positions already discussed in this paper, cf. Blickle, 'Rebellionen'; Suter, *Troublen*, 342–68; Bierbrauer, *Freiheit*, 357–62; Pfister, 'Klientelismus', 34–39; Würgler, *Unruhen*, 97–99, 198; Landolt, *Untertanenrevolten*, 240–48, 427–34, 441–46, 608–10; Suter, *Bauernkrieg*, 225–26, 501; Luebke, 'Factions', 288–300; Luebke, *Rebels*, 212–31. Additionally: Guzzi-Heeb, 'Ribelli', 396–97; Guzzi-Heeb, 'Revolte'.

59 Suter, *Bauernkrieg*, 159–66, 160 ('revolution').

The same was true for the Swiss Confederacy and its cantons. Second, we can say that kinship and clientelism were probably more important in the context of permanent factions (e.g., the French and Spanish "parties") than for temporary factions. Third, we follow Luebke in observing that political and especially tactical options might best explain the choices made by temporary factions in the context of revolts,[60] but were probably less significant in the situation of permanent factions. Political options may also have played a role in the choice of patrons from among different European powers. But fourth, especially when it came to this latter choice, confessional factors were also very important—for Swiss elites' choices between France, Spain and the Netherlands, as well as, in the revolts, for choice of external allies—Reformed or Catholic cantons in the case of the Toggenburg, and Reformed cantons or imperial courts in the case of the prince-bishopric of Basel.

In the end, the actors (individuals, communities, districts, Estates) had options, but not all possible options were available at any given moment. Factions based on tactical options may have had the most flexibility, but they were short-lived compared to those based on confession or kinship, which in turn offered limited choices for action—and (therefore) more stability. Factions based on clientelism only offered choices if a new patron appeared (as did the Spanish in 1587 and the Dutch in 1712). Of course, rivalries might occur within factions as well: members of the French faction might quarrel about who would act as the main connection to the French patron, or about whether to send an embassy to Paris, and members of a confessional faction might divide into "hard" and "soft" camps.

6 Conclusion: Factions or Parties?

"Faction" meant "division" in early modern political discourse. Factions split the body politic into pieces, and dissolved peaceful harmony into quarrelling disorder. As shown above, factions might affect political structures at different levels: small units such as rural or urban[61] communities (e.g. within a rebel movement), territorial states in their monarchical, aristocratic or "democratic" (popular) form, and even the entire Confederacy in connection

60 "Factions represent the aggregation of people united by economic, social, or familial circumstance behind the same general articulation or choice of political options". Luebke, 'Factions', 300.

61 For early sixteenth-century Geneva, cf. the contribution by M. Caesar in this volume, 'The Prince and the Factions'.

with foreign politics, as the nuncio Ranuccio Scotti (1597–1661) observed in his final report to the pope: "In Switzerland one has to negotiate with countless factional persons who are linked with the emperor, or France or Spain" which made, as he noted, the mission to the Confederacy the most difficult of all.[62]

Faction as organised dissent was interpreted as a symptom of crisis because it signalled conflict. As we have seen, for Bodin, factions were an evil. Roman law drew a distinction between unlawful or—under certain circumstances—lawful factions, but they remained undesirable realities. This was true also for Jean-Jacques Rousseau (1712–1778) when he discusses the "general will" in his *Social Contract* (1762): "But when factions arise, and partial associations are formed at the expense of the great association, the will of each of these associations becomes general in relation to its members, while it remains particular in relation to the State: [...] It is therefore essential, if the general will is to be able to express itself, that there should be no partial society within the State, and that each citizen should think only his own thoughts".[63] However, even if factions were disfavoured in early modern political theory, analysis of historical practice has made it clear that factional patterns were endemic to all levels of early modern societies. There seems to be a peculiar coexistence between political discourses praising unity and harmony within political bodies on the one hand, and the actual acceptance and exploitation of factions within these political entities. This can be seen in the representatives of the cantons who gathered regularly at the Swiss Diet: though they secretly fostered the interests of their foreign patrons—the pope or the emperor, the French or Spanish king, the duke of Savoy or the Republic of Venice—they were very eloquent in praising the cantons' reciprocal "love, fidelity and unity" which preserved the Confederacy's "freedom and harmony".[64] This search for harmony and unity was a consistent theme in early modern Swiss pamphlet literature and art as

62 "Nell'Elvetica dovendosi trattare con un'infinità di gente fazionaria chi aderendo all'Imperatore, chi à Francia, e chi a Spagna", quoted in Pierre Louis Surchat, 'Das Corpus Helveticum im Urteil der Nuntien', in Marco Jorio, ed., *1648. Die Schweiz und Europa. Aussenpolitik zur Zeit des Westfälischen Friedens* (Zürich, 1999), 111–19, 112–13.

63 Jean-Jacques Rousseau, *Du contrat social* (Amsterdam, 1762), english trans., G.D.H. Cole 1782, quoted online: http://www.constitution.org/jjr/socon_02.htm [11.8.2015]. The French original uses the term "brigues" instead of "faction". Cf. Luc Bovens, Claus Beisbart, 'Factions in Rousseau's *Du Contrat Social* and federal representation', *Analysis* 67, no. 1 (January 2007), 12–20.

64 Würgler, *Tagsatzung*, 410–23.

well.[65] But political actors, while complaining about the existence of factions, nonetheless tried to exploit them for their needs.

In contrast to Bodin and the Roman law, the Italian philosopher Niccolò Machiavelli (1469–1527) admitted that factional struggles might produce good outcomes in the form of new laws. This was a partially positive judgement about factions which was—as was the case with Machiavelli's ideas in general—not openly and approvingly cited during the early modern period, except by Rousseau. But there were, as Angela de Benedictis has recently shown, a few hidden followers of Machiavelli. One was the German lawyer Johann Wilhelm Neumair von Ramsla (1572–1641), who has become important to recent historiography because he was one of the crucial figures used by the German historian Winfried Schulze to support his thesis that "rebellions might trigger salutary laws".[66] So according to Machiavelli and Neumair, factions could, even if they were undesirable, produce positive new laws, and these positive laws were not unintended consequences simply because they arose from factional debates and the solutions they proposed. Factions did not only engender new laws as the plague might have engendered new sanitation concepts: unlike the plague, one of the goals of factional discourse was to produce solutions.

Yet, factions remained negative entities in the conception of early modern political and legal discourse. There does not appear to be an early modern view of factions that acknowledges this form of organised dissent and accepts factions as "parties" representing legitimate, if specific and partial, interests. Especially town and village communities were characterised as being strongly oriented towards consensus and therefore not really able to tackle open discussions between rival factions.[67] To acknowledge the existence of legitimate partial interests was, according to the political scientist Richard Löwenthal

---

65 Daniel Guggisberg, *Das Bild der "Alten Eidgenossen" in Flugschriften des 16. bis Anfang 18. Jahrhunderts (1531–1712)* (Bern, 2000), 273–356, 618–23, 781–84; for engravings and paintings cf. Würgler, *Tagsatzung*, 512, 533–37.

66 Winfried Schulze, '"Geben Aufruhr und Aufstand Anlass zu neuen heilsamen Gesetzen". Beobachtungen über die Wirkungen bäuerlichen Widerstandes in der frühen Neuzeit', in Winfried Schulze, ed., *Aufstände, Revolten, Prozesse. Beiträge zu bäuerlichen Widerstandsbewegungen im frühneuzeitlichen Europa* (Stuttgart, 1983), 261–85. Cf. Angela De Benedictis, '"According to Bartolo", "according to Baldo". Archives or Knowledge for the Study of Revolt', in Angela De Benedictis, Karl Härter, eds., *Revolts and Political Crime from the 12th to the 19th Century* (Frankfurt am Main, 2013), 17–40, 31–34.

67 Rudolf Schlögl, 'Vergesellschaftung unter Anwesenden. Zur kommunikativen Form des Politischen in der vormodernen Stadt', in Rudolf Schlögl, ed., *Interaktion und Herrschaft. Die Politik der frühneuzeitlichen Stadt* (Constance, 2004), 9–60, 28–42.

(1908–1991), an achievement of early modern representative or parliamentary systems.[68] Yet, the existence of permanent factions in early modern Swiss cities and the existence of long-lasting factions in villages, accepted by political elites in the Swiss cantons in practice, if not in theory, may also be seen as proof that it was possible to dissent within the community. The elites saw the necessity of a relationship with the French or Habsburg factions in order to ensure an adequate flow of resources into the cantons—even if one of the European powers was unable to fulfil their financial obligations. This meant that at least the rival factions accepted the existence of faction. They even jointly defended it against attempts—such as those by the "Landsgemeinden" and by reformed theologians like Zwingli—to abolish all foreign pensions.[69]

Some recent historiography has categorized these types of conflicts as "patron-client-(broker)" relations, and some older as well as more recent research has applied the term "parties" rather than "factions". "Faction", however, is probably a more appropriate label than "party" for this constellation of rivalry among sociopolitical elites and within rebellious movements. The term "party" is still in use and therefore raises potentially misleading associations with early modern "parties" as well as with the political system in which these "parties" operated. The nature of the contemporary party is that of a legal association with written and fixed statutes, a written platform, elected committees and organised procedures in order to foster open and visible competition, to gain the support of voters, and to represent the people in parliament by forming the government, a coalition or the opposition. Early modern factions, however, were rather amorphous, partly secret and generally not transparent groupings, operating by sometimes doubtful means to secure resources needed to achieve the implicit goal of maintaining access to power.

Apart from the differing nature of factions and parties, there are also great differences between the early modern and contemporary political systems. During the early modern period, factions were considered to be an evil, signs of disobedience, disease and corruption, because they were seen as the visible cause of divisions within a political unit which was conceived of as being united and harmonious (community, district, territory, confederation or even realm or empire).[70] In the present day, parties are, by contrast, considered

68 Richard Löwenthal, 'Kontinuität und Diskontinuität. Zur Grundproblematik des Symposions', in Karl Bosl, Karl Möckl, eds., *Der moderne Parlamentarismus und seine Grundlagen in der ständischen Repräsentation* (Berlin, 1977), 341–56.

69 Würgler, *Unruhen*, 198; Luebke, *Rebels*, 85, for the factions in the rural revolt of Hauenstein.

70 Gérard Mairet, 'Présentation', in Jean Bodin, *Les six livres de la République. Un abrégé du texte de l'édition de Paris de 1583* (Paris, 1993), 5–38, 17–21. This does not mean that factions

to be one of the pillars of modern western democracies: the parties organise the open competition of rival political norms and rival solutions to problems within constitutional boundaries—thus guaranteeing an open society and a pluralistic, democratic state under the rule of law. Whereas early modern social and legal theory perceived faction as the division of a united community, contemporary liberal concepts praise parties for uniting individuals.

---

were not considered useful: foreign powers repeatedly profited from factual divisions within the Swiss cantons, Würgler, *Tagsatzung*, 362, 484–90, and town authorities attempted to divide rebellious citizens into rival factions in order to collaborate with one of them against the other, for instance in Basel 1691, Würgler, *Unruhen*, 46–52, 49.

Bibliography

This is a cumulative bibliography of the printed works used by the authors of this volume. Manuscripts and archival sources are not provided here. References to primary sources and abbreviations used may be found at the beginning of each article.

Achón, José Ángel. *A voz de concejo: linaje y corporación urbana en la constitución de la Provincia de Gipuzkoa: los Báñez y Mondragón, siglos XIII–XVI*, San Sebastián, 1995.

Adams, John. 'A Defence of the Constitutions of Government of the United States of America' (1778), in *The Works of John Adams*, vol. IV, Boston, 1851, 374–79.

Adrian, Dominique. 'La chronique de Memmingen', *The medieval Chronicle*, 11 (2016).

Adrian, Dominique. 'La face cachée de la politique. Le chancelier au cœur des tensions politiques à Augsbourg au XVe siècle', *Journal des savants* (janvier-juin 2008), 107–21.

Adrian, Dominique. *Augsbourg à la fin du Moyen Âge: la politique et l'espace*, Ostfildern, 2013.

Affolter, Andreas. *Verhandeln mit Republiken. Die Ambassade des Marquis d'Avaray und die französisch-eidgenössischen Beziehungen im frühen 18. Jahrhundert* (PhD thesis, University of Bern, EPHE Paris, 2015).

Aguirre, Sabino. *Las dos primeras crónicas de Vizcaya. Estudios, textos críticos y apéndices*, Bilbao, 1986.

Albèri, Eugenio. *Relazioni degli ambasciatori veneti al Senato*, 15 vols., Florence, 1839–1863.

Alberti, Leandro. *Descrittione di tutta Italia*, Venice, 1551.

Alcalá-Zamora y Queipo de Llano, José. 'La Monarquía Hispánica y Westfalia', in Bernardo García García, ed. *350 años de la Paz de Westfalia. 1648–1998. Del antagonismo a la integración en Europa*, Madrid, 1999, 21–32.

Aldea Vaquero, Quintín. *España y Europa en el siglo XVII. Correspondencia de Saavedra Fajardo*, 3 vols., Madrid, 1986.

Alexander, Robert J. 'Splinter Groups in American Radical Politics', *Social Research* 20, no 3 (1953), 282–310.

Allegrezza, Franca. 'Alessandro VI e le famiglie romane di antica nobiltà: gli Orsini', in Maria Chiabò et al, eds. *Roma di fronte all'Europa al tempo di Alessandro VI*, vol. 1, Roma, 2001, 330–44.

Allegrezza, Franca. *Organizzazione del potere e dinamiche familiari. Gli Orsini dal Duecento agli inizi del Quattrocento*, Rome, 1998.

Ángel Lema, José. 'Bibliografía y fuentes impresas para el estudio de la Lucha de Bandos en el País Vasco', in *La Lucha de Bandos en el País Vasco. De los Parientes Mayores a la Hidalguía universal. Guipúzcoa, de los Bandos a la Provincia*, Bilbao, 2008, 557–602.

Anna Modigliani, *Congiurare all'antica. Stefano Porcari, Niccolò V, Roma 1453*, Rome, 2013.

Anzulewicz, Henryk. 'Jakob von Paradies, *Determinatio Basiliensis*', in *Polskie traktaty koncyliarystyczne z połowy XV wieku* (*Textus et studia historiam theologiae in Polonia excultae spectantia*), vol. 23 (Warsaw, 1987), 83–115.

Asch, Ronald. 'The Princely Court and Political Space in Early Modern Europe', in Beat Kümin, ed. *Political Space in Pre-industrial Europe*, Aldershot, 2013, 43–60.

Bachmann, Adrian. *Die preussische Sukzession in Neuchâtel. Ein ständisches Verfahren um die Landesherrschaft im Spannungsfeld zwischen Recht und Utilitarismus (1694–1715)*, Zurich, 1993.

Baechler, Blanca. *Petit Conseil de Genève (1460–1540). Étude prosopographique d'une élite dirigeante dans une période de crise politique et religieuse*, 2 vols., Geneva, 1995 (Thèse de doctorat dactylographiée).

Baernstein, Prudence Renée. 'Vita pubblica, vita familiare, e memoria storica nel monastero di San Paolo a Milano', in Gianna Pomata and Gabriella Zarri, eds. *I monasteri femminili come centri di cultura fra Rinascimento e Barocco*, Rome, 2005, 297–312.

Bailey, Michael J. 'Reformers on Sorcery and Superstition', in James D. Mixson and Bert Roest, eds. *A Companion to Observant Reform in the Late Middle Ages and Beyond*, Leiden, 2015, 230–54.

Ballmer, Roger. *Les Etats du pays ou les assemblées d'états dans l'ancien Évêché de Bâle*, Delémont, 1985.

Barbarano de Mironi, Francesco. *Historia Ecclesiastica della Città, Territorio, e Diocese di Vicenza*, 6 vols., Vicenza, 1649–1762.

Barnavi, Élie. 'Centralisation ou fédéralisme? Les relations entre Paris et les villes à l'époque de la Ligue (1585–1594)', *Revue Historique*, CCLIX (1978), 335–44.

Barnavi, Élie. 'La Ligue parisienne (1585–1594); ancêtre des partis totalitaires modernes?' *French Historical Studies* XI, (1979), 29–57.

Barnavi, Élie. *Le Parti de Dieu*, Louvain, 1980.

Barozzi, Nicolò, and Guglielmo Berchet, eds. *Relazioni degli stati europei lette al Senato dagli ambasciatori veneti nel secolo decimosettimo, Serie I, 'Spagna'*, vol. II, Venice, 1860.

Basaglia, Enrico. 'Il banditismo nei rapporti di Venezia con gli stati confinanti', in Gherardo Ortalli, ed. *Bande armate, banditi, banditismo e repressione di giustizia negli stati europei di antico regime*, Rome, 1986, 423–40.

Basas, Manuel. 'La institucionalización de los bandos en la sociedad bilbaína y vizcaína al comienzo de la Edad Moderna', in *La sociedad vasca rural y urbana en el marco de la crisis de los siglos XIV y XV*, Bilbao, 1973, 117–60.

Beaune, Colette, ed. *Journal d'un bourgeois de Paris de 1405 à 1449*, Paris, 1990.

Beceiro, Isabel, and Ricardo Córdoba. *Parentesco, poder y mentalidad. La nobleza castellana, siglos XII–XV*, Madrid, 1990.

Becker, Rotraud, ed. *Nuntiaturen des Giovanni Battista Pallotto und des Ciriaco Rocci (1630–1631)*, Tübingen, 2009.

Beerli, Conrad André. *Le peintre poète Nicolas Manuel et l'évolution sociale de son temps*, Genève, 1953.

Beik, William H. 'Urban factions and the Social Order during the Minority of Louis XIV', *French Historical Studies* 15, no 1 (1987), 36–67.

Bellabarba, Marco. *La giustizia nell'Italia moderna XVI–XVIII secolo*, Rome, 2008.

Beltramini, Guido, and Howard Burns, eds. *Palladio*, London, 2008.

Benedict, Philippe. *Rouen during the Wars of Religion*, Cambridge, 1981.

Benedict, Philippe. 'Were the French Wars of Religion Really Wars of Religion? Contemporary Views, Then and Now', in Wolfgang Palaver, Dietmar Regensburger, and Harriet Rudolph, eds. *The European Wars of Religion. An Interdisciplinary Reassessment of Sources, Myths, and Interpretations*, Farnham, 2016, 61–86.

Bercé, Yves-Marie. *Histoire des croquants. Etude des soulèvements populaires au XVIIe siècle au sud-ouest de la France*, 2 vols., Geneva, 1974.

Bercé, Yves-Marie. *Histoire des croquants*, Paris, 1986.

Bérenger, Jean. 'La Cour impériale de Léopold Ier: partis, clans et clientèles', in Klaus Malettke and Chantal Grell, eds. *Hofgesellschaft und Höflinge an europäischen Fürstenhöfen in der Frühen Neuzeit (15.–18. Jh.)*, Münster, 2001, 257–70.

Bernard, George W. *Power and Politics in Tudor England: Essays*, Aldershot, 2000.

Bernstein, Hilary J. *Between Crown and Community. Politics and Civic Culture in XVIth Century Poitiers*, Ithaca, 2004.

Bianco, Furio. 'Mihi vindictam: aristocratic clans and rural communities in a feud in Friuli in the late Fifteenth and early Sixteenth centuries', in Trevor Dean and Kate J.P. Lowe, eds. *Crime, Society and the Law in Renaissance Italy*, Cambridge, 1994, 249–73.

Bierbrauer, Peter. 'Bäuerliche Revolten im Alten Reich. Ein Forschungsbericht', in Peter Blickle, ed. *Aufruhr und Empörung? Studien zum bäuerlichen Widerstand im Alten Reich*, Munich, 1980, 1–68.

Bierbrauer, Peter. *Freiheit und Gemeinde im Berner Oberland 1300–1700*, Bern, 1991.

Binz, Louis, Jean Emery, and Catherine Santschi, *Le diocèse de Genève. L'archidiocèse de Vienne en Dauphiné*, Bern, 1980 (*Helvetia Sacra* I/3).

Bireley, Robert. *Ferdinand II, Counter-Reformation Emperor, 1578–1637*, Cambridge, 2014.

Bireley, Robert. *Religion and Politics in the Age of the Counterreformation: Emperor Ferdinand II, William Lamormaini, S.J., and the Formation of Imperial Policy*, Chapel Hill, 1981.

Bireley, Robert. *The Jesuits and the Thirty Years War. Kings, Courts, and Confessors*, Cambridge, 2003.

Blickle, Peter. *Landschaften im Alten Reich. Die staatliche Funktion des Gemeinen Mannes in Oberdeutschland*, Munich, 1973.

Blickle, Peter. 'Bäuerliche Rebellionen im Fürststift St. Gallen', in Peter Blickle, ed. *Aufruhr und Empörung? Studien zum bäuerlichen Widerstand im Alten Reich*, Munich, 1980, 215–95.

Blickle, Peter. 'Friede und Verfassung. Voraussetzungen und Folgen der Eidgenossenschaft von 1291', in Hansjakob Achermann, Josef Brülisauer, Peter Hoppe, eds. *Innerschweiz und frühe Eidgenossenschaft*, vol. 1, Olten, 1991, 13–202.

Blickle, Peter. *Kommunalismus. Skizzen einer gesellschaftlichen Organisationsform*, 2 vols., Munich, 2000.

Blickle, Peter. *Unruhen in der ständischen Gesellschaft 1300–*1800, Munich, 2012 (1st ed., 1988).

Bodin, Jean. *The Six Books of the Commonwealth,* abridged and trans. by M.J. Tooley, Oxford, 1955.

Boissevain, James. 'Factions, Parties and Politics in a Maltese Village', *American Anthropologist*, no 66/6 (1964), 1275–87.

Bolognesi, Dante, ed. *1512 La battaglia di Ravenna, L'Italia, l'Europa*, Ravenna, 2014.

Bolzern, Rudolf. *Spanien, Mailand und die katholische Eidgenossenschaft. Militärische, wirtschaftliche und politische Beziehungen zur Zeit des Gesandten Alfonso Casati (1594–1621)*, Lucerne, 1982.

Bonivard, François. *Chroniques de Genève*, ed. Micheline Tripet, 3 vols., Geneva, 2001–2014.

Bonjour, Edgar. *Die Bauernbewegungen des Jahres 1525 im Staate Bern*, Bern, 1923.

Bonora, Elena. *I conflitti della Controriforma. Santità e obbedienza nell'esperienza religiosa dei primi barnabiti*, Florence, 1998.

Bonora, Elena. *Aspettando l'imperatore. Principi italiani tra il papa e Carlo V*, Turin, 2014.

Boockmann, Hartmut. 'Spätmittelalterliche deutsche Stadt-Tyrannen', *Blätter für deutsche Landesgeschichte* 119 (1983), 73–91.

Boone, Rebecca Ard. *War, domination, and the monarchy of France: Claude de Seyssel and the language of politics in the Renaissance*, Leiden, 2007.

Boquet, Damien, and Piroska Nagy. *Sensible Moyen Âge. Une histoire des émotions dans l'Occident medieval*, Paris, 2015.

Borgeaud, Charles. 'Philibert Berthelier, Bezanson Hugues, pères de la combourgeoisie de Genève avec Fribourg et Berne', *Étrennes genevoises* (1927), 18–45.

Boudet, Jean-Patrice. 'Simon de Phares et les rapports entre astrologie et prophétie à la fin du Moyen Âge', in *Les textes prophétiques et la prophétie en Occident (XII–XVI siècle)*, Rome, 1999, 617–48.

Boudet, Jean-Patrice. *Entre science et nigromance: astrologie, divination et magie dans l'Occident médiéval, XII*[e]*–XV*[e] *siècle*, Paris, 2006.

Bovens, Luc, and Claus Beisbart. 'Factions in Rousseau's *Du Contrat Social* and federal representation', *Analysis* 67, no. 1 (January 2007), 12–20.

Bowd, Stephen D. *Venice's most loyal city: civic identity in Renaissance Brescia*, Cambridge, 2010.

Brady, Thomas. *Turning Swiss. Cities and Empire, 1450–1550*, Cambridge, 1985.

Braekevelt, Jonas, et al., 'The politics of factional conflict in late medieval Flanders', *Historical Research*, 85/227 (2012), 13–31.

Brändle, Fabian. *Demokratie und Charisma. Fünf Landsgemeindekonflikte im 18. Jahrhundert*, Zurich, 2005.

Braun, Konrad [Conradus Brunus]. *De seditionibus libri sex, rationibus et exempliss ex omni doctrinarum et Authorum genere locupletati*, Mainz, 1550.

Braun, Rudolf. *Das ausgehende Ancien Régime in der Schweiz*, Göttingen, 1984.

Brettle, Sigismund. *San Vicente Ferrer und sein literarischer Nachlass*, Münster, 1924.

Broggio, Paolo, and Maria Pia Paoli. *Stringere la pace. Teorie e pratiche della conciliazione nell'Europa moderna sec. XV–XVIII secolo*, Rome, 2011.

Bruni, Francesco. *La città divisa: Le parti e il bene comune da Dante a Guicciardini*, Bologna, 2003.

Buchholzer, Laurence, and Olivier Richard, eds. *Ligues urbaines et espace à la fin du Moyen Âge. Städtebünde und Raum im Spätmittelalter*, Strasbourg, 2012.

Buraggi, Gian Carlo. 'Gli statuti di Amedeo VIII di Savoia del 31 luglio 1403', *Memorie dell'Accademia delle scienze di Torino. Classe di scienze morali, storiche e filologiche* 70, no. 2 (1940), 1–38.

Burns, Howard. 'Da naturale inclinatione guidato: il primo decennio di attività di Palladio architetto', in Arnaldo Bruschi, ed. *Storia dell'architettura italiana. Il primo Cinquecento*, Milan, 2002.

Büsser, Nathalie. 'Militärunternehmertum, Aussenbeziehungen und fremdes Geld', in Historischer Verein des Kantons Schwyz, ed. *Geschichte des Kantons Schwyz*, vol. 3, Zurich, 2012, 69–127.

Caesar, Mathieu. *Le pouvoir en ville. Gestion urbaine et pratiques politiques à Genève (fin XIIIe–début XVIe siècles)*, Turnhout, 2011.

Caesar, Mathieu. *Histoire de Genève. La cité des évêques*, Neuchâtel, 2014.

Caillou, François. 'L'essor et l'échec de la Ligue à Tours (1576–1588)', *Annales de Bretagne et des pays de l'Ouest* 114, no 4 (2008), 31–53.

Canaccini, Federico. *Ghibellini e ghibellinismo in Toscana da Montaperti a Campaldino (1260–1289)*, Rome, 2009.

Caro Baroja, Julio. *Linajes y Bandos. A propósito de la nueva edición de las "Bienandanzas e Fortunas"*, San Sebastián, 1956.

Carpi, Olivia. *Une république imaginaire. Amiens pendant les troubles de religion*, Paris, 2005.

Carpi, Olivia. 'L'esprit de la Ligue dans le Nord de la France en 1588', in Véronique Castagnet et al., eds. *Les affrontements religieux en Europe*, Villeneuve-d'Ascq, 2008, 103–116.

Carpi, Olivia. 'Élites citadines et sédition en France à l'époque des troubles de religion', in Philippe Depreux, ed. *Révolte et Statut social de l'Antiquité tardive aux temps modernes*, Munich, 2008, 255–71.

Carpi, Olivia. 'Des vertus de l'oligarchie: la municipalité amiénoise au XVIe siècle', in Laurent Coste, ed. *Liens de sang, liens de pouvoir*, Rennes, 2010, 189–211.

Carpi, Olivia. *Les guerres de religion. Un conflit franco-français*, Paris, 2012.

Carpi, Olivia. 'Élites citadines et sortie de guerre civile en France. Les cas des anciennes villes ligueuses', in Laurent Coste and Sylvie Guillaume, eds. *Élites et crises du XVIe au XXIe siècle. Europe et Outre-mer*, Paris, 2014, 363–75.

Carpi, Olivia. 'Identité civique et sortie de guerre. Le cas d'Amiens au lendemain des guerres de Religion', *Revue du Nord*, Hors-série, 30 (2014), 249–66.

Carpi, Olivia. 'Henri Drouot et la notion de république: réflexion sur l'expérience politique des villes ligueuses du nord-est de la France', *Annales de Bourgogne*, no 87/4 and 88/1 (2015), 83–100.

Carpi, Olivia. 'La milice comme instrument de reconstruction identitaire de la communauté citadine à Amiens dans le premier tiers du XVIIe siècle', in Serge Brunet and José Javier Ruiz Ibáñez, eds. *Les milices dans la première modernité*, Rennes, 2015, 21–34.

Carroll, Stuart. 'The Guise Affinity and Popular Protest during the Wars of Religion', *French History* 9, no 2 (1995), 125–152.

Casanova, Cesarina. 'La riorganizzazione del potere urbano: le fazioni e le famiglie', in *1512 La battaglia di Ravenna*, in Dante Bolognesi, ed. *1512 La battaglia di Ravenna, L'Italia, l'Europa*, Ravenna, 2014, 255–73.

Cassan, Michel. 'Laïcs, Ligue et réforme catholique à Limoges', *Histoire, Économie et Société*, 10e année, no 2 (1991), 159–175.

Cassan, Michel. *Le temps des guerres de Religion. Le cas du Limousin*, Paris, 1996.

Caviglia, Claudio. *Claudio di Seyssel (1450–1520). La vita nella storia de' suoi tempi*, Torino, 1928.

Cazaux, Loïc. 'Les lendemains de la Praguerie. Révolte et comportement politique à la fin de la guerre de Cent ans', in François Pernot and Valérie Tourelle, eds. *Les lendemains de guerre. Les hommes, l'espace et le récit, l'économie et le politique. Actes du colloque de l'Université de Cergy-Pontoise (2008)*, Bruxelles, 2010, 365–74.

Cerman, Ivo. '"Kabal", "Parthey", "Faction" am Hofe Kaiser Leopolds I', in Werner Paravicini and Jan Hirschbiegel, eds. *Der Fall des Günstlings. Hofparteien in Europa vom 13. bis zum 17. Jahrhundert*, Ostfildern, 2004, 235–47.

Chambers, David S. *Popes, Cardinals and War. The Military Church in Renaissance and Early Modern Europe*, London, 2006.

Chaponnière, Jean-Jacques, ed. 'Journal du Syndic Jean Balard ou relation des événements qui se sont passés à Genève de 1525 à 1531', *Mémoires et documents publiés par la Société d'histoire et d'archéologie de Genève* 10 (1854).

Cherubini, Paolo. 'Tra violenza e crimine di stato: la morte di Lorenzo di Oddone Colonna, in Massimo Miglio et al., eds. *Un pontificato ed una città. Sisto IV (1471–1484)*, Città del Vaticano, 1986, 355–80.

Chittolini, Giorgio. 'Private Wars at the End of the Middle Ages: Notes on Italy and Germany in the 15th Century', in Yoshihisa Hattori, ed. *Political Order and Forms of Communication in Medieval and Early Modern Europe*, Rome, 2014, 109–32.

Christin, Olivier. *Vox populi. Une histoire du vote avant le suffrage universel*, Paris, 2014.

Clark, Peter, and Bernard Lepetit, eds. *Capital Cities and their Hinterlands in Early Modern Europe*, Aldershot, 1996.

Cloulas, Ivan. *Giulio II*, Rome, 1993.

Comino, Giancarlo. 'I Ferrero a Mondovì nel Quattrocento e nel Cinquecento: strategie economiche e lotte politiche tra Medioevo e prima età moderna', in Andrea Merlotti, ed. *Nobiltà e Stato in Piemonte. I Ferrero d'Ormea, atti del convegno, Torino-Mondovì, 3–5 ottobre 2001*, Turin, 2003, 121–35.

Comino, Giancarlo. 'Al timone di "una città inquieta": il governatore sabaudo nel Piemonte di antico regime e in particolare a Mondovì', in Gemma Fulcheri, ed. *Il palazzo del Governatore a Mondovì Piazza. Un cantiere tra operatività e conoscenza*, Mondovì, 2012, 63–69.

Constant, Jean-Marie. 'La Ligue vue par les historiens du XVIe siècle à la fin du XXe siècle', in idem, *La Ligue*, Paris, 1996, 467–75.

Constant, Jean-Marie. '*Partis, cabales, factions.* Études des sensibilités politiques dans les Mémoires du temps de Louis XIII', in Malina Stefanovska and Adrien Paschoud, eds. *Littérature et politique. Factions et dissidences de la Ligue à la Fronde*, Paris, 2015, 143–58.

Corbin, Alain, Jean-Jacques Courtine, and Georges Vigarello, eds. *Histoire des émotions*, 3 vols., Paris, 2016.

Coss, Peter. *The origins of the English Gentry*, Cambridge, 2003.

Courbon, Léonard, and Denis Menjot, eds. *La cour et la ville dans l'Europe du Moyen Âge et des Temps Modernes*, Turnhout, 2015.

Courvoisier, Jean. *Le Maréchal Berthier et sa Principauté de Neuchâtel, 1806–1814*, Neuchâtel, 1959.

Courvoisier, Jean. 'Essai sur les projets de cession de Neuchâtel à la France entre 1707 et 1789', *Schweizerische Zeitschrift für Geschichte* 9 (1959), 145–67.

Cozzi, Gaetano. 'Ambiente veneziano, ambiente veneto. Governanti e governati nel Dominio di qua dal Mincio nei secoli XV–XVIII', in Gaetano Cozzi, ed. *Ambiente veneziano, ambiente veneto. Saggi su politica, società, cultura nella Repubblica di Venezia in età moderna*, Venice, 1997, 291–352.

Craig, John. *Reformation, Politics and Polemics: The Growth of Protestantism in East Anglian Market Towns, 1500–1610*, Aldershot, 2001.

Cuendet, Claude. *Les traités de combourgeoisie en pays romands, et entre ceux-ci et les villes de Berne et Fribourg: (XIIIe au XVIe siècle)*, Lausanne, 1979.

Curiel, Iosu. *La parroquia en el País Vasco-Cantábrico durante la baja Edad Media (c. 1350–1530)*, Bilbao, 2009.

Dacosta, Arsenio. *Los linajes de Bizkaia en la baja Edad Media: poder, parentesco y conflict*, Bilbao, 2004.

Dacosta, Arsenio. 'La nobleza vizcaína ante un siglo de cambios', in Arsenio Dacosta et al, eds. *Poder y privilegio. Nuevos textos para el estudio de la nobleza vizcaína al final de la Edad Media (1416–1527)*, Bilbao, 2010, 15–105.

Dacosta Arsenio, et al., eds. *Poder y privilegio. Nuevos textos para el estudio de la nobleza vizcaína al final de la Edad Media (1416–1527)*, Bilbao, 2010.

Dacosta, Arsenio, and José Ramón Díaz de Durana. 'Political identities in conflict: the Lordship of Vizcaya in the fourteenth and fifteenth centuries', *Journal of Medieval Iberian Studies* 7 (2015), 112–34.

De Benedictis, Angela. '"According to Bartolo", "according to Baldo". Archives or Knowledge for the Study of Revolt', in Angela De Benedictis, Karl Härter, eds. *Revolts and Political Crime from the 12th to the 19th Century*, Frankfurt am Main, 2013, 17–40.

De Otazu, Alfonso. *El "igualitarismo" vasco: mito y realidad*, San Sebastián, 1973.

De Otazu, Alfonso, and José Ramón Díaz de Durana. *El espíritu emprendedor de los Vascos*, Madrid, 2008.

De Rouvroy, Louis, duc de Saint-Simon. *Mémoires. Additions au Journal de Dangeau*, ed. Yves Coirault, 8 vols., Paris, 1983–1988.

De Seyssel, Claude. *La Monarchie de France*, ed. Renzo Ragghianti, Paris, 2012.

De Turrecramata, Johannes. *Summa de ecclesia contra impugnatores potestatis Summi Pontificis*, Venice, 1561.

De Vivo, Filippo. *Information and Communication in Venice: Rethinking Early Modern Politics*, Oxford, 2007.

De Vivo, Filippo. 'Rhetoric and government in sixteenth-century Venice: some paradoxes', *The Italianist*, 27 (2007) special issue, Jill Kraye and Laura Lepschy, eds. *Caro Vitto: Essays in Memory of Vittore Branca*, 188–205.

De Vivo, Filippo. *Patrizi, informatori, barbieri. Politica e comunicazione a Venezia nella prima età moderna*, Milan, 2012.

Dei Conti da Foligno, Sigismondo. *Le storie de' suoi tempi dal 1475 al 1510*, 2 vols., Rome, 1883.

Del Vera, Fabrizio. '*Quietis publicae perturbatio*: Revolts in the Political and Legal Treatises of the Sixteenth and Seventeenth Centuries', in Malte Griesse, ed. *From Mutual Observation to Propaganda War. Premodern Revolts in Their Transnational Representations*, Bielefeld, 2014.

Demo, Edoardo. 'Industry and Production in the Venetian Terraferma (15th–18th Centuries)', in Eric R. Dursteler, ed. *A Companion to Venetian History, 1400–1797*, Leiden, 2013, 291–318.

Demo, Edoardo. 'New Products and Technological Innovation in the Silk Industry of Vicenza in the Fifteenth and Sixteenth Centuries', in Karel Davids and Bert De Munck, eds. *Innovation and Creativity in Late Medieval and Early Modern European Cities*, Farnham, 2014, 81–93.

Dendorfer, Jürgen, and Claudia Märtl, eds. *Nach dem Basler Konzil. Die Neuordnung der Kirche zwischen Konziliarismus und monarchischem Papat (ca. 1450–1475)*, Berlin, 2008.

Descimon, Robert. *Qui étaient les Seize? Mythes et réalités de la Ligue parisienne (1585–1594)*, Paris, 1983.

Descimon, Robert. 'Le corps de ville et le système cérémoniel parisien au début de l'âge modern', in Marc Boone and Maarten Prak, ed. *Statuts individuels, statuts corporatifs et statuts judiciaires dans les villes européennes*, Louvain, 1996, 73–128.

Descimon, Robert. 'Power Elites and the Prince: The State as Enterprise', Wolfgang Reinhard, ed. *Power Elites and State Building*, Oxford, 1996, 101–21.

Descimon, Robert. 'Compte-rendu critique de l'ouvrage d'A. Finley-Croswhite', *Annales ESC* 56, no 2 (2001), 545.

Descimon, Robert, and José Javier Ruiz Ibáñez, *Les ligueurs de l'exil. Le refuge catholique français après 1594*, Seyssel, 2005.

Dessì, Rosa Maria. 'I nomi dei guelfi e ghibellini da Carlo I d'Angio a Petrarca', in Marco Gentile, ed. *Guelfi e Ghibellini nell'Italia del Rinascimento*, Rome, 2005, 3–78.

Diacciati, Silvia. *Popolani e magnati: società e politica nella Firenze del Duecento*, Spoleto, 2011.

Díaz de Durana, José Ramón. *Álava en la Baja Edad Media. Crisis, recuperación y transformaciones socioeconómicas (c. 1250–1525)*, Vitoria, 1986.

Díaz de Durana, José Ramón. 'La Reforma municipal de los Reyes Católicos: el Capitulado vitoriano de 1476 y su extensión por el noroeste de la Corona de Castilla', *La formación de Álava*, vol. I, Vitoria, 1986, 213–36.

Díaz de Durana, José Ramón. 'Historia y presente del tratamiento historiográfico sobre la Lucha de Bandos en el País Vasco: balance y perspectivas al inicio de una nueva investigación', in *La Lucha de Bandos en el País Vasco. De los Parientes Mayores a la Hidalguía universal. Guipúzcoa, de los Bandos a la Provincia*, Bilbao, 2008, 21–46.

Díaz de Durana, José Ramón. *Anonymous Noblemen: The Generalization of Hidalgo Status in the Basque Country (1250–1525)*, Turnhout, 2011.

Díaz de Durana, José Ramón, and Jon Andoni Fernández de Larrea. 'El discurso político de los protagonistas de las luchas sociales en el País Vasco al final de la Edad Media', in *Lucha política: condena y legitimación en la España Medieval*, Paris, 2004, 313–36.

Díaz de Durana, José Ramón, and Jon Andoni Fernández de Larrea. 'Las relaciones contractuales de la nobleza y las élites urbanas en el País Vasco al final de la Edad Media', *El contrato político en la Corona de Castilla. Cultura y sociedad políticas entre los siglos X al XVI*, Madrid, 2008, 293–321.

Díaz de Durana, José Ramón, and Arsenio Dacosta. 'La dimensión social del liderazgo del linaje: solidaridad, poder y violencia (País Vasco, siglo XV)', *Studia Zamorensia* 12 (2013), 87–106.

Díaz de Durana, José Ramón and Arsenio Dacosta. 'Culture politique et identité dans les villes cantabriques à la fin du Moyen Âge', *Histoire Urbaine* 40 (2014), 149–55.

Dickinson, Janet. *Court Politics and the Earl of Essex, 1589–1601*, London, 2012.

Dirr, Pius. 'Clemens Jäger und seine Augsburger Ehrenbücher und Zunftchroniken. Zur Kenntnis der Historiographie des 16. Jahrhunderts', *Zeitschrift des Historischen Vereins von Schwaben* 36 (1910), 1–32.

Di Tullio, Matteo. *La ricchezza delle comunità. Guerra, risorse, cooperazione nella Geradadda del Cinquecento*, Venice, 2011.

Dolan, Claire. 'Des images en action: cité, pouvoir municipal et crises pendant les guerres de Religion à Aix-en-Provence', in Laurier Turgeon, ed. *Les productions symboliques du pouvoir*, Québec, 1990, 65–86.

Donati, Claudio. 'The Profession of Arms and the Nobility in Spanish Italy: Some Considerations', in Thomas James Dandelet and John A. Marino, eds. *Spain in Italy. Politics, Society, and Religion 1500–1700*, Leiden, 2007, 299–324.

Duboin, Felice Amato. *Raccolta per ordine di materie delle leggi, cioè editti, patenti, manifesti, ecc. emanate negli Stati di terraferma sino all'8 dicembre 1798 dai sovrani della Real Casa di Savoja*, 23 vols., Turin, 1818–1868.

Duindam, Jeroen. *Vienna and Versailles: The Courts of Europe's Dynastic Rivals, 1550–1780*, Cambridge, 2003.

Duindam, Jeroen. 'Royal Courts', *The Oxford Handbook of Early Modern European History. 1350–1750*, vol. 2: *Cultures and Power*, Hamish Scott, ed. Oxford, 2015, 458–60.

Du Pasquier, Armand. 'Les prétentions de la maison de Mailly-Nesle sur Neuchâtel au XVIIIe siècle', *Musée neuchâtelois* (1921), 10–206.

Du Pasquier, Armand. 'Un mémoire sur la réunion de Neuchâtel à la République française', *Musée neuchâtelois* 48 (1911), 155–229.

Dutour, Thierry. 'Pouvoir politique et position sociale en ville: les factions et leurs chefs à Dijon à la fin du Moyen Âge', in Jacques Paviot and Jacques Verger, eds. *Guerre, pouvoir et noblesse au Moyen Âge, Mélanges en l'honneur de Philippe Contamine*, Paris, 2000, 227–38.

Ehalt, Hubert Christian. *Ausdrucksformen absolutistischer Herrschaft: der Wiener Hof im 17. und 18. Jahrhundert*, Munich, 1980.

Elliott, John H. 'Europa después de la paz de Westfalia', *Pedralbes* 19 (1999), 131–46.

Elliott, John H. *El conde duque de Olivares. El político en una época de decadencia*, Barcelona, 2004.

Elm, Kaspar, ed. *Reformbemühungen und Observanzbestrebungen im spätmittelalterlichen Ordenswesen*, Berlin, 1989.

Emery, Kent. *Dionysii Cartusiensis, Opera Selecta*, Turnhout, 1991.

Enríquez, Javier, et al. 'Política real y control municipal en Vizcaya durante el reinado de los Reyes Católicos (1476–1516)', *Vasconia* 15 (1990), 27–42.

Ernst, Hildegard. *Madrid und Wien 1632–1637. Politik und Finanzen in den Beziehungen zwischen Philipp IV und Ferdinand II*, Münster, 1991.

Esposito Aliano, Anna. 'Famiglia, mercanzia e libri nel testamento di Andrea Santacroce (1471)', in Arnold Esch, ed. *Aspetti della vita economica e culturale a Roma nel Quattrocento*, Rome 1981, 197–220.

Evans, Robert J.W. *Rudolf II and His World. A Study in Intellectual History 1576–1612*, Oxford, 1973.

Fages, Henri. *Notes et documents de l'Histoire de Saint Vincent Ferrier*, Louvain, 1905.

Feger, Otto. *Das Rote Buch*, Constance, 1949.

Felder, Pierre. 'Ansätze zu einer Typologie der politischen Unruhen im schweizerischen Ancien Régime 1712–1789', *Schweizerische Zeitschrift für Geschichte* 26 (1976), 324–89.

Fellner, Thomas, and Heinrich Kretschmayr. *Die österreichische Zentralverwaltung*, 2 vols., Vienna, 1907–1956.

Ferente, Serena. 'Guelphs! Factions, Liberty and Sovereignty: Inquiries about the Quattrocento', *History of Political Thought* 28, no. 4 (2007), 571–98.

Ferente, Serena. *Gli ultimi guelfi. Linguaggi e identità politiche in Italia nella seconda metà del Quattrocento*, Rome, 2013.

Fernández de Larrea, Jon Andoni. 'Las fuerzas de los Parientes Mayores en Álava, Guipúzcoa y Vizcaya en la Baja Edad Media: reclutamiento y organización', *Iura Vasconiae* 4 (2007), 163–88.

Fernández de Pinedo, Emiliano. '¿Lucha de bandos o conflicto social?' in *La sociedad vasca rural y urbana en el marco de la crisis de los siglos XIV y XV*, Bilbao, 1973, 29–42.

Fiedler, Joseph, ed. *Die Relationen der Botschafter Venedigs über Deutschland und Österreich im siebzehnten Jahrhundert*, 2 vols., Vienna, 1866–1867.

Finley-Croswhite, Annette. *Henry IV and the Towns*, Cambridge, 1999.

Firpo, Massimo. 'Il sacco di Roma del 1527 tra profezia, propaganda politica e riforma religiosa', in *Dal sacco di Roma all'Inquisizione. Studi su Juan de Valdés*, Alessandria, 1998, 7–60.

Fletcher, Catherine. *Diplomacy in Renaissance Rome. The Rise of the Resident Ambassador*, Cambridge, 2015.

Folkenflik, Robert. 'Johnson's Politics', in Greg Clingham, ed. *The Cambridge Companion to Samuel Johnson*, Cambridge, 1997, 102–13.

Forclaz, Bertrand. 'Local Conflicts and Political Authorities in the Papal State in the Second Half of the 17th century', in André Holenstein, Wim Blockmans, Jon Mathieu, eds. *Empowering Interactions. Political Cultures and the Emergence of the State in Europe, 14th–19th centuries* (Aldershot, 2009), 65–77.

Fosi, Irene, and Alexander Koller, eds. *Papato e Impero nel pontificato di Urbano VIII (1623–1644)*, Città del Vaticano, 2013.

Friedrich, Karin. *Brandenburg-Prussia, 1466–1806. The Rise of a Composite State*, Basingstoke, 2012.

Friedrichs, Christopher R. *Urban Politics in Early Modern Europe*, London, 2000.

Gal, Stéphane. 'Peurs urbaines et engagements politico-religieux au XVIe siècle: l'exemple de la Ligue grenobloise', *Histoire, Économie et Société*, 20e année, no 1 (2001), 3–21.

Gal, Stéphane. 'Entre loyalisme et rébellion: les assemblées générales de la ville de Grenoble (1588–1598)', *Revue d'Histoire Moderne et Contemporaine*, no 49/3 (2002), 7–25.

Galiffe, James A. *Matériaux pour l'histoire de Genève*, 2 vols., Geneva, 1829–1830.

Galiffe, James A. 'Bezanson Hugues: libérateur de Genève', *Mémoires et documents publiés par la Société d'histoire et d'archéologie de Genève* 11 (1859), 196–524.

Galiffe, James A. et al., *Notices généalogiques sur les familles genevoises*, 7 vol., Geneva, 1829–1895.

García de Cortázar, José Ángel. 'El fortalecimiento de la *burguesía* como grupo social dirigente de la sociedad vascongada a lo largo de los XIV–XV', in *La sociedad vasca rural y urbana en el marco de la crisis de los siglos XIV y XV*, Bilbao, 1973, 283–313.

García de Cortázar, Ángel José, et al., eds. *Vizcaya en la Edad Media: evolución demográfica, económica, social y política de la Comunidad vizcaína medieval*, San Sebastián, 1985.

García Fernández, Ernesto. *Gobernar la ciudad en la Edad Media: Oligarquías y élites urbanas en el País Vasco*, Vitoria, 2004.

Gennaro, Clara. 'La pax romana del 1511', *Archivio della Società Romana di Storia Patria* 90 (1967), 17–60.

Gentile, Marco. ed. *Guelfi e ghibellini nell'Italia del Rinascimento*, Rome, 2005.

Gentile, Marco. 'Discorsi sulle fazioni, discorsi delle fazioni. *Parole e demonstratione partiale* nella Lombardia del secondo Quattrocento', in Andrea Gamberini and Giuseppe Petralia, eds. *Linguaggi politici nell'Italia del Rinascimento: atti del convegno, Pisa, 9–11 novembre 2006*, Rome, 2007, 381–408.

Gentile, Marco. 'Factions and Parties: Problems and Perspectives', in Andrea Gamberini and Isabella Lazzarini, eds. *The Italian Renaissance State*, Cambridge, 2012, 304–22.

Gentile, Marco. 'La vendetta di sangue come rituale. Qualche osservazione sulla Lombardia fra Quattro e Cinquecento', in Francesco Salvestrini, Gian Maria Varanini,

Anna Zangarini, eds. *La morte e i suoi riti in Italia tra Medioevo e prima Età moderna*, Florence, 2007, 209–41.

Gerbet, Marie-Claude. *Les noblesses espagnoles au Moyen Âge. XIe–XVe siècle*, Paris, 1994.

Gern, Philippe. 'Essai sur l'indigénat helvétique de la principauté de Neuchâtel, XVIIIe siècle', *Musée neuchâtelois* 3 (1966), 153–165.

Gießmann, Ursula. *Der Letzte Gegenpapast: Felix V: Studien zu Herrschaftspraxis und Legitimationsstrategien (1434–51)*, Böhlau, 2014.

Giordano, Silvano. *Domenico di Gesù Maria, Ruzola (1559–1630): un carmelitano scalzo tra politica e riforma nella chiesa posttridentina*, Rome, 1991, 187–91.

Goicolea, Javier, et al., eds. *Honra de hidalgos, yugo de labradores: nuevos textos para el estudio de la sociedad rural alavesa (1332–1521)*, Bilbao, 2005.

González Cuerva, Rubén. *Baltasar de Zúñiga. Una encrucijada de la Monarquía hispana (1561–1622)*, Madrid, 2012.

González Cuerva, Rubén, and Valentina Caldari, eds. *The Secret Mechanisms of Courts: Factions in Early Modern Europe*, Journal Special Issue of the *Revista Libros de la Corte, Monográfico* 2 (2015).

Göse, Frank. 'Der "unpolitische Hof"? Zum Verhältnis von Hof und Zentralbehörden in friderizianischer Zeit', *Friederisiko. Friedrich der Grosse. Die Essays*, Munich, 2012, 87–97.

Grendi, Edoardo. *In altri termini: etnografia e storia di una società di antico regime*, Milan, 1994.

Grillo, Paolo. 'L'éta sabauda', in *Storia di Cuneo e del suo territorio 1198–1799*, Rinaldo Comba, ed. Savigliano, 2002, 12–80.

Grillo, Paolo. *Milano guelfa (1302–1310)*, Roma, 2013.

Groebner, Valentin. *Gefährliche Geschenke: Ritual, Politik und die Sprache der Korruption in der Eidgenossenschaft im späten Mittelalter und am Beginn der Neuzeit*, Constance, 2000.

Grubb, James. *Firstborn of Venice*, Baltimore, 1988.

Grubb, James. *La Famiglia, la Roba e la Religione nel Rinascimento. Il caso Veneto*, Vicenza, 1999.

Grubb, James. 'Elite Citizens', in John Martin and Dennis Romano, eds. *Venice Reconsidered. The History and Civilization of an Italian City-State, 1297–1797*, Baltimore, 2000, 339–64.

Guggisberg, Daniel. *Das Bild der "Alten Eidgenossen" in Flugschriften des 16. bis Anfang 18. Jahrhunderts (1531–1712)*, Bern, 2000.

Guichenon, Samuel. *Histoire généalogique de la royale maison de Savoie*, vol. 4: *Deuxième partie*, Turin, 1780.

Günter, Heinrich. *Die Habsburger-Liga 1625–1635. Briefe und Akten aus dem General-Archiv zu Simancas*, Berlin, 1908.

Guzzi-Heeb, Sandro. 'Ribelli innovativi. Conflitti sociali nella Confederazione svizzera (XVII–XVIII secolo)', *Studi storici* 48 (2007), 383–408.

Guzzi-Heeb, Sandro. 'Revolte und soziale Netzwerke. Mechanismen der politischen Mobilisierung in einem alpinen Tal des 18. Jahrhunderts', *Geschichte und Gesellschaft* 36 (2010), 497–522.

Guzzi-Heeb, Sandro. *Passions alpines. Sexualité et pouvoirs dans les montagnes suisses (1700–1900)*, Rennes, 2014.

Haemers, Jelle. *For the Common Good. State Power and Urban Revolts in the Reign of Mary of Burgundy (1477–1482)*, Turnhout, 2009.

Haemers, Jelle. 'Factionalism and State Power in the Flemish Revolt (1477–1492)', *Journal of Social History*, 42 (2009), 1009–39.

Hale, John Rigby, and Michael Edward Mallett. *The Military Organization of a Renaissance State. Venice c. 1400 to 1617*, Cambridge, 1983.

Halliday, Paul. *Politic: Partisan Politics in England's Towns, 1650–1730*, New York, 1998.

Hanvelt, Marc. *The Politics of Eloquence: David Hume's Polite Rhetoric*, Toronto, 2012.

Harding, Robert. 'Revolution and Reform in the Holy League: Angers, Rennes, Nantes', *Journal of Modern History*, no 53 (1981), 379–416.

Hässig, Johann. *Die Anfänge des Toggenburger- oder Zweiten Villmergerkrieges 1698–1706*, Basel, 1903.

Haug, Tilman. *Ungleiche Aussenbeziehungen und grenzüberschreitende Patronage. Die französische Krone und die geistlichen Kurfürsten (1648–1679)*, Köln, 2015.

Head, Randolph C. *Early Modern Democracy in the Grisons. Social Order and Political Language in a Swiss Mountain Canton 1470–1620*, Cambridge, 1995.

Heers, Jacques. *Le clan familial au Moyen Âge. Étude sur les structures politiques et sociales des milieux urbains*, Paris, 1974.

Heers, Jacques. *Parties and Political Life in the Medieval West*, Amsterdam, 1977.

Hegel, Karl, ed. *Die Chroniken der deutschen Städte vom 14. bis ins 16. Jahhrundert*, 36 vols., Leipzig, 1864–1968.

Heller, Henry. 'Putting History Back into the Religious Wars: A Reply to Mack P. Holt', *French Historical Studies* 19, no. 3 (Spring, 1996), 853–61.

Helmrath, Johannes. *Das Basler Konzil: 1431–1449, Forschungsstand und Probleme*, Cologne, 1987.

Hengerer, Mark. 'Court and Communication: Integrating the Nobility at the Imperial Court (1620–65)', *The Court Historian* 5 (2000), 223–29.

Hengerer, Mark. *Kaiserhof und Adel in der Mitte des 17. Jahrhunderts. Eine Kommunikationsgeschichte der Macht in der Vormoderne*, Constance, 2004.

Hengerer, Mark. '*Ab omnibus amatus et aestimatus*: kaiserliche Günstlinge und ihre Gräber im 17. Jahrhundert', in Arne Karsten, ed. *Das Grabmal des Günstlings*, Berlin, 2011, 139–66.

Hengerer, Mark. *Kaiser Ferdinand III (1608–1657): eine Biographie*, Vienna, 2012.

Henry, Philippe. 'Patriciat neuchâtelois, traditions familiales et service étranger. Les Perregaux à la fin du XVIIIe siècle', in Norbert Furrer et al., eds. *Gente ferocissima. Solddienst und Gesellschaft in der Schweiz (15.–19. Jahrhundert)*, Zurich, 1997, 137–48.

Henry, Philippe. 'Libertés neuchâteloises et liberté suisse. Regards étrangers sur les institutions de la principauté de Neuchâtel au XVIIIe siècle', in Philippe Henry, ed. *Des chartes de franchises à la nouvelle Constitution. Une histoire des institutions neuchâteloises*, Neuchâtel, 2002, 143–67.

Herdt, Jennifer A. *Religion and Faction in Hume's Moral Philosophy*, New York, 1997.

Hernando Sánchez, Carlos. 'Nobleza y diplomacia en la Italia de Carlos V: el duque de Sessa embajador en Roma', in Juan Luis Castellano and Francisco Sánchez-Montes González, eds. *Carlos V Europeísmo y Universalidad*, vol 3: *Los escenarios del Imperio*, Madrid, 2001, 205–97.

Hiller, Istvan. 'Gli Ambasciatori della Cappella. Riflessioni sulla perdita del potere', *Nova Corvina* 11 (2003), 8–14.

Hirschbiegel, Jan, and Werner Paravicini, eds. *Der Fall des Günstlings: Hofparteien in Europa vom 13. bis zum 17. Jahrhundert*, Ostfildern, 2004.

Hirschbiegel, Jan, Werner Paravicini, and Jörg Wettlaufer, eds. *Städtische Bürgertum und Hofgesellschaft. Kulturen integrativer und konkurrierender Beziehungen in Residenz und Hauptstädten vom 14. bis in 19. Jahrhundert*, Ostfieldern, 2012.

Historisches Lexikon der Schweiz 13 vols., Basel, 2002–2014.

Höbelt, Lothar. *Ferdinand III. Friedenskaiser wider Willen*, Graz, 2008.

Hofmann, Georg, ed. *Epistolae Pontificiae ad Concilium Florentinum Spectantes*, 3 vols., *1440–45*, Rome, 1940–1946.

Hofmann, Konrad. 'Hans Schneiders historisches Gedicht auf die Hinrichtung des Augsburger Bürgermeisters Schwarz', in *Sitzungsberichte der Königl. Bayerischen Akademie der Wissenschaften zu München*, 1870/1, 500–511.

Holenstein, André. 'Händel—Schiedsgerichte—Vermittlungen. Konflikte und Konfliktlösungen in der alten Schweiz', in Peter Rauscher, Martin Scheutz, eds. *Die Stimme der ewigen Verlierer? Aufstände, Revolten und Revolutionen in den österreichischen Ländern (ca. 1450–1815)*, Vienna, 2013, 387–413.

Holenstein, André. *Mitten in Europa. Verflechtung und Abgrenzung in der Schweizer Geschichte*, Baden, 2014.

Holt, Mack P. 'Putting Religion Back into the Wars of Religion. Review Article', *French Historical Studies* 18, no. 2 (Autumn, 1993), 524–51.

Holt, Mack P.. 'Les réseaux d'autorité et de pouvoir à l'Hôtel de ville et au Parlement de Dijon entre 1580 et 1630', *Annales de Bourgogne* 85, no 1 (2013), 19–35.

Horowski, Leonhard. *Die Belagerung des Thrones. Machtstrukturen und Karrieremechanismen am Hof von Frankreich 1661–1789*, Ostfildern, 2012.

Housley, Norman. *Contesting the Crusades*, Oxford, 2006.

Hubalek, Franz. *Auf dem Briefwechsel des Johannis Schlitpacher von Weilheim (Der Kodex 1767 der Stiftsbibliothek Melk)* (Dissertation thesis, University of Vienna, 1963).

I Ricordi di Marcello Alberini, in Domenico Orano, ed. *Il sacco di Roma nel 1527*, vol. I, Rome, 1901.

Im Hof, Ulrich. 'Ancien Régime', in *Handbuch der Schweizer Geschichte*, vol. 2, Zurich, 1977, 673–784.

Infessura, Stefano. *Diario della città di Roma*, Oreste Tommasini, ed. Rome, 1890.

Ives, Eric. *Factions in Tudor England*, London, 1979.

Izbicki, Thomas M., and Christopher M. Bellitto, eds. *The Church, the Councils and Reform: the Legacy of the Fifteenth Century*, Gerald Christianson (Washington, D.C., 2008).

Kaiser, Wolfgang. *Marseille au temps des troubles. Morphologie sociale et luttes de factions (1559–1596)*, Paris, 1992.

Kälin, Urs. *Die Urner Magistratenfamilien. Herrschaft, ökonomische Lage und Lebensstil einer ländlichen Oberschicht, 1700–1850*, Zurich, 1991.

Kälin, Urs. 'Salz, Sold und Pensionen. Zum Einfluss Frankreichs auf die politische Struktur der innerschweizer Landsgemeindedemokratien im 18. Jahrhundert', *Der Geschichtsfreund* 149 (1996), 105–124.

Keitel, Christian. 'Städtische Bevölkerung und Stadtregiment bis 1397', in Hans-Eugen Specker, ed. *Die Ulmer Bürgerschaft auf dem Weg zur Demokratie*, Ulm, 1997, 96–103.

Knapton, Michael. 'The Terraferma State', in Eric R. Dursteler, ed. *A Companion to Venetian History, 1400–1797*, Leiden, 2013, 85–124.

Knapton, Michael, John E. Law, Alison A. Smith, eds. *Venice and the Veneto during the Renaissance: the Legacy of Benjamin Kohl*, Florence, 2014.

Kneupper, Frances Courtney. *The Empire at the End of Time: Identity and Reform in Late Medieval German Prophecy*, Oxford, 2016, 139–40.

Koller, Heinrich, ed. *Reformation Kaiser Siegmunds*, Stuttgart, 1964.

Körner, Martin. 'Zur eidgenössischen Solddienst- und Pensionendebatte', in Norbert Furrer et al., eds. *Gente ferocissima. Mercenariat et société en Suisse (XVe–XIXe siècle)*, Lausanne, 1997, 193–203.

Kramer, Werner. *Konsens und Rezeption: Verfassungsprinzipien der Kirche im Basler Konziliarismus: mit Edition ausgewählter Texte*, Münster, 1980.

Labayru, Estanislao J. *Historia General de Vizcaya*, Bilbao, 1897.

Landolt, Niklaus. *Untertanenrevolten und Widerstand auf der Basler Landschaft im sechzehnten und siebzehnten Jahrhundert*, Liestal, 1996.

Lantschner, Patrick. *The Logic of Political Conflict in Medieval Cities: Italy and the Southern Low Countries, 1370–1440*, Oxford, 2015.

Lanzinner, Maximilian. 'Geheime Räte und Berater Kaiser Maximilians II (1564–1576)', *Mitteilungen des Instituts für österreichische Geschichtsforschung* 102 (1994), 296–315.

Largiadèr, Anton. *Bürgermeister Rudolf Brun und die Zürcher Revolution von 1336*, Zurich, 1936.

Lavarda, Sergio. 'Banditry and Social Identity in the Republic of Venice. Ludovico da Porto, his Family and his Property (1567–1640)', *Crime, Histoire et Société* 11/1 (2007), 2–24.

Laven, Peter. 'Banditry and lawlessness on the Venetian Terraferma in the late Cinquecento', in Trevor Dean and Kate J.P. Lowe, eds. *Crime, Society and the Law in Renaissance Italy*, Cambridge, 1994, 221–48.

Le Roux, Nicolas. *Les guerres de Religion 1559–1629*, Paris, 2009.

Le Roy Ladurie, Emmanuel. *Saint-Simon ou le système de la Cour*, Paris, 1997.

Leclerq, Jean, et al., eds. *Bernardi, Opera Omnia*, Rome, 1957.

Lema, José Ángel, et al., eds. *Los señores de la guerra y de la tierra: nuevos textos para el estudio de los Parientes Mayores guipuzcoanos (1265–1548)*, San Sebastián, 2000.

Lema, José Ángel, et al. *El triunfo de las elites urbanas guipuzcoanas: nuevos textos para el estudio del gobierno de las villas y de la Provincia (1412–1539)*, San Sebastián, 2002.

Lepetit, Bernard. 'Histoire des pratiques, pratiques de l'histoire', in idem, ed. *Les formes de l'expérience. Une autre histoire sociale*, Paris, 1995, 9–22.

Lerner, Robert E. 'The Jerusalem Rumors: An Addendum', *Rivista di Storia del Cristianesimo* 3, (2006), 541–43.

Lernet, Brigitte. *Maximilian von Trauttmansdorff: Hofmann und Patron im 17. Jahrhundert*, (unpublished PhD thesis, Vienna, 2004).

Les sources du droit du canton de Vaud, ed. Danièle Anex-Cabanis and Jean-François Poudret, vol. B/I. *Droits seigneuriaux et franchises. Lausanne et les terres épiscopales*, Aarau, 1977.

Les villes capitales au Moyen Âge. XXXVIe Congrès de la SHMES (Istanbul, 1er-6 juin 2005), Paris, 2006.

Lindquist, Thea. *The Politics of Diplomacy: The Palatinate and Anglo-Imperial Relations in the Thirty Years' War* (PhD thesis, Madison, 2001).

Lottin, Alain, ed. *Histoire de Boulogne-sur-Mer*, Villeneuve d'Ascq, 2014.

Lowe, Kate J.P. *Church and Politics in Renaissance Italy: The Life and Career of Cardinal Francesco Soderini (1453–1524)*, Cambridge, 1993.

Löwenthal, Richard. 'Kontinuität und Diskontinuität. Zur Grundproblematik des Symposions', in Karl Bosl, Karl Möckl, eds. *Der moderne Parlamentarismus und seine Grundlagen in der ständischen Repräsentation*, Berlin, 1977, 341–56.

Luebke, David Martin. 'Factions and Communities in Early Modern Central Europe', *Central European History* 25, no. 3 (1992), 281–301.

Luebke, David Martin. *His Majesty's Rebels. Communities, Factions, and Rural Revolt in the Black Forest, 1725–1745*, Ithaca, 1997.

Luebke, David Martin. 'Symbols, Serfdom, and Peasant Factions', *Central European History* 34, no. 3 (2001) 357–82.

Lundell, William Paul. *Carthusian Policy and the Council of Basel* (Dissertation thesis, University of Toronto, 1996).

Lundell, William Paul. 'Bartholomeus van Maastricht on Carthusian Allegiance and Unity during the Basel Schism', in Thomas Burman, Mark Meyerson, and Leah Shopkow, eds. *Religion, Text, and Society in Medieval Spain and Northern Europe*, Toronto, 2002, 250–76.

Lutz, Georg. 'Wallenstein, Ferdinand II und der Wiener Hof', *Quellen und Forschungen aus italienischen Archiven und Bibliotheken* 48 (1968), 207–43.

MacHardy, Karin J. *War, Religion and Court Patronage in Habsburg Austria: The Social and Cultural Dimensions of Political Interaction, 1521–1622*, Houndmills, 2003.

Machiavelli, Niccolò. *The Prince*, trans. by W.K. Marriott, Chicago, 1990.

Mairet, Gérard. 'Présentation', in Jean Bodin, *Les six livres de la République. Un abrégé du texte de l'édition de Paris de 1583*, Paris, 1993, 5–38.

Maissen, Thomas. *Die Geburt der Republic. Staatsverständnis und Repräsentation in der frühneuzeitlichen Eidgenossenschaft*, Göttingen, 2006.

Maissen, Thomas. *Schweizer Heldengeschichten—und was dahintersteckt*, Baden, 2015.

Mantel, Alfred. *Über die Veranlassung des Zwölfer- oder zweiten Villmergerkrieges. Die Toggenburgerwirren in den Jahren 1706–1712*, Zürich, 1909.

Marchal, Guy P. 'Wilhelm Tells Geburt', in Guy P. Marchal, *Schweizer Gebrauchsgeschichte*, Basel, 2007, 283–303.

Marek, Pavel. 'La diplomacia española y la papal en la Corte Imperial de Fernando II', *Studia Historica* 30 (2008), 109–44.

Marek, Pavel. *La embajada española en la corte imperial (1558–1641). Figuras de los embajadores y estrategias clientelares* (Praga, 2013), 175–83.

Marín, José Antonio. *"Semejante Pariente Mayor". Parentesco, solar, comunidad y linaje en la institución de un Pariente Mayor en Guipuzkoa. Los señores de Oñaz y Loyola (siglos XIV–XVI)*, San Sebastián, 1998.

Marschke, Benjamin. *Absolutely Pietist. Patronage, Factionalism, and State-Building in the Early Eighteenth-Century Prussian Army Chaplaincy*, Tübingen, 2005.

Marshall, Alan. *The Age of Faction: Court Politics, 1660–1702*, Manchester, 1999.

Martin, Dennis. 'Carthusians as Advocates of Women Visionary Reformers', in Julian M. Luxford, ed. *Studies in Carthusian Monasticism in the Late Middle Ages*, Turnhout, 2008, 142–52.

Martin, Dennis. 'Carthusians as Public Intellectuals: Cloistered Religious as Advisors to Lay Elites on the Eve of the Protestant Reformation', in Christopher Bellitto and David Flanagan, eds. *Reassessing Reform, A Historical Investigation of Church Renewal*, Washington D.C., 2012, 232–53.

Mat'a, Petr, and Thomas Winkelbauer, eds. *Die Habsburgermonarchie 1620 bis 1740. Leistungen und Grenzen des Absolutismusparadigmas*, Stuttgart, 2006.

McGinn, Bernard. *Visions of the End: Apocalyptic Traditions in the Middle Ages*, New York, 1979 (repr. 1998).

Mears, Natalie. 'Courts, courtiers and culture in Tudor England', *Historical Journal* 46, no. 3 (2003), 703–22.

Mecenseffy, Grete. 'Philipp IV von Spanien und seine Heirat mit Maria Anna von Österreich', in *Historische Studien. A.F. Pribram zum 70. Geburtstag dargebracht*, Vienna, 1929, 41–70.

Mecenseffy, Grete. *Im Dienste dreier Habsburger. Leben und Wirken des Fürsten Johann Weikhard Auersperg (1615–1677)*, Vienna, 1938.

Mecenseffy, Grete. *Habsburger im 17. Jahrhundert. die Beziehungen der Höfe von Wien und Madrid während des Dreißigjährigen Krieges*, Vienna, 1955.

Meier, Ludwig. *Die Werke des Erfurter Kartäusers Jakob von Jüterbog in ihrer handschriftlichen Überlieferung'*, Münster, 1955.

Meijknecht, Ton. *Bartholomeus van Maastricht, monnik en conciliarist*, Assen, 1982.

Melchiorre, Matteo. *Conoscere per governare. Le relazioni dei Sindici inquisitori e il Dominio veneziano in Terraferma (1543–1626)*, Udine, 2013.

Merki-Vollenweider, Martin. *Unruhige Untertanen. Die Rebellion der Luzerner Bauern im Zweiten Villmergerkrieg (1712)*, Luzern, 1995.

Mertens, Dieter. *Iacobus Carthusiensis: Untersuchungen zur Rezeption der Werke des Kartäusers Jakob von Paradies (1381–1465)*, Göttingen, 1976.

Metzler, Sally. *Bartholomeus Spranger: Splendor and Eroticism in Imperial Prague*, New York, 2014.

Meuthen, Erich. *Das Basler Konzil als Forschungsproblem der Europäische Geschichte*, Opladen, 1985.

Micaleff, Fabrice. 'Comment la bonne Ligue sauva la monarchie. 1593 selon Nicolas Lefèvre de Lezeau', *Les Dossiers du Grihl*, [online November 29, 2011, http://dossiersgrihl.revues.org/4708].

Michel, Kaspar. 'Regieren und Verwalten', in Historischer Verein des Kantons Schwyz, ed. *Geschichte des Kantons Schwyz*, vol. 3, Zurich, 2012, 9–67.

Miles, Pattenden. 'Rome as a "Spanish Avignon"?' in Piers Baker-Bates and Miles Pattenden, eds. *The Spanish Presence in Sixteenth-Century Italy: Images of Iberia*, Aldershot, 2015, 65–84.

Minnich, Nelson H. *Councils of the Catholic Reformation: Pisa I (1409)-Trent (1545–63)*, Aldershot, 2008.

Molà, Luca. *The Silk Industry of Renaissance Venice*, Baltimore, 2000.

Molas i Ribalta, Pere. *Familia i politica al segle XVI català*, Barcelona, 1990.

Molas i Ribalta, Pere. 'Austria en la orden del Toisón de Oro, siglos XVI–XVII', *Pedralbes* 26 (2006), 123–52.

Monsalvo Antón, José María. 'Parentesco y sistema concejil. Observaciones sobre la funcionalidad política de los linajes urbanos en Castilla y León (siglos XIII–XV)', *Hispania* 185 (1993), 939–41.

Monsalvo Antón, José María. 'Violence between Factions in Medieval Salamanca: Some Problems of Interpretation', *Imago Temporis Medium Aevum*, 3 (2009), 139–70.

Montandon Léon, et al. *Neuchâtel et la Suisse*, Neuchâtel, 1969.

Monter, William. *Calvin's Geneva*, New York, 1967.

Mori, Elisabetta. *L'Archivio Orsini. La famiglia, la storia, l'inventario*, Rome, 2016.

Morsolin, Bernardo. *Giangiorgio Trissino. Monografia di un letterato nel secolo XVI*, Florence, 1894.

Mousnier, Roland. *Les hiérarchies sociales de 1450 à nos jours*, Paris, 1969.

Muir, Edward. *Mad Blood Stirring: Vendetta and Factions in Friuli During the Renaissance*, Baltimore, 1993.

Muir, Edward. 'Was There Republicanism in the Renaissance Republics? Venice after Agnadello', in John Martin and Dennis Romano, eds. *Venice Reconsidered. The History and Civilization of an Italian City-State, 1297–1797*, Baltimore, 2000, 137–267.

Müller, Heribert, ed. *Das Ende des konziliaren Zeitalters (1440–1450): Versuch einer Bilanz* Munich, 2012.

Munita, José Antonio, et al., eds. *En tiempo de ruidos y de bandos. Nuevos textos para el estudio de los linajes vizcaínos: los Barroeta de la merindad de Marquina (1355–1547)*, Bilbao, 2014.

Naef, Henri. *Fribourg au secours de Genève: 1525–1526*, Fribourg, 1927.

Naef, Henri. 'Bezanson Hugues, son ascendance et sa postérité, ses amis fribourgeois (notes et documents inédits)', *Bulletin de la Société d'histoire et d'archéologie de Genève*, 5 (1934), 335–573.

Naef, Henri. *Les origines de la Réforme à Genève*, 2 vols., Genève, 1936–1968.

Naef, Henri. 'L'occupation militaire de Genève et la combourgeoisie manquée de 1519', *Revue d'histoire ecclésiastique suisse*, 52 (1958), 48–86.

Naphy, William G. *Calvin and the consolidation of the Genevan Reformation*, Manchester, 1994.

Niccolini, Enrico. *3 luglio 1548. Mezzogiorno di sangue a Vicenza*, Vicenza, 1985.

Noflatscher, Heinz. 'Regiment aus der Kammer? Einflußreiche Kleingruppen am Hof Rudolfs II', in Werner Paravicini and Jan Hirschbiegel, eds. *Der Fall des Günstlings. Hofparteien in Europa vom 13. bis zum 17. Jahrhundert*, Ostfildern, 2004, 209–34.

Nussdorfer, Laurie. 'The Vacant See: Ritual and Protest in Early Modern Rome', *The Sixteenth Century Journal* 18 (1987), 173–89.

Offenstadt, Nicolas. 'Guerre civile et espace public à la fin du Moyen Âge. La lutte des Armagnac et des Bourguignons', in Laurent Bourquin and Philippe Hamon, eds. *La politisation. Conflits et construction du politique depuis le Moyen Âge*, Rennes, 2010, 111–29.

Olivieri, Achille. 'Alessandro Trissino e il movimento calvinista vicentino del Cinquecento', in *Rivista di Storia della Chiesa in Italia*, 21 (1967), 54–117.

Onnekink, David, and Gijs Rommelse, eds. *Ideology and Foreign Policy in the Early Modern Age (1650–1750)*, Farnham, 2011.

Opheim, Bente. 'Political networks and factions: Online Prosopography of Medieval Scandinavian Sagas', *History and Computing* 12, no. 1 (2000), 43–57.

Panciera, Walter. 'Vicenza. L'età moderna (1516–1813)', in Giuseppe Gullino, ed. *Storia di Vicenza*, Verona, 2014, 137–40.

Panzer, Georg. *Ulrich Schwarz, der Zunftbürgermeister von Augsburg 1422–1478*, Munich, 1913.

Paravicini, Werner, and Jörg Wettlaufer, eds. *Der Hof und die Stadt. Konfrontation und Integration in Spätmittelalter und Früher Neuzeit*, Ostfildern, 2006.

Paris, James. 'La députation de la vénérable classe à Berlin en 1726', *Musée neuchâtelois* XLVIII (1911), 187–268.

Partner, Peter. *The Pope's Men. The Papal Civil Service in the Renaissance*, Oxford, 1990.

Pastore, Stefania. 'Una Spagna anti-papale. Gli anni italiani di Diego Hurtado de Mendoza', *Roma moderna e contemporanea* XV (2007), 63–94.

Patrouch, Joseph F. *Queen's Apprentice. Archduchess Elizabeth, Empress Maria, the Habsburgs, and the Holy Roman Empire, 1554–1569*, Leiden, 2010.

Patschovsky, Alexander, and Ivan Hlaváček, eds. *Reform von Kirche und Reich zur Zeit der Konzilien von Konstanz und Basel*, Constance, 1996.

Paul Joachimsohn. 'Spottverse von Basler Konzil', *Neues Archiv der Gesellschaft für Ältere Deutsche Geschichtskunde* 18 (1893), 693–94.

Pellegrini, Marco. *Ascanio Maria Sforza. La parabola politica di un cardinale principe del Rinascimento*, 2 vols., Rome 2002.

Pellegrini, Marco. 'A Turning-Point in the History of the Factional System in the Sacred College. The Power of Pope and Cardinals in the Age of Alexander VI', in Maria Antonietta Visceglia and Gianvittorio Signorotto, eds. *Court and Politics in Papal Rome 1492–1700*, Cambridge, 2002, 8–30.

Penzi, Marco. '*Damnatio memoriae*: la Ligue catholique française e la storiografia, tra politiques, rivoluzionari, mistici e liberali », *Quaderni storici* 118, (2005), 236–84.

Pez, Bernhard, and Philibert Hueber, eds. *Codex diplomatico-historico-epistolaris*, Augsburg, 1729.

Pfister, Ulrich. 'Politischer Klientelismus in der Schweiz', *Schweizerische Zeitschrift für Geschichte* 42 (1992), 28–68.

Piergentili, Pierpaolo, and Gianni Venditti, eds. *Scorribande, lanzichenecchi e soldati ai tempi del sacco di Roma. Papato e Colonna in un inedito epistolario dall'Archivio Della Valle-Del Bufalo*, Rome, 2009.

Pillorget, René. 'Luttes de factions et intérêts économiques à Marseille de 1598 à 1618', *Annales ESC*, 27e année, no 3 (1972), 705–730.

Pils, Susanne Claudine, and Jan Paul Niederkorn, eds. *Ein zweigeteilter Ort? Hof und Stadt in der Frühen Neuzeit*, Vienna, 2005).

Polo, Regina. *El régimen municipal de la Corona de Castilla durante el reinado de los Reyes Católicos: organización, funcionamiento y ámbito de actuación*, Madrid, 1999.

Porebski, Stanisław A. *Jakub z Paradyza. Opuscula inedita. Wydal, wstepem i notami krytycznymi opat*, Warsaw, 1978.

Portilla, Micaela. *Torres y casas fuertes en Álava*, Vitoria, 1978.

Poudret, Jean-François. *La Maison de Savoie évincée de Lausanne par Messieurs de Berne*, Lausanne, 1962.

Povolo, Claudio. 'Crimine e giustizia a Vicenza. Secoli XVI–XVII. Fonti e problematiche per l'approfondimento di una ricerca sui rapporti politico-giudiziari tra Venezia e la Terraferma', in Amelio Tagliaferri, ed. *Venezia e la Terraferma attraverso le relazioni dei Rettori*, Milan, 1981, 411–32.

Povolo, Claudio. *L'intrigo dell'onore. Poteri e istituzioni nella Repubblica di Venezia tra Cinque e Seicento*, Verona, 1997.

Povolo, Claudio. *Furore. Elaborazione di un'emozione nella seconda metà del Cinquecento*, Verona, 2015.

Price, J.L. *Holland and the Dutch Republic in the Seventeenth Century. The Politics of Particularism*, Oxford, 1994.

Prosperi, Adriano. *Tra evangelismo e controriforma: G.M. Giberti (1495–1543)*, Rome, 1969.

Prosperi, Adriano. 'Carlo V e i papi del suo tempo', *Archivio storico per le province napoletane* 119 (2001), 239–47.

Prügl, Thomas. 'Herbst des Konziliarismus?: Die Spätschriften des Johannes von Segovia', in Müller, ed. *Das Ende des konziliaren Zeitalters*, 153–74.

Pursell, Brennan C. *The Winter King: Frederick V of the Palatinate and the Coming of the Thirty Years' War*, Aldershot, 2003.

Raeymaekers, Dries. *One Foot in the Palace. The Habsburg Court of Brussels and the Politics of Access in the Reign of Albert and Isabella, 1598–1621*, Leuven, 2013.

Raggio, Osvaldo. *Faide e parentele. Lo stato genovese visto dalla Fontanabuona*, Turin, 1990.

Raveggi, Sergio, et al., eds. *Guelfi e Popolo grasso: I detentori del potere politico a Firenze nella seconda metà del Dugento*, Florence, 1978.

Raveggi, Sergio, et al. 'La lotta politica e sociale', in *Storia della civiltà Toscana*, Folorence, 2000, vol. 1: Franco Cardini, ed. *Comuni e signorie*, 117–36.

Rebel, Herman. 'What do the Peasants Want Now? Realists and Fundamentalists in Swiss and South German Rural Politics, 1650–1750', *Central European History* 34, no. 3 (2001), 313–56.

Reddy, William M. *The Navigation of Feeling: A Framework for the History of Emotions* New York, 2001.

Rehberg, Andreas. '*Etsi prudens paterfamilias...pro pace suorum sapienter providet*. Le ripercussioni del nepotismo di Martino V a Roma e nel Lazio', in Maria Chiabò *et al.*, eds. *Alle origini della nuova Roma Martino V (1417–1431)*, Rome, 1992, 225–82.

Rehberg, Andreas. 'Alessandro VI e i Colonna: motivazioni e strategie nel conflitto tra papa Borgia e il baronato romano', in Maria Chiabò *et al.*, eds. *Roma di fronte all'Europa al tempo di Alessandro VI*, vol. I, Rome, 2001, 345–86.

Reinhard, Wolfgang. 'Papal Power and Family Strategy in the Sixteenth and Seventeenth Centuries', in Ronald G. Asch and Adolf M. Birke, eds. *Princes, Patronage, and the Nobility: The Court at the Beginning of the Modern Age, c.1450–1650*, London, 1991, 229–356.

Reinhard, Wolfgang. *Geschichte der Staatsgewalt. Eine vergleichende Verfassungsgeschichte Europas von den Anfängen bis zur Gegenwart*, Munich, 1999.

Ricciardelli, Fabrizio. *The Politics of Exclusion in Early Renaissance. Florence*, Turnhout, 2007.

Rivero Rodríguez, Manuel. 'Crisis sucesoria en la Corona de Aragón', in José Martínez Millán, ed. *La corte de Carlos V*, Madrid, 2000, 150–66.

Roberts, Penny. *A City in Conflict. Troyes during the French Wars of Religion*, Manchester, 1986.

Rogge, Jörg. *Für den gemeinen Nutzen. Politisches Handeln und Politikverständnis von Rat und Bürgerschaft in Augsburg im Spätmittelalter*, Tübingen 1996.

Rogger, Philippe. *Geld, Krieg und Macht. Pensionsherren, Söldner und eidgenössische Politik in den Mailänderkriegen 1494–1516*, Baden, 2015.

Rohmann, Gregor. *"Eines Ehrbaren Raths gehorsamer Amptman". Clemens Jäger und die Geschichtsschreibung des 16. Jahrhunderts*, Augsburg, 2001.

Romano, Dennis. 'The Limits of Kinship: Family Politics, Vendetta, and the State in Fifteenth-Century Venice', in Michael Knapton, John E. Law, Alison A. Smith, eds. *Venice and the Veneto during the Renaissance: the Legacy of Benjamin Kohl*, Florence, 2014, 87–102.

Rosenwein, Barbara H. *Generations of feeling: a history of emotions, 600–1700*, Cambridge, 2016.

Rospocher, Massimo. *Il papa guerriero. Giulio II nello spazio pubblico europeo*, Bologna, 2015.

Rossi, Giovanni. '*...partialitas in civitate est tanquam vermis in caseo...*: il giudizio (negativo) sulle fazioni politiche in Giovanni Nevizzano (1490 ca-1540)', in Marco Gentile, ed. *Guelfi e Ghibellini nell'Italia del Rinascimento*, Rome, 2005, 79–108.

Roth, Friedrich. *Augsburgs Reformationsgeschichte*, 4 vols., Munich, 1901–1911.

Roussanov, Jessica, and Robert E. Lerner. 'The Jerusalem Rumors: The Earliest Stage of the 'Master of Rhodes' Letter on the Birth of Antichrist', *Rivista di Storia del Cristianesimo* 2, (2005), 157–72.

Rousseau, Jean-Jacques. *Du contrat social*, Amsterdam, 1762 (english trans., G.D.H. Cole *The Social Contract*, 1782).

Rousset, Maurice. 'Bulletin critique sur *L'Histoire de la Ligue* de Charles Valois', *Revue d'Histoire de l'Église de France* 6, no 33 (1920), 505–6.

Ruggiu, François-Joseph. 'Pour une étude de l'engagement civique au XVIIIe siècle', *Histoire urbaine*, no 2 (2007), 145–64.

Ruppert, Karsten. *Die kaiserliche Politik auf dem Westfälischen Friedenskongreß (1643–1648)*, Münster, 1979.

Rusconi, Roberto. *L'attesa della fine: Crisi della società, profezia ed Apocalisse in Italia al tempo del grande scisma d'Occidente*, Rome, 1979.

Sabean, David. 'The Communal Basis of Pre-1800 Peasant Uprisings in Western Europe', *Comparative Politics* 8 (1976), 355–64.

Santarelli, Daniele. *Il papato di Paolo IV nella crisi politico-religiosa del Cinquecento: le relazioni con la Repubblica di Venezia e l'atteggiamento nei confronti di Carlo V e Filippo II*, Rome, 2008.

Santschi, Catherine. 'Les mandements changent de maîtres', in Matthieu De La Corbière, Martine Piguet et Catherine Santschi, eds. *Terres et châteaux des évêques de Genève. Les mandements de Jussy, Peney et Thiez des origines au début du XVIIe siècle*, Geneva, 2001, 331–456.

Sartori, Giovanni. *Parties and Party Systems. A Framework for Analysis*, Cambridge, 1976.

Savio, Andrea. *Strategie nobiliari. La famiglia Godi fra Vicenza e l'Europa (1480–1588)* (PhD thesis, XXV cycle, tutor Alessandro Pastore, Università degli Studi di Verona, 2013).

Sbriccoli, Mario. *Crimen laesae maiestatis. Il problema del reato politico alle soglie della scienza penalistica moderna*, Milan, 1974.

Scheurer, Rémy, Louis-Edouard Roulet, and Jean Courvoisier. *Histoire du Conseil d'Etat neuchâtelois. Des origines à 1945*, Neuchâtel, 1987.

Scheutz, Martin. '... *hinter Ihrer Käyserlichen Majestät der Päbstliche Nuncius, Königl. Spanischer und Venetianischer Abgesandter*. Fronleichnamsprozessionen im frühneuzeitlichen Wien', in Richard Bösel et al., eds. *Kaiserhof—Papsthof (16.–18. Jahrhundert)*, Vienna, 2006, 173–205.

Schick, Sébastien. *Des liaisons avantageuses. Action des ministres, liens de dépendance et diplomatie anglaise dans le Saint-Empire romain germanique (années 1720–1750)* (PhD thesis, Université Paris I Panthéon-Sorbonne, Ludwigs-Maximilians Universität München, 2015).

Schiller, Friedrich. *Geschichte des dreissigjährigen Kriegs*, Frankfurt, 1792.

Schläppi, Daniel. '*In allem übrigen werden sich die Gesandten zu verhalten wissen*. Akteure in der eidgenössischen Aussenpolitik des 17. Jahrhunderts. Strukturen, Ziele und Strategien am Beispiel der Familie Zurlauben von Zug', *Der Geschichtsfreund* 151 (1998), 5–90.

Schlögl, Rudolf. 'Vergesellschaftung unter Anwesenden. Zur kommunikativen Form des Politischen in der vormodernen Stadt', in Rudolf Schlögl, ed. *Interaktion und Herrschaft. Die Politik der frühneuzeitlichen Stadt*, Constance, 2004, 9–60.

Schmitt, Carl. *Gespräch über die Macht und den Zugang zum Machthaber*, Pfullingen, 1954.

Schneider, Karin. *Deutsche mittelalterliche Handschriften der Universitätsbibliothek Augsburg: Die Signaturengruppen Cod.I.3 und Cod.III.1.*, Wiesbaden, 1988, 60–79.

Schnerb, Bertrand. '*Familiarissimus domini ducis*. La succession des favoris à la cour de Bourgogne au début du XVe siècle', in in Werner Paravicini and Jan Hirschbiegel, eds. *Der Fall des Günstlings. Hofparteien in Europa vom 13. bis zum 17. Jahrhundert*, Ostfildern, 2004, 177–89.

Schreiber, Renate. *'ein galeria nach meinem humor'. Erzherzog Leopold Wilhelm*, Vienna, 2004.

Schreiber, Renate. '"Gnedigster Herr und vilgeliebter Herr Brueder ...". Private Briefe von Erzherzog Leopold Wilhelm an und über Kaiser Ferdinand III', *Frühneuzeit-Info* 18/1 (2007), 39–43.

Schulze, Winfried. '"Geben Aufruhr und Aufstand Anlass zu neuen heilsamen Gesetzen". Beobachtungen über die Wirkungen bäuerlichen Widerstandes in der frühen Neuzeit', in Winfried Schulze, ed. *Aufstände, Revolten, Prozesse. Beiträge zu bäuerlichen Widerstandsbewegungen im frühneuzeitlichen Europa*, Stuttgart, 1983, 261–85.

Schwarz, Henry Frederick. *The Imperial Privy Council in the 17th Century*, Cambridge, 1943.

Scott, Tom. *Die Freiburger Enquete von 1476. Quellen zur Wirtschafts- und Verwaltungsgeschichte der Stadt Freiburg im Breisgau im fünfzehnten Jahrhundert*, Freiburg im Breisgau, 1986.

Serio, Alessandro. 'Modi, tempi, uomini della presenza hispana a Roma tra la fine del Quattrocento e il primo Cinquecento (1492–1527)', in Francesca Cantù and Maria Antonietta Visceglia, eds. *L'Italia di Carlo V: Guerra, religione e politica nel primo Cinquecento*, Rome, 2003, 433–75.

Serio, Alessandro. '*Nationes* hispanas y facción española en Roma durante la primera Edad Moderna', in Carlos J. Hernando, ed. *Roma y España un crisol de la cultura europea en la Edad Moderna*, Madrid, 2007, 241–48.

Serio, Alessandro. *Una gloriosa sconfitta. I Colonna tra papato e impero nella prima età moderna (1431–1530)*, Rome, 2008.

Shaw, Christine. *Iulius II: The Warrior Pope*, Oxford, 1993.

Shaw, Christine. 'The Roman Barons and the Guelf and Ghibelline Factions in the Papal States', in Marco Gentile, ed. *Guelfi e Ghibellini nell'Italia del Rinascimento*, Roma, 2005, 475–94.

Shaw, Christine. *The Political Role of the Orsini Family from Sixtus IV to Clement VII. Barons and Factions in the Papal States* (Roma 2007), 100–102.

Shaw, Christine. 'The Roman Barons and the Popesi', in Marco Gentile and Pierre Savy, eds. *Noblesse et États princiers en Italie et en France au XVI*^e^ *siècle*, Roma, 2009, 101–24.

Shepherd, Robert. 'Court Factions in Early Modern England', *The Journal of Modern History* 64, no. 4 (December 1992), 721–45.

Sigmund, Paul E. 'Nicholas of Cusa on the Constitution of the Church', in Chandler Brooks, Gerald Christianson, and Thomas M. Izbicki, eds. *Nicholas of Cusa on Christ and the church: essays in memory of Chandler McCuskey Brooks for the American Cusanus Society*, Leiden, 1996, 127–34.

Simms, Brendan. *The Impact of Napoleon. Prussian High Politics, Foreign Policy and the Crisis of the Executive, 1797–1806*, Cambridge, 1997.

Smail, Daniel Lord. 'Factions and Vengeance in Renaissance Italy. A Review Article', *Comparative Studies in Society and History* 38, no. 4 (October, 1996), 781–89.

Smoller, Laura. *History, Prophecy, and the Stars: The Christian Astrology of Pierre D'Ailly*, Princeton, 1994.

Smoller, Laura. 'Apocalyptic Calculators of the Later Middle Ages' (unpublished paper, *Knowing the Time, Knowing of a Time*, 3rd Annual Conference of the Center of Millennial Studies Boston, Dec 6–8 1998, Conference Proceedings. http://www.mille.org/publications/Confpro98/confprodec98.html).

Smoller, Laura. *The Saint and the Chopped-Up Baby: The Cult of Vincent Ferrer in Medieval and Early Modern Europe*, Ithaca, 2014.

Sommer-Mathis, Andrea. 'Ein *pícaro* und spanisches Theater am Wiener Hof zur Zeit des Dreißigjährigen Krieges', in Andreas Weigl, ed. *Wien im Dreißigjährigen Krieg: Bevölkerung, Gesellschaft, Kultur, Konfession*, Köln, 2001, 651–91.

Sösemann, Bernd, and Gregor Vogt-Spira, eds. *Friedrich der Grosse in Europa. Geschichte einer wechselvollen Beziehung*, 2 vols., Stuttgart, 2012.

Spruyt, Hendrik. *The Sovereign State and Its Competitors: An Analysis of Systems Change*, Princeton, 1996, 130–50.

Stefanovska, Malina. *La politique du cardinal de Retz: Passion et factions*, Rennes, 2008.

Steiner, Carlo. 'Informelle Netzwerke in der Aussenpolitik der eidgenössischen Orte. Das labile Kräfteverhältnis in der Beziehung zwischen dem Zuger Solddienstunternehmer Beat II. Zurlauben und dem französischen Ambassador Jean de la Barde', *Argovia* 122 (2010), 45–65.

Stella, Aldo. 'Le minoranze religiose', in Franco Barbieri and Paolo Preto, eds. *Storia di Vicenza. L'età della Repubblica Veneta (1404–1797)*, III/1, Vicenza, 1989, 199–219.

Stieber, Joachim. *Pope Eugenius IV, the Council of Basel, and the Secular and Ecclesiastical Authorities in the Empire: The Conflict over Supreme Authority and Power in the Church*, Leiden, 1978.

Stribrny, Wolfgang. 'Die Neuenburger Wirren—Friedrichs des Grossen schwerster innenpolitischer Konflikt', in Jürgen Ziechmann, ed. *Fridericianische Miniaturen*, vol. 2 Bremen, 1991, 133–46.

Stribrny, Wolfgang. *Die Könige von Preussen als Fürsten von Neuenburg-Neuchâtel (1707–1848). Geschichte einer Personalunion*, Berlin, 1998.

Surchat, Pierre Louis. 'Das Corpus Helveticum im Urteil der Nuntien', in Marco Jorio, ed. *1648. Die Schweiz und Europa. Aussenpolitik zur Zeit des Westfälischen Friedens*, Zurich, 1999, 111–19.

Suter, Andreas. *"Troublen" im Fürstbistum Basel (1726–1740). Eine Fallstudie zum bäuerlichen Widerstand im 18. Jahrhundert*, Göttingen, 1985.

Suter, Andreas. *Der schweizerische Bauernkrieg von 1653. Politische Sozialgeschichte—Sozialgeschichte eines politischen Ereignisses*, Tübingen, 1997.

Suter, Andreas. 'Korruption oder Patronage? Aussenbeziehungen zwischen Frankreich und der Alten Eidgenossenschaft als Beispiel (16.-18. Jahrhundert)', *Zeitschrift für Historische Forschung* 37 (2010), 187–218.

Suvanto, Pekka. *Wallenstein und seine Anhänger am Wiener Hof zur Zeit des zweiten Generalats 1631–1634*, Helsinki, 1963.

Tabacco, Giovanni. *Lo Stato sabaudo nel sacro romano impero*, Turin, 1939, 59–66.

Tagliaferri, Amelio, ed. *Relazioni dei Rettori veneti in Terraferma.* Vol. VII: *Podestaria e Capitanato di Vicenza*, Milan, 1976.

Tamponi, Michele. *Nino Visconti di Gallura. Il dantesco Giudice Nin gentil tra Pisa e Sardegna, guelfi e ghibellini, faide cittadine e lotte isolane*, Rome, 2010.

Tarpley, Webster G. *Paolo Sarpi, his networks, Venice and the coming of the Thirty Years' War*, (PhD thesis, Washington D.C., 2009).

Tena, Maria Soledad. *La sociedad urbana en la Guipúzcoa costera medieval: San Sebastián, Rentería, y Fuenterrabía (1200–1500)*, San Sebastián, 1997.

Ter Braake, Serge. 'Parties and Factions in the Late Middle Ages: The Case of the Hoeken and Kabeljauwen in The Hague (1483–1515)', *Journal of Medieval History* 35, (2009), 97–111.

Tercero Casado, Luis. 'A Fluctuating Ascendancy: The "Spanish Party" at the Imperial Court of Vienna (1631–1659)', in Rubén González Cuerva and Valentina Caldari, eds. *The Secret Mechanisms of Courts: Factions in Early Modern Europe*, Journal Special Issue of the *Revista Libros de la Corte*, Monográfico 2 (2015), 39–53.

Teuscher, Simon. *Bekannte—Klienten—Verwandte. Soziabilität und Politik in der Stadt Bern um 1500*, Cologne, 1998).

Tilly, Charles. *Coercion, Capital, and European States, AD 990–1990*, Cambridge, 1990.

Tóth, Ferenc. 'La mission secrète du baron de Tott à Neuchâtel en 1767', *Revue historique neuchâteloise*, 2003, 133–59.

Truchuelo, Susana. *Gipuzkoa y el poder real en la Alta Edad Moderna*, San Sebastián, 2004.

Ulbert, Jörg. 'Der Leiter der preussischen Aussenpolitik Heinrich Rüdiger von Ilgen (1654–1728) als Informant der französischen Diplomatie. Anwerbung—Bezahlung—Gegenleistung', in Sven Externbrink, Jörg Ulbert, eds. *Formen internationaler Beziehungen in der Frühen Neuzeit. Frankreich und das Alte Reich im europäischen Staatensystem. Festschrift für Klaus Malettke zum 65. Geburtstag*, Berlin, 2001, 274–96.

Van Berchem, Victor. 'Amé Lévrier: à l'occasion du 4e centenaire de sa mort (13 mars 1524)', *Étrennes genevoises* (1925), 5–37.

Van Berchem, Victor. 'La mort de Berthelier', *Étrennes genevoises* (1928), 28–64.

Vehse, Carl Eduard. *Geschichte der deutschen Höfe seit der Reformation*, Section 2: *Geschichte des österreichischen Hofs und Adels und der österreichischen Diplomatie*, Hamburg, 1852.

Ventura, Angelo. *Nobiltà e popolo nella società veneta del '400 e '500*, Bari, 1964.

Vergani, Raffaello. 'Gli inizi dell'uso della polvere da sparo nell'attività mineraria: il caso veneziano', *Studi veneziani*, nuova serie 3 (1979), 104–15.

Vergani, Raffaello. 'L'argento veneto: mito e realtà nei secoli XV–XVI', *Ricerche Storiche*, anno XIV n. 1 (January-April 1984), 143–61.

Vianello, Francesco Maria. 'Cloths for Peasants and the Poor: Wool Manufactures in Vicenza Countryside (1570–1700)', in Giovanni Luigi Fontana and Gérard Gayot, eds. *Wool: Products and Markets (13th–20th Century)*, Padua, 2004, 411–17.

Vianello, Francesco Maria. 'Rural Manufactures and Pattern of Economic Specialization: Cases from the Venetian Mainland', in Paola Lanaro, ed. *At the Center of the Old World. Trade and Manufacturing in Venice and Venetian Mainland (1400–1800)*, Toronto, 2006, 347–61.

Villacorta, Consuelo. *Libro de las buenas andanças e fortunas que fizo Lope Garçía de Salazar* (Bilbao, 2015).

Visceglia, Maria Antonietta. '«Farsi imperiale»: faide familiari e identità politiche a Roma nel primo Cinquecento', in Francesca Cantù and Maria Antonietta Visceglia, eds. *L'Italia di Carlo V. Guerra, religione e politica nel primo Cinquecento*, Rome, 2003, 477–508.

Visceglia, Maria Antonietta. 'Napoli e la politica internazionale del papato tra la congiura dei baroni e il regno di Ferdinando il Cattolico', in Giuseppe Galasso and Carlos José Hernando Sánchez, eds. *El reino de Nápoles y la Monarquía de España entre agregación y conquista (1485–1535)*, Madrid, 2004, 453–83.

Visceglia, Maria Antonietta. 'Guerra e riti di pacificazione: le spedizioni di Giulio II a Bologna nelle pagine del cerimoniere del papa (1506–1512)', in Gian Mario Anselmi and Angela de Benedictis, eds. *Città in guerra. Esperienze e riflessioni nel primo '500. Bologna nelle "guerre d'Italia"*, Bologna, 2008, 85–117.

Visceglia, Maria Antonietta. *Morte e elezione del papa. Norme, riti, conflitti. L'età moderna*, Rome, 2013.

Von Birk, Ernst, et al., eds. *Monumenta conciliorum generalium saeculi decimi quinti*, 4 vols., Wien, 1857–1935.

Von Liliencron, Rochus. *Die historischen Volkslieder der Deutschen vom 13. bis 16. Jahrhundert*, 4 vols., Leipzig, 1865–1869.

Von Thiessen, Hillard. *Diplomatie und Patronage. Die spanisch-römischen Beziehungen im Pontifikat Pauls V. Borghese 1605–1621 in akteurszentrierter Perspektive*, Epfendorf, 2010.

Von Thiessen, Hillard. 'Switching Roles in Negotiation: Levels of Diplomatic Communication between Pope Paul V Borghese (1605–1621) and the Ambassadors of Philip III', in Stefano Andretta et al., eds. *Paroles de négociateurs: l'entretien dans la pratique diplomatique de la fin du Moyen Âge à la fin du XIX*[e] *siècle*, Rome, 2010, 151–72.

Walker, Greg. *Persuasive Fictions: Faction, Faith and Political Culture at the Court of Henry VIII*, Aldershot, 1996.

Walker, Jonathan. 'Bravi and Venetian Nobles, c.1550–1650', *Studi veneziani* 26 (1998), 85–113.

Walter, François. *Histoire de la Suisse*, vol. 2, Neuchâtel, 2009.

Watts, John. *The Making of Polities*, Cambridge, 2009.

Weber, Dieter. *Geschichtsschreibung in Augsburg. Hektor Mülich und die reichsstädtische Chronistik des Spätmittelalters*, Augsburg, 1984.

Weber, Nadir. 'La principauté de Neuchâtel et la diplomatie prussienne: un croisement fructueux', in Elisabeth Crettaz-Stürzel, Chantal Lafontant Vallotton, eds. *Sa Majesté en Suisse. Neuchâtel et ses princes prussiens*, Neuchâtel, 2013, 106–13.

Weber, Nadir. *Lokale Interessen und grosse Strategie. Das Fürstentum Neuchâtel und die politischen Beziehungen der Könige von Preussen (1707–1806)*, Cologne, 2015.

Weigel, Petra. 'Reform as Paradigma: Konzilien und Bettelorden', *Konstanzer Arbeitskreis Vorträge und Forschungen* 67 (2007), 289–335.

Wick, Markus René. 'Der Glarner "Landhandel". Strukturgeschichtliche und konfliktsoziologische Hypothesen zum Glarner Konfessionsgegensatz', *Jahrbuch des Historischen Verein des Kantons Glarus* 69 (1982), 49–240.

Wiget, Josef. 'Der Stand Schwyz im 18. Jahrhundert', in Historischer Verein des Kantons Schwyz, ed. *Geschichte des Kantons Schwyz*, vol. 4, Zurich, 2012, 9–43.

Willman, Robert. 'The Origins of Whig and Tory in English Political Language', *The Historical Journal* 17, no. 2 (June, 1974), 247–64.

Wilson, Peter H. *The Thirty Years War: Europe's Tragedy*, Cambridge, 2009.

Windler, Christian. '"Ohne Geld keine Schweizer". Pensionen und Söldnerrekrutierungen an den eidgenössischen Patronagemärkten', in Hillard von Thiessen, Christian Windler, eds. *Nähe in der Ferne. Personale Verflechtung in den Aussenbeziehungen der Frühen Neuzeit*, Berlin, 2005, 105–33.

Witschi, Rudolf. *Friedrich der Grosse und Bern*, Bern, 1926.

Wittwer, Wilhelm. 'Catalogus Abbatum monasterii SS. Udalrici et Afrae Augustensis', ed. Anton von Steichele, *Archiv für die Geschichte des Bisthums Augsburg* 3 (1860), 10–437.

Woelki, Thomas. 'Die Kartäuser und das Basler Konzil', *Zeitschrift für Kirchengeschichte* 121, (2010), 305–22.

Wührer, Jakob. 'Ein teilausgebautes Haus ohne Fundament? Zum Forschungsstand des frühneuzeitlichen Wiener Hofes am Beispiel der Organisationsgeschichte', *Mitteilungen des Instituts für Österreichische Geschichtsforschung* 117 (2009), 23–50.

Wünsch, Thomas. *Konziliarismus und Polen: Personen, Politik, und Programme aus Polen zur Verfassungsfrage der Kirche in der Zeit der mittelalterlichen Reformkonzilien*, Paderborn, 1998.

Wünsch, Thomas. 'Vom Konziliarismus zur 'Devotio Moderna': Die Transformation der Reformidee bei dem polnischen Theologen Jakob von Paradies in den Jahren 1440 bis 1450', in Heribert Müller, ed. *Das Ende des Konziliaren Zeitalters (1440—1450)*, Munich, 2012, 175–96.

Würgler, Andreas. *Unruhen und Öffentlichkeit. Städtische und ländliche Protestbewegungen im 18. Jahrhundert*, Tübingen, 1995.

Würgler, Andreas. 'Zwischen Verfahren und Ritual. Entscheidungsfindung und politische Integration in der Stadtrepublik Bern in der Frühen Neuzeit', in Rudolf Schlögl, ed. *Interaktion und Herrschaft. Die Politik der frühneuzeitlichen Stadt*, Constance, 2004, 63–91.

Würgler, Andreas. '"The League of the Discordant Members" or How the Old Swiss Confederation Operated and How it managed to Survive for so long', in André Holenstein, Thomas Maissen, and Maarten Prak, eds. *The Republican Alternative. The Netherlands and Switzerland compared*, Amsterdam, 2008, 29–50.

Würgler, Andreas. 'Verflechtung und Verfahren. Individuelle und kollektive Akteure in den Aussenbeziehungen der Alten Eidgenossenschaft', in Hillard von Thiessen, Christian Windler, eds. *Akteure der Aussenbeziehungen. Netzwerke und Interkulturalität im historischen Wandel*, Cologne, 2010, 79–93.

Würgler, Andreas. 'Symbiose ungleicher Partner. Die französisch-eidgenössische Allianz 1516–1798/1815', *Jahrbuch für Europäische Geschichte* 12 (2011), 53–75.

Würgler, Andreas. 'Formen der Konfliktlösung im Vergleich. Unruhen in Schwaben und in der Schweiz (1650–1800)', in Wolfgang Wüst, ed. *Mitregieren und Herrschaftsteilung in der Frühen Neuzeit* (Erlangen, 2016), 147–69.

Würgler, Andreas. *Die Tagsatzung der Eidgenossen. Politik, Kommunikation und Symbolik einer repräsentativen Institution im europäischen Kontext*, Epfendorft, 2013, 485–90.

Zarri, Gabriella. *Le sante vive: profezie di corte e devozione femminile tra '400 e '500*, Turin, 1990.

Z'Graggen, Bruno. *Tyrannenmord im Toggenburg. Fürstäbtische Herrschaft und protestantischer Widerstand um 1600*, Zurich, 1999.

Zorzi, Andrea. *La trasformazione di un quadro politico. Ricerche su politica e giustizia a Firenze dal comune allo Stato territoriale*, Florence, 2008.

Zürn, Martin. *"Ir aigen libertet". Waldburg, Habsburg und der bäuerliche Widerstand an der oberen Donau*, Tübingen, 1998.

Index

The index covers both text and footnotes.

Abbeville 147
Abruzzo 84, 90, 102
Adams, John 195
Adams, Simon 1
Adrian, Dominique 6, 8, 10
Africa 52
Aggsbach, Carthusian monastery of 75, *see also* Vincent of Aggsbach
Agnadello, battle of 125
Álava 37–55
Albe 84, 89
Alberini, family 99
Alberini, Marcello 103
Albert V (Duke of Bavaria) 168
Alberti, Leandro 122
Alembert, Jean Le Rond d' 12
Alexander VI (Pope) 92–93, 94n38
Almerico, family 128
Almerico, Giuseppe 130
Alphonse V, the Magnanimous (King of Aragon) 84
Alps 4, 203–204
Altieri, family 102
Altieri, Lucrezia 98
Altieri, Marco Antonio 96, 97n46, 98
Amadeus VIII (Duke of Savoy) 62
ambassadors 9–10, 56, 61, 93, 96, 99–100, 103–104, 109–111, 113, 115n46, 119, 121, 134–135, 155–156, 158, 159n10, 162, 165–166, 170, 172–173, 177, 179, 181–182, 184, 186, 188–190, 192–194, 199, 206–207, *see also* court; patron-client relations
Amelia, *see* Pontani, Giovan Battista
America 52
Amiens 6, 8, 10, 137–154
Ammannati, Jacopo 87n15
Añacino, family 12
Angaran, family 126
Angelini, Augustino 193n43
Angers 146
Angevins 84
Anguillara, county of 91
Anguillara, family 85, 88
Anjou, François, Duke of 137
Anvers 122
Appenzell 205–206
Aragon, House of 84, 87–93, *see also* Alphonse V; Ferdinand II; Giovanna d'Aragona; Maria Cecilia d'Aragona
Aramayona 52
Argon, Peter von 8, 16, 20–21, 29, 32
Arzt, Ulrich 32
Astalli, family 88
Augsburg 6, 8, 10, 18–36
Aumale, *see* Guise, Charles de
Avaray, Claude-Théophile Bésiade, Marquis d' 188
Avendaño, family 45
Avendaño, Pedro de (the Elder) 54

Baden, margrave of 207
Baglioni, family 96
Balard, Jean 113
Baldo degli Ubaldi 196
Baltasar Carlos (Prince of Asturias) 173
banishment, *see* exile
Barbatia, Andreas 197
Bari 170
Barnabites 132–134
Barnavi, Élie 143
Bartholomeus of Maastricht 58, 69–71, 74
Basel 115n49, 208, 210, 215n70
Basel, Council of 15, 56–81
Basel, prince-bishop of 202, 210
Basel, rural areas of 204
Basque country 6, 37–55
Baud, family 106
Bavaria, Duke of 22n11, *see also* Albert V, Maximilian I
Bayonne 46
Becan, Martin 162, 167
Beik, William 140
Benedict XIII (Pope) 78
Benedictines 61–62, 67, 75, *see also* Wittwer, Wilhelm
Benedictis, Angela de 213
Benevento 91
Bentivoglio, family 96

Bercé, Yves-Marie 200
Bérenger, Jean 159
Bergamo 124
Bergeon, Charles-François 186, 188–189
Berlin *see* court, Prussian
Bern 8, 104, 105n6, 106–110, 114–119, 176, 179, 186–188, 192–193, 202–208, 210
Bernard of Clairvaux 77
Bernard, Antoine 146–147
Bernard, George 1
Bernardino da Siena 13
Berny, Antoine de 144
Berthelier, Philibert 109, 112, 114, 118
Besançon 107, 111
Bésiade, *see* Avaray, Claude-Théophile Bésiade
Bigant, François 145
Bilbao 51
Blanchet, Jean 112
Blickle, Peter 201–202
Blois 144
Blois, Treaty of 94
Bodin, Jean 13, 196, 204, 212–213
Bohemia, chancellor of 160
Bologna 61, 95–96, 103
Bonivard, François (chronicler) 109, 112–113
Bonnac, Jean-Louis d'Usson, Marquis de 190
Borgia, family 93–94
Borgia, Cesare 94
Borgia, Girolama 93
Borromeo, Carlo (cardinal) 133n29, 134
Bourbon, Duke of 183, 189n32, *see also* Louis IV Henri
Bourbon, François-Louis de (Prince de Conti) 179–182
Bourbon, Henri of (King of Navarre) 137, *see also* Henri IV
Bourbon, Louis Armand de (Prince de Conti) 183
Bourbon, Louis IV Henri de, prince de Condé, Duke of 187–188
Bourbon-Soissons, Louise-Léontine 181
Bouret, François 181
Boves, *baronnie* of 144
Brady, Thomas 107
Brandenburg, Frederick of *see* Frederick I
Brändle, Fabian 205
Branzo, family 126
Braun, Konrad 197
Brescia 124, 136
Breu, Jörg (the Elder) 35n44
Bridget of Sweden (Saint) 77
Bruges 8n
Brun d'Oleyres, Jean-Pierre 186, 187n25, 188–191
Brun, Rudolf 21
Brussels 144
Büeler, family 209
Burgos 39
Burgundian Wars 106
Burgundy 184
Burgundy, Duke of 8n25
Butrón, family 45
Butrón y Múgica, Gómez de 52
Byzantium 3

Cadereyta, Marquis of 172n61
Caetani, family 85
Callixtus III (Pope) 86
Calvin, John 121
Cantabria 39
Capra, family 126, 128–129, 131, 136
Capra, Francesco 126
Capranica, family 88
Capuchins 167
Carafa, Carlo (nuncio in Vienna) 167
cardinals, *see* Borromeo, Carlo; Cesarini, Alessandro; Cesarini, Giuliano; Colonna, Giovanni; Colonna, Pompeo; Della Rovere, Giuliano; Della Valle, Andrea; Farnese, Alessandro; Guise, Louis; Klesl, Melchior; Mazarin, Jules; Medici, Giulio de'; Numai, Cristoforo
Carmelites 167
Caro Baroja, Julio 46
Caroldo, Gian Giacomo 121
Carpi, Olivia 6, 8, 10–11, 15
Carthusians 58–65, 69–76
Carvajal, Bernardino 93
Casati, Gabrio 133
Castañeda, marquis de (Spanish ambassador) 170
Castilian Civil War (1475–1479) 49
Castille 41, 45, 49, 52n22
Cavalieri di Masciolo, Bernardino de' 98
Cavalieri di Masciolo, Bernardo de' 98

Cavalieri di Masciolo, Marzia de' 98
Cavalieri, family 98
Cayet, Palma 143
Cecil, Robert (Earl of Salisbury) 14
Cerman, Ivo 159
Cerveteri 91
Cesarini, family 89
Cesarini, Alessandro (Cardinal) 98n54, 102
Cesarini, Giuliano (Cardinal) 93
Chambrier d'Oleyres, Jean-Pierre de 192
Chambrier, family 185, 188–189
Chambrier, François de 182, 189n34
Chambrier, Jean de 186–187, 194
Chamillart, Michel 181
Charles II (Duke of Savoy) 104–121
Charles IV (Holy Roman Emperor) 116
Charles V (Holy Roman Emperor) 28n32, 31, 35n45, 50, 54, 99–100, 103, 116n52, 117, 125, 134
Charles VIII (King of France) 93
Chevalier, Simon 186n23
Chièvres, *see* Croy, Guillaume de
Chittolini, Giorgio 87
Choiseul, Duke of 193
chroniclers 12, 16, 19, 21 28–34, 45, 83, 87–88, 109, *see also* Bonivard, François; Conti, Sigismondo; García de Salazar, Lope; Gherardi da Volterra, Iacopo; Infessura, Stefano; Meisterlin chronicle; Mülich, Hector; Rem, Wilhelm; Sanudo, Marino; Vascho, Antonio de; Zink, Burkhard
Clement VII (Pope) 101–102, *see also* Medici, Giulio de'
clientelism, *see* patron-client relations
Cognac, league of 101
Collemont (*maieur* of Amiens) 148
Cologne 70
Cologne, archbishop of 61
Cologne, Cistercian Abbey of 68
Cologne, university of 61, 70n
Colonna, family 82–103, 158
Colonna (di Genazzano) 84, 88, 94, 101
Colonna, Agnese 98
Colonna, Antonio 87
Colonna, Ascanio 98, 100–102
Colonna, Caterina 88n20
Colonna, Fabrizio 88–89, 93, 96–98
Colonna, Geronimo 87–88
Colonna, Giovanna *see* Giovanna d'Aragona
Colonna, Giovanni (Cardinal) 88–89, 95
Colonna, Giovanni (di Palestrina) 88
Colonna, Girolamo 88
Colonna, Lorenzo (di Genazzano) 88–89
Colonna, Lorenzo Oddone 89
Colonna, Marco Antonio 94–95
Colonna, Oddone *see* Martin V
Colonna, Odoardo 89
Colonna, Pompeo (Cardinal) 96–102
Colonna, Prospero 88–89, 93, 98
Colonna, Sciarra 98
Colonna, Stefano (di Palestrina) 101
Colonna, Vespasiano 100, 103
common good 8, 27, 32–34, 108, 140, 150–152, *see also* political language
conspiracy 11, 20, 24, 34, 84, 107, 118, 138–139, 141–149, 170, 197–198, 201n18, 208, *see also* court; murders; revolts; trust; tyranny
Constance 19, 107
Constance, council of 59–60
Constantinople 69, 76, 81
Conti, family 85, 89, 96
Conti, Giacomo 88
Conti, Sigismondo dei (chronicler) 87n15
Corbie 142
corruption 29–32, 71, 77, 155–156, 169n52, 172, 199, 209, 214
councils
  urban 10, 18–35, 96, 105–106, 111–115, 118–119, 124–129, 136, 146–147, 198, 204, 207–208
  ecclesiastical 56–81, 83, 100, 150, *see also* Basel, Constance, Ferrara, Florence, Trent
  privy (imperial) 161–163, 167–168, 171, 173
Coureux, Robert 146–148
court
  in general 2, 5, 9–10, 12, 134–135, 161, 176
  Burgundian 16
  French 2, 160, 176, 178, 180–181, 183, 186–188, 193
  Imperial 2, 6, 9, 116n53, 134, 155, 175
  Papal 62, 76, 81, 83–86, 90, 95, 98, 103, 158
  Prussian 6, 177–178, 184–190, 193, 195
  Sabaudian 121
  Spanish 47, 128, 160, 171
  Tudor 1, 14
  See also conspiracy; murders; trust

craftsmen 18–22, 29
Crescenzi, family 85, 89
Cressier 182
Crèvecoeur, *see* Gouffier, François
Crotone, bishop of 98
Crotone, diocese of *see* Della Valle, Andrea
Croy, Guillaume de 99
Cuerva, Rubén Gonzalez 6, 15
Cuneo 119
Cybo Franceschetto 91
Cybo Giambattista, *see* Innocent VIII

Da Monte, family 128
Da Porto, family 126–129, 131, 136
Da Roma, family 126, 128
Da Roma, Galeazzo 130
Da Roma, Leonardo 130
Da Schio, family 128
Dacosta, Arsenio 6, 41, 45–46
death sentence 26–29, 35, 112, 124
Della Rovere, family 87, 100
Della Rovere, Bianca 84
Della Rovere, Felicia 95
Della Rovere, Francesco Maria 96
Della Rovere, Giuliano (Cardinal) 84, 91, 93, *see also* Julius II
Della Rovere, Leonardo 84
Della Rovere, Luchina 95
Della Valle, family 85–87, 90, 97–98
Della Valle, Andrea (Cardinal) 98, 101–102
Della Valle, Bartolomeo 98
Della Valle, Bernardino 90
Della Valle, Fabrizio 98
Della Valle, Filippo 86, 98
Della Valle, Francesco 86
Della Valle, Laura 99n55
Della Valle, Lelio 86
Della Valle, Lelio II 98, 101
Della Valle, Livia di Lelio 86
Della Valle, Nicola 86
Della Valle, Paolo 86, 90
Della Valle, Pietro 86
Della Valle, Valerio 99
Dendrich, Ulrich 32
Denis the Carthusian 58, 65–67, 76–77
Descimon, Robert 3
Diaz de Durana, José Ramón 6
Dickinson, Janet 1
Diderot, Denis 12
Dijon 3, 145–146
diplomatic relations, *see* ambassadors; court
Domingo de Jesús María (Carmelite) 167
Dominicans 13, 64, 67, 78
Dominici, Michele (Franciscan) 13
Donauwörth, *see* Heiligkreuz
Doullens 142 -143
Dragonzino, Giovanbattista (da Fano) 122
Duindam, Jeroen 2, 14
Dutch Republic 207, 211

Eber, Valentin 31n
economic factors 6, 19, 21, 40, 45–47, 49, 53–54, 88, 90, 125–126, 139, 155, 169, 175–177, 178n6, 200–201, 205, 210, 211n60, *see also* guilds; merchants; trade
Egen, Peter 21n7, *see also* Argon, Peter von
Eggenberg, Hans Ulrich von 156–158, 160, 162, 163n30, 166, 169, 174
Ehalt, Hubert 160
Ehem, Thomas 24
Emmanuel Philibert (Duke of Savoy) 136
emotions 15–16, 82, 85, 88–90, 95–96, 131, 141, *see also* friendship
Empire, *see* Holy Roman Empire
England 52, 122, 142, 195n, *see also* court, Tudor; Henry VIII
Enrique IV (King of Castile) 41, 47
Épernon, Duke of 142, 147, 149–150
Erfurt, Charterhouse of 72
Erfurt, university of 61
Erlbach, Heinrich 8, 22, 24–25, 26n24, 29, 33–34, 36
Estrées, Antoine III d' (*sieur* de Coeuvres) 142, 147
Eugenius IV (Pope) 56, 59–62, 64, 67–68, 70, 72, 80, 88
exile 21, 24, 35, 48, 85, 93, 98, 124, 144, 151–152

factions
- composition 2, 7, 13, 20, 32, 34, 49–50 101, 136, 177, 186, 205–206, *see also* craftsmen; merchants; jurists; lawyers; noble lineages
- generic terms 11–12, 29, 31, 82, 135, 138–139, 153, 192, 196–198, 200, 203, 205, 209, 212n, 214

historiographical debate 1–2, 4–5, 39, 46, 82, 108–109, 116–117, 139, 155–157, 177n2, 198, 205, 209, 213–214
identity 6–7, 30, 100, 126, 139, 141, 146–153, 169, 206, 209
leaders 7–8, 15–16, 20–24, 32–36, 45, 55, 105–106, 108, 118, 126, 137–138, 143–144, 150, 168, 170, 192, 205
names 12–13, 25, 45, 113–114, 120, 158–159, 201–202, 205–206, *see also* Guelphs and Ghibellines
political language 3, 6, 10, 15–16, 28–34, 36, 67–69, 82, 98, 107n15, 123, 127, 141, 177n2, *see also* chroniclers; common good; emotions; friendship
programs and propaganda 7, 14, 22–34, 30, 47, 95, 109–113, 153
religion 4, 12, 99–100, 121, 131–134, 139–140, 146–152, 155–156, 160, 167, 201, 208–211
See also ambassadors; conspiracy; corruption; court; death sentence; exile; modern state; patron-client relations; feuds; revolts; trust; tyranny; violence
Farnese, Alessandro (Cardinal) 93
Farnese, Giulia 93, 95
Felix v (Pope) 56, 62, 68, 70n, 78
Ferdinand I (Holy Roman Emperor) 161
Ferdinand I (King of Naples) 84–85, 89, 93
Ferdinand II (Holy Roman Emperor) 155–169, 174
Ferdinand II (King of Aragon) 53, 99–100
Ferdinand III (Holy Roman Emperor) 155–156, 159, 162–165, 169–175
Ferdinand IV (King of Romans) 173
Fernández de Pinedo, Emiliano 47
Ferrara 84, 87, 95
Ferrara, council of 56, 62
Ferrara, war of 89
Ferrer, Vincent 57, 64, 66, 78
feuds 2, 46, 83–92, 107–108, 127, 130, 135–136, *see also* honour; murders
Finley-Croswhite, Annette 145
Flanders 52, 108n16
Fleckenstein, family 209
Florence 2–3, 85, 87, 91
Florence, council of 56
Fondi, duchy of 93
Fouache, Gaspard 149
Fournel, Robert 145
Foys, Jean de 114
France 11, 52, 93–96, 99, 106, 134, 137–154, 172–174, 176, 178, 183, 186–195, 200, 202, 206–207, 209, 211–212, *see also* court, French; Charles VIII; Francis I; Henri III; Henri IV; Louis XI; Louis XIV; Paris
Franche-Comté 176
Franche-Comté, *parlement de* 182
Franciotti, Niccolò 95
Francis I (King of France) 94, 99
Franciscans 13, 20n6, 83, 102
Frascati 91
Frederick I (King of Prussia) 176, 180
Frederick II (King of Prussia) 191
Frederick V (Elector Palatine, King of Bohemia) 167
Frederick William I (King of Prussia) 187, 189
Frederick William III (King of Prussia) 194
Freiburg im Brisgau 23
French Wars of Religion 137–154, 156
Fribourg (Switzerland) 8, 104–110, 112n37, 114–120, 180n8, 192–193, 208
Frickinger, Andreas 22–25, 27
Friedrich III (Holy Roman Emperor) 62, 70
friendship 16, 21, 26n, 40, 90, 95, 99, 103, 105, 109, 128, 141, 145, 164, 180, 183–184, 197, *see also* emotions; political language
Fuenterrabía 46

Gamboa, family 45
Gand 3
Gara, Lucrezia 95
García de Cortázar, José Ángel 4
García de Salazar, Lope (chronicler) 38–39, 46, 54
Garzadori, family 128, 136
Garzadori, Ottaviano 127n15
Gattinara, Mercurino da 100
Gaudot, Claude 193
Gaudot, Josué 190
Geneva 6, 8, 12, 104–121, 192n42, 211n61
Germany 107
Gerolamo d'Estouteville 91

Gessenay 110
Gherardi da Volterra, Iacopo (chronicler) 87n15
Ghibellines, *see* Guelphs and Ghibellines
Giberti, Gian Matteo 101n62, 132
Gigault 142
Giovanna d'Aragona (Illegitimate daughter of Ferdinand I of Naples) 84
Giovio, Paolo 96, 97n46
Glarus 205n34
Godi, family 126, 128, 132, 134, 136
Godi, Girolamo 127n15
Golden Bull 113n39, 117
Gonzaga, Eleonora (Empress) 162, 164, 166
Gonzaga, Louis of (Duke of Nevers) 138, 143
Gouffier, François (*sieur* de Bonnivet et de Crèvecoeur) 142
Granada 48, 52
Grangier, Bastien 113n38
Gregory XV (Pope) 175
Grisons 208n43
Gualdo, family 125–126, 128, 132, 133n27, 134
Guelphs and Ghibellines 2–3, 10, 12–13, 82, 84–85, 90, 94, 96, 100, 102, 107, 114n43, 120n77, 121, 135–136, 158
Guicciardini, Francesco 96, 97n46
guilds 18–36, 86n11, 187, *see also* merchants; trade
Guipzcoa 37–55
Guise, family 144
Guise, Charles de (Duke of Lorraine and Aumale) 142, 144, 149–150
Guise, Henri I of (Duke of Lorraine) 137, 142–143
Guise, Louis of (Cardinal) 138, 144
Guy, François Charles de 186n23

Habsburg 198
Habsburg Austria 207
Habsburg Spain 156, 207
Hagen Johannes 58, 69n24, 72n30
Halluin, Charles de (*sieur* de Piennes et marquis de Maignelay) 142
Halluin, Duke of 149
Harrach, family 169
Harrach, Carl 158n10
Heers, Jacques 4
Heidelberg, university of 70
Heiligkreuz (Observant Benedictine abbey in Donauwörth) 67
Henri I (Prince of Condé) 137, 151
Henri III (King of France) 137–138, 140, 148–150
Henri IV (King of France) 143, 150, *see also* Bourbon, Henri of
Henry VIII (King of England) 1
Henwart, Lucas 27
Henwart, Peter 27
Höbelt, Lothar 163
Hohenzollern-Hechingen, *see* Zollern
Holland 13
Holt, Mack P. 4, 145
Holy Roman Empire 21n8, 25, 56–81, 100, 105n4, 107, 118, 121, 125n11, 126–128, 135–136, 155–175, 202, *see also* Charles IV; Charles V; Ferdinand I; Ferdinand II; Ferdinand III; Friedrich III; Leopold I; Matthias; Maximilian I; Maximilian II; Rudolf II; Sigismund
honour 2, 30, 46, 49, 101n62, 112, 127, 130–131, 136, 147–148, 166, 169, 181, *see also* feuds, murders, noble lineages
Hugues, Besançon 105–106
Hume, David 12
Hungary 101n62
Hungary, King of 162, *see also* Ferdinand III

Ilgen, Heinrich, Rüdiger von 185, 187
Infessura, Stefano (chronicler) 87n15
Innocent VIII (Pope) 87n15, 90, 92
Isabella I (Queen of Castile) 55
Italian wars 204
Italy 4, 8, 93

Jacinto da Casale (Capuchin) 167
Jacobacci, family 102
Jacob of Jütebog, *see* Jacob of Paradise
Jacob of Paradise 69, 71, 73–75
Jäger, Clemens 28n30
Jankov, battle of 171, 173
Janssen, Geert 15
Jean de Bruges 56
Jesuits 14, 134, 156–157, 162, 167
John of Ragusa 58
John of Segovia 58, 71n26
Johnson, Samuel 12

Juan II (King of Castile) 41, 47
Julius II (Pope) 87n15, 92, 95–96, *see also* Della Rovere, Giuliano
jurists 107, 116, 124, 130, 134, 145, 196–197, *see also* lawyers

Kaiser, Wolfgang 139
Kepler, Gebhard 24–25
Khevenhüller, Franz Christoph von 158n10, 166
Khuen, Johann Eusebius 158
Klesl, Melchior (Cardinal) 156, 158
Kneupper, Frances Courtney 6, 15
Knyphausen, Friedrich Ernst Freiherr zu Innhausen und 188, 190
Krakow, university of 71
Kunzelmann, Ulrich 20
Kurz von Senftenau, Ferdinand Siegmund 173

L'Aquila 91
La Baume, Pierre de 115n47
La Chapelle-Marteau, Michel 145
La Marthonie, Geoffroy de 144
Labourd 39
Lamentana, family 88
Lamormaini, William 162, 166–167
Langenmantel, Heinrich 24, 34
Lannoy, Charles de 100
Latium 88
Lausanne 118n63
lawyers 86, 151, 213, *see also* jurists
Lazcano, family 45
Le Crotoy 142
Le Landeron 182
Le Roy Ladurie, Emmanuel 177n2
Le Scellier 145
Leni, family 88
Lentulus, Robert Scipio von 193
Leo X (Pope) 92
Leopold I (Holy Roman Emperor) 164
Leopold Wilhelm (Archduke) 164
Leroy, Nicolas 144
Leroy, Vincent 144
Lesdiguières, Duchesse de 181
Lesdiguières, Duke of 150
Liguria 83
Lombardy 10, 124
London 186n23
Longueville, duchess of 143
López de Chinchilla, Garci 51
López de Lazcano, Juan 54
Lorraine (Duke of), *see* Guise
Loschi, Davide 126
Louis XI (King of France) 142
Louis XIV (King of France) 140, 176, 179–181
Löwenthal, Richard 213
Lucerne 115n49, 180n8, 193, 203–204, 208–210
Luebke, David Martin 211
Luisa di Savoia 102
Lundell, William Paul 60
Lutz, Georg 169
Luynes, Duke of 186
Lyon 122

Machiavelli, Niccolò 92, 213
Madrid *see* court, Spanish
Magré, family 128
Mailly, marquise de 181
Mailly-Nesle, house of 183, 191n38
Mailly-Nesle, Louis III de (Marquis) 190
Mailly-Nesle, Louise Julie 191n38
Mainz, archbishop of 61
Mair, Paul Hector 22n10, 24n18, 26n25
Malvezzi, family 96
Mantua 88
Mantua, Duke of 107–108, 162
Manuel, Juan (Spanish ambassador) 99n58
Marche 122
Margani, family 85, 90
Margani, Gerolama 98
Margani, Paolo 90
Margani, Pietro 85–86
Maria Anna of Austria (Spanish *Infanta*) 162, 164–166, 170–172, 174–175
Maria Cecilia d'Aragona (Illegitimate daughter of Ferdinand I of Naples) 89, 95
Maria Theresa (Spanish *Infanta*) 173
Mariana of Austria (daughter of Ferdinand III) 173
Marín, José Antonio 40
Marino 88
Marseille 10, 139–140
Martin V (Pope) 59, 70, 86, 88
Martínez de Álava, Diego 55

Massimi, family 102
Matignon, comte de 181–182
Matissart, Philippe 145
Mattei, family 88, 90
Matthias (Holy Roman Emperor) 155
Maximilian I (Duke of Bavaria) 155, 159, 165, 167–168, 173, 175
Maximilian I (Holy Roman Emperor) 99, 116
Maximilian II (Holy Roman Emperor) 168
Maximilian III (Archduke of Austria) 156
Mayenne, Duke of 143
Mazarin, Jules (Cardinal) 175
Medici, family 92, 94, 97, 99–100, 102
Medici, Giulio de' (Cardinal) 99–100, *see also* Clement VII
Medici, Lorenzo de' (d. 1492) 91, 97
Medici, Piero de' 91
Meggau, Leonhard Helfried von 158, 168
Meisterlin chronicle 25n21
Melk Abbey, *see* Schlitpacher of Weilheim
Memmingen 19
merchants 18–19, 21, 24, 27, 45–46, 86n11, 122, 145, 151, 206, *see also* guilds; trade
Merveilleux, Jean-Jacques de 186–188
Mettam, Roger 177n2
Metternich, Ernst von 182
Milan 87, 91, 93, 99, 132–134
Milan-Spain 207–208
Mileto, diocese of, *see* Della Valle, Andrea
modern state 3, 51–55, 176–181, 185, 194–195, 211–212
Moncada, Hugo de 100–101
Mondovì 107–108, 119–120
Mondragón 47
Monsalvo, José Maria 45
Mont, von, family 208n43
Montefeltro, Agnese di 88, 97
Montefeltro, Guidantonio da 88n20
Montefeltro, Guidobaldo da 96
Monterotondo 88
Montmollin, family 185, 188–189
Montmollin, Georges de 180
Montmollin, Jean Henri de 185
Montreuil 142
Monza, family 126, 128, 130, 136
Monza, Giovanni Battista 127n15, 130
Moreel, Willem 8n25
Mulhouse 107
Mülich, Hector (chronicler) 19, 25n21, 28–30, 33
Münster 174
Muralt, Kaspar von 190n37
murders 24, 48, 73, 86, 126, 130–131, 169–170, *see also* feuds; honour, violence

Nantes 146
Naples 83–84, 94, 100
Naples, kingdom of 83, 87–89, 91, 93–94, 101n62, 102, *see also* Ferdinand I; Giovanna d'Aragona; Maria Cecilia d'Aragona
Napoleon (Emperor) 194
Navarre 39, 52, *see also* Bourbon, Henri
Navis, André 112
Negri, Paola Antonia 132–134
Nemours, Treaty of 137
Netherlands (Spanish) 142
Netherlands, *see* Dutch Republic
Neuchâtel 6, 8, 13, 176–194
Neumair von Ramsla, Johan Wilhelm 213
Neumüller, Marx 35
Nibat, Nicolas de 144
Nicholas of Cusa 58, 67
Nicholas V (Pope) 63, 72
Nieder, Johannes 67
Nievo, family 128
noble lineages 5, 9, 15, 19, 21 37–55, 82–103, 122–136, 148–149, 160, 197, *see also* Almerico, Añacino; Angaran; Anguillara; Avendaño; Borgia; Branzo; Butrón; Capra; Caetani; Colonna; Conti; Da Monte; Da Porto; Da Roma; Da Schio; Della Rovere; Della Valle; Gamboa; Garzadori; Godi; Gualdo; Lazcano; Magré; Margani; Mattei; Medici; Mailly-Nesle; Monza; Nievo; Onãz; Orsini; Pogliana; Porcari; Riario; Santacroce; Savelli; Scroffa; Tebaldi; Thiene; Trento; Trissino; Valmarana; Velo; Zambeccari
Normant, Jacques 145
Norway 3
Numai, Cristoforo (Cardinal) 102
Nürnberg, Diet of 70n

Offischer, family 110
Oldenburg, Philipp Andreas 196

Olivares, Gaspar de Guzmán, count-duke of 159, 163, 169
Oñate, count of, Spanish ambassador in Vienna 156, 158, 170
Onãz, family 45
Orléans, Duke of 183, 186–197
Orléans, Henri II d' (Duc de Longueville) 179
Orléans, Jean-Louis d' (Abbé d') 179
Orléans, Marie d' (Duchesse de Nemours) 179–180
Orléans-Longueville, house of 176
Orsini, family 82–103, 158
Orsini (Bracciano) 84–85, 88
Orsini (Neapolitan line) 84
Orsini, Alfonsina (di Tagliacozzo) 91, 97
Orsini, Camillo 100
Orsini, Clarice 91
Orsini, Gentile Virginio 85, 91, 93, 95
Orsini, Giangiordano di Gentile Virginio 89, 94–95
Orsini, Giovan Battista (Cardinal) 95
Orsini, Giulio 96
Orsini, Giustina 88
Orsini, Latino (Cardinal) 89
Orsini, Laura 95
Orsini, Maddalena 91
Orsini, Napoleone 84–85
Orsini, Paolo (di Lamentana) 89
Orsini, Roberto 84, 100
Orsini, Virginio 89n25
Osnabrück 174
Österreicher, Georg 35n45
Ostervald, Jean-Frédéric 189n34
Otazu, Alfonso de 47
Ottoman Empire, *see* Turks
Oyarzun 46

Padua 132
Pagliarino, Bartolamio 127n15
Paliano 90
Palladio, Andrea 122
Papacy 60–63, 71, 79–81, 82–103, 156, 167, 177n2, 207, *see also* court, papal; Rome; Alexander VI; Benedict XIII; Callixtus III; Clement VII; Eugenius IV Felix V; Gregory XV; Innocent VIII; Julius II; Leo X; Martin V; Nicholas V; Paul III; Sixtus IV; Urban VIII
Papal Wars 82–103
Paris 119n71, 137, 140–143, 145, 148, 150–151, 186n23, *see also* court, French; France
parties, *see* factions
passions, *see* emotions
patronage, right of 40, 47–48, 51
patron-client relations 2, 8–9, 15, 21, 24–26, 98, 101, 136, 143, 162–169, 172, 174–175, 177–182, 199, 207, 209–214, *see also* court
Paul III (Pope) 132
Pavia, battle of 99–100
Pellegrin, Marco 93
Peneysans (Genevan faction) 111n30
Perregaux, family 183
Perregaux, François-Frédéric 192
Perregaux, Théophile 188–191
Perugia 96
Petrucci, Alfonso 97
Pfyffer, family 207n43
Philip II (King of Spain) 137
Philip IV (King of Spain) 159, 162, 165–166, 168–173, 175
Philippe II (King of Spain) 144
Philippe, Jean 106
Picardy 142, 144, 152
Piccolomini, Giovanni (Cardinal) 102
Piennes, *see* Halluin
Pillorget, René 140
Pisa 96
Pitigliano 88
plot, *see* conspiracy
Pogliana, family 136
Poland 195n, *see also* Polish War of Succession
Polisensky, Josef 157
Polish War of Succession 191n38
Pontani, Clelia 99
Pontani, Giovan Battista 99
Pontecorvo 91
Pont-Rémy 142
Porcari, conspiracy 84n5
Porcari, family 88, 99
Porral, Ami 106
Postel, Jean 145
Pozzetti, Ferdinando (Cardinal) 102
Prague, defenestration of 156
Prügl, Thomas 71n26

Prussia, *see* court, Prussian; Frederick I; Frederick II; Frederick William I; Frederick William III
Pury, Abram de 186, 192
Pury, Daniel de 180
Pury, David de 192
Pury, Samuel de 182, 190–191
Puyzieulx, Roger Brulart de Sillery, Marquis de 181

Quiroga, Diego de (Capuchin) 170–173

Radauer, Leonhard 24
Ravenna 97
Reding, family 207n, 209
Rehberg, Andreas 88
Reinhard, Wolfgang 95, 177n2
Religious orders, *see* Barnabites; Benedictines; Capuchins; Carmelites; Carthusians; Dominicans; Franciscans; Jesuits
Rem, Wilhelm (chronicler) 29–31
Rennes 146
Rentería 46
Retz, Jean François Paul de Gondi de 14
revolts 6, 11–12, 90, 94, 101, 104–110, 117–118, 121, 137–138, 149, 160, 167n43, 184, 190–194, 196–198, 200–206, 210–214, *see also* conspiracy; tyranny; violence; warfare
Riario, family 87
Riario, Girolamo 84, 88–90
Riario, Pietro (Cardinal) 84
Richelieu, Armand-Jean du Plessis de (Cardinal) 163
Ridolfi, Niccolò (Cardinal) 132
Rieti, diocese *see* Colonna, Pompeo; Pontani, Giovan Battista
Roermond, charterhouse of 70
Romagna 83–84, 95, 102
Rome 9, 64–65, 75–76, 81–103, 125n11, 133, 158n, *see also* court, papal; papacy
Rome, sack of 100–103
Rossbach, battle of 191
Rottembourg, Conrad-Alexandre, Comte de 187
Rottweil 107
Rouen 137, 146
Rougement, François Antoine de 186n23
Rousseau, Jean-Jacques 192n43, 212–213
Rudolf II (Holy Roman Emperor) 156, 165
Ruiz de Avendaño, Martín 52

Sabean, David 200
Saint Ulrich (monastery in Augsburg) 25
Saisseval, *see* Senicourt
Salvemini, Gaetano 2
San Sebastián 46
Sandoz-Rollin, David-Alphonse 194
Santacroce, family 85–86, 89, 98
Santacroce, Andrea 85–86
Santacroce, Giorgio 87
Santacroce, Livia 86
Santacroce, Prospero 85–86
Sanudo, Marin 109
Sarpi, Paolo 158n7
Sauli, Alessandro 134
Sauli, Domenico 133–134
Sauvage, Jean de 99
Savelli, family 85, 91, 94, 96
Savelli, Giovan Battista (Cardinal) 89
Savelli, Sabella 86
Saveuse, *see* Tiercelin
Savio, Andrea 6, 13
Savoy, House of 6, 8, 13, 104–121, 207, 209, 212, *see also* court, Sabaudian; Geneva; Amadeus VIII; Charles II; Emmanuel Philibert; Luisa di Savoia
Sbriccoli, Mario 196–197
Schaffhausen 115n49
Schiller, Friedrich 155–156, 198
Schlitpacher of Weilheim, Johannes 75
Schneider, Hans 25n22
Schnerb, Bertrand 16
Schulze, Winfried 213
Schunde, Johannes 70n
Schwarz, Ulrich 8, 18, 23–30, 32–36
Schwyz 204n33, 205–209
Scotland 142
Scotti, Ranuccio 212
Scroffa, family 128
seditions, *see* revolts
Senicourt, François de (*sieur* de Saisseval) 142, 147
Senigallia 94
Sessa, Duke of 100
Seven Years' War 191
Seyssel, Claude de 119–121

Sfondrati, Niccolò (cardinal) 134
Sforza, Caterina 84
Sforza, Ascanio Maria (Cardinal) 93
Shaw, Christine 82, 85
Sicily 101n
Sigismund (Holy Roman Emperor) 61–62, 86
Sixtus IV (Pope) 83–84, 86–87, 89, 90n31, 92
Smail, Daniel Lord 10
Soderini, Fracesco 97
Solothurn 104–107, 109–110, 115n49, 180n8, 183, 188, 189n32, 190, 192–193, 208, 210
Soriano 94
Spain 37–55, 94–96, 99, 133–136, 155–156, 162, 168, 170n55, 171, 173, 175, 209, 211–212, *see also* court, Spanish; Habsburg Spain; Milan-Spain; Philip II; Philip IV
St. Gallen, prince-abbot of 201–203
state-building, *see* modern state
Steiger, Isaak 189
Stieber, Joachim 61
Strauß, Jörg 18n, 22, 24–25, 27, 34
Strünckede, Friedrich Konrad von 184–189
Stückl, Johann 168
Suter, Andreas 202–203
Suvanto, Pekka 169
Sweden 174
Swiss Confederacy 6, 8, 10, 13, 105–116, 118–120, 122, 134, 176, 177n2, 179n8, 183, 192–194, 196–215, *see also* Appenzell; Basel; Bern; Fribourg; Geneva; Glarus; Grisons; Lucerne; Schaffhausen; Schwyz; Solothurn; St. Gallen; Uri; Zurich
Swiss Peasants' War 203, 210

Tagliacozzo 89, 93, 94n38
taxation 19, 22, 26, 29, 151, 192, 194, 202–206
Tebaldi, family 99
Tebaldi, Marco di Simone de' 99n55
Tell, William 198
Tena, Soledad 45
Tercero Casado, Luis 6, 15
Terracina 91
Terranova, Duke of 172
The Hague 3
Thiene, family 126–129, 131
Thiene, Adriano 127n15
Thiene, Marcantonio 126, 127n15
Thiene, Marco 126
Thirty Years' War 122, 155–175
Thou, Jacques Auguste de 143
Thun, Christoph Simon von 159, 162, 166
Tiercelin, Charles de (sieur de Saveuse) 142, 144
Tivoli, peace of 94n38
Toggenburg, valley of 201–203, 210
Torcy, Jean Baptiste Colbert, Marquis de 181
Tott, François de 192
Town Wars 19–20
trade 20, 53, 85, 122, 183, *see also* guilds; merchants
Traetto, duchy of 93
Trauttmansdorf, Maximilian von 159, 162–164, 166, 168, 170–171, 173–174
Trent, Council of 150
Trento, family 128
Tretto di Schio 123
Trevor-Roper, Hugh 157
Tribolet, David de 186
Trier, archbishop of 61
Trissino, family 125–126, 128
Trissino, Achille 127
Trissino, Giangiorgio 126
Trissino, Giovanni 126
Trissino, Marco 127
Troyes 146
Truchuelo, Susana 53
trust 9, 66, 74, 98, 103, 110–111, 120–121, 159, 163, 165, 182, 186, 188, 206, *see also* court; patron-client relations
Turks 57, 59, 72, 76, 78, 81 83, 94
tyranny 20, 29, 96, 101, 109–111, 116, 197–198, 201, *see also* revolts

Ulm 21
Umbria 90
Urban VIII (Pope) 167, 175
Urbino 88, 96–97
Urbino, Duke of 88
Uri 205n34
Usson, *see* Bonnac, Jean-Louis
Utrecht, Treaty of 176

Valagin 184–185, 189
Valdés, Alfonso de 100
Valdés, Juan de 103

Valmarana, family 125–126, 128–129, 131–134, 136
Valmarana, Alberto 130
Valmarana, Giacomo 127n15
Valmarana, Maddalena 132
Valmarana, Niccolò 130
Valmarana, Tommaso 130
Vandel, Robert 114
Vandel, Thomas 106
Vascho, Antonio de (chronicler) 87–88
Vattel, David 189n
Vattel, Emer de 190n34
Vehse, Eduard 157
Velo, family 126, 128–129
Velo, Bernardino 127n15
vengeance, *see* feuds
Venice 6–7, 13, 89, 95–96, 122–136, 158, 162, 170n55, 207, 208n43, 212
Venier, Bernardo 129
Verona 132
Vetter, Hans 27
Vicenza 6, 8–9, 122–136
Vich, Jéronimo de 96
Vicovaro 91
Vienna 31n, *see also* court, imperial
Vienna, university of 61
Villarreal de Álava 52
Villars, *maréchal* de 176
Villeroy, duc de 181
Vincent of Aggsbach 58, 69, 75, 77
violence 2, 18, 39–40, 47, 49–50, 53–54, 73, 83, 86, 90, 92, 104, 110, 115, 120, 124, 126–127, 130–131, 135, 146, 202, *see also* feuds; murders; revolts; warfare
Visceglia, Maria Antonietta 6, 15
Vitelleschi, Muzio 14
Vitelli, Vitellio 101
Vitelli, Vitellozzo 94
Vitoria 45, 51
Vittel, family 27
Vittel, Hans 23–26, 29
Vittel, Leonhard 25–26, 29
Vizcaya 37–55

Walker, Greg 1
Wallenstein, Albrecht von 157, 165, 169–170
War of the Mantuan Succession 162
War of the Spanish Succession 176, 209
warfare 3–4, 8–9, 12, 14, 38, 47–55, 82–92, 110, 116n54, 125, 127, 130, 136, 144, 193, 196–197, 206–208, *see also* Burgundian Wars; Castilian Civil War; Ferrara; French Wars of Religion; Italian Wars; Papal Wars; Polish War of Succession; Seven Years' War; Swiss Peasants' War; Town Wars; War of the Mantuan Succession; War of the Spanish Succession
Weber, Nadir 6, 8, 13
Welser, Bartholome 27
Westphalia, peace of 156, 172–173, 175
White Mountain, battle of 160, 167n43
Wittwer, Wilhelm 23
women 54, 71, 84, 88–89, 93, 91, 95, 98–99, 132–133, 143, 145 162, 173, 191n38, *see also* Altieri, Lucrezia; Borgia, Girolama; Bourbon-Soissons, Louise-Léontine; Cavalieri di Masciolo, Marzia de'; Colonna, Agnese, Caterina; Della Rovere, Bianca, Felicia, Luchina; Della Valle, Laura, Livia di Lelio; Farnese, Giulia; Gara, Lucrezia; Giovanna d'Aragona; Gonzaga, Eleonora; Isabella I; Lesdiguières, duchesse de; Longueville, duchess of; Luisa di Savoia; Margani, Gerolama; Maria Anna of Austria; Maria Cecilia d'Aragona; Maria Theresa; Montefeltro, Agnese di; Negri, Paola Antonia; Orléans, Marie d'; Orsini, Clarice, Giustina; Laura, Maddalena; Pontani, Clelia; Santacroce, Livia; Sforza, Caterina
Worms, Diet of 99
Würgler, Andreas 6, 8, 10, 13

Zaccaria, Antonio Maria 132
Zambeccari, family 96
Zink, Burkhard (chronicler) 16, 21, 29
Zollern, Johann Georg von 168
Zug 115n49, 205–206, 208–209
Zurich 21, 107, 115, 118, 204, 206–208
Zurlauben, family 209
Zwingli, Ulrich 214

www.ingramcontent.com/pod-product-compliance
Ingram Content Group UK Ltd.
Pitfield, Milton Keynes, MK11 3LW, UK
UKHW021421091026
15624UKWH00010B/338

9 789004 344150